AMERICA'S FOUNDING AND THE STRUGGLE OVER ECONOMIC INEQUALITY

AMERICA'S FOUNDING AND THE STRUGGLE OVER ECONOMIC INEQUALITY

CLEMENT FATOVIC

UNIVERSITY PRESS OF KANSAS

Published by the University Press of Kansas (Lawrence, Kansas 66045),
which was organized by the Kansas Board of Regents and is operated and funded
by Emporia State University, Fort Hays State University, Kansas State University,
Pittsburg State University, the University of Kansas, and Wichita State University

Library of Congress Cataloging-in-Publication Data

Fatovic, Clement, 1973–
America's founding and the struggle over economic inequality / Clement Fatovic.
    pages cm. — (Constitutional thinking)
    Includes index.
    ISBN 978-0-7006-2173-6 (hardback) — ISBN 978-0-7006-2151-4 (ebook)
    1. Equality—United States. 2. Income distribution—United States. 3. United
    States—Social policy—1775–1783. 4. United States—History—Revolution,
    1775–1783. I. Title.
    HN90.S6F38 2015
    305.50973—dc23
    2015026842

British Library Cataloguing-in-Publication Data is available.

Printed in the United States of America

10 9 8 7 6 5 4 3 2 1

The paper used in this publication is recycled and contains 30 percent postcon-
sumer waste. It is acid free and meets the minimum requirements of the American National Standard for Permanence of Paper for Printed Library Materials
Z39.48-1992.

For Rebecca

CONTENTS

FOREWORD

For centuries Americans have been resistant to the idea that government has a role in reducing economic inequality. Against the expectations of thinkers such as Alexis de Tocqueville, who imagined that commitments to popular sovereignty and political equality would, over time, incline citizens to favor equality more generally, Americans have historically embraced economic inequality as a necessary consequence of equality of opportunity. The Horatio Alger myth so seized the American imagination that throughout US history most Americans have opposed redistribution on the expectation that with enough effort and talent anyone could become wealthy and ought to be able to keep the fruits of one's labor and enjoy one's wealth. As political scientist Jennifer Hochschild showed in her classic book *What's Fair: American Beliefs about Distributive Justice*, Americans cherish political equality but also are very comfortable with economic inequality. Most Americans have seen no necessary connection between these two kinds of equality. This attitude found political sustenance in appeals to the authority of the American founders, who arguably resisted pure democracy in favor of a complex republic designed to dampen the tendency of the idea of equality to intrude upon a commitment to liberty. If Americans are free to pursue their dreams and develop their talents, it has been thought, some will inevitably succeed and others fail, but—in principle—anyone could become very rich. It is this attitude that fuels the Tea Party movement today.

In recent years this optimistic and idyllic picture has been challenged by the fact that economic inequality is as great as or greater than it was in the era of the robber barons and by pessimistic prognostications of some economists who see this problem getting still worse in the future. French economist Thomas Piketty published a 700-page book, *Capital in the Twenty-First Century*, that became a best-seller. A year into his second term, President Barack Obama gave a speech in which he asserted that the problem of growing economic inequality is the "defining challenge of our time." The economic gap between the few super-rich citizens and most Americans has become so massive that even Obama's Republican opponents have taken notice and pledged to do something about it. It is likely that a prominent issue in the 2016 presidential campaign will be the problem of inequality and what to do about it.

What changed since 1982, when Hochschild wrote her book documenting Americans' comfort with economic inequality, and 2014, when economic inequality became the defining issue of our time? Over the past thirty years, evidence has mounted that the American dream is a myth. Economic inequality has become more pronounced, and wealth has become more entrenched. More importantly, the idea that everyone would be better off financially even if worse off relative to the wealthy has proven untrue. The income and standard of living of most Americans has stagnated even while the super-rich have accumulated unprecedented wealth. Economists are beginning to revise standard accounts of the logic of capitalism, and other social scientists are exposing other adverse consequences of inequality, such as increased crime and other social costs. A robust economic and social debate today upends conventional understandings of the logic of capitalism. In sum, conventional economic understandings are under siege today.

In the book that you have before you, Clement Fatovic recasts this economic and social debate as a political and constitutional problem. Fatovic challenges the idea that inequality is a necessary consequence of liberty by showing that *a concern for equality is a necessary condition for freedom, properly understood.* Returning to the debate surrounding the founding of the American republic, Fatovic shows that the conventional and instinctive appeal to the founders as authority for the proposition that no legitimate constitutional argument supports governmental support for redistributive policy is mistaken. Thomas Jefferson, James Madison, and Thomas Paine, to say nothing of less well-known thinkers of the founding era such as Noah Webster and Abraham Clark, all thought it imperative that government resist inequality in order to make political freedom viable and vital. If this book did nothing more than correct mistaken appeals to authority, it would be a signal contribution to the contemporary debate. Fatovic makes an irrefutable case that leading politicians of the founding generation and early history of Congress thought that governmental efforts to avoid or mitigate economic inequality were uncontroversial and legitimate legislative issues. Of course, there was much debate and contest regarding particular proposals, and many were defeated, but modern-day libertarian antipathy to any and all redistributive policy finds little support in the thinking of influential founders and statesmen at the origin of our constitutional order.

Still more important than the issue of original intentions and misinformed appeals to authority is Fatovic's project to enlarge and enlighten contemporary political debate. In his account of a huge array of political issues—including suffrage and representation, tax policy, regulation of militias, revenue plans, and even the design and ratification of the Constitution itself—Fatovic shows the economic concerns surrounding equality were nested in a larger political conundrum. As I mentioned above, today's partisans often assume that economic inequality is a by-product of the nation's commitment to freedom. The burden of this book is to show the reader how today's conventional wisdom rests on a mistaken and narrow view of freedom. For the founding generation, political freedom—the ability of ordinary citizens to participate in politics—requires a modicum of economic equality. Conversely, pronounced and serious levels of inequality render ordinary citizens unfree. Americans have lost the understanding and practice of debating public policy from this more capacious perspective on equality and freedom. This book recovers the resources needed, along with a refreshingly original argument necessary, to reframe democratic discourse about a defining issue of our time.

Jeffrey K. Tulis
Coeditor, *Constitutional Thinking*

PREFACE AND ACKNOWLEDGMENTS

Economic inequality in the United States today is approaching un-precedented levels. The concentration of wealth has reached a point unseen since the eve of the Great Depression, when the top 0.1 per-cent controlled nearly 25 percent of all wealth in the country. At present, the top 0.1 percent owns more than 22 percent of all wealth in the United States, while the top 1 percent controls more than 40 percent of the nation's wealth.[1] The six heirs to the Walmart fortune alone possess more wealth than the bottom 40 percent of Ameri-cans combined.[2] In some ways the distribution of income is now even more skewed than it was during the Roaring Twenties. Ap-proximately 24 percent of all income went to the top 1 percent the year before the stock market crash of 1929.[3] In recent years, the top 1 percent has taken in more than 90 percent of all income gains.[4] The economic gap between the top and the bottom has grown so large that leaders in both major political parties have been forced to take notice. In an address that received extensive media commentary, Democratic president Barack Obama called rising inequality the "defining challenge of our time."[5] During a major campaign-style event, former Republican governor of Florida and 2016 presidential hopeful Jeb Bush observed that a widening "opportunity gap" has made the "American dream . . . a mirage for too many."[6]

Disparities in wealth and income had been growing rapidly since the late 1970s, but it took the worst economic downturn since the Great Depression to draw sustained public attention to this trend. The 2008 financial crisis, which plunged millions into poverty, threw millions more out of work, decimated savings, and left many homeowners underwater on their mortgages, laid bare the struc-tural imbalances in the economy and exposed just how vulnerable middle- and working-class households are to forces beyond their control. The sluggish and uneven recovery that followed the Great Recession has contributed to the sense that economic inequality is growing out of proportion. Although the stock market has more than doubled in value, and compensation for top executives at major corporations is now at or near an all-time high, median wages have barely budged in real terms since 2009.

A few scholars and journalists had been warning for years about the growing divide between haves and have-nots as well as the related decline in upward mobility,[7] but it was collective acts of political protest that finally forced the media and political establishments to begin focusing on these developments. Since the financial crash of 2008, low-wage workers, the unemployed and underemployed, and grassroots activists have staged demonstrations, strikes, and sit-ins throughout the country to demand improved pay and better benefits for workers, increases in the minimum wage, higher taxes on the wealthy, and stricter regulations on and accountability from the financial sector, which many blamed for the country's economic woes. Members of the Occupy Wall Street movement, which began in Manhattan's financial district in September 2011 and soon spread to cities around the country (and other parts of the world), raised public awareness of growing class divisions with their slogan "We Are the 99 Percent." Highly publicized protests and occupations of financial institutions, boardrooms, college campuses, and other spaces spurred national conversations about corporate malfeasance, the corruption of the political process, the erosion of democracy, and other problems linked to economic inequality. Although the Occupy movement has largely dissipated, the language of the 1 percent and the 99 percent it popularized continues to frame debates over economic inequality and public policy in the United States.

Despite these and other efforts to address growing economic stratification, there has been considerable resistance to treating the issue as an appropriate matter for public policy. One of the major challenges to placing economic inequality on the political agenda is a persistent and powerful strain of laissez-faire thinking dating back to the revolutionary period that is inimical to most forms of government involvement in the economy. In particular, opponents of policies designed to reduce economic inequality frequently invoke the American founders to support their claims that government action in this area is illegitimate. Contemporary critics—most notably within the Tea Party movement—allege that political efforts to deal with economic disparities violate the founders' beliefs in limited government and individual freedom. Although the founders were certainly concerned about maintaining limited government, they were also deeply concerned about economic inequality. Indeed, many of the founders worried about economic inequality precisely because they viewed it as a threat to freedom. As I demonstrate below, some of the most important political debates during the founding were framed in terms of the impact different policies would have on economic inequality.

Much of the resistance to government action on economic inequality in recent decades has drawn on a very different tradition in American political thought. Even as the American welfare state was undergoing its greatest expansion since the New Deal, laissez-faire ideas experienced a revival in the 1960s and 1970s thanks to the concerted efforts of libertarian politicians, newly established think tanks, prominent scholars, and business groups advocating smaller government, lower taxes, and freer markets.[8] Since the 1970s, this powerful strand of American political thought has contributed to a formidable conservative backlash against the perceived excesses and failures of the welfare state (as well as the high wages, benefits, and workplace protections the labor movement secured after World War II). Republican president Ronald Reagan encapsulated modern hostility toward government that had grown too bureaucratic, taxed too much, spent too much, and accomplished too little with the line "Government is not the solution to our problem; government *is* the problem."[9] This line of thinking provided a crucial justification for the wave of deregulation, privatization, tax cutting, and reductions in domestic spending that occurred over the next few decades under the rubric of "neoliberal reform."[10] The notion that government should generally stay out of the economy except to maintain a climate friendly to business became so well entrenched within the established two-party system that Democratic presidential candidate Bill Clinton made the promise to "end welfare as we have come to know it" one of the centerpieces of his campaign.[11]

The resilience of laissez-faire ideas in American political thought would have presented a major obstacle to efforts to deal with economic inequality in any circumstances, but the emergence of the Tea Party in 2009 has probably posed the most serious challenge in recent years to the notion that government has a legitimate role to play in alleviating economic hardships or minimizing disparities in wealth and income. The Tea Party movement was initially formed in opposition to a nearly $800 billion stimulus package championed by the Obama administration because its grassroots members and their benefactors believed such spending was fiscally irresponsible and highly unlikely to achieve its goal of boosting economic output. It did not take long for Tea Party members to make the additional argument that many forms of government intervention in the economy favored by the president—including those begun by his predecessor at the height of the financial crisis—violated the Constitution and betrayed the principles of the American founding. Members of the various Tea Party organizations and their supporters in the media frequently invoked the slogans and symbols of the American Revolution to support their claims that government attempts to regulate (or bail out) big business or to minimize economic inequalities are antithetical to American ideals of limited government, individualism, and freedom.

These ideas about the limited role of government in the economy have also been combined with other ideas that have served to delegitimize policies aimed at addressing economic inequality. Chief among these is the belief that government assistance creates pernicious forms of dependency that degrade personal dignity and undermine individual liberty. Many of these arguments were advanced in response to proposals aimed at improving the material conditions of ordinary Americans, including increases in the minimum wage, assistance to homeowners struggling to pay their mortgages, extensions in unemployment benefits, an ambitious plan to overhaul the health-care system, and tax hikes on the rich to help pay for all of this. As 2012 Republican vice presidential nominee Paul Ryan said of the welfare programs that existed in the 1960s in a campaign speech shortly before the election, "This top-down approach created and perpetuated a debilitating culture of dependency, wrecking families and communities."[12] Resistance to more egalitarian policies has also been reinforced by an assertion that even acknowledging the existence of economic inequality in public is to engage in a crass and disreputable politics of envy. In response to the attention the issue was receiving during the 2012 election, Republican presidential standard-bearer Mitt Romney opined, "You know, I think it's about envy. I think it's about class warfare."[13]

If attacking large disparities between rich and poor constitutes a form of class warfare, then the struggle against economic inequality is arguably the longest-running war in American history. Battles over the powers and responsibilities of the government have been waged in terms of class since the very beginning of the Republic, if not before. The issues that agitated Americans during the founding are not necessarily identical to the issues that trouble many Americans now, but economic inequality was just as much a preoccupation then as it is today—if not more so.

Economic inequality was a pervasive topic in legislative debates, newspaper articles, political pamphlets, private correspondence, religious sermons, public orations, and official addresses during the American founding. The subject generally entered political discussions in one of two main ways. One was in response to the perceived effects that policies under consideration would have on the economic conditions of particular classes. Almost any proposal could be—and often was—evaluated for its possible effects on relations between the classes. Economic inequality was one of the factors that frequently entered into calculations about the costs and benefits of different proposals. In particular, these debates would often focus on the expected impact a policy would have on the well-being and opportunities of the lower classes. The topic of economic inequality also came up independently of any policy proposal already on the political agenda. Tackling economic inequality was sometimes the main impetus behind proposals to guarantee a wide distribution of landed property, to establish free public schools, to institute a more progressive tax system, and to provide various forms of assistance to those facing hardships. These and other initiatives specifically designed to preserve or promote greater economic equality were proposed by venerable figures including Thomas Jefferson, Thomas Paine, Noah Webster, and Abraham Clark. Countless other actors from this period supported similar measures in pursuit of greater equality among classes—sometimes through regular political channels, sometimes through direct political action and violence.

The debates that took place during the founding are important not just because they provide insights into perceptions about the causes, consequences, and extent of economic inequality in early American thought. They are also of interest because they provide a richer and deeper understanding of the politics of major legislative and constitutional undertakings during that period. The politics of economic inequality helped shape the outcome of debates over some of the most important political, economic, and constitutional controversies following independence. Indeed, some of the conflicting ideas about the role of government in the economy that divide Americans today were first formulated in debates that centered on questions of class and inequality. As discussed in the following chapters, economic inequality figured prominently in debates over suffrage and representation during the Revolution, tax policy and the repayment of war debt during the Confederation period, the creation and ratification of the Constitution, the establishment of the national bank and other key features of Alexander Hamilton's economic program during the Washington administration, the disposition of western lands, rules for regulating the militia, and virtually every revenue plan Congress considered during the first few years of its existence. Although efforts to achieve more egalitarian outcomes did not always succeed, hardly anyone questioned the pursuit of economic equality as a legitimate political consideration.

Early American discussions of economic inequality are not simply of historical interest. They are also relevant to contemporary debates over wealth and income inequality because they help us understand why economic inequality is so troubling. Projections that the concentration of wealth is likely to get even more extreme in the future as the rate of return on capital outpaces the rate of economic growth in the United States and elsewhere around the world make it all the more urgent to understand the consequences of economic inequality.[14]

Many of the arguments advanced in favor of promoting economic equality during the founding are similar to the ones supporters of greater equality make today. Proponents of more egalitarian policies relied on appeals to feelings of compassion for the needy and underprivileged, moral outrage at perceived unfairness in the distribution of wealth, and nationalist sentiments about maintaining the distinctive character of American society. In addition, a few (most notably Paine) urged action on the grounds that economic inequality erodes the bases of social trust and solidarity, engenders undesirable social behaviors in rich and poor alike, contributes to increases in crime, weakens the overall performance of the economy, and leads to greater social and political instability—claims that find support in contemporary scholarship today.[15] However, the overriding considerations focused on the political consequences of economic inequality. In particular, many founders supported policies designed to promote economic equality because they believed it contributes significantly to the maintenance of free government.

Although many of the arguments now advanced against addressing economic inequality through public policy are carried out in the name of freedom, the most important arguments made in favor of minimizing economic inequality through public policy during the founding were also framed in terms of freedom. Contemporary arguments against government efforts to promote greater equality usually conceptualize freedom in economic terms, but the founders' arguments developed in support of public policies conducive to greater economic equality typically invoked a more participatory conception of freedom. According to this understanding of freedom, economic independence, which requires a wide but not perfectly equal distribution of property, is a precondition for political independence. The ability to participate effectively in the political process depends not just on those legal and political rules that ensure formally equal access to the ballot, political office, and the ears of politicians but also on material conditions that enable citizens to exercise their political rights on free and equal terms. As many founders understood it, greater equality in the economic sphere makes it possible to achieve greater equality in the political sphere. In the words of lexicographer Webster, "A general and tolerably equal distribution of landed property is the whole basis of national freedom."[16]

These arguments were based on a widespread belief, rooted largely in the republican ideology nearly every American professed to support, that excessive levels of economic inequality undermine the conditions necessary for the preservation of self-government. Their fear was that extreme concentrations of economic resources would result in dangerous concentrations of political power. Although many at the time generally believed (somewhat erroneously) that economic conditions in America were already fairly equal, they worried about the prospects of free government if economic inequality ever grew so extreme that it started to undermine political equality. The great danger was that dominance in the economic sphere would eventually translate into dominance in the political sphere. For that reason, reducing economic inequality was not only a legitimate function of government; it was also a political imperative for many founders. Nothing less than the fate of republican government was at stake.

———

This book could not have been completed without help from a variety of institutions and individuals. My first debt of gratitude is to Isaac Kramnick, a wonderful scholar, teacher, and mentor who sparked my interest in American political thought and urged me to pay more attention to issues of class in studying the history of ideas. However, I might not have even undertaken this particular project at all if it were not for the early encouragement of Sandy Levinson and Jeff Tulis, who have provided tremendous support and wise counsel for years. I am deeply obliged to them and to Fred Woodward for the faith they placed in this project when it was little more than a vague idea. Chuck Myers deserves my gratitude for skillfully—and very patiently—shepherding the manuscript through every stage of its development. Chuck provided excellent suggestions on how to frame the argument and link the topic to contemporary concerns about economic inequality.

I am also thankful for the opportunities I received to present parts of this book to other scholars. Comments and questions from discussants and audience members at various academic conferences, including the annual meetings of the American Political Science Association, the Midwest Political Science Association, and the Western Political Science Association led to improvements both big and small. Michael Gillespie, the director of the Center for the Humanities in an Urban Environment at Florida International University, kindly invited me to share some preliminary findings and ideas with an engaged and helpful audience at the center's Annual Faculty Advisory Board Lecture in April 2013. My engagement with this diverse and multidisciplinary crowd enriched my own understanding of the founding and reaffirmed my belief in the value of conversations across disciplinary boundaries.

A one-semester sabbatical leave in the fall of 2012 provided a welcome respite from administrative duties that enabled me to complete drafts of two chapters. The staffs at Green Library at Florida International University and in the Special Collections and University Archives of Alexander Library at Rutgers University provided expert assistance.

Throughout the process of researching and writing this book, I was fortunate to receive constant encouragement, support, and advice from people in every part of my life. I benefited immensely from conversations with friends, students, and colleagues who asked probing questions, pushed me to broaden my analysis, offered helpful suggestions, steered me away from errors, and introduced me to some very useful resources: Iqbal Akhtar, Kevin Evans, Craig Ewasiuk, Alan Gibson, Kate Gordy, Harry Gould, Carson Holloway, Michael Jimenez, Julia Maskivker, Brian Nelson, Mindy Peden, Joaquin Pedroso, Laurie Shrage, Markus Thiel, Megan Thomas, Chantalle Verna, José Vilanova, Sean Walsh, and Michael Zuckert. I am especially grateful to those who also generously read portions of this book and provided constructive feedback and useful suggestions that greatly improved the quality and coherence of the argument. Ron Cox, Andrew Dilts, Ken Kersch, Sandy Levinson, Bryant Sculos, Jeff Tulis, an anonymous reviewer for the University Press of Kansas, and my wife, Rebecca, offered suggestions that vastly improved both the content and the style of this book.

Most of all, I am grateful for the unconditional love, patience, and support of my family. They tolerated and accommodated my unconventional work schedule, provided unstinting encouragement, and offered a welcome break whenever I needed it.

Clement Fatovic

1

THE AMERICAN REVOLUTION AND THE IDEAL OF EQUALITY

The ideal of equality has been central to the meaning of America ever since the colonies declared independence from Great Britain. Along with the concepts of freedom, democracy, and individual rights, the concept of equality has helped define the idea of America around its highest aspirations as opposed to its sometimes-ugly realities. There have always been discrepancies large and small between stated commitments to these ideals and actual practices, but the ideal of equality has consistently fired the American imagination. However, like the other ideals that shape the American public's understanding of itself, the meaning and application of equality have always been contested. Even if it was "self-evident" to the generation that founded the Republic "that all men are created equal," it has never been obvious exactly what that equality actually means, how it gets implemented, or who is promised its benefits. Some conceptions of equality have been more readily accepted than others. Even though bitter and costly struggles have been waged over the ideas of equality under the law, equal opportunity, and equal rights, legal and political conceptions of equality are now generally far less controversial than the ideal of economic equality. The advancement of equality in the spheres of law and politics is one thing, but the promotion of equality in the sphere of economics is quite another. In fact, it is often assumed today that the pursuit of economic equality involves undesirable or even illegitimate trade-offs with freedom or other important values. As a result, many Americans today are willing to tolerate levels of inequality in the economic realm they would find unconscionable in law and politics.

For those Americans who participated in the creation of the Republic, however, equality in the spheres of law and politics was very closely connected to equality in the sphere of economics. Whatever their disagreements over the meaning and application of equality, Americans in that period generally agreed that legal and political equality depend to some degree on economic equality. Following the first stirrings of the American Revolution, more and more Americans came to understand that some measure of economic equality is a precondition for the preservation and promotion of political and legal equality. For that reason, many of them voiced concerns in letters, pamphlets, essays, books, sermons, orations, and legislative debates about the ways in which economic inequalities threaten to introduce and exacerbate legal and political inequalities.

Even more striking than the connections many Americans made between different forms of equality were the links they established between economic equality and political freedom. It was widely assumed that economic relations significantly affect the conditions under which citizens participate in the political process. Equality and freedom were not necessarily seen as distinct or opposing ideals that had to be balanced against each other, but as complementary and mutually constitutive ideals that sustained one another. In particular, economic equality was viewed as essential to political freedom. That is, a rough degree of economic equality creates the conditions for the effective exercise of citizenship.

These ideas grew out of a sober acknowledgment of the dangers excessive levels of economic inequality pose to self-government. Many expressed anxiety that disparities in economic resources would eventually translate into disparities in political power that ultimately weaken the foundations of free government. Concentrations of wealth make it much easier for the rich to gain undue influence in government and dominate the political process. By the same token, lack of material resources makes it much more difficult for the poor to gain a voice and participate in the political process. The most worrisome feature of economic inequality concerned the relations of dependence and domination that formed between members of different classes. Many feared that large concentrations of wealth would give members of the upper classes the ability to determine not only the availability and prices of goods, employment opportunities, working conditions, and the wages of those in the lower classes but also the tax policies, spending priorities, and other public policies that affected the lives of ordinary citizens. If the political process were skewed in favor of the few at the expense of the many, support for the institutions of free government would gradually erode over time, eventually threatening the freedom of rich and poor alike.

To combat the dangers economic inequality poses to political freedom, many Americans looked to the government to prevent economic inequality from becoming excessive. The use of public policy to minimize or prevent the growth of economic inequality was viewed as a legitimate function of government by a wide spectrum of political actors, from middling farmers such as Revolutionary War veteran William Manning and urban champions of the laboring classes such as Thomas Paine to wealthy planters such as Thomas Jefferson and intellectual elites including Noah Webster. Even though many of these and other important figures generally favored small and limited governments, they were open to the use of public policy to minimize the damaging effects of economic inequality on the kind of government they wished to preserve. Religious and humanitarian considerations frequently entered into arguments in favor of public policies designed to address economic inequality, but political considerations revolving around the links between the maldistribution of wealth and imbalances of power ultimately justified a more active role for government than many were otherwise willing to accept.

Attitudes toward Inequality and Hierarchy during the Founding

The presence of slavery and indentured servitude throughout all thirteen colonies and states serves as an obvious reminder that various forms of extreme inequality were well entrenched if not always accepted. A variety of cross-cutting and overlapping hierarchies characterized social and political life in eighteenth-century America. As historian Gordon Wood notes, "Most of colonial society was vertically organized."[1] Colonial society was stratified along racial, gender, religious, occupational, and financial lines. Although Americans were conscious of belonging to different economic strata, antagonisms stemming from differences in occupation, national origin, and other markers of identity hampered the development of a politicized class identity or general class-consciousness.[2] Relations of subordination between whites and blacks, men and women, Protestants and Catholics, professionals and laborers, native-born citizens and immigrants, and rich and poor existed throughout the country, but there were notable regional differences in manners and sensibilities, especially when it came to relations between classes.[3] Class distinctions were much more rigid in the South than in the North. Hierarchical patterns of behavior and vertical structures of power were also far more prevalent in the southern states compared with their northern counterparts, with large planters continuing to model their behavior and consumption patterns on that of the English gentry.[4]

Those in the lower ranks of society were expected to exhibit appropriate levels of respect toward their "betters" and submit to their judgments about what was best for the community as a whole. Norms of deference required certain forms of address, posture, and gesture in social intercourse between members of different social and economic classes that were taught in guidebooks and enforced through social norms.[5] Official rules reflected and reinforced these inequalities. Property qualifications for voting and officeholding throughout the colonies gave institutional expression to the notion that the propertied were more fit for public service and concentrated political power in the hands of the wealthy. As a result of these political rules and social attitudes, members of more prestigious and lucrative professions, including lawyers, merchants, and large landowners, were heavily overrepresented in assemblies, whereas farmers, artisans, and other laborers were badly underrepresented.[6] In addition, the tax system in the colonies generally favored landed aristocrats and imposed heavy burdens in the form of poll taxes on citizens of more modest means.[7]

What scholars have labeled the "politics of deference" was a well-established feature of public culture before the Revolution.[8] Despite periodic challenges to the pretensions of elites and the subordination of the lower ranks, the prevailing social order was never in any real danger of being overturned during the colonial period. Even some of those who contested the British Parliament's right to govern the colonies defended the right of the "better sort" to rule within the colonies. For instance, the same writer who proclaimed the right of the people to resist tyrannical or corrupt government asserted that individuals must remain subordinate and obedient to their superiors: "The welfare, nay, the nature of civil society requires, that there should be subordination of order, or diversity of ranks and conditions in it; that certain men or orders of men be appointed to superintend and manage such affairs as concern the public safety and happiness."[9] Defenders of hierarchy could find justifications in a variety of authoritative sources that considered inequalities rooted in nature or in divine reason, from ancient texts such as the Bible and Aristotle's *Politics* to modern classics such as Alexander Pope's *Essay on Man*.[10]

After the Revolution got under way, Americans became more outspoken in questioning hierarchical attitudes and practices.[11] The notion that the rich have a right to govern the rest was an early target of patriots.[12] Going back to the seventeenth century, there were critics who condemned elite pretensions to superiority, reformers who sought to lower barriers to political participation, moments of popular resistance to established structures of power and privilege, boycotts against public markets that seemed to benefit wealthy merchants at the expense of small retailers and vendors, religious denunciations of the acquisitiveness of the rich and their stinginess toward the poor, and even occasional physical attacks on the property of the rich.[13] One of the major differences was that various forms of inequality that had been widely accepted started to come under attack from Americans of all ranks, including those who stood at the top of the social hierarchy. Challenges to social and economic inequality that used to grow out of and be confined largely to local circumstances were being mounted on an increasingly larger scale with national implications. For instance, the political and military need to mobilize the people in the struggle for independence compelled elites to rethink the role of the marginalized and subordinated. It was getting more and more difficult to reconcile institutions such as slavery, habits of deference, and great disparities of wealth with the animating principles of the Revolution. Increasing numbers of Americans began to argue that social and political hierarchies were incompatible with revolutionary ideals of liberty, self-rule, balanced government, and most of all equality.

According to Wood, "Equality was in fact the most radical and most powerful ideological force let loose in the Revolution."[14] The ideal of equality, which was articulated in pamphlets, sermons, addresses, newspapers, correspondence, and, most memorably, in the Declaration of Independence, inspired patriots to expand the franchise, eliminate vestiges of feudalism in property law, curtail indentured servitude, and challenge the morality of slavery. It also reshaped Americans' ideas about social relations between upper and lower classes. Many men enlisted in the Revolutionary Army with the expectation that they would get to choose their own officers.[15] Newspaper and pamphlet writers urged the adoption of annual elections and rotation in office to instill a sense of "humility" in elected gentlemen who might otherwise avoid and develop contempt for their inferiors.[16] The use of honorific titles such as gentleman, esquire, and honorable—never very rigid or well defined to begin with—continued to fade in importance.[17] By the same token, the use of pseudonyms such as "A Farmer," "A Mechanick," and "A Husbandman" by pamphleteers from all backgrounds indicated the changing political status and mobilization of those in the laboring classes.

As the ideal of equality became more firmly established in both popular and elite opinion, Americans also began to question existing distributions of wealth and power. Indeed, participants on both sides of the war for independence viewed the conflict at least partly in terms of class.[18] For a moment, ideas and interests converged in opposition to various forms of inequality. Attacks on the rule of economic elites often went hand in hand with attacks on British rule because so many of the wealthiest inhabitants in the colonies were Loyalists. Samuel Adams cast the British as plutocratic exploiters who grew "rich and powerful" by seizing the "honest earnings of those industrious emigrants" in order to "support themselves in their vanity and extravagance."[19] One of the chief grievances Pennsylvanians voiced against British rule was the swelling concentration of wealth and power in the hands of the "few." They complained that the political system was dominated by a "minority of rich men" who considered the lower classes "their property, their beasts of burden, born only to be ruled by these Lords of Creation."[20] Loyalists, in turn, portrayed the rebels as "levelers" intent on demolishing the established social order and undermining property rights.[21] As Americans began to reject the legitimacy of British rule, they started increasingly to question the legitimacy of economic inequality in general. Most Americans still accepted economic inequality as a fact of life, if not a law of nature, but more and more of them started to believe extreme levels of economic inequality were incompatible with those political ideals that animated the struggle for independence. For the next few decades, the ideal of economic equality would play a significant role in debates over public policy and the prospects of republicanism in the United States.[22]

No one argued that economic inequality could or should be eliminated entirely, but leading revolutionaries including Jefferson, Adams, and Paine, along with (now) lesser-known figures such as Abraham Clark, James Sullivan, and Manning expressed concerns that extremes of inequality threatened vital political values. As lexicographer and education reformer Webster put it, "The basis of a democratic and a republican form of government, iz [*sic*], a fundamental law, favoring an equal or rather a general distribution of property. It iz [*sic*] not necessary nor possible that every citizen should hav [*sic*] exactly an equal portion of land and goods, but the laws of such a state should require an equal distribution of intestate estates, and bar all perpetuities."[23] Whatever their impressions of the actual distribution of wealth in America, those who described economic inequality as a political problem generally accepted some form of public action to limit the maldistribution of wealth and mitigate its effects. As discussed in the following chapters, almost every area of public policy, from the tax system and the disposition of public lands to inheritance law and education, provided opportunities to promote economic and political equality.

Critics of economic inequality could draw upon a wide assortment of intellectual traditions and historical precedents that shaped the colonial experience, from the religiously inspired social radicalism of the Great Awakening to the experiments of reformers seeking to lift the unemployed out of poverty and the sometimes violent forms of crowd action directed against the privileges of elites in the "urban crucible."[24] In their battle against excessive economic inequality, critics found ample stores of intellectual ammunition in a variety of religious and secular sources. Critics drew from scripture, Lockean natural rights theory, and various schools of Enlightenment philosophy to develop an eclectic mix of religious, moral, economic, and humanitarian arguments against excessive economic inequality. Although religious, moral, economic, and humanitarian ideals figured prominently in many critiques of economic inequality, political considerations were usually supreme. With increasing frequency and urgency, many Americans came to perceive economic inequality as a threat to a host of interrelated political ideals, including civic virtue, social solidarity, political stability, equality under the law, and above all political freedom.

A variety of political thinkers and traditions dear to Americans at the time addressed the political costs associated with high levels of economic inequality. The one that supplied the overarching frame-work for understanding how ideals such as civic virtue, social solidar-ity, political stability, equality under the law, and political freedom were interconnected and how they were imperiled by economic im-balances was republicanism. Central to the idea of republicanism is the notion that the preservation of freedom in a republic ultimately depends on the quality of its citizens. In particular, the virtue and active participation of equal and independent citizens are considered essential to the maintenance of a free way of life. Republicans from Aristotle, Cicero, and Machiavelli to James Harrington, Algernon Sidney, and Jean-Jacques Rousseau have recognized the role of in-stitutions—including a balanced constitution, general laws, annual elections, and rotation in office—in creating and perpetuating free government, but they also emphasized the importance of social, economic, and moral factors in making these institutions work. Of paramount importance was the virtuous citizen, committed to the commonweal and prepared to subordinate private interest for the sake of the public good.[25] As Samuel Adams explained, virtue is critical to the preservation of liberty: "While the People are virtuous they cannot be subdued."[26]

According to long-standing republican tradition, the virtue of the citizen does not spring automatically from human nature: it has to be cultivated by a proper education and the right set of socio-economic conditions. For citizens to develop and exercise the virtue necessary for the maintenance of republicanism, they must be in-dependent. That is, they have to be capable of exercising their own judgment and will, free from the control or dominance of others. To a significant degree, the basis of this autonomy is material: politi-cal independence depends on economic independence. For many re-publican thinkers, economic equality is considered indispensable to the preservation of republicanism. Without it, individuals would not enjoy the independence required to use their own judgment, protect their liberties, exercise their responsibilities, or fulfill their duties as citizens. Lack of independence makes citizens susceptible to de-ception, manipulation, and exploitation by others. As Revolution-ary War veteran and newspaper editor Robert Coram explained in 1791, "If they are dependent, they can neither manage their private concerns properly, retain their own dignity, or vote impartially for their country; they can be but tools at best."[27] The achievement of economic independence does not require an equal distribution of property for republicans, but it does require a minimum degree of property to keep poorer citizens from becoming so desperate they sell their votes to richer ones and to prevent richer citizens from becoming so powerful they dominate the poorer ones.[28] As Webster explained, one of the most important lessons taught by the history of ancient republics is that "vast inequality of fortunes" is ultimately fatal to free government.[29]

Although there are several varieties of republicanism, including more aristocratic and more democratic variants, virtually every thinker in that tradition taught Americans the same lesson about the relationship between economics and politics: power follows property.[30] Republicans were aware that shifts in the distribution of power could produce shifts in the distribution of wealth, but thinkers such as Harrington, who exerted a strong influence on revolutionary thinking, believed political power was ultimately determined by property ownership, especially property in land. As Harrington put it in *The Commonwealth of Oceania*, "Equality of estates causeth equality of power, and equality of power is the liberty not only of the commonwealth, but of every man."[31] Conversely, unequal property was closely associated with unequal power. An uneven distribution or concentration of power jeopardized both individual and collective freedom. As political theorist Michael J. Thompson explains, opposition to economic inequality within the republican tradition and among the Americans guided by it was based on fears of the political inequality and domination it tended to produce and maintain.[32] Economic inequality is so destructive to liberty that Harrington went so far as to assert, "Where there is inequality of estates, there must be inequality of power, and where there is inequality of power, there can be no commonwealth."[33]

Republicans devised a variety of measures to prevent domination of the political process resulting from excessive levels of economic inequality. To borrow a distinction drawn from James Madison's account of the problem of factions in republics, they proposed to deal with the problem of economic inequality either by controlling its effects (e.g., by giving the people institutional means of controlling elites and holding them accountable or by redistributing property after its distribution became too unbalanced), by eliminating its causes (e.g., by taking steps to ensure the distribution of property did not become too unequal in the first place), or by some mixture of the two.[34]

Republican thought on the political effects of economic inequality exerted a profound influence on the thinking of Americans during the revolutionary period. Thompson may go too far in claiming arguments over economic inequality were *"central* to the political debates that spurred America's political and social development,"[35] but there is no question that growing numbers of Americans came to see economic inequality as a danger to individual and collective freedom, the moral character of individuals,[36] and the very idea of the public good in the decades following the struggle for independence.[37] The republican ideal of economic equality was reiterated in speeches, sermons, pamphlets, essays, and private correspondence throughout the closing decades of the eighteenth century (and well into the next one).[38]

Perhaps the most important and widely voiced republican objection to excessive economic inequality was the claim that it threatens political freedom. In keeping with the teachings of republican thinkers throughout the ages, many Americans began to sense that republican government could not succeed where property was distributed too unevenly. Webster summed up the conventional republican wisdom on this point, proclaiming, "An equality of property, with a necessity of alienation, constantly operating to destroy combinations of powerful families, is the very *soul of a republic*—While this continues, the people will inevitably possess both *power* and *freedom*; when this is lost, power departs, liberty expires, and a commonwealth will inevitably assume some other form."[39] Excessive inequality undermines the ability of ordinary citizens to participate effectively in the political system not only because their material conditions make it harder for them to get involved but because they are more easily overpowered by those with great concentrations of wealth. For that reason, Connecticut Congregational minister and historian Benjamin Trumbull cautioned, "It will be highly politic in every free state, to keep property as equally divided among the inhabitants as possible, and not to suffer a few persons to amass all the riches and wealth of a country."[40] By the same token, broadly distributed property serves as a check against concentrations of political power in the hands of a few. In a letter to Jefferson, Yale University president Ezra Stiles opined that government would never "acquire a Power dangerous to liberty so long as Property in the United States is so minutely partitioned and transfused among the Inhabitants."[41] What Benjamin Franklin had described as a "happy mediocrity of condition" gave citizens the material resources and independence necessary to resist encroachments on liberty.

Critics argued that economic inequality erodes the conditions that make individual liberty and free government possible. As one petition circulated in Pennsylvania put it, "No observation is better supported, than this that, a country cannot long preserve its liberty, where a great inequality takes place. Is it not therefore the most dangerous policy in this infant republic, to combine the wealthy in order to make them powerful?"[42] Preachers numbered the "baneful effects of exorbitant wealth" among the factors "inimical to a free, righteous government."[43] William Findley, an Irish immigrant who represented the Pennsylvania backcountry in Congress, warned, "Enormous wealth possessed by individuals, has always had its influence and danger in free states." However, "wealth in many hands operates as many checks" against the possibility of dependence on a few.[44] According to Revolutionary War veteran and Massachusetts farmer Manning, free government is lost for two main reasons. One is the conniving and scheming of the few; the other is the ignorance and inattention of the many. The result in both cases is dependence.[45]

One of the most persistent critics of economic inequality was radical republican Clark of New Jersey, a signer of the Declaration of Independence and a leading figure in state politics in the decade following the start of the Revolutionary War. Clark argued, "Inequality of property . . . is detrimental in a republican government" because it undermines the independence necessary for citizens to exercise their political rights.[46] Like many other republicans, Clark supported egalitarian measures for a variety reasons, but the decisive factor behind his support for reforms was an interest in maintaining the conditions that made republican self-government possible. Sympathy for the plight of the poor and middling classes may help explain why he and other like-minded republicans sought to reduce court costs, lower the tax burdens on the poor, and provide relief to distressed debtors (policies he successfully pursued in New Jersey), but it does not necessarily explain their opposition to pensions for military officers or payments to speculators. What mattered to egalitarians such as Clark was not just the *absolute* condition of citizens but their *relative* status. Any policy that increased the distance between the social classes was worrisome even if the material well-being of the lower orders did not suffer because that policy would undermine the socioeconomic foundations of republican government. Clark feared that great disparities in wealth would produce great disparities in power, transforming a republic of equal and independent citizens into a hierarchical society of "lords and tenants."[47] If left unchecked, economic inequality would eventually lead to political inequality incompatible with republicanism.

Critics argued excessive economic inequality threatened other political values as well. In a 1792 pamphlet that examined the history of banking institutions, including their most recent incarnations at both the state and national levels, Boston lawyer and politician Sullivan argued inequality was antithetical to the republican values that animated the Revolution. Large gaps between the rich and the rest of the public are worrisome because they engender passions detrimental to the solidarity republicanism requires among citizens. Privileges, especially those created and dispensed by government, stimulate the "corrosive passion of envy" that gives rise to the social competition and political factitiousness so destructive to "civil society."[48] Sullivan concluded his analysis of money and banking policies in the United States by reminding readers of the principles that ought to guide decision making in a republic: "Government ought to move uniformly, on fixed, rational, honest, and regular principles. It is intended to preserve the equal rights of all the citizens, and to protect the weak against the powerful, and the poor against the rich. But these important ends can never be accomplished where the measure of wealth, and medium of trade, is unsteady and capricious, or where the powers of government, by an undue influence, are made subservient to the gratification or emolument of particular associations, or of individuals in the civil community."[49]

Of course, these egalitarian ideas did not meet universal assent. Some conservatives expressed concerns that the equality of liberty championed by republicans would endanger property rights. One of the most outspoken critics of the egalitarian ideals that grew out of the Revolution was Gouverneur Morris, a fervent nationalist who played a leading role in the creation of the Constitution. He noted, "Where political Liberty [which he defined as the right to give or withhold consent from any law to which a man would be subject] is in excess Property must always be insecure and where Property is not secure Society cannot advance."[50] Many propertied men and political elites agreed with Morris's views, but he did not speak for all conservatives. In fact, some of the most prominent conservatives agreed with their more radical contemporaries about the tensions between republicanism and inequality. In a letter to Sullivan, John Adams expressed wholehearted approval of republican theorist Harrington's observation that "power always follows property," writing, "The balance of power in a society, accompanies the balance of property in land. The only possible way, then, of preserving the balance of power on the side of equal liberty and public virtue, is to make the acquisition of land easy to every member of society; to make a division of land into small quantities, so that the multitude may be possessed of landed estates. If the multitude is possessed of the balance of real estate, the multitude will take care of the liberty, virtue, and interest of the multitude, in all acts of government."[51] Speaking from the floor of the House of Representatives in 1796, Massachusetts arch-Federalist Fisher Ames attributed the vitality of free government in America to its lack of poverty. The possibility of political turmoil and social disorder is remote, he claimed, because so many Americans have the opportunity to achieve literacy. However, he worried about how long liberty would endure if conditions became less equal: "Can liberty, such as we understand and enjoy, exist in societies where the few only have property, and the many are both ignorant and licentious?"[52]

Americans from across the ideological spectrum also condemned the moral values and social behaviors that seemed to spring from excesses of inequality. Critics denounced conspicuous displays of wealth as antithetical to the egalitarian spirit of republicanism. In his 1783 Fourth of July oration in Boston, John Warren, a Revolutionary War surgeon and founder of Harvard Medical School, reminded listeners of the "opulence of individuals, which when exorbitant, must always be injurious to the common interest."[53] John Adams and others supported sumptuary taxes on luxuries to discourage the consumption of goods that accentuated differences between the classes and bred social resentment. Some displays of affluence were deemed inimical to social solidarity and republican virtues of simplicity and frugality. For instance, the establishment in 1785 of a social club that would meet in Boston every other week to dance and play cards led to a hysterical outcry that can be explained only by the fact that detractors, who derisively dubbed the Tea Assembly the Sans Souci Club, perceived the luxury and idleness it represented as a fundamental threat to republican virtue and simplicity. Even defenders of the social club acknowledged that the ideal of republican equality is bound to make anything that stimulates social competition suspect

in the eyes of observers.[54] Samuel Adams went even further by attacking the acquisitive spirit behind the accumulation of wealth as
a threat to republican government: "The inordinate love of gain, will
make a shameful alteration in the character of those who have here-
tofore sacrificed every enjoyment to the love of their country."[55]

Political writers and preachers also condemned ostentatious displays of wealth for setting bad examples that the poor and middling
classes tried to emulate. West Springfield, Massachusetts, Congregationalist minister Joseph Lathrop advised Americans to "live according to our rank and ability," but he also exhorted the wealthy to live
more modestly so "that their example may encourage moderation
among others" and so that the savings from their frugality could
"be applied to some charitable purpose."[56] Others, such as Sullivan,
contended that great disparities, especially those resulting from government policy, give those with less wealth a perverse incentive to
pursue get-rich-quick schemes rather than engage in more productive and virtuous activities: "A great part of our wants are factitious,
arising from what we see in the possession of others; and therefore,
when a few men, by an inequality of operation in the laws of the ruling power, accumulate fortunes, and live in unequalled splendour,
it corrupts the taste of the other part of the community, and draws
their attention from their ordinary means of business. It produces a
spirit of envy, and renders those unhappy, who before had been quite
contented with their situation."[57] The ideal of equality emboldened
some writers to vent their hostility toward the wealthy. Contrary to
those who claimed that the lower orders are irresponsible, vicious,
or dangerous to liberty, Manning asserted that the greatest threats
to free government stem from the insatiable appetites of the upper
class: "It is a solemn truth that the higher a person is raised in stations of honor, power, and trust the greater are his temptations to do
wrong and gratify those selfish principles."[58]

Beliefs about the Level of Economic Equality in America

Despite their awareness that their societies were structured by various differences in wealth, status, and class, Americans frequently asserted that they lived in an egalitarian country. Even as they issued
dire warnings about the dangers of economic inequality to the political health of the Republic, their diagnoses of the existing distribution

of property were overwhelmingly favorable. Indeed, the idea that America was a land of equality—at least for white men—was a general point of national pride and superiority.[59] Whatever disparities in wealth or income Americans observed were generally thought to fall within tolerable limits from a republican standpoint.[60] How did Americans reconcile their claims of equality with acknowledged disparities in wealth and income? How could the very same people who viewed political conflicts through the prism of class proclaim that a general state of equality prevailed? How could those who used terms such as *lower orders, superiors, rich,* and *poor* to describe their societies claim they were anything but unequal?

An important part of the answer to these questions lies in the fact that many Americans believed the distribution of wealth fell within a relatively narrow range, with the vast majority falling somewhere in the middle. Three interrelated arguments were usually offered to justify claims of relative economic equality. The most common argument was that America was equal compared with other countries, especially those in Europe. Another was that any inequalities that did exist were largely insignificant because they were only temporary. Yet another argument was that any economic inequalities that did exist were not especially severe or widespread.

Favorable comparisons with countries in Europe were critical to sustaining the notion that America was an egalitarian country.[61] Americans from different backgrounds and parts of the country were united in their belief that economic conditions in their own country were remarkably equal compared with the conditions they and their ancestors left behind. In contrast to the extremes of poverty and wealth that characterized European societies, the "middling ranks" constituted the largest share of the population and of property owners. Self-described laborer Manning flatly asserted, "We are on an equality as to property [compared] to what they are in the old countries."[62] Robert Goodloe Harper, a Princeton-educated representative from South Carolina, boasted that America was nothing like Europe: "Fortunately for America, there are few *sans-culottes* among her inhabitants, very few indeed. Except some small portions of rabble in a few towns, the character is unknown among us; and hence our safety. Our people are all, or very nearly all, proprietors of land, spread over a vast extent of country, where they live in ease and freedom; strangers alike to oppression and want."[63] Webster expressed the views of many Americans when he observed that this relatively equal division of land was enough to "prezerv [*sic*] a government in the united states [*sic*], very different from any which now exists or can arize [*sic*] in Europe."[64] Perhaps Franklin summed up the differences between the New World and the Old World best of all:

Whoever has travelled thro' the various Parts of Europe, and observed how small is the Proportion of People in Affluence or easy Circumstances there, compar'd with those in Poverty and Misery; the few rich and haughty Landlords, the multitude of poor, abject and rack'd Tenants, and the half-paid and half starv'd ragged Labourers; and views here the happy Mediocrity that so generally prevails throughout these States, where the Cultivator works for himself, and supports his Family in decent Plenty, will, methinks, see abundant Reason to bless divine Providence for the evident and great Difference in our Favour, and be convinc'd that no Nation that is known to us enjoys a greater Share of human Felicity.[65]

The conviction that America was more equal than countries in Europe was also based on the belief that social mobility made differences in wealth and income transitory, and therefore largely inconsequential. Boasts that it was possible for the lowliest laborer to achieve economic independence with enough pluck and hard work could be heard throughout the land. The absence of legal impediments to upward mobility and the general lack of institutional support for the aristocracy helped explain the fact that the "rich and the poor are not so far removed from each other as they are in Europe" for French immigrant Michel Guillaume Jean de Crèvecœur.[66] Encomiums to social mobility and opportunity even became standard motifs in oratory commemorating the Fourth of July.[67] In one of the earliest Fourth of July orations ever delivered, South Carolina historian David Ramsay made the political implications of economic opportunity abundantly clear to his listeners, proclaiming, "The poorest school-boy may prosecute his studies with increasing ardour, from the prospect, that in a few years he may, by his improved abilities, direct the determinations of public bodies, on subjects of the most stupendous consequence."[68]

As French political thinker Alexis de Tocqueville would explain after his journeys throughout the United States in the nineteenth century, equality of conditions did not mean wealth was distributed equally among individuals or families. It meant no one's economic status was fixed: the distribution of wealth was not determined by a rigid class hierarchy propped up by the legal and political systems. In contrast to the situation in Europe, no one could count on the government to prevent the loss of wealth and status, and everyone could hope to achieve wealth and status without interference from government. According to this way of thinking, Americans were equal in the sense that they were equally subject to the same dynamic forces that constantly unsettle and destabilize class relations. The idea that anyone could experience a sudden reversal of fortune—for good or ill—was a mainstay of eighteenth-century social and political thought in America. Even the most wealthy and powerful men in America were vulnerable to the vicissitudes of life. In a midcentury essay calling for the establishment of a hospital that would minister to rich and poor alike, Franklin observed, "The Circumstances and Fortunes of Men and Families are continually changing; in the Course of a few Years we have seen the Rich become Poor and the Poor Rich; the Children of the Wealthy languishing in Want and Misery, and those of their Servants lifted into Estates."[69] Robert Morris, a well-connected and well-to-do merchant who served as superintendent of finance during the final years of the Revolution, expressed the same idea a few decades later: "Those who are now most rich, may then be poor, and those who are poor, become rich."[70] Proving the point, the merchant and financier fell from his perch as one of the wealthiest men in North America and landed in a debtor's prison.[71] Though the height from which Morris fell made his descent particularly spectacular, there were so many other prominent men who lost their fortunes and ended up in debtor's prisons that it became easy for Americans to believe that the class structure was truly—and perhaps terrifyingly—fluid and unstable.[72]

The availability of land reinforced this belief in social mobility. Historian Frederick Jackson Turner's famous thesis that the availability of inexpensive but productive land on the frontier provided settlers the opportunity to achieve independence was already an article of faith in the eighteenth century. Franklin also succinctly articulated the thinking accepted by generations of Americans: "Land being thus plenty in America, and so cheap as that a labouring Man, that understands Husbandry, can in a short Time save Money enough to purchase a Piece of new Land sufficient for a Plantation, whereon he may subsist a Family."[73] As long as land was plentiful, the country could avoid the poverty, inequality, and social tensions that afflicted European societies.[74]

When Americans did acknowledge the possibility that conditions might not be equal everywhere, they usually insisted their own cities and states were free of significant disparities. Writing of New York City, Judge Thomas Jones explained, "With respect to riches, there is not so great an inequality as is common in Boston and some other places. . . . Every man of industry and integrity has it in his power to live well, and many are the instances of persons who came here distressed by their poverty who now enjoy easy and plentiful fortunes."[75] Pennsylvania representative Albert Gallatin believed economic disparities in his state were so small that "an equal distribution of property has rendered every individual independent, and there is among us true and real equality."[76]

The belief that such class distinctions as did exist were not especially significant was reinforced by another favorable comparison with Europe. Next to the extravagant and ostentatious displays of wealth by Europe's aristocrats, the lifestyles of America's economic elites seemed modest. Many of the wealthiest Americans, including prosperous merchants in cities along the eastern seaboard and landed gentry in the South, did live in grand style, but their opulence paled in comparison with the magnificence of the European nobility and commercial elites. American travelers to Europe were awestruck by the exquisite elegance and exotic luxuries they encountered. The ordinarily prolix John Adams confessed to his wife that the abundance and variety of wealth on display in Paris was so overwhelming that the "richness, the magnificence, and splendor is beyond all description."[77]

If there were extremes of wealth in Europe not found in America, there were also extremes of destitution in Europe not noticed in America. Americans who traveled through Europe could not help but remark upon the extent and depth of poverty that plagued the Continent. One of the first things that struck John Adams upon his arrival in France was the existence of such abject poverty in the midst of so much abundance. There was beauty everywhere he turned, "yet every place swarms with beggars."[78] On his return trip to France, Adams was forced to travel over the Pyrenees and through the Spanish countryside, where he saw "nothing but signs of poverty and misery among the people. A fertile country, not half cultivated, people ragged and dirty, and the houses universally nothing but mire, smoke, fleas, and lice."[79] When asked by a European about poverty in the United States, Adams proudly proclaimed, "As to poverty, there is hardly a beggar in the country. As to dejection, I never saw, even at the time of our greatest danger and perplexity, so much of it as appears in England or France upon every intelligence of a disastrous event."[80] Writing as an "American Farmer," French immigrant Crèvecœur boasted that his adopted country had no "real poor" thanks in part to the fact that "those who through age and infirmities are past labour are provided for by the township to which they belong."[81] Similar claims about the abject condition of the poor in Europe and the absence of such misery in the United States were made by Franklin,[82] Jefferson, and many other Americans who spent time in Europe.

In spite of these claims, many Americans and foreign visitors did acknowledge the existence of class differences. Not surprisingly, those who spoke for ordinary laborers and yeomen were particularly conscious of class distinctions. In a speech at the New York State Ratifying Convention, anti-Federalist Melancton Smith, a businessman from Poughkeepsie, expressed the views of many when he observed, "Every society naturally divides itself into classes" because of differences in "birth, education, talents, and wealth."[83] Manning also took it for granted that societies are always divided between the rich and the poor, or what he referred to as "the Few and the Many."[84] Much as Madison had argued in *Federalist* 10, Manning maintained that variations in the "capacities, strength, and abilities" of individuals will always produce a "very unequal distribution of property in the world."[85] The inescapable consequence of the "difference of interest between those that labor for a living and those that get a living without bodily labor" was class conflict. The few will always seek to exclude the many from the privileges that set them apart.[86] Although Manning's contemporaries could agree that societies have always been divided between rich and poor, many of them continued to believe America had avoided the extremes that had fractured other societies. In their view, America was not a country divided into rich and poor but a country dominated by a solid middle class.

Many foreign accounts reinforced the image of America as a country generally devoid of the extremes found in Europe. For instance, French abolitionist Brissot de Warville remarked in 1788 that he "saw none of those livid, ragged wretches that one sees in Europe, who, soliciting our compassion at the foot of the altar, seem to bear witness . . . against our inhumanity."[87] However, a number of European visitors challenged the self-flattering claims of Americans that poverty was nonexistent in the United States. The marquis de Chastellux reported that he first witnessed poverty among whites "in the midst of those rich plantations [in Virginia], where the negro alone is wretched." He was shocked to find whites living in "miserable huts" and wearing "wane looks" and "ragged garments" that "bespeak poverty" of a kind he had not encountered in his previous travels. Instead of giving away or selling even small portions of their vast estates, the greatest proprietors clung to hundreds and thousands of acres of unproductive land in the hopes of one day acquiring enough slaves to cultivate these vast estates.[88] The duc de La Rochefoucault Liancourt described the conditions he observed on his journey from Philadelphia to what would become Washington, DC, in almost exactly the same horrid terms that Franklin, John Adams, and Jefferson used to describe the plight of the poor in Europe: "In the most remote and uninhabited parts of America that I have visited, I have never seen a greater proportion of wretched habitations. The men and women who are seen issuing from their huts are badly clothed, and bear every mark of poverty. The children are in rags, and almost naked."[89]

As it turns out, these foreigners were more astute observers of actual conditions than Americans themselves were.

The Actual Distribution of Wealth and Income in America after the Revolution

The actual distribution of wealth matched neither the ideal nor the perception of most Americans. The reality is that significant inequalities existed between different sections of the country, between urban and rural communities, and between the frontier and more-settled communities. Available evidence suggests that the duc de La Rochefoucault Liancourt's observations that conditions varied tremendously from one part of the country to another and even within the same state were much closer to the mark than the rosy descriptions provided by most Americans. Analyses of tax lists, probate records, and other documents suggest that Americans who boasted about the economic equality of their country failed to appreciate just how great the disparities between rich and poor actually were in the late eighteenth century.

Although levels of inequality fluctuated over time and varied widely from place to place, it is possible to make a few generalizations. Wealth tended to be more highly concentrated in the South than in the North, in older communities than in recently settled ones, and in cities than in farming communities.[90] Poverty also tended to be higher in places where the distribution of wealth was skewed toward the top. Levels of wealth and poverty also varied across different occupations. At the bottom were slaves, indentured servants, and unskilled laborers, with lawyers, merchants, and large landowners usually at the top. Substantial disparities sometimes existed even within the same states, communities, and occupations.

In general, higher levels of inequality were associated with higher levels of wealth and urbanization. Higher levels of inequality, as distinct from poverty, can be affected dramatically by what goes on at the top as well as at the bottom. Satisfying the demand for goods from around the country and across the globe gave merchants in bustling seaports opportunities to amass huge fortunes that increased disparities between these commercial elites and ordinary laborers.[91] In Boston just before the start of the Revolution, the top 10 percent owned almost 60 percent of the city's wealth.[92] In New York, higher levels of inequality accompanied the city's rising prosperity at the end of the century and beyond.[93] In Philadelphia, the most populous and prosperous city in the country, the assets of the city's top 0.05 percent of property owners exceeded the combined taxable property of the bottom 75 percent.[94]

High levels of inequality were not limited to cities. Wealth disparities in commercial farming societies, especially in the South, sometimes exceeded the differences found in even the most stratified urban centers. Rates of landownership provide an important indication of how unevenly wealth was distributed in these areas. In the prosperous commercial farming communities of the Virginia Tidewater and South Carolina eastern parishes, about 10 percent of families controlled more than half of all land, whereas almost half of the white men remained landless.[95] The distribution of land alone did not account for large wealth disparities in the South. Much of the extremely high inequality in Maryland (compared with northern states) could be attributed to the mercantile activities of a few merchants scattered throughout the state.[96]

Just as levels of inequality varied from one place to another, so too did they vary from one period to another. Inequality trended upward throughout the colonial period as property—and power—became concentrated in fewer and fewer hands. However, the Revolution brought about a major wealth realignment because Loyalist property was confiscated, old hierarchies were dismantled, and new economic opportunities were opened up.[97] However, during the critical period between the end of the war and the creation of the Constitution, inequality in most places began to creep back up. Transformations in the nature of production away from bespoke production by cordwainers, tailors, and other skilled artisans toward mass manufacturing by less-skilled wage laborers contributed to an uptick in economic disparities toward the end of the century.[98] In some states, landownership became increasingly concentrated thanks to speculative activity, whereas the number of landless men started to creep upward. By the end of the century, the top 10 percent controlled 40–45 percent of all wealth in many places.[99]

In many respects, Philadelphia exemplified several of these trends. As the port city became more affluent, it also became more unequal. In 1760, half of the city's wealth was owned by the top 10 percent, whereas less than 10 percent of its wealth was held by those in the bottom 60 percent.[100] The distribution of wealth in the Quaker City became more equal shortly after the start of the Revolution,[101] but a trend in the opposite direction set in after 1780. At the start of that decade, the bottom 90 percent owned 56 percent of property; at the end of the decade that number declined to 33 percent; and by the middle of the next decade, the total was just 18 percent.[102]

If conditions in the country were relatively equal early in the eighteenth century, evidence suggests that things changed by the end of the eighteenth century. Exact data are unavailable or unreliable for most of the eighteenth century, but an inventory of real estate values conducted as part of a national tax assessment in 1798 provides a treasure trove of information about the distribution of wealth near the end of the century. Based on a statistical analysis of the information gathered by the Treasury Department on the value of land, houses, wharves, and other real estate subject to the 1798 tax (discussed at greater length in chapter 4), economist Lee Soltow finds that wealth was distributed more unevenly than most Americans imagined. A handful of wealthy Americans, such as the Bingham family of Philadelphia, lived in magnificent homes costing upwards of $30,000 and decorated with expensive imported goods that managed to impress even the most discerning European visitors, whereas tens of thousands of Americans eked out existences in homes valued at less than $10—and sometimes as little as $1.[103]

Not only was inequality far greater than many Americans acknowledged but also there were deeper pockets of poverty than many Americans realized. In spite of the country's self-image as a land of plenty, workers throughout the country often lived a hand-to-mouth existence and faced the possibility of extreme privations whenever the economy took a downturn.[104] The well-to-do generally had little direct contact with the poor and rarely had good reason to venture into the places where they were most likely to congregate.[105] Elite comparisons of the conditions of the poor and laboring classes in America to those in other parts of the world failed to take into account their personal experiences of economic insecurity and material deprivation. Those who were aware of how much poverty actually existed sometimes lamented the ignorance of the upper classes about the plight of the poor.[106] Poverty—like inequality—tended to be much higher in cities than in the countryside and more prevalent in bigger cities than in smaller ones. Anywhere from one-fourth to one-third of urban residents in America were impoverished (compared with a full one-third of city dwellers in Europe).[107] Seasonal variations in the availability of work contributed to the vulnerability—and inequality—of many kinds of laborers. Farmhands, construction workers, carpenters, masons, draymen, and others often struggled to make ends meet when the weather turned cold and rivers froze over, making it impossible to do certain kinds of work.

Even though conditions in America were far less equal than many Americans believed, they were right about one thing: their country was still more equal than any country in Europe.[108] Despite the great disparities among property owners—not to mention between those who did and those who did not own property—rates of ownership were far higher in America than in Europe. Ownership of land, the most significant form of property both in terms of its economic value and its political import in establishing the right to participate, was comparatively widespread on the eve of the Revolution. Whereas only 10 to 30 percent of adult men in many European countries owned real estate, approximately 50 percent of men in America did.[109] Although the most desirable land (in terms of soil quality and proximity to navigable waters) often fetched prices beyond the reach of the lowliest laborers, it was relatively easy to acquire land for anyone willing to settle the frontier. The low price of frontier land and the ability to acquire it on credit made it possible for artisans, mechanics, and even indentured servants to achieve landownership within a few years.[110] Landholdings varied in size from plots of just a few acres in subsistence farming communities in New England to southern plantations consisting of thousands of acres, but middling farmers owned anywhere from a few dozen to more than 200 acres— a quantity more than sufficient to achieve the economic independence Jefferson and others believed necessary for free government. In eastern New Jersey between 1778 and 1780, roughly two-thirds of men owned at least some land, and more than one-third owned enough to support an average-sized family and produce a modest surplus for the market.[111] Thanks to this relatively broad ownership of land, between 50 percent and as many as 75 percent of free adult men were eligible to vote in America compared with just 15 percent in Britain.[112]

Americans at the time were also right about the levels of social mobility that existed on their side of the Atlantic. Even though wealth was concentrated at the top, it was possible for those born into modest circumstances to make it into the ranks of the wealthy. To be sure, the upper echelons were populated with men—and even a few women—who inherited their riches. In states such as Virginia, 80 percent of the commonwealth's richest men in 1787 had inherited much of their wealth.[113] However, lists of the propertied in other parts of the country, especially north of Pennsylvania, were filled with the names of men who started out with little. Among Boston's wealthiest men during the 1770s and 1780s, anywhere from one-third to one-half could be described as "self-made." The percentage of self-made men in Philadelphia and New York during this period was similar.[114] In fact, upward mobility seems to have increased somewhat from these levels in the years immediately following the Revolution. By the time the Constitution was ratified, more than half of the wealthiest men in these cities had risen from humble origins.[115] By definition, it was impossible for everyone to make it to the top, but it was reasonable for every white man—including an indentured servant—to think he could improve his condition. Perhaps as many as 95 percent of those in the lower class could expect to rise to a higher level in the course of their lifetimes.[116] Even if Franklin's "happy mediocrity" did not prevail, the ability of white men to move into the "middling ranks" kept that ideal alive throughout the early history of the Republic.

Dealing with Inequality and Poverty

Notwithstanding claims that America was largely free of the poverty and inequality that afflicted European societies, there were policies in place to deal with both of these social ills. Public programs to alleviate poverty had existed at the local level in all thirteen colonies since the seventeenth century. Outside of these antipoverty measures, however, there were few policies in place designed specifically to address economic inequality. After all, why would Americans enact policies to address a problem they did not believe existed? However, prominent figures including Jefferson, Paine, and Clark did propose measures to reduce existing disparities in wealth and, even more importantly, prevent new ones from emerging. What is most remarkable about their proposals is that they made them at all in light of the fact that so many of them failed to appreciate the actual extent of economic inequality at the time. Their proposals can best be understood as preventative measures designed to inoculate the country against the ills of social and economic inequality. An examination of the policies that actually existed at the time provides an important indication of attitudes concerning the government's proper role in dealing with poverty and inequality.

Poverty relief during the colonial period had always been administered at the local level. However, changes in the size and composition of towns and cities between the seventeenth century and the middle of the eighteenth century contributed to significant changes in attitudes toward the poor and understanding of community responsibilities. The kinship ties that reinforced a sense of collective responsibility for all the poor in the community without distinction gave way to more discriminating judgments about who deserved help and why.[117] Whether and how to assist the poor came to depend more heavily on what one believed to be the causes of poverty. Poverty was attributed to a wide variety of causes including character flaws, dissolute and extravagant lifestyles, alcoholism, accidents,

illness, disability or old age, widowhood, general economic down-
turns, risky commercial ventures, poor investments, and just plain
bad luck.[118] Perhaps even more important than the cause of poverty was the character of the pauper. The kind and quantity of aid
the poor received—and under what conditions—often depended on
perceptions of their moral worth. The most common distinction
was that between the "laboring" poor and the "idle" poor, with the
former described as worthy and virtuous and the latter vilified as
undeserving and vicious.[119] Those incapable of providing for themselves—those who were elderly or had disabilities—could almost
always count on aid from their communities.

One of the defining features of public assistance in America
throughout its history has been "local variation."[120] Not only were
there differences in the political units that actually administered aid
to the poor (generally speaking, towns and counties in the North and
parishes in the South) but also the amount, kind, and conditions of
aid could vary significantly from place to place, even within the same
state.[121] Numerous private organizations were established to address
the plight of the poor in general or the hardships that confronted particular segments of the community, including the Boston Society for
Encouraging Industry and Employing the Poor (which used public
and private funds to build a spinning factory that would employ the
poor)[122] and industry-specific mutual-aid societies such as the New
York General Society of Mechanics and Tradesmen (which provided
social insurance to members and their families in case of illness,
poverty, and death).[123] A variety of other eleemosynary institutions
sprang up after the Revolution. In 1786, Philadelphia physician and
social reformer Benjamin Rush helped establish the Philadelphia
Dispensary—the first of its kind in the country—for the purpose of
"relieving such sick, poor, and indigent persons as are unable to procure medical aid."[124] However, these private institutions were far
less significant in number and impact than the public provision of
aid. One constant across the country and throughout the eighteenth
century was the predominance of public aid over private sources of
relief. According to welfare historian Michael B. Katz, public assistance to the poor has outweighed relief from private sources since
the very beginning of the country's history.[125]

Public assistance has always served multiple purposes, with reduction of poverty being just one—and not always the central—
objective.[126] Attempts to deal with poverty in Philadelphia after the

Revolution exemplified the mixed motives of reformers. Easing the misery of the poor was seldom the only—if it was even the primary—consideration. Many programs, both public and private, were also designed to improve the behavior and character of the poor, to instill proper habits of deference toward social superiors, to root out and deter criminality, to maintain social order, and to promote industry, among other ends.[127]

Public relief generally took four main forms: (1) outdoor relief, (2) poorhouses, (3) auctions, and (4) resettlement.

The oldest type of assistance in America, outdoor relief was aid delivered outside of institutions such as almshouses and asylums.[128] Assistance usually took one of two forms: cash or relief in kind. The amounts of both varied from one jurisdiction and period to another. Where it was given, relief in the form of money might be sufficient to cover the costs of rent but not much else. Relief in kind included the provision of goods as varied as medicine, meat, turnips, grain, potatoes, rice, molasses, chocolate, and the use of town-owned livestock, with fuel for winter being perhaps the most common form of assistance in kind.[129]

In some places, the poor were auctioned off to the lowest bidder, who agreed to provide material support in exchange for a public subsidy and the labor of the poor. It was a system that lent itself to abuse on both sides. On one side, neglect, mistreatment, abuse, and even death could result at the hands of successful bidders who exploited their charges. On the other side, some poor people got themselves auctioned off to their own family members to make extra money for themselves.[130]

Resettlement involved the relocation of the poor from one jurisdiction to another. This practice often resulted in extended litigation as paupers were shuffled from town to town regardless of the season or their health conditions.[131]

Because of the expenses and abuses associated with these forms of relief, states and cities began experimenting with a variety of institutions to provide assistance to and—just as importantly—monitor the poor. Several states authorized the construction of almshouses during the colonial period, but these facilities did not become common in America until the mid-nineteenth century.[132] When localities began experimenting with poorhouses, they were justified as reform measures that would bring an end to the harsh and abusive practices of auctioning off and resettling the poor.[133] Advocates argued that poorhouses would eliminate the abuses associated with other programs, reduce the costs of assisting paupers, reform the moral character of the poor, discourage alcoholism and other behaviors thought to contribute to poverty, improve the lives of poor children, and inculcate a strong work ethic. There was a great deal of variation—in the amount and type of aid paupers received, the rules that governed them, and the discretion wielded by overseers, among other things—but there were a few things they had in common. In nearly every instance, members of the upper class took a leading role in directing and managing these facilities. The poor often received aid in the form of fuel (e.g., wood for heat), money, food, medicine, clothing, and burial. Some almshouses were built at taxpayer expense, whereas others were privately funded. In some cases, workhouses were combined with almshouses. The main impetus behind this eventual move toward almshouses was the anticipated reduction in costs of maintaining the poor.[134] However, much of the cost savings was attributable to the fact that those in need were reluctant to avail themselves of almshouses except in the most extreme cases. Those who made use of "indoor relief" were expected to work under highly regimented conditions. The work requirement was imposed not simply as a means of maintaining these facilities but also to instill proper work habits and moral values in the poor.[135] Overseers expected everyone in their charge, including the old and the infirm, to perform some kind of work for their own support, sometimes offering incentives in the form of (additional) monetary allowances, tea, sugar, meat, coffee, clothing, tobacco, and other material goods.[136]

Responses to Economic Inequality

If the programs in place to assist the poor had only a minimal impact on inequality that is because they were not specifically designed to narrow the gap between rich and poor. Much like antipoverty programs today, their contributions to equality were indirect and focused on economic conditions at the bottom, not the top. By contrast, policies specifically designed to address the maldistribution of wealth could be directed at the bottom, the top, or the middle. Those who worried about economic inequality proposed measures that would improve conditions at the bottom, prevent excessive growth

at the top, or shore up the middle. As the ideal of political equality gained increasing acceptance, proposals to address economic inequality at all of these levels became more common. Unlike the
various forms of poor relief administered locally, postrevolutionary
measures to reduce economic inequality were proposed at the local,
state, and national levels.

Egalitarians did not necessarily think it was either desirable or
possible to establish perfect equality of property. Even some of the
most outspoken critics of economic inequality, such as Findley, believed that disparities in wealth were compatible with the requirements of republican (and democratic) government—but only up to a
point.[137] The threshold was crossed when wealth became so concentrated that it gave a privileged few the ability to lord it over others
and translate their economic advantages into political ones, or, in
Clark's words, when husbandmen and mechanics became "tenants
to those moneyed men" who live off the labor of others.[138] Egalitarians generally did not think the country had reached that point, but
at several critical junctures in state and national politics after the
Revolution they worried the country was veering dangerously toward the consolidation of economic and political power in the hands
of a few. Because they doubted inequality had swelled to the proportions that made republican government difficult if not impossible
in Europe, they focused their attention more on preventing than on
rectifying economic inequality.

Maintaining the political and socioeconomic conditions that make
equality possible was the priority for egalitarians. At a minimum,
preserving those conditions meant the government would have to
avoid actions that worsened or introduced economic disparities. As
Sullivan argued in *The Path to Riches*, "The rules and regulations
adopted by civil society, ought always to be such, as not to afford to
any individual, or particular company of men, an accidental opportunity, or a superior privilege, for the acquirement of property."[139]
Sometimes acting on that principle meant dismantling existing legal and political structures that propped up privilege and inequality.
The most notable example was Jefferson's successful bid to get the
State of Virginia to abolish the laws of entail and primogeniture,
which required landed aristocrats to pass their entire estate without
division into the hands of the firstborn male heir. Undoing this ves-
tige of aristocracy would become a priority for republicans in other
states as well.[140]

Support for economic equality also entailed opposition to proposals that might contribute to disparities between the rich and everyone else. Egalitarians and their allies mounted the strongest opposition to policies that tipped the balance in favor of the wealthy or allowed the few to reap enormous financial rewards at the expense of the many. Because any action the government takes has the potential to affect the absolute well-being and relative position of different groups one way or the other, any policy disagreement had the potential to turn into a conflict over economic inequality. And many did. Alexander Hamilton's plan to restore national credit and spur economic growth through the establishment of a national bank, the imposition of new taxes, the assumption of state debt, and the promotion of domestic manufacturing triggered the most heated and prolonged debates over class and inequality at the national level following the ratification of the Constitution. Virtually every measure dealing with property in any form was debated in terms of its distributional effects—no matter how slight or indirect. Every proposal dealing with taxes, spending, the disposition of public lands, the public debt, salaries for public officials, military pay, veterans' benefits, education, relief for disaster victims, and mandates on members of the militia and other select groups offered an opportunity for legislators, editors, pamphleteers, and ordinary citizens to consider the impact on economic inequality.

Every aspect of the revenue system at both the state and the national levels was apt to set off a debate over economic inequality. Rules requiring taxes to be paid in specie rather than paper money, penalties imposed for nonpayment of taxes, taxes raised from the sale of basic necessities, and excise taxes that disproportionately affected the livelihoods of farmers and laborers met popular resistance and criticism from egalitarian writers.

Those who argued for more fairness in the tax system did not simply react to regressive tax policies. In fact, the egalitarian impulse was most commonly expressed in calls for the creation of more progressive taxes. There was broad acceptance of the idea that taxes should be allocated based on the ability to pay. As Jefferson put it in a letter to Madison, "Taxes should be proportioned to what may be annually spared by the individual."[141] Early in the revolutionary period, there was a shift, especially in New England and the mid-Atlantic states, away from heavy reliance on regressive poll taxes toward the adoption of ad valorem taxes based on the actual value of real and personal property and the imposition of taxes on luxuries, such as wine, pleasure carriages, and watches.[142] In 1776, Pennsylvania's revolutionary government enacted a progressive tax code that included taxes on speculative holdings following more than a decade of unsuccessful pleas for higher taxes on the wealthy.[143] Maryland went so far as to declare in its Declaration of Rights "that the levying [of] taxes by the poll is grievous and oppressive, and ought to be abolished; that paupers ought not to be assessed for the support of government; but every other person in the State ought to contribute his proportion of public taxes, for the support of government, according to his actual worth, in real or personal property, within the State."[144] In calling for protectionist duties on imports to encourage the development of manufacturing in New Jersey, Clark also recommended that a "considerable tax be laid on those who make use of superfluities, for that would compel the rich and splendid to pay something in proportion to their grandeur."[145] Egalitarians during the first few Congresses enjoyed some success in getting goods consumed heavily by the lower classes to be taxed at lower rates or exempted from taxation altogether and in getting carriages, luxury items, and other goods consumed mainly or exclusively by the wealthy to be taxed at relatively high rates. Although egalitarians did not win every battle over taxation, they did prevail in the rhetorical war over the legitimacy of a more progressive tax system. Even conservative leaders such as Gouverneur Morris felt compelled to express approval of more progressive taxes, writing, "It is confessed on all hands that taxes should be raised from individuals in proportion to their wealth."[146]

Egalitarianism was not limited to opposition to policies that had the potential to increase economic inequality. Proponents of equality also went on the offensive and proposed a variety of measures designed to maintain the conditions necessary for economic equality. Webster identified two in particular he believed were "essential to the continuance of republican government." Both regulations were designed to empower citizens, especially the poor, to participate fully in the political and economic life of the community. One was a system of universal public education that provides students both the practical skills and knowledge necessary for a good livelihood. The other was a distribution of property that allowed citizens to achieve a modicum of economic independence. Both are necessary to overcome the exclusive privileges associated with "monarchical" institutions. In Webster's view, republican principles must not be limited to formal constitutional rules but must extend as well to educational and economic arrangements if a free system of government is to survive.[147]

Other leading figures, including Jefferson, Joel Barlow, Samuel Adams, and Rush, also proposed public education as a means of redressing the persistence of inequality.[148] Not only would it lead to economic opportunities that would lift the poor out of poverty, it would also promote egalitarian values necessary for free government. In a proclamation drafted for Massachusetts governor James Bowdoin, Adams promoted education for the "sons of the poor and the rich" as a way to preserve "those principles of Equality which are essential to the Republican form of our government."[149] In Rush's view, it was imperative for republican societies to educate their citizens because ignorance gives rise to and sustains various forms of hierarchy.[150] Toward that end, he proposed a tax on all estates in and around Philadelphia that would provide a dependable source of funding for free public schools aimed specifically at educating the children of the poor. Prominent leaders were joined by now-forgotten voices, including that of Revolutionary War veteran, anti-Federalist, and editor of the *Delaware Gazette* Coram. After detailing how the progress of civilization had generated the "unequal distribution of property [that] was the parent of almost all the disorders of government," Coram proposed a publicly funded system of education available to children of all classes as the best means of alleviating the "miseries, without disturbing the established rules of property."[151]

Some of the more radical egalitarians proposed measures that would have an even more direct and immediate effect on equality. The most common approach involved the (re)distribution of land. Republicans looked to the sale of western lands as the chief means of expanding and equalizing ownership of land without upsetting existing distributions of property. As discussed in chapter 4, they favored the sale of these lands in small plots in order to make them more accessible to ordinary farmers as opposed to wealthy speculators (who preferred to purchase tracts in much larger sizes). Jefferson went even further and proposed giving up to fifty acres of land to any adult male who owned less than that amount in his home state of Virginia. Instead of changing the distribution of landed property as a way to foster more equality, Paine proposed direct money transfers to compensate the propertyless for what he argued was the loss of their birthright to an equal share of the earth.

The most ambitious proposals came from the pen of Paine. The revolutionary writer who proclaimed that "government even in its best state is but a necessary evil" went on to propose the development of a welfare state that guaranteed social insurance to the unemployed, the elderly, and the disabled; provided free public education to all children; offered financial assistance to young families and their elders; and raised revenue through a highly progressive system of taxation, among other things. It would take several generations before some of Paine's reforms would be enacted into law, but some proposals to provide targeted forms of assistance to particular groups, including low-wage sailors who faced special hardships in their line of work, did make it into the law books during one of the early Congresses.

Egalitarians were not always successful in their efforts to reduce existing levels of inequality or even to prevent its growth. Proposals designed to address economic inequality often encountered stiff opposition from forces who prioritized other values over equality or simply wanted to preserve their own privileges under the status quo. However, what is remarkable about the objections generally offered is that they seldom rejected egalitarian ideals in principle. In fact, even the most vigorous opponents of egalitarian proposals often paid lip service to the ideal of economic equality. Whether sincere or not, they sometimes protested that their own positions were more conducive to the cause of equality than that of the self-proclaimed egalitarians. Even some of those founders widely reputed to have been champions of the upper classes—particularly financier Robert Morris and his protégé Hamilton—were not necessarily averse to designing public policy in ways that would promote the interests of the lower classes.

The following chapters survey the most significant debates over economic inequality during the postrevolutionary period. Many of these debates took place within the context of critical battles that helped to determine the structure of the political system, the shape of the financial and economic systems, and the nature of social relations in the United States. Early contests over tax policy at the state and national levels, different schemes of representation under the Constitution, plans for the repayment of Revolutionary War debt, proposals to establish banks, alternatives for disposing of western lands, and many other important issues often focused on the impact they would have on the distribution of wealth—and therefore on power. Debates over economic inequality—and the closely related topics of class and poverty—were central to the struggles that helped to establish defining American ideals and institutions.

2

CLASS CONFLICT AND CRISIS UNDER THE ARTICLES OF CONFEDERATION

The reforms enacted during the revolutionary period opened up the political system to segments of the free male population that had been excluded or discouraged from formal participation during the colonial period. Efforts to expand the role of ordinary citizens in the political process included the erection of public galleries that made it possible for almost anyone to attend legislative proceedings, the periodic publication of legislative debates, the use of the secret ballot to insulate laborers from undue influence and intimidation by their employers, and changes in electoral rules.[1] The reduction or total abolition of property qualifications for voting and officeholding throughout the United States weakened the power of economic elites who had dominated the political process throughout the colonies.[2] Artisans, mechanics, and small farmers used their new political freedoms to elect representatives more sympathetic to their economic interests, troubles, and aspirations. Merchants, lawyers, and large landowners were still overrepresented in legislative assemblies after the enactment of electoral changes, but they lost ground to those in the middling ranks, particularly yeoman farmers.[3] Just as important as these changes in the composition of state and local assemblies were changes in thinking about the purpose of representation. The idea that representatives ought to mirror their constituents and follow their instructions began to eclipse the notion that the people ought to defer to the decisions of public officials possessed of superior education and judgment.

The expansion of suffrage and accompanying changes in the composition of government also affected the kinds of policies that representatives pursued. Elected officials were expected to advocate policies that promoted the interests of the economic groups they represented. The infusion of lawmakers from the middling ranks made state legislatures more responsive to the demands of Americans looking for relief from the heavy economic burdens brought on by wartime conditions. Newly enfranchised men sought legislative relief from the rising commodity prices, high taxes, scarcity of hard money, and periodic food shortages that disproportionately affected those near the bottom. Lawmakers were also giving voice to developing resentments over the growing disparities between the masses of laboring peoples struggling to earn a living and pay their taxes and the privileged few making enormous profits from government contracts and market scarcities they sometimes helped to create. Hard-pressed voters urged their representatives to create bankruptcy law more protective of debtors, issue paper money to make it easier for the laboring classes to pay their taxes and discharge their debts, establish land banks that would provide loans to small farmers, discriminate between original bondholders and speculators in making interest payments on debt, and redistribute the tax burden from the poor and middling ranks to the upper classes. In many states, legislatures responded with laws that provided various forms of relief to debtors,[4] required interest payments to be made to original creditors before subsequent purchasers, increased access to western lands, taxed land on the basis of assessed value rather than acreage, gave tax abatements to the poor, established property taxes according to the ability to pay, and made paper money legal tender.[5]

The wave of popular politics that swept through the country was not confined to the corridors of statehouses and other formal institutions of power. When government failed to enact the changes demanded by the laboring classes, they resorted to a variety of actions "out of doors" to redress their grievances. Protests, marches, demonstrations, violent attacks, and other forms of direct crowd action that had been directed against British authorities and policies that violated the rights of colonists beginning with the Stamp Act Crisis were now being staged against American authorities and policies that threatened the interests of the lower and middling ranks.[6] Popular anger over the failure of government to improve the conditions of the lower orders often culminated in actions that, from the point of view of the gentry, threatened to destabilize the established political and social order. Throughout the country, North and South, anger over perceived inequities in public policies led to assaults on tax collectors, closures of courts ordering foreclosures, and interruptions of sheriffs' auctions.[7] Simmering class tensions sometimes boiled over into violent outbursts, including a labor strike in 1779 by sailors seeking higher wages;[8] an assault on the home of James Wilson in 1779; a riot at a Camden County, South Carolina, courthouse in 1785;[9] and—most important of all—Shays's Rebellion, an insurgency in western Massachusetts in 1786 that would reverberate throughout the nation.

It was in this context that leading nationalists called for a convention to revise the Articles of Confederation. As early as 1780, nationalists such as Alexander Hamilton had insisted that an overhaul of the Articles of Confederation was necessary if the government were ever to carry out a respectable foreign policy, maintain a strong national defense, raise sufficient revenue, restore the credit of the United States, and—most important of all—preserve the Union itself. Leading nationalists including Hamilton, James Madison, John Jay, George Washington, Gouverneur Morris, Robert Morris, and others attributed most of the country's problems to inadequate powers and structural deficiencies in the frame of government itself. However, many of them also blamed the country's troubles—especially its persistent economic woes and the inability to address them—on the "excesses of democracy" at the state level. In their view, state legislatures were *too representative* of the people and *too responsive* to their demands. State lawmakers had not done enough, they believed, to resist the popular urge for policies that ultimately undermined the economic stability and financial creditworthiness of the still-fragile republic. Nationalists inveighed against the new breed of representatives that rose to power in the aftermath of the Revolution as flatterers and panderers who indulged every passion and whim of the people, who themselves were proving irresponsible in their exercise of power, indifferent to the rule of law, and hostile to property rights.[10]

In Madison's view, both the people and their representatives were shaking confidence in the stability and virtue of republican government. The political experiment that began with the Revolution failed to produce a unified republic of virtuous citizens willing to put aside their particular interests in selfless pursuit of the public good and resulted instead in faction-ridden societies fractured by religious, regional, and economic differences. Out of all of these, the ones that troubled Madison and his allies most were the factions divided along economic lines: "creditors or debtors—Rich or poor—husbandmen, merchants or manufacturers."[11] Conflicts between these economic groups were responsible for the "mutability," "multiplicity," and "injustice" of laws that contributed to economic stagnation, led to rising inflation, produced revenue shortfalls, undermined national credit, and ultimately threatened the right to private property.[12] The threat to property was so serious that Madison contemplated a plan of representation according to population and property even though he recognized that the latter would "offend the sense of equallity [*sic*] which reigns in a free Country."[13]

Placing the creation of the Constitution within the context of class-based politics during this tumultuous decade is vital to understanding why elite opinion toward the role of the lower orders in politics underwent such a radical transformation. Each state experienced class conflicts shaped by memories of political battles from its own colonial history, its unique economic conditions, and its particular distribution of wealth and power. Developments in any one of the states always had the potential to spill over into other states and onto the national stage. However, events in two particular states ultimately had the profoundest impacts on the course of national politics. From the beginning of the Revolution, whatever transpired in Pennsylvania reverberated throughout America because it was home to the capital of the young republic throughout most of this period. Philadelphia was the scene of some of the most significant political and economic battles in the early history of the new nation. The Quaker City was doubly important because it was also the seat of the state capital and the largest and most dynamic urban center at the time. Many of the controversies that raged there offered a preview of the high-stakes debates that would take place after the US Constitution took effect. Events in Massachusetts in late 1786 and early 1787 helped pave the way for the creation of the Constitution. Although Boston was the birthplace of the American Revolution, Massachusetts did not receive any special attention from national leaders until an uprising of middling farmers in the western part of the state threatened the established order. Unlike other disturbances that periodically flared up in other settings, Shays's Rebellion took on national significance and finally convinced many national elites that popular politics had gone too far.

Class Conflict in the Confederation's Capital

After the Continental Congress made the decision that the colonies ought to separate from Great Britain, one of the first orders of business was to revise the form of government in each of the newly independent states. In response to the May 15, 1776, congressional resolution authorizing the creation of new written constitutions, the states reorganized their governments according to the political ideals of freedom, equality, consent, and limited government that had animated the struggle for independence. State leaders generally reconfigured their institutions to create a stricter separation of powers and weaken the powers of the executive, and they altered their suffrage rules to give the people a greater voice in politics. As a result, the distribution of power both inside and outside state government underwent a profound transformation. Not only were royal appointees and Loyalists to be replaced by patriots committed to the cause of independence but also the political system was generally broadened to incorporate men from those ranks of society marginalized and excluded under colonial government. States moved toward abolishing religious tests for office, eased or eliminated property qualifications for voting or officeholding, granted the right to vote to anyone who served in the army or militia, and in a few cases even extended the franchise to free blacks. In New Jersey, wealthy women enjoyed the right to vote until the state altered its constitution in 1807.[14]

In Pennsylvania, long-simmering tensions between different classes bubbled to the surface in the debate over the Pennsylvania Constitution. The efforts of radicals to replace the traditional power structure, which was organized around a proprietary party that served the interests of the Penn family and an antiproprietary party associated with leading Quakers and their allies, turned into a struggle against the power of economic elites more generally. Populists inspired by Thomas Paine's plainspoken plea for a simple and more democratic form of government pushed for institutional changes that would make government more representative of and responsive to the people. Defenders of the status quo warned that proposals to enfranchise the unpropertied would give those with "nothing to lose" the ability to throw the state into "public convulsions."[15] However, conservative forces were unable to hold back the democratic tide. Many radicals believed formal changes in the structure of government and rules of suffrage alone would not be enough to guarantee an equal voice to the people. Fearing economic inequality would threaten political equality, radicals looked for ways to limit the power and influence of the affluent. James Cannon, a schoolteacher and mathematician who became one of Philadelphia's leading radical voices, proclaimed, "Great and over-grown rich Men will be improper to be trusted, they will be too apt to be framing Distinctions in Society, because they will reap the Benefits of all such Distinctions."[16] Just how far some radicals were prepared to go to prevent the wealthy from dominating the political process can be seen in a proposed constitutional statement that would have permitted the state legislature to limit the size of estates. The proposal declared, "An enormous Proportion of Property vested in a few Individuals is dangerous to the Rights, and destructive of the Common Happiness of Mankind; and therefore every State hath a Right by its Laws to discourage the Possession of such Property."[17]

Although the provision concerning limits on acquisition was not adopted, Pennsylvania went further than any other state in democratizing and equalizing its political system. When all was said and done, radicals succeeded in removing property qualifications for voting and officeholding,[18] extending the franchise to free blacks, preventing the establishment of an upper chamber in its state legislature to check the people, instituting annual elections, requiring rotation in office, denying veto power to the executive council, and establishing government-operated loan offices that provided low-interest, long-term loans to farmers who put their land up as collateral.[19]

Throughout the war, the Pennsylvania Constitution would serve as an example to members of Congress of what was possible when radicals controlled the political process.[20] Within Pennsylvania itself, members of the gentry initially acquiesced in, if they did not fully support, these changes. However, the economic troubles brought on by the war and the perception that democratic politics failed to solve these problems and even exacerbated them convinced many Pennsylvanian elites that the experiment in democratic governance was a failure. Although many artisans from the middling ranks would join members of the upper classes in calling for reforms to the state's democratic constitution, participants on both sides framed the debate in terms of class antagonism between the "few and the many . . . aristocraticks [sic] and democraticks [sic]."[21]

The dispute over the state constitution led to the formation of political parties closely identified with distinct economic classes. Critics of the Pennsylvania Constitution, who called themselves the Republican Party, were led by a coterie of political and commercial elites organized around wealthy merchant and financier Robert Morris, who would occupy a number of key positions in state and national government. The Morris circle came to include prominent conservatives such as James Wilson, George Clymer, Gouverneur Morris, and Thomas Fitzsimons. Supporters of the existing political system, known as Constitutionalists, included urban radicals such as Cannon and George Bryan as well as rural activists such as William Findley and John Smilie. For the better part of a decade, the partisan contest over the state constitution would be shaped by conflicting visions of the economic foundations of society and government. Whereas Morris's party believed the economy and the government ought to be guided by a class of "moneyed men" who possessed the knowledge and resources to lead America to greatness, the Constitutionalists argued that the laboring classes were the building blocks of both the economy and republican government.

The economic woes brought on by the war exacerbated class tensions in Philadelphia. Things came to a head in 1779, during the worst economic slump of the Revolution. The British market for domestic goods was already closed, but now shipping in this port city came to a virtual standstill, production of goods for domestic consumption and foreign export was interrupted, and the price of goods—especially imports—skyrocketed. Many struggling laborers blamed rising prices for necessities on market manipulations by large merchants such as Morris, accusing them of engrossing, monopolizing, and forestalling in order to create and then profit from wartime scarcities.[22] Because food usually made up the biggest part of the household budget, any increase in the cost of basic foodstuffs could spell disaster for members of the lower orders.[23] Some artisans drew upon the labor theory of value to argue that their work in constructing, supplying, and loading the ships that merchants sent to more lucrative markets entitled them to a say in how and where those ships were used.[24] Members of the militia who were already furious that the burdens of fighting a war that seemed more and more to benefit the wealthier parts of the community were falling largely on "the Mid[d]ling and poor" demanded that the government take action to stop price manipulation by monopolizers and forestallers.[25] After numerous town meetings and petitions failed to produce results, members of the militia decided to take matters into their own hands and put an end to war profiteering. On October 4, 1779, an armed force of 150 to 200 militiamen "arrested" four men perceived as obstacles to price controls and forced them to march through the streets of Philadelphia. Sensing that he might be the next target on their list, Wilson gathered some allies in his home, where they armed and barricaded themselves. In what would come to be known as the Fort Wilson Riot, a gun battle erupted when the agitated crowd assembled in front of Wilson's home. The militiamen failed to take Wilson's home and suffered heavy casualties in the process, but their actions did force the state government to respond to their demands. Within a week, the supreme executive council and the Pennsylvania Assembly agreed to distribute 100 barrels of flour in Philadelphia and to levy fines according to wealth against those who refused to serve in the militia. By the end of the month, the council warned merchants engaged in price gouging that they could no longer expect the protection of the government from crowd action and mob violence.[26]

Some of the most significant political battles waged on the national stage featured many of the same players behind the attempts to reform the Pennsylvania democratic government. Once again, the leading protagonist was Robert Morris. The financier had already served on a number of vital committees in Congress since the start of the war when he was tapped in 1781 to fill the all-important role of superintendent of finance. As the best-connected merchant in the country and one of its foremost nationalists, Morris was ideally suited for a position in what was essentially the first national executive office. Before Morris would accept this position, though, he demanded two conditions from Congress. One was that he be allowed to keep his existing private business interests intact. The other was that he be given nearly dictatorial powers to manage the finances and administration of the country. After a protracted debate in which critics asked how such demands could possibly be reconciled with basic republican principles, Congress eventually relented and gave Morris everything he asked.[27]

The country's finances were in tatters when Morris assumed his post. The national debt continued to mount, the public credit had all but evaporated, revenue was nearly impossible to raise, and supplies for the army were in desperately short supply.[28] On several occasions during his three-year tenure, Morris was compelled to expend his own funds and borrow money on his personal credit to keep the government running. Although the so-called financier of the American Revolution was excoriated for continuing his business activities while he handled sensitive financial matters for the Confederation, the most severe criticisms were directed at his policies.

Virtually every measure Morris pursued touched off a heated debate over its implications for economic inequality and the future of republican government—none more so than his bank initiative.[29] Only three days into his term, Morris submitted a plan for the establishment of a national bank much along the lines suggested to him by Hamilton in a lengthy and detailed letter.[30] The Bank of North America would be chartered by the national government and receive deposits from Congress, but it would operate as a private, independently run institution serving the interests of its shareholders. Like his young protégé, Morris believed the creation of a national bank was indispensable to the restoration of the national credit and therefore to strengthening the Union. In the minds of both men, the bank would accomplish these objectives by securing the confidence of those moneyed men essential to the support of government and the growth of the economy. Their determination to win the support of moneyed men reflected their assumption that economic and political affairs were best managed from the top down and not the bottom up as so many had claimed at the start of the Revolution.[31]

The details of the bank left little doubt it was designed to attract—and benefit—moneyed men. However, even some of those who took up their pens in defense of the bank—a group that included Paine—conceded that the bank contributed to economic inequality. Both its structure and its operation excluded all but the wealthiest individuals from participation. Morris settled the initial capitalization of the bank at $400,000 (just one-tenth of the $4,000,000 Hamilton thought was necessary) with shares to be sold at $400 apiece—an amount that priced out all but the wealthiest individuals. In addition, those shares could be purchased only in gold or silver, which were in scarce supply and unlikely to be in the purses of laborers and yeomen. Furthermore, the bank would issue only short-term loans due within thirty or sixty days, as was customary among merchants and bankers. Morris expected the loans to circulate as a form of paper currency that would obviate the need for paper money issued by the government. In his estimation, a privatized medium of exchange would be able to maintain its value much better than the highly volatile notes irresponsibly printed by government presses. To top it all off, Morris insisted that the bank enjoy monopoly status to protect it from competition from land banks favored by small farmers and retailers.

Initial support for the Bank of North America eventually gave way to widespread criticism that it privileged a few at the expense of many—a perception powerfully reinforced by Morris's successful effort to preserve the bank's monopoly status against a campaign to charter a competitor in Philadelphia.[32] Despite Morris's claims that the bank would fill the void left by land banks, which were greatly preferred by small farmers because they accepted land as collateral, almost every loan the Bank of North America made went to wealthy citizens, most of whom were concentrated in Philadelphia. Out of 1,806 loans the bank made to residents of Pennsylvania in its first year of operation, only 2 went to farmers.[33]

By 1784, an organized movement was under way in Pennsylvania to revoke the bank's charter. Not only had the bank failed to produce the economic benefits its supporters had promised but it had also contributed to widening disparities between the mercantile community centered in Philadelphia and farmers in the rest of the state. The privileges and inequalities associated with the bank were simply intolerable to critics who viewed the institution as a betrayal of revolutionary ideals. Newspapers blasted the bank as part of a larger scheme to ensure that "all power may be centered in the hands of one man—Robert Morris and his Creatures."[34] In the eyes of critics, the bank was fundamentally incompatible with the principles of social and political equality. An official statement by a committee of the Constitutionalist-controlled Pennsylvania Assembly attacked the bank not just for economic policies that resulted in a severe shortage of money but also for political consequences detrimental to republican ideals: "The accumulation of enormous wealth in the hands of a society, who claim perpetual duration, will necessarily produce a degree of influence and power, which cannot be intrusted in the hands of any set of men whatsoever, without endangering public safety."[35] Debate over the fate of the bank raged for more than a year as petitions from across the state streamed into the assembly and pamphleteers took up their quills on both sides of the issue. When the assembly finally took its vote, the bank's charter was revoked by the lopsided margin of two to one.[36]

Morris and his allies refused to let matters stand there. By this point, he had resigned his post as superintendent of finance, but he was still actively involved in both national and state politics. Emboldened by the gains the Republican Party made in the 1785 election, the bank's supporters launched an all-out public relations campaign to renew its charter. To the great surprise and disappointment of the state's radicals, Morris managed to enlist the aid of his erstwhile political enemy Paine, who had denounced the financier for corrupt practices and associations during the Silas Deane affair. The author of *Common Sense* now wrote a series of essays defending the bank as a patriotic enterprise that contributed to the growth of commerce and agriculture, strengthened public credit, eliminated the need for unstable paper money, and facilitated foreign investment.[37] Radicals in the state assembly such as Findley reiterated the charge that the bank was antithetical to republican principles because it promoted economic inequality and gave "undue and impartial advantage to one set of men."[38] Contrary to the contentions of the Continentalists, Paine argued that experience with public banks in other countries showed that they actually benefited all economic groups—including the poor—by increasing the circulation of money.[39] Philadelphia businessman Peletiah Webster offered a different response to concerns that the bank exacerbated inequality. He warned that the Constitutionalist plans to prevent the growth of economic and political inequality by revoking the bank's charter could result in capital flight destructive to the entire state economy. Instead of abolishing the bank "for fear it should gain too much influence in government," Webster suggested, "It would be much more politic to make a leveling act [a steep tax on estates, presumably], to prevent the great wealth of individuals, who are much more likely to become dangerous to the State, than any aggregate bodies of men."[40] Thanks to these efforts and additional victories in the next election, the Republicans ultimately succeeded in their efforts to renew the bank's charter.

The bank was hardly the only initiative that sparked debate over inequality during Morris's tenure as superintendent of finance. Even more important than the bank to his plans for strengthening the country's financial system was the report on credit he issued to Congress on July 29, 1782. A forerunner to the report on public credit that Hamilton would produce as the country's first treasury secretary, Morris's ambitious plan called for a raft of new taxes to fund the country's mushrooming debts in order to restore the national credit and strengthen the economy. Much like his proposal for the bank, Morris's funding plan was explicitly designed to boost the confidence of moneyed men in the beleaguered national government, which desperately needed a steady stream of revenue to show it could honor its debts in full. The more faith they had in their government, the more likely they would be to invest their capital in domestic enterprises. In Morris's view, their investments were critical to the growth and diversification of the country's struggling economy. As one of his biographers explains, the objective of the funding plan was to increase the flow of investment capital "into those Hands which could render it most productive."[41]

Even more troubling to critics than Morris's assumption that the affluent were the engines of economic growth was the possibility that they would get even richer off the backs of the poor. Morris's plan called for the redemption of government debt at full face value even though much of this debt was in the hands of speculators who had purchased it at a fraction of its nominal value from poor and middling citizens who could not afford to hold on to rapidly depreciating securities when they had bills to pay. Critics pointed out that the repayment of this debt would involve a massive redistribution of wealth from ordinary taxpayers—many of whom had been forced to sell these securities at a loss—to unscrupulous speculators. In addition, the interest payments Morris proposed offered the prospect of an additional income stream to those who seemed to need it least. Some supporters of the funding plan disputed suggestions that only the wealthy stood to gain, claiming that prompt and complete interest payments were necessary to help the most disadvantaged: "Among these are to be found The Widow, the Orphan, the Aged, and the Infirm, whose only Hope to Screen them from the most wretched Poverty, depends on the Payment of the stipulated Interest."[42] Congressional opponents such as Abraham Clark of New Jersey viewed Morris's policies as nothing more than naked schemes to promote the interests of financial and commercial elites at the expense of the lower classes.[43]

Morris's reputation in his own day and among scholars today as an elitist champion of the "monied classes" who sought an upward redistribution of wealth rests in large part on the solicitude he always exhibited for the interests of creditors.[44] As he confessed in a letter to Richard Butler, "I am sorry to say that this most worthy Part of the Community have been too little attended to and been

treated with very unjust neglect. To obtain sufficient Funds for placing them on a proper Footing is the Object which lies nearest to my
Heart."[45] Morris frankly acknowledged that many of the policies he
favored would disproportionately benefit some groups over others.
Ideally, the benefits and burdens of government would be equally
distributed, but he understood that every policy would have uneven
redistributive effects. Certain taxes would fall harder on some individuals, industries, or states than others. As he explained in his 1782
report on credit, "If exact numerical Proportion be sought in Taxes,
there would be no End to the Search. Not only might a Poll Tax be
objected to as too heavy on the Poor and too light on the rich, but
when that Objection was obviated, the phisical [*sic*] Difference in
the human Frame would alone be as endless a Source of Contention,
as the different Qualities of land."[46]

There is no question Morris's policies were designed to benefit
the entrepreneurial classes who held much of their wealth in securities and other financial instruments. However, close examination of
Morris's 1782 report on public credit complicates the familiar picture of the financier as an oligarch indifferent to the effects his policies would have on inequality or the less fortunate. Morris made no
apologies for the benefits his policies would bring to the wealthy.
However, he often went out of his way to reassure readers of his
report that his plan would not disadvantage the poor. In fact, the arguments he offered in support of his tax proposals reveal that he was
not opposed in principle to egalitarian ends. Where he parted ways
from his critics was on the appropriate means of achieving greater
economic equality.

In addition to the 5 percent duty on imported goods Congress had
already approved, Morris proposed a land tax, a poll tax on all freemen, a tax on most male slaves, and an excise tax on spirits. Each
of these taxes would fall more heavily on some segments of the
community than on others, but they would not necessarily impose
special burdens on the lower orders. As Morris had explained in a
letter written months before he submitted his proposal, a tax on
land struck hardest at owners of large estates. To exempt land from
taxation, as some favored, would do nothing to help the poor, but
it would be an enormous favor to the rich.[47] In his report, Morris
argued that the land tax could actually prove to be a boon to small
farmers and aspiring landowners. Morris surmised that the expense
of paying the tax on vast tracts of uncultivated land would compel

investors to sell parcels of their land to farmers who would actually settle and develop the land to support themselves:

> To him who cultivates from one to five hundred Acres, a Dollar per hundred is a trifling Object; but to him who owns an hundred Thousand it is important. Yet a large Proportion of America is the Property of great Landholders, they monopolize it without Cultivation; they are (for the most Part) at no Expense either of Money or personal Service to defend it; and, keeping the Price higher by Monopoly than otherwise it would be, they impede the Settlement and Culture of the Country. A Land Tax, therefore, would have the salutary Operation of an Agrarian Law, without the Iniquity. It would relieve the Indigent, and aggrandize the State, by bringing Property into the Hands of those who would use it for the Benefit of Society.[48]

What is most striking about this passage is Morris's endorsement of a tax on land because it could achieve the egalitarian objectives of an agrarian law that redistributes property from the landed to the landless without the coercion.

At first glance, the poll tax seems even more objectionable than the tax on land. After all, a tax that applies equally to rich and poor is inherently regressive. However, Morris contended that the poll tax under consideration would not be nearly as "oppressive" as it was in Europe. Labor was so dear and well compensated in America that "three Days of labor produce Sustenance for a week," making it much easier for laborers to meet their obligations. By Morris's calculation, it would take just two days of labor out of the entire year for the typical laborer to meet the obligation. He acknowledged that the tax would be "next to Nothing" for the rich and "of little consequence" to the "middling Ranks," but he believed that the exemption of any person unable to labor mitigated the regressiveness of the tax.[49]

Of course, allegations that Morris's schemes were intended to enrich financial and mercantile elites at the expense of others forced Morris and his allies to address the effects of his policies on inequality. Even if the claims that his tax proposals would alleviate inequality were nothing more than cynical rationales fabricated to deflect attention from the inegalitarian consequences of his policies, the fact that he felt compelled to offer them at all is indicative of how powerfully egalitarian values informed public opinion. Morris's private correspondence indicates that the effects his policies would have on the lower classes factored into his own thinking as well. In a letter to George Washington, the financier noted that creditors would not be the only ones who would benefit from increased government revenue. New taxes would help the government do justice to both the wealthy creditors who had amassed public debt and the lowly workers who produced supplies for the army. Without a steady stream of revenue, those laborers who produced food, clothing, and other materiel for the army would go unpaid. "And thus while People who live in Ease and even in Luxury avoid under various Pretexts the Payment of taxes a great Portion of the Public Expense is borne by poor Women who earn their daily Bread by their daily Labor."[50]

Despite his best efforts and a threat to resign if his financial plan did not pass, Congress failed to act. That failure had less to do with any debate over economic inequality than with the structure of the Confederation government itself. Under the Articles of Confederation, Congress lacked the power to raise revenue on its own authority. All it could do was make requests to the states. Unless all thirteen states agreed—which they seldom did—the national government and the army were left strapped for funds. Morris and other nationalists, including Madison, Washington, Hamilton, and Jay, agreed that no revenue plan would succeed without a fundamental alteration in the powers of the national government. One of the biggest obstacles standing in their way was the resistance of states reluctant to relinquish any of their powers to a more powerful and more centralized national government. Nothing would change in Philadelphia without dramatic changes in the rest of the country. The nationalist cause received just the boost it needed from events that transpired in western Massachusetts.

Popular Resistance to the Massachusetts Constitution and the Specter of Leveling

The radicalism of the Pennsylvania Constitution was met with mixed reactions in other states. Although radicals looked to the Keystone State's democratic and egalitarian reforms as models for their own efforts, more conservative Americans worried that similar changes in their own states could jeopardize the respect for property rights and social rank they believed was critical to the maintenance of law and order. Even as radicals in Philadelphia were agitating for changes in their state political system, John Adams, who was leading the Massachusetts delegation in Congress, began warning of the dangers associated with opening up the political process to the poor and propertyless. For the same reasons women and children were not given the right to vote, Adams explained in a letter to Boston attorney James Sullivan, grown men "wholly destitute of Property, are also too little acquainted with public Affairs to form a Right Judgment, and too dependent upon other Men to have a Will of their own." Each of these groups lacked the independence required to exercise their own will, according to him.[51] Citing English republican James Harrington's dictum, "Power always follows Property," the revolutionary leader proposed that the best way to preserve a balance of liberty and power would be to "make the Acquisition of Land easy to every Member of Society: to make a Division of the Land into Small Quantities, So that the Multitude may be possessed of landed Estates. If the Multitude is possessed of the Ballance [*sic*] of real Estate, the Multitude will have the Ballance [*sic*] of Power, and in that Case the Multitude will take Care of the Liberty, Virtue, and Interest of the Multitude in all Acts of Government." When it was not possible to achieve the broad distribution of wealth he thought necessary for the exercise of self-government, Adams was unwilling to make an exception to the requirement that power follow property. As he put it, to allow "every Man, who has not a Farthing . . . [to] demand an equal Voice with any other in all Acts of State . . . [will] confound and destroy all Distinctions, and prostrate all Ranks, to one common Levell [*sic*]."[52] As the years passed, Adams became increasingly pessimistic about the ability of the poor—and the rich, for that matter—to surmount their narrow economic interests in pursuit of the commonweal. Instead of equalizing differences between different classes, Adams pinned his hopes for republicanism on the possibility of balancing those classes.[53]

Adams got the chance to put his ideas about a balance of interests into practice when he was selected in 1779 to serve as a delegate to his state constitutional convention in Boston. The year before, the state rejected a proposed constitution that established relatively low property qualifications for voting and officeholding. As Gordon Wood explains, several states sought to "reverse the democratic tendencies of the early constitutions," but none would go as far as

Massachusetts in reducing the role of the lower orders and their representatives in the legislature.[54] Adams was given the opportunity to write the first draft of the constitution as a member of the three-person subcommittee tasked with this responsibility by the convention. The document Adams produced drew extensively upon the principles he laid out in his 1776 essay, "Thoughts on Government," a response to what he considered Paine's misguided call for simplicity in government in *Common Sense*.

Adams's draft began with a statement of republican principles that affirmed the state's commitment to the protection of individual rights, the ideal of government under law, the principle of popular sovereignty, and the idea that "government is instituted for the common good." However, the actual frame of government represented a departure from the egalitarian ideals that shaped the Pennsylvania Constitution and informed early revolutionary politics in Adams's own state. Both the structural arrangements and the suffrage rules in Adams's draft were designed to check the power of popular majorities. These features reflected Adams's growing acceptance of the idea that the maintenance of freedom in a republic requires political institutions that balance the ineradicable social divisions between the few and the many. In keeping with his strong defense of the separation of powers and checks and balances in "Thoughts on Government," Adams's draft established three branches of government, a bicameral legislature, and a strong executive with an absolute veto over legislation. Representation in the senate would not be determined by population size but "by the proportion of the public taxes paid" in each district.[55] In addition, Adams created escalating property requirements to vote for the statehouse, the senate, and the governor and lieutenant governor. The property qualifications to hold one of these offices were even higher. In both instances, the requirements were substantially higher than the ones stipulated in the rejected constitution. Foreshadowing the fuss he would make over the proper way to address the president of the United States during the first Congress, Adams stipulated that the titles of the governor and lieutenant-governor would be "His Excellency" and "His Honor," respectively.[56]

The state constitutional convention made a few alterations to Adams's plan—including a revision that allowed the legislature to override the governor's veto—but kept the basic structure of Adams's design intact. Adams and his allies were able to get their way in part because many delegates from the western part of the state were unable to make it to Boston because of harsh winter conditions.[57] Critics pointed out that the constitution would weaken the Bay State's democratic character and violate its own declaration of principles. Not only were the new property qualifications repugnant to the "principle of personal equality" but they also undermined the idea that citizens should be subject only to laws made by their own consent.[58] When all was said and done, the Massachusetts Constitution raised property qualifications for voting and officeholding by substantial margins (doubling the amount of wealth required to be eligible for the governorship and the upper chamber), established the upper house of the legislature on the basis of taxes rather than population, insulated both the governor and the judiciary from popular control, and established what many considered an excessively low quorum requirement that enabled a coterie of officials near the capital to pass laws without the participation of representatives from the western part of the state. According to historian Leonard Richards, the constitution "shifted power from the rural backcountry to Boston, from the poor to the rich, and from town meetings to the state senate and the governor's office."[59] As a result of these changes, Massachusetts ended up with the highest property qualifications of any state.

This shift in power would have profound implications for the way the legislature handled matters that pitted different economic groups against each other. The repayment of state debt was an especially fraught issue. Although the notes were worth just one-fortieth of their face value when the legislature took up the matter in 1781, lawmakers backed by mercantile elites pressed for consolidation of the war debt and full repayment at face value. Critics pointed out that the plan would be a huge windfall for a small handful of speculators who often purchased notes at only a fraction of their face value from impoverished soldiers forced to sell just to make ends meet. As in many other states, a tiny group of investors ended up with the vast majority of certificates.[60] Speculators in the Boston area ended up with almost 80 percent of all the notes, with half of this total falling into the "hands of just thirty-five men."[61] To make matters even worse, critics argued, the repayment plan was based on an extremely regressive and burdensome tax plan. In addition to new impost and excise duties, the plan called for interest payments in hard money (in scarce supply); property taxes on livestock, land, and barns; and poll taxes on males sixteen years old and above.[62] Under this tax system, Massachusetts farmers faced a tax burden four to five times higher than the one they faced under British rule.[63] Just as galling to them was the fact that a higher proportion of those taxes would now come from regressive polls than they did before the Revolution.[64] To add to the consternation of hard-pressed farmers, the majority of taxes collected by the state was used to service the debt.

The legislature also seemed to side with creditors over debtors. Massachusetts was the only state that mandated the payment of all taxes and private debts in specie. Under state laws dating back to the seventeenth century, creditors could have debtors imprisoned until they made good on their obligations.[65] Communities in rural parts of the state repeatedly petitioned the legislature to reform a system that proved costly to both creditors and debtors. The law actually created perverse incentives to sue even trustworthy debtors who had every intention of fulfilling their obligations. Instead of distributing a debtor's property equally among creditors, the system gave preference to the first creditor to file suit. Anxiety about being left with nothing encouraged creditors to file suit much earlier than they otherwise would—if they would have filed any suit at all. As a result, the courts were kept busy with proceedings between neighbors—to the benefit of lawyers, judges, and court officials. When citizens complained that the system advantaged no one but this narrow group of legal professionals, the state legislature responded with a few temporary measures that failed to make any fundamental changes.[66]

These and other policies led to a growing divide between the eastern and western parts of the state that actually predated the start of the war. Often, these tensions boiled over into violence. According to Wood, the "towns west of the Connecticut River were in a state of virtual rebellion from the governing authorities in the East" throughout the revolutionary period.[67] In 1782, for instance, a Congregationalist minister and Revolutionary War veteran named Samuel Cullick Ely led an attempt to close the Northampton County Court in protest against the state constitutional government that resulted in his arrest and subsequent escape from jail with help from supporters.[68] In 1786, these popular uprisings against the political domination of economic elites and the injustice of their policies culminated in what has come to be called Shays's Rebellion. The insurgency, which involved numerous war veterans and distressed farmers in the western part of the state, shut down the courts in five counties to prevent foreclosures and attempted to seize the federal arsenal at Springfield Armory before it was finally put down in February 1787.

The rebellion is often characterized as a failure, but it did prod the legislature to adopt some of the changes urged by the insurgents and their supporters. In response to the rebellion, the state government adopted a number of changes that had the effect of lightening the burdens on ordinary citizens, including easing tax-collection efforts, allowing taxpayers to pay their taxes in goods, reducing direct taxes, and permitting debtors to repay creditors in personal property rather than specie.[69]

The effect of the rebellion at the national level was very different. National elites seized on the events in western Massachusetts as a sign of impending class warfare that demonstrated the need for a stronger national government capable of quelling domestic unrest and protecting property. As news of the insurgency spread, alarms were raised about the possibility of redistribution throughout the other states. Much of the information that elites in other states received was based on the account of General Henry Knox. Commissioned by Congress to investigate the disturbances in western Massachusetts, Knox produced a report that misrepresented both the size and the composition of the rebel forces. His claims that the number of insurgents exceeded 15,000 (when the number was actually just a fraction of that estimate) contributed to fears of a mass uprising by the lower orders that threatened the existing social and political order. Even more misleading were claims that the insurgents consisted of "levellers" hell-bent on destroying existing property relations. Knox claimed that the Shaysites were "determined to annihilate all debts public and private."[70]

These exaggerations actually worked to the advantage of nationalists in other states. Many of them played up the economic character of the insurgency in order to discredit the Shaysites as levelers hostile to property, largely ignoring their political and constitutional grievances against the concentration and misuse of power by commercial elites. Virtually every account critical of the rebellion characterized it as an attack on property. General Henry Lee told Washington, "Their object . . . [was] the abolition of debts, the division of property, and re-union with G. Britain."[71] Elbridge Gerry, one of the wealthiest men in Massachusetts, warned darkly of the "livilling [*sic*] spirit" that seemed to animate the Shaysites.[72] Washington's former aide David Humphreys wrote that the insurgents were driven by a "leveling principle; a desire of change; & a wish to annihilate all debts public & private."[73] These reports produced such a powerful effect on Washington that he quoted long passages about the threat of leveling in a letter to Madison about the state of national affairs.[74] In a letter to his father, Madison explained that the insurgents "profess to aim only at a reform of their constitution and of certain abuses in the public administration, but an abolition of debts public and private and a new division of property are strongly suspected to be in contemplation."[75]

Contrary to reports, the insurgents were not all impoverished and indebted farmers. Not even the namesake of the uprising, Revolutionary War veteran Daniel Shays, was a pauper.[76] According to Richards, there was "no correlation—none whatsoever—between debt and rebel towns."[77] In fact, there were just as many creditors as there were debtors in the ranks of the Shaysites.[78] The rebels were united less by class membership than by shared grievances against the policies that favored Boston mercantile elites at the expense of the state's rural population. In Richards's view, the insurgents viewed themselves as regulators seeking to hold officials accountable to the people (just like the eponymous group that fought against official corruption and exorbitant legal fees in colonial North Carolina). In petitions submitted to the state government prior to the start of hostilities, aggrieved citizens complained about mandates that debts and taxes be paid in extremely scarce hard currency, numerous court fees citizens were required to pay at every stage of legal proceedings, and even placement of the capital in Boston as opposed to a more central location in the middle of the state. Petitioners argued that legislators passed these laws to enrich themselves and line the pockets of lawyers who collected state-mandated fees. Little of this was mentioned in the stories that nationalists circulated in their efforts to gin up support for a more powerful and more centralized national government.

Conclusion

Regardless of the truth of the matter, elite perceptions of Shays's Rebellion played a decisive role in the push for revisions to the Articles of Confederation. Since the beginning of the decade, many national-ists had already concluded that the country was in a state of "cri-sis." Developments since the end of the war throughout America had convinced men such as Madison, Washington, Hamilton, and the Morrises that the lower classes wielded too much power at the state level. The "rage for paper money," the passage of laws favoring debtors over creditors, and similar policies in Rhode Island and sev-eral other states demonstrated that democratic politics threatened property rights and public credit.[79] Shays's Rebellion showed them that the people could be even more dangerous when they acted out-side the formal channels of power. For years, leading nationalists had been arguing that the national government needed additional powers to carry out effective foreign policy and protect the country from foreign domination. Now, many of them were arguing that a strong national government was also required to deal with domestic threats. Efforts to reform the political system had failed because na-tionalists could not persuade enough state leaders of the necessity for change. An attempt to revise the Articles of Confederation at the Annapolis Convention in September 1786 could not even reach a quorum because only twelve delegates from just five states showed up: delegates from four states never arrived, and four states never bothered to appoint any delegates at all. Nationalists exploited fears of more Shays's Rebellions cropping up in other states to convince Congress to call for another convention in Philadelphia in 1787.

3

THE CONSTITUTIONAL BACKLASH AGAINST THE "EXCESSES OF DEMOCRACY"

The creation of the US Constitution was a direct response to the class conflict that roiled state politics throughout the 1780s. One of the top priorities of many who attended the Constitutional Conventional was to establish protections for property against the excesses of democracy and unruliness of popular action seen in places such as Philadelphia and western Massachusetts. The framework of government that emerged out of Philadelphia in September 1787 expressly limited the power of popular majorities to enact some of the redistributive policies pursued at the state level since the start of the American Revolution. In particular, the Constitution restricted the ability of the states to enact legislation that favored debtors over creditors and prohibited them from issuing paper money to ease the shortage of specie. Although the framers declined to make a full enumeration of the rights of Americans, they did make it a point to protect the sanctity of contracts in Section 10 of Article I and to guarantee the rights of creditors in Article VI. Critics immediately pointed to these and other provisions of the Constitution as evidence of class bias toward the wealthy. Even the more general shift in power from the states to the national government was viewed through the prism of class politics. Opponents of the Constitution contended that the small number of representatives in the House of Representatives, the selection of senators by state legislators rather than direct election by the people, and the lifetime appointment of federal judges would sharply curtail popular control of government and enhance the power and influence of elites.

Ever since Progressive historian Charles Beard published his groundbreaking study on the economic origins of the Constitution, scholars have debated the extent to which the economic interests of the framers and the ratifiers determined their support for the Constitution. Beard's controversial thesis was that the "dynamic element in the movement for the new Constitution" came primarily from commercial and financial elites who sought to stem the rising tide of a democratic politics that threatened their holdings in public securities and other forms of personal property.[1] In particular, those who had accumulated large holdings in devalued public securities at steeply discounted prices expected to reap windfall profits under a new government that would redeem these notes at full face value. Scholars such as Robert E. Brown and Forrest McDonald have disputed Beard's claim that support for the Constitution was motivated principally by the prospect of economic gain, arguing that sizable portions of framers and ratifiers with and without substantial holdings in real and personal property could be found among the Constitution's most vigorous supporters and most vocal opponents alike.[2]

In recent decades scholars from various fields have drawn renewed attention to the critical role of class conflict in the creation and ratification of the Constitution. However, they offer a modified version of Beard's thesis as far as leading proponents of the Constitution are concerned. Supporters did not necessarily back the Constitution because they sought to enrich themselves but because they wanted to protect property rights in general from the threats posed by democratic politics at the state and local levels—a point conceded even by some of Beard's critics.[3] In particular, they sought to limit the ability of popular majorities to enact paper money laws and other policies that would threaten private property, damage the credit of the United States, drive away capital investment, and ultimately hamper economic development. Historians, political scientists, and legal scholars who have examined the politics surrounding the creation and ratification of the Constitution also argue that much of the opposition to the new government came precisely from those classes (and their representatives) whose political power would be curtailed. Terry Bouton characterizes the enactment of the Constitution as the culmination of an elite "counterrevolution" that enacted many of the same policies decried as tyrannical when imposed by the British in the 1760s and 1770s.[4]

Some of the leading sponsors of the Constitution, such as Gouverneur Morris, had been suspicious of, if not downright hostile to, democratic politics since the very beginning of the Revolution.[5] However, many of those who wanted to curtail the power of popular majorities, especially in matters pertaining to the economy, arrived at their positions gradually based on their experiences with popular government in the years after the Revolution began. In spite of all the changes that occurred, national elites did not necessarily reject the egalitarian ideals of the Revolution altogether. Some of the recent scholarship that has taken a critical view of the founders' motives has exaggerated or distorted the extent of their hostility toward the ideal of economic equality. Although they sought safeguards against the kinds of redistributive measures popular majorities had pursued, they did not openly repudiate the republican idea that the preservation of political freedom requires a rough degree of economic equality. When presented with the opportunity to curtail the role of ordinary citizens in the political process, even the more conservative forces shied away from the most antidemocratic options. If nothing else, their reluctance (or inability) to adopt more restrictive measures testifies to the tenacity of republican ideals in the opinion of the public at large.

Inequality in the Constitutional Convention

The official purpose of the Constitutional Conventional, which met behind closed doors in Philadelphia from May to September 1787, was to recommend revisions to the Articles of Confederation. It was widely understood that this would require changes in the powers of the national government to enable it to regulate commerce between the states, raise revenue without relying on requisitions from the states, carry out unified foreign policy, and protect national security. Most of the delegates who attended the convention believed structural reforms that changed the balance of power between the states and the national government were necessary to overcome the problems that had plagued the country since gaining independence. However, most of them believed these changes would not be sufficient unless they also addressed the "excesses of democracy."[6] It was also necessary to limit the power of popular majorities to pursue the kinds of policies that, in the view of nationalists, had contributed to the financial instability, sluggish economic growth, and fiscal troubles that wracked the country. In addition, it was necessary to strengthen the national government to prevent insurgencies like Shays's Rebellion from spilling over into other states—a fear only reinforced by a tax uprising of farmers in Greenbrier County, Virginia, that took place just as the Constitutional Conventional was about to get under way.[7]

Looking back on the work of the convention more than a decade after it concluded, Gouverneur Morris recalled that the delegates instituted a variety of countermajoritarian checks because "they knew by experience the violence of popular bodies."[8] The counterdemocratic objectives of the leading delegates were not a secret slowly unveiled over time: they were announced at the very beginning of the convention. In an early speech on the defects of the Articles of Confederation, Edmund Randolph of Virginia asserted, "Our chief danger arises from the democratic parts of our constitutions." He also lamented, "None of the constitutions have provided sufficient checks against the democracy."[9] The reason they feared democracy so much was that they identified it with the self-interested rule of the lower classes. As James Madison explained to his fellow delegates, the "evils which had perhaps more than any thing [*sic*] else, produced this convention" were the "Interferences" of the states with the "security of property rights, and the steady dispensation of Justice."[10] Debates over representation, eligibility requirements for officeholding, the tax power, and other important subjects revealed just how much delegates associated the excesses of democracy with the debtor relief legislation, paper money laws, and other class-based policies favored by distressed farmers, artisans, and laborers throughout the states.

The nationalists faced a dilemma. They could not weaken the influence of the people too much without undermining their primary objective of strengthening the powers and authority of the national government. Men such as Madison and James Wilson realized that any new system of government would have to draw its strength and legitimacy as directly as possible from the people themselves, or sovereignty would continue to reside in the states—a situation that would undermine attempts to establish coherent and effective national policies.[11] As a consequence, most delegates ultimately resisted efforts to limit popular representation as a means of curbing the influence of the lower classes. Instead, they opted to curtail the ability of the lower classes to enact policies that might upset existing property relations by removing certain matters from state jurisdiction altogether. The debates revealed that many of those keenest on limiting redistributive activities in the states contemplated a variety of restrictions on popular participation before they finally settled instead for limits on the powers of the states in economic matters.

Class differences figured into debates on some of the most contentious issues from the very start of the convention. With the exception of wealthy South Carolina planter Charles Pinckney, the delegates recognized that there were widening class differences that threatened political and social stability.[12] Few subjects were more controversial or pertinent to the question of class than representation in the national legislature. On May 31, the committee of the whole took up the proposal in the Virginia Plan to have the first branch of the national legislature popularly elected. The reaction was mixed. Whereas Wilson and Madison argued that a branch drawn directly from the people was essential to the success of any new government, Roger Sherman of Connecticut and Elbridge Gerry of Massachusetts contended that the people were too ignorant and incompetent to make responsible choices. Gerry reminded his colleagues that the "evils we experience flow from the excess[es] of democracy." For Gerry those excesses were exemplified by the redistributive policies being pursued in his home state. Although he still considered himself a supporter of republican government, he confessed that his enthusiasm had been dampened by the "levilling spirit" that had manifested itself in Shays's Rebellion.[13] George Mason of Virginia agreed that there had been democratic excesses "but was afraid we [should] incautiously run into the opposite extreme." He thought it was shortsighted of his fellow delegates to contemplate changes that would weaken the influence of the people because the country was so dynamic and class membership was so fluid that they could very well end up disenfranchising their own children: "We ought to attend to the rights of every class of the people. He had often wondered at the indifference of the superior classes of society to this dictate of humanity & policy; considering that however affluent their circumstances, or elevated their situations, might be, the course of a few years, not only might but certainly would, distribute their posterity throughout the lowest classes of Society. Every selfish motive therefore, every family attachment, ought to recommend such a system of policy as would provide no less carefully for the rights and happiness of the lowest than of the highest orders of Citizens."[14]

The counterdemocratic and antiegalitarian aims of leading delegates were most pronounced in debates over what would become the Senate. Many of the delegates looked to the system of balances in the Massachusetts Constitution as a model for the upper house of the national legislature. The most explicit plea for changes aimed at preventing the kinds of redistributive measures being pursued in the states occurred on June 26 during a debate over the appropriate length of office for members of the upper house. Several delegates spoke out in favor of frequent elections as the only arrangement consistent with republicanism, but the debate came down to a choice between six-year terms and nine-year terms for members of the second branch. Madison explained that one of the purposes of the Senate was to protect the people from their own errors and passions by entrusting power to a "portion of enlightened citizens, whose limited number, and firmness might seasonally interpose agst. impetuous counsels."[15] However, Madison was also concerned about protecting the interests of the propertied few from the dispossessed many. The great danger in any popular government was that the majority "might under sudden impulses be tempted to commit injustice on the minority." Economic differences between creditors and debtors and between farmers and merchants created worrisome divisions, but the "distinction of rich & poor" constituted the gravest threat. Madison did not think the gap between rich and poor was very great at the time, but he expected the country to become much more unequal in the future. Because the convention ought to create a system that will "last for ages," it was imperative to understand what was in store for the country and plan accordingly. In Madison's estimation, population growth would contribute to a rise in inequality as the demand for land eventually outstripped the supply necessary to preserve economic independence for most citizens: "An increase of population will of necessity increase the proportion of those who will labour under the hardships of life, & secretly sigh for a more equal distribution of its blessings. These may in time outnumber those who are placed above the feelings of indigence."[16] The country was fortunate that "no agrarian attempts [i.e., land redistribution measures] have yet been made," but Madison reminded fellow delegates, "Symptoms of a leveling spirit, as we have understood, have sufficiently appeared in a [*sic*] certain quarters to give notice of the future danger." The danger could not be eliminated without abandoning republicanism altogether, but it could be minimized by making the Senate as independent of democratic majorities as possible. The best way to do this would be to make Senate terms "considerable" enough to insulate members from the "transient impressions" of the people.[17] According to Robert Yates's notes, which often cast Madison in a more conservative light than his own version of the debates did, the Virginian argued for a lengthy term of office in order to "protect the minority of the opulent against the majority" of propertyless citizens who could be expected to emerge after commerce and manufacturing overtook agriculture as the dominant economic interests in the country.[18]

Alexander Hamilton was even more outspoken in pushing for a class-based understanding of the two houses of Congress. His ideas on the proper functions of political institutions in the United States were premised on his belief "that nothing like an equality of property existed." He explained that such inequality would always "exist as long as liberty existed, and that it would unavoidably result from that very liberty itself." If the first branch of Congress, like the Roman Tribunate, was designed to protect the interests of the "poorer orders of citizens," then it was entirely appropriate for the second branch to look after the concerns of the rich.[19]

The following week, Gouverneur Morris expanded on these explanations of the class-based function of the upper house. He reminded colleagues that its main purpose was to "check the precipitation, changeableness, and excesses of the first branch," especially when its members threatened personal safety, liberty, and private property.[20] In order for them to perform this function well, members of what Morris called the "checking branch" would not only have to possess the "virtues and abilities" necessary in the first branch, they would also have to possess "great personal property" and the "aristocratic spirit." Acting as a curb against the excesses of democracy would not be the only function of the second house. It would also provide a safety valve against the pressure of the rich for more power and influence. Morris made the counterintuitive argument that forming the wealthy into a separate interest would actually *diminish* their tendency to dominate the rest of the population. Although it sounded like a nakedly self-serving proposal (especially coming as it did from the aristocratic Morris), the idea that giving elites their own institutions could provide an effective way to keep them in check had actually been a staple of republican practice and thought for ages.[21] Not only would having their very own branch of the legislature satisfy the ambitions of the rich, it would also make it easier for the people to keep an eye on them.[22] Assuming the two branches would actually represent the interests of distinct classes, neither Morris nor any of the other delegates ever addressed how or whether the influence of the wealthy would be confined to the upper chamber.[23]

When the question of how to determine representation in the lower house came up, a few delegates suggested that apportionment ought to be based on property as well as population. Gouverneur Morris explained that the protection of property was the primary object of society. Rejecting the idea that government is established to protect life and liberty along with property, Morris reasoned—in striking contrast to the views of Thomas Hobbes, John Locke, and other social contract theorists—that the former were actually secure in the state of nature. Property, however, was imperiled in the "savage state."[24] "If property then was the main object of Govt. certainly it ought to be one measure of the influence due to those who were to be affected by the Governmt."[25] John Rutledge, a plantation owner from South Carolina, agreed with Morris's assessment but added a sectional twist to the argument in favor of representing property along with persons. Looking ahead to the way population growth would unfold, he argued that representation for property would protect the Atlantic states from being outvoted by more populous but poorer western states in the future.[26] The next day, Gerry of Massachusetts and Pierce Butler of South Carolina joined this chorus.[27] It was not until July 13, when the convention was deliberating on whether and how to represent slaves, that anyone mounted a serious challenge to these assertions. Wilson observed that government ought to protect more than just property, proclaiming, "The cultivation & improvement of the human mind was the most noble object." In any case, he added, wealth and numbers often went hand in hand, so there was no need to make special provisions for property in the scheme of representation.[28] When the matter came to a vote, Wilson's position prevailed: nine states (with Delaware divided) agreed to strike out the word "wealth" from the language on representation.[29]

On July 26, the convention once again took up the question of property qualifications for members of Congress. A number of leading delegates favored some kind of wealth requirement but could not agree on the amount or kind of property that should qualify a man for office. The debate that ensued exposed the degree to which sectional differences in wealth divided the delegates from different parts of the country. Shifting from the position he took earlier in the convention, Mason, who owned a large plantation, proposed that the committee of detail draft language "requiring certain qualifications of landed property & citizenship" and "disqualifying" anyone in debt from being eligible for Congress.[30] Gouverneur Morris was the first to object but not because he favored a more egalitarian system. The sometime merchant and close ally of Robert Morris objected because the prohibition against persons with "unsettled accounts" would apply so broadly that it would end up excluding merchants and others whose businesses regularly required them to borrow money.[31] Rufus King was even more explicit, arguing, "There might be great danger in requiring landed property as a qualification since it would exclude the monied interest, whose aids may be essential in particular emergencies."[32] The only speaker to take a principled republican stand against property qualifications tout court was John Dickinson, who argued that the effect would be to exclude worthy individuals from different backgrounds. Even though he was one of the wealthiest men in the country, he opposed the "policy of interweaving into a Republican constitution a veneration for wealth. He had always understood that a veneration for poverty & virtue, were the objects of republican encouragement."[33] Madison proposed a compromise solution by calling for the word "landed" to be removed. However, he sounded a more egalitarian note when he spoke against high property qualifications as such because it would be "politic as well as just that the interests & rights of *every* class should be duly represented & understood in the public councils."[34] The convention agreed to Madison's proposal (with ten states in favor and only Maryland opposed) and voted in favor of Mason's amended proposition eight to three (with Connecticut, Delaware, and Pennsylvania voting in the negative).[35]

However, these votes did not settle the matter. Debate continued over the language excluding debtors and those with "unsettled accounts." Ultra-elitist Gerry argued that the exclusion was necessary to keep Congress free of "public debtors, pensioners, placemen & contractors."[36] John Langdon of New Hampshire was the only speaker who raised any democratic objections, declaring, "So many Exclusions . . . would render the system unacceptable to the people."[37] The convention ultimately rejected proposals to insert property qualifications in the Constitution, but not everyone objected to them on principle. Delegates such as King opposed "requiring landed property as a qualification since it would exclude the monied interest," not because it would exclude individuals with little or no property.[38] Others who spoke out against the exclusion also objected to the way it would affect members of the moneyed class. Gouverneur Morris, Oliver Ellsworth, and Pinckney pointed out that the rule would end up excluding merchants, land speculators, and purchasers of public securities but made no mention of small farmers or laborers.[39]

As Madison's remarks on June 26 about the dangers of a propertyless class indicate, many of the delegates were just as concerned about threats to property in the distant future as they were about threats to property in the present. There was wide agreement that the country's much-vaunted equality would erode over time as it transitioned from a predominantly agrarian economy with relatively broad ownership of property to a mixed or industrial economy with concentrations of property ownership antithetical to republican ideals. Their great fear was that the growth of inequality would produce a large class of dependent laborers incapable of responsibly carrying out the duties of citizenship.[40] However, the delegates who pointed to these expected trends did not seek ways to minimize the growth of inequality or guarantee access to property. Instead, some of them sought to minimize the influence of the propertyless in politics.

This was the approach Gouverneur Morris took when the subject of voting qualifications came up during consideration of the committee of detail report in August. Morris's remarks echoed long-standing republican beliefs about the connection between property and independence. Instead of using the link between material resources and political power to justify greater economic equality, Morris used it to call for restrictions on political participation. Arguing that the "ignorant & the dependent can be as little trusted with the public interest" as children can be, Morris proposed to limit suffrage to "freeholders."[41] Looking ahead to the socioeconomic changes in store for the country, he worried that the expansion of wage labor would create a class of economically dependent workers unable to exercise their own political judgment and will. He argued that the Constitution must erect a seawall against the rising tide of manual laborers "who will receive their bread from their employers." "Give the votes to the people who have no property, and they will sell them to the rich who will be able to buy them."[42] Backtracking from his earlier remarks, Dickinson supported Morris's suggestion as a way to protect property owners from the "dangerous influence of those multitudes without property & without principle, with which our Country like all others, will in time abound."[43] Madison defended the right of suffrage as "one of the fundamental articles of republican Government" but said he feared that anticipated economic changes would imperil free government in the long run. "In future times a great majority of the people will not only be without landed, but any other sort of, property." In those circumstances, there could be only two equally dangerous outcomes: either the propertyless would unite to pursue their narrow material interests or they would "become the tools of opulence & ambition." In either case, republican liberty would be at an end.[44]

These views did not go unopposed. Some, such as Ellsworth, objected on the grounds that a freeholder qualification would exclude "wealthy merchants" and other kinds of property owners,[45] whereas several others rejected the idea of property qualifications in principle. Those who did so were members of an older generation that still expressed confidence in the virtues and abilities of the "common people." Mason vehemently rejected the insinuation that freeholders possessed a monopoly on concern for the "common interest."[46] Benjamin Franklin reminded his colleagues of the heroic patriotism demonstrated by the "common people" during the Revolutionary War and questioned the right of the elected to "narrow the privileges of the electors."[47] Rutledge warned that any attempt to limit the franchise would only serve to "make enemies of all those who should be excluded."[48]

Proponents of property qualifications for office made one more serious attempt to restrict access to national office before the convention ended. On August 10, the delegates took up the question of property qualifications for the national executive office. Pinckney stated he preferred to set the minimum at the astounding level of $100,000 for the president but proposed leaving the amount blank for the time being. It was no surprise that the reply to Pinckney came from Franklin, the Pennsylvania delegate most closely associated with the radicalism of his state's constitution. The aging statesman vigorously disputed the assumptions underlying Pinckney's proposal by reiterating his earlier objections and introducing new ones. Even if the possession of great wealth were associated with certain positive qualities, Franklin argued, "it was not less true that the possession of property increased the desire of more property." His stance was premised on a vision of America as an open and inclusive land of opportunity that was the envy of the enlightened world and a magnet for immigrants.[49] Whether it was the force of Franklin's arguments or lack of enthusiasm for Pinckney's proposal to begin with, the motion was soundly rejected. With that vote, the convention essentially laid to rest the possibility of restricting suffrage to particular classes of property owners in the Constitution itself.

The most significant defeat for nationalists concerned a national power Madison believed was "absolutely necessary" to the success of the new plan of government.[50] Throughout the convention, Madison argued strenuously for giving the national legislature a veto over state legislation in order to prevent encroachment on federal authority, violation of treaties, and infringement of rights. An original part of the Virginia Plan introduced at the start of the convention, the "negative," as Madison called it, would have applied to "all laws passed by the several States."[51] As Madison's reference to "rights" suggests, legislation affecting property was of greatest concern. In a letter to Thomas Jefferson written shortly before the convention met, Madison explained that the negative was necessary to prevent states from passing laws that "oppress the minority within themselves by paper money and other unrighteous measures which favor the interest of the majority."[52] The idea met stiff opposition from states' rights advocates. After all, a veto on state laws meant the end of state sovereignty. However, some of those who rejected the national veto as an encroachment on states' rights favored limits on the power of the states to enact legislation that eroded property rights, including the "power of emitting paper money."[53]

Although an absolute veto over all state law was too much for most members of the convention to swallow, they did accept narrower restrictions on the ability of the states to pass the kinds of class-based legislation that motivated so many of the delegates to seek sweeping institutional reforms in the first place. The most significant restrictions on the states included the prohibitions in Article I, Section 10 against future emissions of paper money and laws "impairing the Obligations of Contracts." The draft of the Constitution prepared by the committee of detail actually made it possible for states to issue bills of credit with the permission of Congress, but on August 28 Wilson and Sherman successfully moved to make the prohibition absolute.[54] The final version did not require the states to remove any paper money still in circulation, but it did eliminate an important tool used to alleviate the financial hardships of citizens poor in hard money. In doing so, its authors scored a major victory for the moneyed interests whose support they believed would be critical to acceptance of the Constitution.

The delegates were so confident that the Constitution protected property that some of them argued against the inclusion of additional guarantees as needlessly provocative. Not content with likely restrictions on the ability of states to issue paper money, Gouverneur Morris moved on August 16 to prevent the national government from emitting bills of credit on the grounds that the "Monied interest will oppose the plan of Government, if paper emissions be not prohibited." The principal objection to this motion was that it would be dangerous to limit the powers of the government to deal with unforeseeable emergencies when it might be necessary to resort to paper money, but John Francis Mercer of Maryland warned that any additional benefits to moneyed men would only serve to alienate the "opposite class of Citizens." In any case, he was confident that the "people of property would be sure to be on the side of the plan." Although the state delegations voted nine to two to strike out the words "and emit bills on the credit of the U. States,"[55] no one doubted Mercer's assumption that propertied men would generally support the Constitution.

Closely related to the limits on the states were the obligations the national government would be required to assume. The debate over language stipulating that the national government "*shall* fulfill the engagements and discharge the debts of the U.S." offered a preview of the controversy that would erupt over Hamilton's funding plan a few years later. When the section authorizing Congress to levy taxes for the payment of public debts came up near the end of the convention, Revolutionary War veteran Butler of South Carolina fulminated against the idea: "The Blood-suckers who had speculated on the distresses of others" would be entitled to compensation on the same terms as "those who had fought & bled for their country."[56] Butler and Mason led the charge in favor of a clause allowing the government to discriminate between original owners and subsequent purchasers in order to prevent speculators from profiting. Mason, who drew a sharp distinction between original holders of these certificates and those who "fraudulently" acquired these certificates by taking advantage of the "ignorant and distressed," believed that the Constitution would end up compounding these injustices. He

predicted that the use of the word "shall" would "beget specula-
tions and increase the pestilent practice of stock-jobbing."[57] Those
who stood up in defense of the original language asserted that they
were personally disinterested in the matter before Gerry argued that
the opprobrium heaped on so-called stock-jobbers was undeserved
because, without them, the value of the certificates would be even
lower, and "there would be no market" at all, whereas Gouverneur
Morris let his case rest on an appeal to "public faith."[58]

Anxiety over class conflict also shaped the objectives identified in
the preamble. As subsequent debates in Congress would reveal, the
meaning and implications of phrases such as the "general Welfare"
were not entirely clear even among those who had a hand in drafting
this language. However, there was much stronger agreement on the
meaning of the declaration in the preamble that the Constitution
was created to "establish Justice" and "insure domestic Tranquility." The reference to "domestic Tranquility" was undoubtedly included in response to Shays's Rebellion and the other uprisings by
distressed debtors, taxpayers, and laborers that had occurred in recent years. The meaning of "Justice" would be contested over time,
but one of its most basic and widely accepted meanings at the time
included the protection of property rights.[59] Although the objectives
laid out in the preamble sound innocuous and broad-minded enough
today, they sent an important signal about the particular values and
interests the proposed system would serve.

The Class Critique of the Constitution

In many respects, the debate over the ratification of the Constitution was a debate over the legacy of the Revolution. Critics of the
Constitution, saddled with the unfortunate label of anti-Federalists,
raised a host of (sometimes inconsistent) objections to the powers,
structure, and composition of the proposed government. Their major
criticisms of the Constitution—its lack of a bill of rights, its consolidation of power in the national government, its grant of virtually unlimited tax power to the national government, the undefined powers
of the legislature and the executive branch, and inadequate representation in Congress—boiled down to the claim that it betrayed
the ideals of the Revolution. The understandings of republicanism
forged in the crucible of revolutionary struggle influenced the way in

which anti-Federalists framed their critiques and the way in which Federalists structured their defenses of everything from the constitutional separation of powers to the system of representation. Those very same republican ideals shaped debates over the constitutional implications for class politics.

The debate over the ratification of the Constitution exposed a number of cleavages in American politics, including the division between large and small states, the conflict between free and slave states, and differences between the "carrying" states and the "producing" states. The debate also stripped away any illusions that the country was free from the kinds of class conflicts that fractured European societies. Many of the most controversial features of the Constitution were viewed through the prism of class differences. Everything from the establishment of a bicameral legislature and the shift of power from the states to the national government to the system of representation and the tax power was debated at least partly in terms of its implications for relations between the few and the many. In many instances, urban artisans and laborers on the bottom rungs of society joined wealthy seaport merchants in support of the Constitution, whereas large planters sided with small backcountry farmers in opposition, but that did little to halt accusations that the proposed government would benefit the upper classes at the expense of the lower and middling classes.

Class did not necessarily predict whether someone supported or opposed the Constitution, but it did significantly factor into some of the reasons he or she offered for or against it. As Patrick Henry asserted at the Virginia Ratifying Convention, "I dread the operation of it on the middling and lower class of people: It is for them I fear the adoption of this system."[60] The irony in pointing out how differently the Constitution would affect the rich and the poor is that the anti-Federalists ended up acknowledging that the country already lacked the kind of homogeneity so many of them believed was indispensable to the survival of republican government.[61]

A few critics of the Constitution responded directly to many elites' assumption that the greatest threat to liberty came from the rapaciousness of the multitudes by arguing that the most serious threats came from the ambitiousness of the few. The letters of "Centinel," most likely penned by Pennsylvania judge and legislator George Bryan or his son Samuel, advance some of the sharpest criticisms of the role the wealthy had played in American politics since the

Revolution. In a long-running and widely reprinted series of essays that reached a broad audience thanks in large part to a clear and accessible style that avoided the purple prose found in much contemporary writing, the letters of "Centinel" cast the struggle over the Constitution as a clear-cut conflict between the classes. Representing a strain of "plebeian populism" that set these essays apart from many other anti-Federalist writings,[62] "Centinel" pointed out that the "wealthy and ambitious, who in every community think they have a right to lord it over their fellow creatures," exploited the instability that followed the war to advance their own interests at the expense of other classes.[63] The creation of the Constitution represented the culmination of their efforts to undermine the foundations of free government. Even a seemingly innocuous provision such as the prohibition against ex–post facto laws, "Centinel" contended, was installed to "screen the numerous public defaulters" from any investigations into their speculative activities, war profiteering, and handling of public funds. It was no surprise that the Constitution was designed to advance the interests of speculators when the convention included so many "of this description in the deputation from the state of Pennsylvania." Chief among these was Robert Morris: "The late Financier alone, in the capacity of chairman of the commercial committee of Congress, early in the late war, was entrusted with millions of public money, which to this day remain unaccounted for, nor has he settled his accounts as Financier."[64]

Many anti-Federalists detected the seeds of aristocracy in the Constitution.[65] Before the convention even adjourned, Mason warned that the "moderate aristocracy" set out in the Constitution would eventually turn into either a monarchy or a "corrupt, tyrannical <oppressive> aristocracy."[66] Perhaps the most commonly voiced criticism of the Constitution was that it would eventuate in an aristocracy of wealth. According to some critics, the aristocratic tendencies of the Constitution could have been predicted from even the most cursory review of the delegates to the Constitution. Without identifying anyone by name, the "Federal Farmer" pointed out that the Pennsylvania delegation (which included well-known conservatives and members of the state Republican Party such as Wilson, Robert Morris, and Gouverneur Morris) was made up "principally of those men who are esteemed aristocratical."[67] The Dissent of the Minority of the Convention of Pennsylvania similarly noted that six of those who represented the state were known enemies of the state democratic constitution.[68]

Evidence of the aristocratic designs of the Constitution did not rest on the identity of its framers alone. The composition, structure, powers, and language of the proposed system offered further proof that supporters of the Constitution aimed to shift power and wealth into the hands of the few. Although some critics of the Constitution did complain about the lack of property qualifications,[69] most claimed to speak for the poor and middling classes, who would lose power.

Many anti-Federalists argued that the size of Congress was much too small to provide adequate representation to the multitudes. The fewer members there were in the House of Representatives, the more it would be dominated by the wealthy. Because each Congressman would represent a large number of constituents, anti-Federalists reasoned, those who are already well known across a large area would have an enormous electoral advantage over those who enjoyed only a local reputation. As a result, both chambers would be dominated by the "better sort," the "well-born," and the wealthy. Most Federalists did not see this as a drawback because they assumed a strong positive correlation between the kind of broad reputation needed to attract enough votes to get elected and the kinds of virtues needed to govern wisely and effectively. In any case, Federalists wanted representatives with more extensive views. However, many anti-Federalists challenged the rosy assumption that aristocrats would pursue the best interests of the entire community. In their view, the wealthy lacked both the knowledge and the sympathy required to represent the lower classes.

One of the earliest and most influential anti-Federalist writings to make this case was the Dissent of the Minority to the Pennsylvania Ratifying Convention, which circulated widely in other states. Even though it was a very populous state, Pennsylvania was to send only ten representatives to Congress. According to the dissent, the system of representation would give a decided advantage to the "lordly and high-minded." The minority spelled out exactly what this would mean in starkly class-conscious language. The Pennsylvania Delegation would consist of "men who will have no congenial feelings with the people, but a perfect indifference for, and contempt of them; they will consist of those harpies of power, that prey upon the very vitals; that riot on the miseries of the community."[70] The lack of solidarity between the classes meant the poor and middling classes would have to send members from their own ranks if their interests were to be represented. Other critics also charged that the ratio of representatives to the population would enhance the influence of economic elites. Maryland lawyer (and future Supreme Court justice) Samuel Chase explained that he objected to the Constitution "because the representatives will not be the representatives of the people at large, but really of a few rich men. . . . In fact, no order or class of people will be represented in the House of Representatives— called the Democratic branch—but the rich and wealthy. They will be ignorant of the sentiments of the middling (and much more of the lower) class of citizens."[71]

Poughkeepsie businessman Melancton Smith made a similar argument at the New York State Ratifying Convention. He too argued that an inadequate number of representatives would result in the election of aristocrats unacquainted "with the common concerns and occupations of the people."[72] However, Smith went even further than the Pennsylvania minority in explaining why members of the upper class could never effectively represent individuals from lower classes. Not only were they ignorant of "how the burdens imposed [by taxes] will bear upon the different classes,"[73] they were also oblivious or indifferent to the everyday struggles of the classes below them. Smith cast the "few" as arrogant and callous aristocrats who "do not feel for the poor and middling class." To him, the "reasons are obvious—they are not obliged to use the pains and labour to procure property as the other.—They feel not the inconveniences arising from the payment of small sums. They consider themselves above the common people—entitled to more respect— do not associate with them—they fancy themselves to have a right of pre-eminence in every thing [*sic*]."[74] The only solution was to increase the number of yeomen sent to Congress. Echoing Aristotelian ideas about the superiority of the middle class, Smith argued that members of this class would make ideal legislators because they are capable of sympathizing with the interests of those above and below them. They are most capable of looking after the public interest because they will reject policies either injurious to property or that impose undue burdens on the poor.[75]

"Brutus," who was most likely New York judge and delegate to the Constitutional Convention Robert Yates, pressed these points with even greater theoretical rigor. In response to claims by Madison and other Federalists that the purpose of representation is to "refine and enlarge the public views, by passing them through the medium of a chosen body of citizens" superior in judgment and virtue to their constituents,[76] "Brutus" argued that representatives in a republic ought to mirror their constituents in every respect. According to this theory of representation, free government is impossible where representatives are ignorant of or indifferent to the particular sentiments, interests, and opinions of their constituents. The more extensive the territory that a lawmaker represents, the less likely he is to know the "minds of the people."[77] The implications of inadequate representation were especially troubling for the poor and middling classes. As the number and diversity of interests expand, the groups that can form coalitions to advance their mutual interests will enjoy a decided advantage over those that lack similar material resources and associational skills. According to "Brutus" the yeomanry will almost always be outmaneuvered by the wealthy because it is much easier for the latter to organize and maintain unity in pursuit of their interests. Aside from the fact that the wealthy already enjoy the kind of name recognition critical to electoral success in large districts, "Brutus" claimed that their interests are so similar, it will be much easier for them to maintain a united front against other classes.[78] Although divisions among propertied elites in New York made the claim about the cohesiveness of the wealthy somewhat dubious, "Brutus" pointed to another sociological fact that gave them an indisputable advantage. The wealthy have such "large family connections" and "dependents" that their influence will easily extend beyond their actual numbers.[79] In the face of these well-known advantages, "Brutus" feared that mechanics and farmers would be discouraged from even seeking office in the first place: "It will and must be esteemed a station too high and exalted to be filled by any but the first men in the state, in point of fortune; so that in reality there will be no part of the people represented, but the rich, even in that branch of the legislature, which is called the democratic."[80] As a consequence, there will be a government "of the few to oppress and plunder the many."[81]

In developing this argument, "Brutus" identified a threat to republicanism far more insidious than the lack of rotation, the possibility of a standing army, or any other institutional arrangement. Apathy among citizens had always been considered a dire condition ultimately fatal to republicanism, but it was usually understood in moral, not sociological, terms. That is, apathy signified a loss of public virtue among citizens. However, "Brutus" was suggesting that the poor and middling classes would become apathetic not because they suffered from a moral defect that inclined them to prioritize private matters over public business but because the new government was designed in a way that would effectively exclude from power anyone in their socioeconomic condition. As a consequence of their exclusion, they would lose interest and faith in the political system, which in turn would make it even easier for the upper classes to consolidate their power. The result would be a vicious cycle that reinforced social and political inequalities.

The idea that the structure of the Constitution favored the rich came out most explicitly in critiques of the judiciary. Many critics feared that the establishment of a national judiciary would place the courts beyond the reach of ordinary citizens. The authors of the Dissent of the Minority to the Pennsylvania Ratifying Convention expected that "rich and wealthy suitors would eagerly lay hold of the infinite mazes, perplexities and delays" in the legal process to gain an advantage, so that the "poor man" would just "drop his demand in despair."[82] The appellate system was particularly objectionable because it imposed burdens that would not fall evenly on all classes. The costs and inconveniences associated with traveling to courts far from home would be so great that poor people would just give up their claims against wealthy adversaries.[83] One of the objections to the proposed judiciary raised by Mason was that federal jurisdiction over conflicts between citizens of different states would require parties to travel long distances at their own expense, making it impossible for poor men to get justice.[84] Likewise, "Brutus" argued that the expense of traveling "many hundred miles" with a train of lawyers and witnesses to the Supreme Court would be so prohibitive that the "poorer and midling [sic] class of citizens will be under the necessity of submitting to the demands of the rich and the lordly."[85]

Some of the express new powers the Constitution gave Congress were also viewed through the prism of class. The expansive tax powers of the national government drew fierce and widespread criticism. Most of that criticism—including charges that it would be used to consolidate power in the national government, that taxes would fall unequally on different states, that methods of enforcement would be highly intrusive, that it would result in a proliferation of tax collectors and excessive growth in the size of government, and that it would extend to so many objects that the states would be left with no revenue sources of their own—spoke to fears that resonated with all classes. However, anti-Federalists also raised concerns specific to the poor and middling classes. For instance, because there were no limits on how the tax power could be used, there would be nothing to prevent Congress from passing regressive taxes on items consumed more heavily by the lower classes. "Brutus" predicted that the need for revenue would make Congress turn to the "real necessaries of life."[86] Perhaps even worse than taxes on articles of consumption would be direct taxes, which "Brutus" described as being "so oppressive, as to grind the face of the poor, and render the lives of the common people a burden to them."[87] Mason advanced a similar argument during a prolonged debate over the tax power at the Virginia State Ratifying Convention. Reiterating points he had made about the dangers of a distant national government, Mason argued that those selected to devise and administer the tax system would lack "fellow-feeling" for ordinary Virginians. Because the Constitution would result in a "government where the wealthy only are represented," the federal government would end up imposing polls and other regressive taxes that fall "light on the rich, and heavy on the poor." Mason did not let his case rest on speculative arguments alone. He paused to read aloud a letter from Robert Morris proving that the Federalists contemplated the use of taxes that "will be ruinous and unequal [to the states if not to individuals], and will be particularly oppressive on the poorest part of the people."[88]

The enumerated powers were not the only ones that gave rise to charges that the proposed government would disadvantage the poor and middling classes. One of the most common criticisms involved the indeterminate and ambiguous language scattered throughout the Constitution. The likelihood that the federal government would rely on the doctrine of implied powers to augment its own powers at the expense of individuals and the states was a central theme in the writings of "Brutus" and many others.[89] Critics warned that vague phrases such as "general welfare" and "necessary and proper" would be construed as general grants of power open to any interpretation members of Congress chose to put on them. Such open-ended language expanded the powers of Congress and made the character of elected officials all the more important as a check against misuses and abuses of discretionary authority.[90] Even under the best of with acknowledgments that the system was designed to attract "men who possess the most attractive merit and the most diffusive and established characters."[94] Critics suspected that this talk of "fit characters" superior in virtue and ability was coded language for the wealthy. The disparaging remarks many Federalists made about the abilities of the lower classes only reinforced suspicions that they linked virtue and wealth in their thinking on representation.

Proponents of the Constitution sometimes admitted that support for the Constitution divided along class lines. According to Hamilton, one of the groups arrayed in support of the proposed government comprised propertied men who wanted a government strong enough to "protect them against domestic violence and the depredations which the democratic spirit is apt to make on property." Among the factors working against the Constitution, he noted, was the "opposition of all men much in debt" along with the "democratical jealousy of the people, which may be alarmed at the appearance of institutions that may seem calculated to place the power of the community in few hands and to raise a few individuals to stations of great preeminence."[95]

Many Federalists also admitted that they aimed to curb democracy and restore the "better sort" to power. One of the most hostile critics of popular government was "Caesar," who dismissed the people as an "unthinking mass" too ignorant and uninformed to make a sound judgment about the best form of government.[96] Similarly, "Atticus" described the people as too fickle and unstable for any "regular system of action."[97] "State Soldier" opined that justice was better protected the "more independent a government is . . . of the people."[98] Even Noah Webster, who championed economic equality as a prerequisite of republican government, bemoaned the inferior judgment of the lower orders, writing, "The middle states are receiving emigrations of poor people, who are not at once judges of the characters of men, and who cannot be safely trusted with the choice of legislators."[99]

Hamilton agreed that society is divided into different classes, but he rejected the mirror theory of representation advanced by "Brutus" and others. Hamilton ridiculed the idea that each class of occupations should be represented as something "altogether visionary."[100] Not only was such representation impossible, it was unnecessary. In his view, members of certain occupations were ideally suited to represent a broad range of interests. Denying the idea that distinct classes necessarily have conflicting interests, Hamilton contended that the interests of manufacturers, mechanics, and merchants were actually so closely aligned that all of them could and would be best represented by merchants. Hamilton also challenged the common assumption that members of the same industry share the same interests, pointing out that rivalries within segments of the economy are sometimes even more intense and significant than rivalries between different segments of the economy.[101] Hamilton also disputed claims that there is more virtue in some classes than in others. "Look through the rich and the poor of the community, the learned and the ignorant, where does virtue predominate? The difference indeed consists, not in the quantity, but kind, of vices which are incident to various classes; and here the advantage of character belongs to the wealthy." Despite this seemingly even-handed assessment, Hamilton claimed that the vices particular to the rich rendered them less dangerous to the public: "Their vices are probably more favorable to the prosperity of the state, than those of the indigent; and partake less of moral depravity."[102]

Other Federalists took a more moderate position. They accepted inequality as an unavoidable fact of life, but they agreed that excessive levels of inequality could threaten republican government. In their view, inequality was not (necessarily or only) the product of law and government policy but the result of natural talent, hard work, education, and perhaps even divine ordination. For instance, Nicholas Collin insisted that social order is ordained by God, but he recognized the dangers of extreme inequality: "Great disparity of property is bad; but some must arise from the inequality of genius and industry, inheritance, and chance, which in fact is the disposition of providence." In Collin's view, the United States was blessed to have a system where anyone can earn a decent living, even if the majority can never obtain riches. With the help of a strong national government, the United States could continue to enjoy an ideal position "equally removed from poverty, and the danger of wealth."[103]

Some Federalists did speak approvingly of the people as judges of the merits and characters of their rulers, but they often stressed that this was all the people could be entrusted to do. These Federalists expressed support for the idea of popular government but envisioned a fairly passive role for the people in most political matters. For instance, Benjamin Rush rejected the idea that sovereignty resides *in* the people in favor of the idea that "all power is derived *from* the people." According to his principle, the people possess power "only on the days of their elections. After this, it is the property of their rulers, nor can they exercise or resume it, unless it is abused."[104]

Madison sought to reconcile the tensions between the elitist tendencies of the Constitution and the egalitarian ideals of the Revolution by redefining republicanism. His claim in *Federalist* 10 that a "republic" is simply a "government in which the scheme of representation takes place" made no requirement of regular or active participation by the people, as republican thinkers from Aristotle to Rousseau demanded.[105] Madison drew a sharp contrast between the stability and order that obtain under a republic (i.e., representative government) and the "turbulence and contention" that constantly beset democracy.[106] One of the great advantages of a republic in Madison's view is that it limits the ability of the people to act in a collective capacity. Under Madison's new minimalist conception of republicanism, the people would satisfy the requirements of citizenship merely by voting for "fit characters" who possessed superior wisdom and virtue. In making these points, Madison was less explicit about the role the upper classes would play in the new government, but anti-Federalists could read between the lines when he mentioned the "substitution of representatives whose enlightened views and virtuous sentiments render them superior to local prejudices and schemes of injustice."[107] Although Madison identified a number of factors that contributed to the rise of factions in small republics—from trivial divisions over personal loyalties to more substantial differences over religious and political opinions—he singled out the "various and unequal distribution of property" as the "most common and durable source of factions." Conflicts of interest that arise between different sectors of the economy do lead to the formation of dangerous factions, but nothing contributes as much to social divisions as the differences between "those who hold and those who are without property."[108]

Madison left little doubt that the "fit characters" he expected to rise to national office under the new government would also be able to rise above the popular clamor for paper money, debtor relief laws, and other redistributive measures he considered "unjust." Because they would be elected in districts considerably larger than any that existed at that time, it was unlikely that any single set of interests would dominate. The unlikelihood that any particular interest, or faction, would achieve majority status within these enlarged districts would diminish pressure on representatives to cater to the demands of debtors and the poor. These representatives were to pursue the public interest, not the interest of any particular segment of society. Madison acknowledged that "enlightened statesmen will not always be at the helm," but when they were they could be expected to uphold principles of justice against the demands of self-interested groups.

Exactly what Madison considered just and unjust around this time is evident from the notes he composed, "The Vices of the Political System of the United States," in preparation for the Constitutional Convention. One of the most "alarming" vices of republican government in the United States, he wrote, was the tendency of the people and their representatives in the states to enact "unjust laws" that called "into question the fundamental principle of republican Government, that the majority who rule in such Governments, are the safest Guardians both of [the] public Good and of private rights." There, he still referred to a republic as a system in which the "majority however composed, ultimately give [sic] the law" without reference to any "enlargement" or "refinement" by representatives.[109] Madison offered religious tests as an example of the kinds of unjust laws he had in mind, but he devoted most of his attention to economic measures that had redistributive objectives favored by debtors and laborers. The main culprits were "paper money, instalments of debts, occlusion of Courts, making property a legal tender."[110] Madison objected to these measures not because he favored policies that benefited the rich instead of the poor but because he believed any measures that threatened property rights ultimately threatened the interests of rich and poor alike. He (and many other Federalists) insisted the policies favored by debtors were actually detrimental to their own interests, and their economic situations would improve after legislatures stopped giving in to their demands. Like many other Federalists, Madison doubted that the people were always the best judges of the public good or their own interests. His chief argument in favor of representative government over pure democracy was that the "public voice, pronounced by the representatives of the people, will be more consonant to the public good than if pronounced by the people themselves, convened for the purpose."[111]

Madison, along with many other Federalists, equated justice with the protection of property rights. Majority rule was an important element of his political thought, but the "rules of justice" always won out whenever they came into conflict with each other.[112] Majorities could be fluctuating, evanescent, driven by vicious motives, and wrong about their interests, but justice was grounded in the permanent and inalienable natural rights of individuals, including the right to property. Of course, the exercise of those rights according to one's own reason and abilities led to the social and economic differences that gave rise to factions. Madison acknowledged, "The diversity in the faculties of men, from which the rights of property originate, is not less an insuperable obstacle to a uniformity of interests." However, he maintained, "the protection of these faculties is the first object of government. From the protection of different and unequal faculties of acquiring property, the possession of different degrees and kinds of property immediately results; and from the influence of these on the sentiments and views of the respective proprietors, ensues a division of the society into different interests and parties."[113] If any statement in support of the Constitution signaled the abandonment of the egalitarian aspirations within the republican worldview that shaped the revolutionary period, it was certainly Madison's announcement that government was instituted to protect the causes of inequality.

Conclusion

The ratification of the Constitution did not settle the matter of popular participation in the United States. However, the arguments presented on both sides did offer a preview of the battles that would take place in coming years over the role of the people, the meaning of republican government, and the ideal of equality. In many respects, the battles that took place over the Constitution were the same ones that gave rise to demands for a new frame of government in the first place. Once a stronger centralized government capable of exercising a range of powers without the permission of the state governments was in place, nationalists could finally get to work securing reliable sources of revenue, repaying the massive war debt, restoring the nation's tattered credit, and stabilizing the country's fragile economy. Although some of the combatants on the front lines of these conflicts changed, the arguments they deployed for and against different

detractors alike, but perhaps no other founder has had his reputation defined so thoroughly by his enemies as Hamilton. At various points in his life and after his death, he has been described as a monarchist bent on subverting republican government, a champion of unilateral executive power unfettered by constitutional constraints, and an imperialist and militarist determined to assert US power abroad. Most of these images have been qualified if not debunked, but one image that has persisted is that of Hamilton as a spokesperson for the interests and the superiority of the wealthy. The dominant portrait of Hamilton today was first outlined by Thomas Jefferson and his allies, who used broad and unflattering brushstrokes to portray the architect of the young Republic's economic and financial system as an apologist for the plutocracy.[1] Philip Freneau, editor of the Jeffersonian-Republican *National Gazette*, set the tone by arguing that Hamilton's program was designed to enrich financial elites at the expense of the "industrious mechanic, the laborious farmer, and generally the poorer class of people."[2] That image has been embellished by generations of scholars and politicians who have continued to depict the first secretary of the treasury as a man who not only accepted but even promoted the divide between the haves and the have-nots. More measured writers characterize Hamilton as someone who "saw that stratification between the wealthy and the mass of workers was to be a permanent feature of a developed economy,"[3] whereas others simply assert, "Hamilton always spoke out for protection only for the 'rich and well-born.'"[4] From the beginning, critics have portrayed Hamilton as a man who subscribed to the age-old belief that the people are too ignorant and incompetent to exercise power responsibly, and more recent writers have relied on anachronistic categories to paint him as someone who "believes in the trickle-down theory."[5] In the end, the picture that emerges is that of a brilliant but ruthless champion of the "monied interests" indifferent to both the political effects and the human costs of inequality. This Hamilton was willing to stretch the constitutional powers of the national government to the limit in pursuit of policies that would advance the economic interests of the upper classes even if those policies also worsened the condition of the lower classes.

Like any caricature, this one does capture prominent features in Hamilton's thinking about issues of class and inequality, but it ultimately distorts more than it reveals. Not only does it leave out important details that qualify and complicate Hamilton's views on the supposed moral qualities and politicoeconomic contributions of the wealthy but also it grossly exaggerates his attitude toward members of the "lower orders" and what can or should be done to alleviate their condition.[6] Hamilton's expansive views of the government's powers in the economy were not limited to policies that advanced the interests of moneyed men. Though he was largely untroubled by economic inequality—especially when compared with his more egalitarian contemporaries—he was hardly indifferent to the hardships created by poverty and other forms of economic distress. His reputation as a coldhearted defender of privilege ignores a variety of measures he proposed to mitigate the burdens faced by the poor and laboring classes. Although it is true Hamilton never devoted anything like the kind or amount of attention to poverty or inequality someone such as Thomas Paine did, it is not true that he simply accepted and promoted policies that would exacerbate these problems, as so many of his critics have alleged. In fact, at various points in his public career he supported and even proposed modest measures to minimize some of the burdens experienced by the poor.

One reason Hamilton's interest in addressing the underprivileged has been easy to overlook is that he was not one to employ the kinds of emotional appeals or florid rhetoric often used by others who tackled the problems of poverty and economic hardship. His penchant for logically rigorous and empirically weighty argumentation is apt to give the impression Hamilton was unmoved by the plight of those who faced material deprivation. Perhaps an even more important reason this dimension of Hamilton's thinking has gone largely unnoticed is that he never developed a systematic theory or program that addressed the underlying causes of poverty or inequality. Instead, his proposals were limited mainly to ad hoc efforts to mitigate the distresses experienced by specific groups. Contrary to claims that "Hamilton envisaged a national government that confined itself to the great objects of government: commerce, finance, diplomacy, and war,"[7] Hamilton was willing to use the powers of the federal government to develop the kinds of policies now associated with a modern, activist welfare state. His expansive views of the government's economic powers extended to measures in support of ends more likely to find favor among his political and ideological counterparts than among close associates such as Robert Morris or Gouverneur Morris.[8] The economic policies he supported were not limited to advancing the interests of capital or promoting general economic prosperity. His support for higher pay for public servants, health care for sick sailors, and more progressive tax policies suggests he considered policies aimed at mitigating economic hardships and inequality as legitimate goals for the positive state he envisioned.

The Hamiltonian System

Hamilton began to develop his views on the proper role of the government in the economy even before the United States secured its independence from Great Britain. In lengthy letters to Robert Morris and James Duane in 1780, when the country was still struggling to win its independence, the young artillery officer turned his attention away from military affairs toward the state of politics. The official adoption of the Articles of Confederation was still several months away, but Hamilton already sensed the need for a much more powerful and centralized national government. James Madison, Washington, and many others would eventually come to see that the articles failed to provide all the powers the national government needed to regulate commerce, raise revenue, and repay the mounting war debt, but Hamilton was among the first to conclude that the credit and prosperity of the nation would require far more power and discretion in the government than many thought were compatible with the ideals of republicanism. In this period he was already beginning to formulate ideas about the notion of sovereignty, the relation between means and ends, and constitutional interpretation that would come to define Federalism for a generation.

The bedrock principle of his theory of government, which he would explicate in defense of his economic program as treasury secretary, was that government is defined by its purposes rather than its constraints. That belief underlies his assertion to Duane that "undefined powers are discretionary powers, limited only by the object for which they were given," a conviction he held and acted on throughout his entire life in politics.[9] On the basis of this belief he suggested that Congress under the Articles of Confederation could actually do many of the things it seemed legally powerless to do if only representatives disabused themselves of the mistaken notion that they lacked full sovereign powers. This does not mean Hamilton believed that every matter of public concern fell within the purview of the national government. For instance, he did not think these powers should include any jurisdiction over "internal police, which relates to the rights of property and life among individuals and to raising money by internal taxes."[10] Even though he acknowledged that certain matters were beyond the proper scope of national power, he observed that these jurisdictional boundaries were often very difficult to observe in practice. As he stated in "A Letter from Phocion," "It is impossible for Congress to do a single act which will not directly or indirectly affect the internal police of every state."[11]

Hamilton's numerous attempts to strengthen and expand the powers of the national government—from his efforts to revise the Articles of Confederation at the abortive Annapolis Convention to his ultimately successful scheme to craft an entirely new Constitution at the Philadelphia Convention, from his defense of the proposed Constitution during the ratification struggle in New York to the financial and economic program he developed as a member of the Washington administration—were based on the assumption that the government could play a positive and even leading role in society and the economy. Of all the founders, none was as critical of the idea of a naturally self-regulating economic order as Hamilton.[12] However, in his view, express grants of power were not necessary to authorize all the activities he considered legitimate functions of government. Some powers were implied in the very idea of sovereignty, whereas others were implied by the various ends assigned to government. One of the few maxims Hamilton was willing to allow in the science of politics was the idea that "the means ought to be proportioned to the end; that every power ought to be commensurate with its object; that there ought to be no limitation of a power destined to effect a purpose, which is itself incapable of limitation."[13]

These ideas guided the development of his ambitious plans to restore the credit and strengthen the economy of the United States through the assumption and funding of the Revolutionary War debt, the establishment of a national bank, and the promotion of domestic manufacturing. Each component of this ambitious three-part program was controversial for a variety of reasons. For instance, individuals from states that had already paid off their Revolutionary War debts complained that his proposal to have the national government assume state debts compelled responsible states to subsidize the irresponsible ones. Southerners feared that the placement of the bank in a northern city would lead to the further erosion of their influence over national affairs. Supporters of agrarianism warned that manufacturing would undermine republican values by creating new relations of dependence and increasing levels of inequality. The fiercest opposition was often grounded in constitutional objections that parts of Hamilton's program exceeded the powers expressly granted to Congress or subverted the idea of limited government—the very same points many anti-Federalists had made during the ratification contest. Much of the opposition to Hamilton's program was also rooted in class politics. Both the avowed purposes and the apparent tendencies of Hamilton's proposals seemed to confirm anti-Federalist allegations that the Constitution had been designed to enrich the privileged and well-connected few at the expense of the many.

Hamilton did little to contradict these allegations. In fact, he openly admitted that parts of his economic program were designed to benefit the interests of moneyed men so they would be more inclined to support the newly established government.[14] Hamilton always insisted his programs would benefit the economy and the country as a whole, but he did little to dispel suspicions that the benefits would flow mainly to those in the upper echelons of society. Although scholars have generally vindicated Hamilton's claims that his plans would stabilize and improve the overall state of the economy,[15] they have tended to side with critics who argued that his policies (deliberately) exacerbated economic inequality.

Hamilton's policies did have the effect described by his detractors, but not because Hamilton believed men of wealth were necessarily morally or intellectually superior or entitled to more political power than others. The benefits his policies provided to the wealthy were not ends in themselves but means to the attainment of larger ends he did not think could be accomplished in any other way. Further complicating the picture of Hamilton as a champion of the propertied classes is that he recommended measures designed to mitigate economic hardships, whether they were brought on by his policies or not.

Hamilton's Funding Plan and the Problem of Speculation

Article VI of the Constitution stipulates, "All Debts contracted and Engagements entered into, before the Adoption of this Constitution, shall be as valid against the United States under this Constitution, as under the Confederation." Despite this constitutional acknowledgment of the validity of old debts, the details of Hamilton's plans to fund the debts of the United States provoked considerable controversy. His proposal to have the national government assume the war debts of the various states divided politicians mainly along state lines, with those from states with outstanding debts generally in favor and those from states that had already paid off their debts generally opposed. His proposal to pay current holders of the debt at face value divided politicians along ideological lines, with more egalitarian politicians usually opposed. Hamilton argued that both the assumption plan and the plan to pay off the debt at par were absolutely necessary to stabilize the economy and put the finances of the United States in order.

Looking to Great Britain as a model, Hamilton laid out his program in his 40,000-word *Report on Public Credit*. The plan to reimburse current holders of government certificates at full face value was explicitly designed to appease anxious creditors.[16] Hamilton believed it was imperative for the government to fulfill its contractual obligations if it were to enlist the support of economic elites. In his view, that meant the government would have to pay current holders of government securities their full face value even though many of these individuals were speculators who had purchased the certificates at only a tiny fraction of their original value. He was steadfastly opposed to any "discrimination" between original holders and subsequent purchasers (whom he declined to call speculators) because it would constitute a breach of contract and violate the constitutional guarantee that all debts entered into under the Articles of Confederation would still be valid. The maintenance of public credit—and the preservation of national honor—required "punctual performance of contracts."[17] Despite his insistence that justice requires strict fulfillment of contractual obligations, his plan did reduce the interest rates paid to creditors below those that had been promised.

Though Hamilton acknowledged that many sold their certificates under duress, he denied that they had any reason to complain now. They had received whatever price the market was willing to bear when they sold the securities. Besides, these sellers had shown little faith in their country. Despite the fact that enormous numbers of Americans had lost confidence the government would ever honor its obligations, he asserted that everyone knew the "public were bound to pay to those, to whom they should convey their title, the sums stipulated to be paid to them."[18] If the government reneged on its promise now, it would suffer a serious and potentially permanent blow to its credit and its honor.

One of the effects of the funding plan would be to provide wind-fall profits to those who had purchased these securities at depressed prices, sometimes as low as ten cents on the dollar. This included those who had bought certificates when it was far from certain the government would ever repay investors and those who used insider information to buy up certificates from unsuspecting holders when details of Hamilton's plan began to emerge. When word got out that Hamilton was planning to have the government redeem these cer-tificates at face value, speculators and their agents traveled south all along the eastern seaboard scooping up as many of these certifi-cates as unwitting holders were willing to sell. However unsavory these activities were, none of that relieved the government of its "moral obligation" to uphold property rights and fulfill its contrac-tual obligations.[19] Hamilton flatly rejected proposals to discriminate between past and current holders by paying members of each group whatever amount they paid minus whatever amount they received as both an administrative nightmare and an affront to justice.

The reasons for Hamilton's opposition to discrimination between original and current possessors of public securities extended beyond moral arguments about the obligations to fulfill contracts and pro-tect property rights. Hamilton also made the pragmatic political argument that the specific plan he proposed was absolutely nec-essary to win the support of financial and commercial elites. The need to engage moneyed men in any plan to restore the credit of the United States was a theme Hamilton sounded early and often in his career.[20] The attachment of "that description of Men, who are in every society the only firm supporters of government" was so critical at this delicate juncture in the country's history that it outweighed any concerns about the inequality, unfairness, or vices his plan might stimulate.[21] The treasury secretary conceded that the funding plan "fosters a spirit of gambling," but he believed these tendencies were limited to those actually engaged in "jobbing in the funds." However, he rejected as "malignant and false" the notion that investment and trading in public securities "furnished effectual means of corrupting."[22] To be sure, there were spectacular profits to be made, but it was a "strange perversion of ideas, and as novel as it is extraordinary, that men should be deemed corrupt & criminal for becoming proprietors in the funds of their Country."[23]

Hamilton did not deny that those who already possessed substantial wealth in financial instruments would reap the lion's share of benefits from his funding plan. In fact, the prospect of huge profits for investors was critical to the success of his program. However, Hamilton also believed the funding plan would be advantageous to "every class of the community" because it would help facilitate commerce, promote agriculture and manufacturing, and make borrowing easier and less costly for everyone.[24] In his view, the expected drop in interest rates to 5 and perhaps as little as 4 percent was something that would benefit all classes in the long run.[25] That access to credit would improve the circulation of money, thereby facilitating investment and promoting economic expansion to the benefit of all.

Congressional Debate over the Funding Plan

Although Hamilton seemed unperturbed by the possibility that his funding system would intensify economic inequality, the plan's likely effects provoked a bitter outcry inside and outside of Congress. Ordinary citizens drafted petitions, wrote newspaper articles, and organized protests against Hamilton's plans. Massachusetts farmer and Revolutionary War veteran William Manning considered those "measures so glaringly unjust" that he felt compelled to engage as a political writer for the first time in his life. Disavowing any personal stake whatsoever in the repayment of war debt, Manning argued that Hamilton's proposal would "eventually prove the destruction of our dear-bought liberties and of all the state governments."[26] In response to the secretary's claim that national honor required the government to fulfill its promises, Manning pointed out that the government had *already* broken its promise to needy soldiers who were told they would get paid after a few months but had to sit on their securities for years: "Did the poor soldiers—when they had the promise of [the] government to be paid once in three months and had waited two years or three for their pay, and were then discharged and sent home to their needy families with nothing but certificates stating that there was so much due to them from a government that had broken its promises so many times already and had neither funds established nor time set for the payment thereof—I say, did these poor soldiers act voluntarily in selling their certificates under par? Surely, no."[27] Against Hamilton's claim that the government cannot be expected to rectify or alleviate the unfairness of market forces, Manning pointed out that government policies had actually contributed to the hardships that forced many soldiers and others to sell their certificates. Because the supply of hard money was inadequate, state policies that required private debts and taxes to be paid in specie compelled certificate holders who were poor to sell their certificates.[28]

The effects of Hamilton's funding plan on inequality also became the subject of intense and prolonged debate in Congress. Deliberations over Hamilton's funding plan provided the occasion for the first major congressional debate on questions of class, inequality, and fairness. Congress members' positions on the funding plan generally coincided with their overall attitude toward the administration, but concerns about the effects of the plan on the distribution of wealth cut across the partisan lines just beginning to form. Even some of those who would become staunch Federalists expressed reservations about the plan's implications for economic equality.

Much of the debate within Congress revolved around competing conceptions of justice. Among critics of Hamilton's plan, the idea of justice was rooted in considerations of fairness and equity they used to judge the legitimacy of legal rules and contractual agreements. In their view, the law had to conform to standards of justice that took into account the circumstances surrounding the acquisition and transfer of holdings. Their conception of justice also permitted violations of the law if strict enforcement would produce unfortunate or intolerable effects. Among Hamilton's supporters, in contrast, justice was closely associated with the protection of property rights and the enforcement of contracts. As they saw it, justice militated against interference with existing property arrangements as long as the acquisition and transfer of holdings took place according to established rules of law. According to their conception of justice, the most important effects were the ones that contributed to stability and order in the market.

Some of the most vociferous criticism in the early stages of the debate focused on the wave of speculation unleashed based on rumors about the plan to repay securities at face value. The perennial administration critic James Jackson of Georgia cried that speculation had run amok after Hamilton unveiled his *Report on Public Credit*: "Since this report has been read in this House, a spirit of havoc, speculation, and ruin, has arisen, and been cherished by people who had an access to the information the report contained, that would have made a Hastings blush to have been connected with, though long inured to preying on the vitals of his fellow men" (January 28, 1790, 1st Cong., 2nd sess., 1132).[29] Jackson was especially outraged that predatory opportunists were profiting from the misfortunes of others. He viewed these opportunistic speculators as "rapacious wolves seeking whom they may devour, and preying upon the misfortunes of their fellow-men, taking undue advantage of their necessities" (January 28, 1790, 1st Cong., 2nd sess., 1137). To make matters worse, the funding plan called for taxes that would fall hardest on the very people who had been swindled. Moreover, Jackson believed the plan would do little to stimulate economic growth because it would tax laborers to "pay the indolent and idle creditor who receives them, to be spent and wasted in the course of a year, without any hope of a future reproduction" (February 9, 1790, 1st Cong., 2nd sess., 1181). To remedy the "distress" created by news of Hamilton's proposal, Jackson came out in support of a policy of discrimination. He argued that discrimination was justified to set right a wrong Congress itself had helped to create (January 28, 1790, 1st Cong., 2nd sess., 1138).

Several proadministration representatives actually joined Jackson in condemning the speculative frenzy. Theodore Sedgwick of Massachusetts, usually one of the administration's most reliable allies in the House, explained that he was not opposed to all speculation, but "when it is extended too far, it becomes a real evil, and requires the administration to divert or suppress it. . . . A spirit of gambling is of such evil tendency, that every legislative endeavor should be made to suppress it" (January 28, 1790, 1st Cong., 2nd sess., 1135). Thomas Scott of Pennsylvania was even more direct. He argued that the government must repay its foreign debt without discrimination but suggested that Congress had the power to discriminate among holders of domestic debt: "It is very clear to me, that we have the power to administer justice and impartiality among the members of the Union" (February 9, 1790, 1st Cong., 2nd sess., 1188).

Of all those who identified as Federalists, perhaps none was as deeply disturbed by the consequences and implications of the funding plan as Pennsylvania senator William Maclay. He immediately understood that the plan would be an enormous boon to speculators.[30] He objected to the funding plan because it would lay excessive burdens on the people and enrich a self-interested class of court-iers and speculators.[31] In opposition to those who argued that strict compliance with the law required full compensation of current debtholders, Maclay maintained that the ideal of justice sometimes requires departures from unfair laws. In an essay he wrote for the *Independent Gazeteer*, Maclay cited several historical examples—including the jubilee year practice of redistributing property among the ancient Hebrews—in support of the idea that it is sometimes necessary to mitigate the severity of the law for the sake of jus-tice.[32] As legislators, he told his colleagues, they should follow the demands of justice, which "had been the guide of all Just legislation, from the Jewish Jubilee to the present day."[33] Though it is doubtful Maclay was actually calling for the redistribution of land, forgive-ness of debts, and emancipation of slaves by invoking the jubilee year,[34] that reference, along with an approving remark on courts of chancery, leaves little question that he took a very different view of property rights and contracts than most supporters of the funding plan within Congress. In fact, Maclay reiterated his appeal to justice for the original holders of the debt on several other occasions but had little success persuading his colleagues in the Senate, including fellow Pennsylvanian senator Robert Morris.[35]

Leading the charge for discrimination in the House of Representa-tives was Madison. His support for discrimination signified a rever-sal of the position he had taken as a member of the Confederation Congress.[36] Although the supposed "mutability" and "injustice" of laws affecting private property had helped convince Madison of the need for a strong national government that could stand up to popu-list pressures in the states, he was now convinced that consider-ations of justice and humanity justified a policy of discrimination. The conception of justice Madison invoked in this debate was not identified with the protection of property rights (as it had been in his writings before and after the Constitutional Convention) but with a notion of fairness that permitted departures from the strict letter of the law. Dividing creditors into four distinct classes (original credi-tors who kept their securities, original creditors who sold them, cur-rent holders who bought them, and intermediate holders), Madison argued that the government's obligations toward each group must be guided by the principles of public justice, public faith, public credit, and public opinion (February 11, 1790, 1st Cong., 2nd sess., 1234).

Everyone could agree on how to treat the first and last classes of creditors, but the middle two classes posed special challenges.

In taking up the cause of original creditors who ended up selling their certificates, the ordinarily abstract and analytical Madison relied on sentimental appeals more characteristic of his friend and ally Jefferson. At one point, Madison even went so far as to assert "that, in great and unusual questions or morality, the heart is the best judge" (February 18, 1790, 1st Cong., 2nd sess., 1309). He was particularly troubled by the plight of original holders who ended up selling their securities at substantial losses. In his view, that class "may appeal to humanity, for the suffering of the military part of the creditors can never be forgotten, while sympathy is an American virtue. To say nothing of the singular hardship, in so many mouths, or requiring those who have lost four-fifths of seven-eighths of their due, to contribute the remainder in favor of those who have gained in the contrary proportion" (February 11, 1790, 1st Cong., 2nd sess., 1235). Madison acknowledged it would be impractical to repay the two middle groups at full value, but doing nothing for them was morally intolerable. "To reject wholly the claims of either is equally inadmissible; such a sacrifice of those who possess the written engagements would be fatal to the proposed establishment of public credit; it would moreover punish those who put their trust in the public promises and resources. To make the other class the sole victims is an idea at which human nature recoils" (February 11, 1790, 1st Cong., 2nd sess., 1236). These appeals to the humanity of his colleagues would set the tone for the debate over the next two weeks.

Throughout these debates, with the exception of Samuel Livermore of New Hampshire, no one ever questioned claims about the hardships faced by those who sold their securities (February 19, 1790, 1st Cong., 2nd sess., 1338). Even firm opponents of discrimination such as Federalist (and one-time Hamilton mentor) Elias Boudinot of New Jersey emphasized that they understood how someone such as Madison could be "led away by the dictates of his heart, for he believed he really felt for the misfortunes of his fellow-citizens, who had been prey of avaricious men" (February 11, 1790, 1st Cong., 2nd sess., 1238). An interest in relieving the economic distresses and misfortunes of citizens was a legitimate consideration in formulating public policy, Boudinot acknowledged, but he could not support discrimination "on account of its impracticability" (February 11,

1790, 1st Cong., 2nd sess., 1239). Other opponents of discrimination were just as adamant in asserting their sympathy for original holders who sold out of desperation. William L. Smith of South Carolina strenuously objected to any plan that would "take money out of the pocket of one man, to put into that of another," but he suggested that Congress might be able to provide relief to original possessors. Where it could be proven that they "sold from absolute distress," Smith proclaimed, "he would yield to no member in his alacrity to give them every just compensation, and to indemnify them for their sufferings" (February 15, 1790, 1st Cong, 2nd sess., 1254, 1255).

The proposal to compensate original holders who had sold their certificates encountered stiff resistance. Arguments against discrimination fell into three distinct but interrelated categories. One set of arguments concerned the logistical difficulties of administering any such plan. The chain of ownership was often so long that it could be impossible to figure out who sold what and for how much. Another set of arguments focused on the injustice of the remedy. Fisher Ames of Massachusetts, the leading Federalist in the House, echoed the points Hamilton had made in his *Report on Public Credit* when he asserted that Madison's plan would "violate the sacred rights of property" (February 15, 1790, 1st Cong., 2nd sess., 1264). To allow the government to do whatever it wanted in this instance would leave property rights in general insecure (February 9, 1790, 1st Cong., 2nd sess., 1195). A third set of arguments concerned the powers of Congress. Some critics denied that Congress even had the authority to alter the terms of a contract. In particular, they claimed any change to the conditions governing these securities would be tantamount to an ex post facto law clearly proscribed by the Constitution.

These arguments provoked a furious retort from arch-republican John Page of Virginia. He complained that representatives were using tortured reasoning to deny that "justice ought to be done." Indeed, the notion of justice was being perverted to protect the interests of wealthy speculators at the expense of those they had duped. If the arguments advanced by critics of discrimination prevailed, Congress would never be able to remedy any wrongs in the future. Page offered a litany of hardships the government would be unable to address if the arguments against the justice of discrimination prevailed: "We must not contemplate the restoration of the starving soldier, with his humble wife and numerous and naked offspring, to a more eligible situation; we must not restore confidence to the man of honor, who is buried in abject poverty, because it is addressing a language to the heart, which the haughtiness of the head disdains to hear; but, in doubtful cases of justice, the heart is the best director on this subject; happy will it be for us, if, as I think, they both concur to give their approbation to the present measure" (February 17, 1790, 1st Cong., 2nd sess., 1285).

In the end, the House rejected Madison's discrimination proposal by the lopsided vote of thirteen to thirty-six (February 22, 1790, 1st Cong., 2nd sess., 1344). However, that vote did not end debate on the distributive consequences of Hamilton's funding plan. Both the assumption plan and the taxes proposed to fund the debt provoked further discussion on how the government policies might affect different classes. Some members continued to remind their colleagues that the poor were forced to sell their securities out of necessity (see, e.g., remarks of Alexander White, February 25, 1790, 1st Cong., 2nd sess., 1409). Others complained that the tax plan could give an unfair advantage to "men of property" who would seek to monopolize articles that would be taxed: "The speculator would be enriched, and the poor oppressed, without benefiting, in the least degree, the Government or the public creditors" (Theodore Sedgwick, March 2, 1790, 1st Cong., 2nd sess., 1449–1450). Despite these and other objections, the main features of Hamilton's funding plan were eventually passed after a deal over the permanent location of the capital was struck with Madison and Jefferson and a complex compromise was reached on rates of interest to be paid on different certificates.[37]

The Debate over the National Bank

The debate over Hamilton's *Report on Public Credit* was mild in comparison with the firestorm that erupted over his plan to establish a national bank. In this case, allegations that the proposal would enrich financial elites were combined with claims that it was unconstitutional.

The idea for a national bank was nothing new. Hamilton first proposed the idea for a national bank in an important letter to Duane in 1780. At the time, he forthrightly acknowledged it was necessary to "engage a number of monied men of influence to relish the project and make it a business."[38] However, Hamilton was more circumspect about the possible benefits to financial and commercial elites in his *Report on a National Bank* to Congress in December of 1790.

His report highlighted the benefits to the public at large, declaring, "Public utility is more truly the object of public Banks, than private profit."[39] The main benefits included increases in the circulation (and therefore the productivity) of capital; facilitation of the government's ability to borrow money, especially in a time of war or other emergency; and improvements in the ability of the public to pay taxes, whether through greater access to loans or simply through increases in the overall money supply.[40] In addition, the bank would spur industry in the United States and help keep interest rates low.[41]

Though Hamilton emphasized the advantages of a national bank to the public at large, he downplayed the fact that these benefits would be much less direct—and less certain—than the benefits to those more immediately connected with the bank. Hamilton's Bank of the United States would operate in much the same way Morris's Bank of North America did. For one thing, private investment in the bank would be limited either to those who already possessed substantial amounts of liquid capital or to those who could pool their resources with others. This was because the capital stock of $10,000,000 would be divided into 25,000 shares worth $400 apiece, an amount generally out of reach for all but the most wealthy or well connected.[42] For another thing, the bank was structured to ease credit for members of the entrepreneurial class located in cities—not farmers, mechanics, or other laborers located in the backcountry. Whether by design or not, the banking system would prove to be a huge bonanza for members of the country's mercantile and financial elite.[43] Records indicate that the bank would actually make only a small fraction of its loans to small borrowers.[44]

Congressional debate over the bank would touch on questions of class, inequality, and privilege, but legislators first had to tackle the question of its constitutionality. The debate ranged over a variety of constitutional provisions, including the commerce clause, the general welfare clause, the preamble, and the tax power, but the one that dominated deliberations was the necessary and proper clause, which George Mason had dubbed the "sweeping clause" at the Constitutional Convention. The two most sophisticated and outspoken advocates for the two sides were Madison and Ames.

Madison controlled the proceedings on February 2. Before he turned to the bank itself, he expounded on the nature of the Constitution and outlined some principles for its proper interpretation. "It is not a general grant, out of which particular powers are excepted," he explained. "It is a grant of particular powers only, leaving the general mass in other hands" (February 2, 1791, 1st Cong., 3rd sess., 1945).[45] The fact that the Constitution limited the federal government to a set of specific powers dictated the way it ought to be interpreted. "Where a meaning is clear," the exercise of power was to be judged by its "consequences." However, where the meaning is unclear, Madison suggested the original "meaning of the parties to the instrument" could serve as a "proper guide." Based on the plain meaning of the text and the weight of evidence concerning the understanding of those who ratified the Constitution, Madison concluded Congress lacked the authority to establish the bank. Neither the plain meaning of the Constitution nor the understandings of those involved in its ratification supported claims that the general welfare clause, the borrowing clause, or the necessary and proper clause authorized Congress to establish a bank. Any attempt to justify the bank in terms of the general welfare clause "would give Congress an unlimited power; would render nugatory the enumeration of particular powers; would supercede all the powers reserved to the State Governments" (February 2, 1791, 1st Cong., 3rd sess., 1946). Likewise, efforts to find an independent grant of power in the necessary and proper clause would destroy the "essential characteristic of the Government, as composed of limited and enumerated powers" (February 2, 1791, 1st Cong., 3rd sess., 1947–1948). The doctrine of enumerated powers was so essential to the very idea of limited government that even if the framers had neglected to include something as basic as a treaty-making power, reasoned Madison, the "defect could only have been lamented, or supplied by an amendment of the Constitution" (February 2, 1791, 1st Cong., 3rd sess., 1950).

The next day, Ames countered with a radically different theory of constitutional government and alternative doctrine of constitutional interpretation. In fact, he developed a defense of the implied powers of Congress even more expansive than the one Hamilton would develop in his "Opinion on the Constitutionality of a National Bank." Ames essentially argued that the general ends outlined in the Constitution determined the means at the government's disposal with only a few key exceptions and exclusions. "Congress may do what is necessary to the end for which the Constitution was adopted, provided it is not repugnant to the natural rights of man, or to those which they have expressly reserved to themselves, or to the powers which are assigned to the States. . . . That construction may be maintained to be a safe one which promotes the good of the society, and the ends for which the Government was adopted, without impairing the rights of any man, or the powers of any State" (February 3, 1791, 1st Cong., 3rd sess., 1956).[46] The legitimate ends of government were not restricted to those objects specified in Article I, Section 8 of the Constitution; they also included those general ends contained in the preamble. These, in Ames's view, permitted the establishment of the bank (February 3, 1791, 1st Cong., 3rd sess., 1959).

Echoing arguments Madison himself had made in *Federalist* 37, Ames contended that no constitution could ever specify in advance all the powers it would be necessary and proper for the government to exercise because the "ingenuity of man was unequal to providing, especially beforehand, for all the contingencies that would happen." The Constitution is not a detailed rulebook that covers every situation that may come before the government; it is a statement of "principles" requiring the continuing exercise of judgment (February 3, 1791, 1st Cong., 3rd sess., 1954). If Madison were right about the nature and proper interpretation of the Constitution, then almost everything Congress had done in the nearly two years since it came into being was invalid, "for we have scarcely made a law in which we have not exercised our discretion with regard to the true intent of the Constitution. Any words but those used in that instrument will be liable to a different interpretation. We may regulate trade; therefore we have taxed ships, erected light-houses, made laws to govern seamen, &c., because we say they are the incidents to that power" (February 3, 1791, 1st Cong., 3rd sess., 1954). The bank, he argued, was no less necessary or proper to the achievement of legitimate ends than any of the other measures Congress had already adopted to deal with commerce or the common defense.

In the days that followed, speakers continued to debate the constitutionality of the bank in the terms laid out by Madison and Ames. Supporters of the bank pressed the claim that the use of powers by construction and implication was unavoidable. Sedgwick maintained that "no instrument for the delegation of power could be drawn with such precision and accuracy as to leave nothing to necessary implication." To prove his point, Sedgwick reminded his fellow legislators that Madison himself had relied on the interpretive principles he now rejected as illegitimate when he successfully argued that the removal power should be placed in the president

(February 4, 1791, 1st Cong., 3rd sess., 1960). The hypocrisy and inconsistency of some bank opponents were so great, alleged John Laurance of New York, that they relied on the very same mode of interpretation whose validity they denied when it was used by bank proponents in their own references to what would become the Tenth Amendment (February 4, 1791, 1st Cong., 3rd sess., 1965). Boudinot conceded that there was no explicit grant of power to erect a national bank, but he argued "that it was necessarily deduced by the strongest and most decisive implication" from the ends of the Constitution, which could be gleaned from the preamble (February 4, 1791, 1st Cong., 3rd sess., 1972). Congress had already acted by implication on numerous occasions, including the debate over the removal power, in delegating power to legislate for the Western Territory, and in building lighthouses and piers (February 4, 1791, 1st Cong., 3rd sess., 1976). In fact, the need to act by implication was such a basic and uncontroversial activity that Congress had even done it under the far more constricting confines of the Articles of Confederation (February 4, 1791, 1st Cong., 3rd sess., 1975).

Opponents of the bank responded by warning that the principles advanced by its supporters would place Congress on a slippery slope toward unfettered discretion. If the bank were allowed, Jackson admonished, then anything goes (February 4, 1791, 1st Cong., 3rd sess., 1967). Jackson denied that either the necessary and proper clause or the general welfare clause could be used to justify the bank. The necessity of the bank was disproved, he claimed, by the fact that the country's economy was doing just fine without such an institution. In fact, the country was flourishing. Jackson also disputed claims that the bank would promote the general welfare because he believed that it would end up benefiting some parts of the country more than it did others. The general welfare clause would become a pretext for all sorts of sectional legislation because it could mean anything at all and "justify the assumption of every power" (February 4, 1791, 1st Cong., 3rd sess., 1969). Michael Jenifer Stone of Maryland agreed that the "end of all Government is the public good," but he rejected the idea that the Constitution left the choice of means up to legislators. He suggested that there was no point in the Constitution at all if members of Congress could find authorization for legislation in the preamble because there is virtually nothing it would prohibit (February 5, 1791, 1st Cong., 3rd sess., 1983). Stone's most compelling constitutional argument pertained to the meaning of the necessary and proper clause. Contrary to assertions that the clause granted or expanded the powers of Congress, Stone maintained that it served to restrict the way the national legislature exercised its enumerated powers (February 5, 1791, 1st Cong., 3rd sess., 1986).

Congressional critics of the bank did not limit their arguments to points of constitutional interpretation. They also developed moral and political arguments that attacked the bank for being an antirepublican institution that would create new forms of inequality. In a letter to fellow southerner Jackson, former delegate to the Constitutional Convention Pierce Butler asserted, "The wealth and influence this Bank must and will give can not [sic] be a proper engine in the hands of a few." He added, "It is establishing an Aristocratick [sic] influence subversive of the spirit of our free, equal government."[47] Jackson repeated Butler's complaint that it would create exclusive benefits antithetical to republican values (February 1, 1791, 1st Cong., 3rd sess., 1941). Madison voiced a related objection about the unequal operation of the Bank Bill. He pointed out that the portion of the bill dealing with the disposition of western lands treated different classes of creditors differently, giving unfair advantages to those already in privileged positions. This provision violated the political principle that the "public good is most essentially promoted by an equal attention to the interests of all" (February 8, 1791, 1st Cong., 3rd sess., 2012).

In the Senate, Maclay perceived the bank as yet another scheme by Hamilton's supporters to enrich the few at the expense of the many. Though Maclay was no egalitarian, he was an old-fashioned republican who believed that the purpose of government was to promote the common interest. He described the bank as an "Aristocratic engine" likely to operate "like a Tax in favor of the Rich against the poor, Tending to the Accumulating in a few hands, And Under this View may be regarded As opposed to republicanism. And Yet Stock Wealth Money or property of any kind Wherever Accumulated has a Similar effect."[48] To make matters even worse, the group that would benefit under this scheme was made up of idle speculators, of all people. Maclay considered all banking systems "Machines for promoting the profits of unproductive Men," but this one was especially deplorable because it allowed them to subscribe in government certificates, whereas it required members of the public to put up specie.[49]

On the final day of debate in the House, Madison made one last effort to refute the dangerous constitutional ideas promoted by Hamilton's allies—and to salvage his reputation from accusations of inconsistency. He rejected the use of the preamble as an independent source of authority as an unacceptable constitutional innovation (February 8, 1791, 1st Cong., 3rd sess., 2009). Madison then went on to argue that those instances in which he had accepted a more liberal interpretation of the Constitution involved special circumstances. He conceded he had used the very same reasoning he now rejected in dealing with the question of the Western Territories, but he insisted this congressional departure from proper constitutional principles was justifiable because that "was a case *sui generis*, and therefore cannot be cited with propriety." In response to the point that Morris's Bank of North America had been established under the Articles of Confederation, Madison argued that had been a wartime measure that should not be used as a precedent in peacetime (February 8, 1791, 1st Cong., 3rd sess., 2011). Despite his efforts to distinguish Hamilton's proposal from previous measures approved by Congress, the Bank Bill passed by the comfortable margin of thirty-nine to twenty.

Before Washington agreed to sign the bill into law, he had to be persuaded of its constitutionality. To help him make up his mind, he sought the opinions of his cabinet members. Needless to say, Hamilton defended the constitutionality of the bank he had proposed, but his colleagues, Attorney General Edmund Randolph and Secretary of State Jefferson, issued separate opinions disputing the constitutionality of the Bank Bill. Everyone agreed that the Constitution gave Congress no explicit authority to charter a bank, so the dispute came down to the proper interpretation of the necessary and proper clause.

Jefferson insisted the necessary and proper clause gave Congress no additional powers beyond those "specially enumerated" in Article I. In his view, the necessary and proper clause was not an additional grant of power but a *limitation* on the powers of Congress. It did not specify any further ends Congress was authorized to pursue. Instead it restricted Congress to means actually necessary to the achievement of those narrowly defined ends. In fact, Jefferson noted, the "very power now proposed *as a means*, was rejected as *an end*, by the Convention which formed the constitution."[50]

Hamilton responded with a detailed critique of the interpretive theory underlying these arguments and a forceful articulation of his own theory of constitutional interpretation. He began by pointing out that the interpretive principles espoused by Jefferson and his allies "would be fatal to the just & indispensable authority of the United States."[51] According to Hamilton, those ideas were based on fundamentally mistaken notions about the nature of government and sovereignty that would lead to utterly absurd consequences. Citing congressional authorization for the erection of lighthouses as an example of how the government could not avoid exercising powers by construction, he argued that Jefferson's insistence on "adherence to the letter of its powers would at once arrest the motions of the government."[52] Jefferson's understanding of the word "necessary" was so restrictive that it treated the term "as if the word *absolutely* or *indispensably* had been prefixed to it."[53] To accept the secretary of state's interpretation would be to impose limitations on government not required by the text of the Constitution itself. "There are few measures of any government, which would stand so severe a test. To insist upon it, would be to make the criterion of the exercise of any implied power *a case of extreme necessity*; which is rather a rule to justify the overleaping of the bounds of constitutional authority, than to govern the ordinary exercise of it."[54] Necessity was not an either-or proposition that could be applied in a mechanical manner but a matter of degree that required the exercise of discretionary judgment about the best fit between means and ends. The necessary and proper clause should not be interpreted in such a narrow fashion that it prevented the government from achieving the ends for which it was established; it "ought to be construed liberally, in advancement of the public good."[55] Of course, Hamilton did not emphasize these points when he tried to allay worries about the necessary and proper and supremacy clauses in *Federalist* 33.[56]

Hamilton also turned the tables on Jefferson by using the proposed constitutional amendments Jefferson supported against him. Whereas Jefferson had pointed to the reserved powers language of what would become the Tenth Amendment as expressing the very "foundation" of the Constitution, Hamilton used the language of proposed amendments against the very groups that supported them. He argued that there would have been no reason for anti-Federalists to propose amendments expressly prohibiting Congress from granting monopolies or erecting corporations unless they believed the Constitution already allowed the federal government to do these things. Why would they go to such trouble to deny these powers to Congress unless they believed it already possessed them?[57]

Hamilton insisted his interpretation was more consistent with both the spirit and the letter of that document than was Jefferson's. In Hamilton's view, the powers of the national government were not restricted to those explicitly granted to it by the Constitution. Rather, they included "express" powers delegated by specific language in the Constitution, powers "implied" as means or instruments of "carrying into execution any of the specified powers," and "resulting" powers based on a combination of express and implied powers that come into being in novel circumstances.[58] Hamilton's defense of the authority of Congress to erect the bank rested on the proposition that "implied powers are to be considered as delegated equally with express ones."[59] As long as it was possible to show that an institution or program had a "relation" to "one or more of the specified powers of the government," it was constitutional.[60] The "welfare of the community" is the only legitimate standard to apply, but what qualifies as conducive to the welfare of the community is not a matter of strict application of rules; it "must be a matter of conscientious discretion."[61]

This assertion of constitutional authority did not mean Congress could do whatever it wanted. From the outset Hamilton admitted the powers of government were limited in ways even Jefferson had not acknowledged. In many respects, the powers of the national government were far more expansive than Jefferson would ever allow, but they were still restricted to those means that "are not precluded by restrictions & exceptions specified in the constitution; or not immoral, or not contrary to the essential ends of political society."[62] Paradoxically, whereas Jefferson's strict constructionism confined the limits on the government's powers to the four corners of the constitutional text, Hamilton's loose constructionism allowed him to look for limits beyond the explicit language of the text. Though Hamilton was willing to acknowledge extratextual limits on the powers of government, he did not think any of them applied in this case.

Debate over the bank did not cease after Washington signed the bill into law on February 25, 1791. Some critics continued to question the constitutionality of the Bank of the United States well into the nineteenth century, but most opposition tended to focus on its incompatibility with republican principles. One of the harshest and most inveterate critics was Jeffersonian politician and agrarian theorist John Taylor of Caroline. The Virginian charged Hamilton and his allies with creating a corrupt system that betrayed the democratic and egalitarian ideals of the Revolution. Pointing to the large number of Congressmen who became stockholders in the very same institution they were supposed to oversee, Taylor argued that the national legislature was no longer representing the general interest but instead serving special interests. In addition, by creating an aristocratic institution that enabled a few to amass great wealth without having to labor ("the enriching of a favored few at the public expence"), the supporters of the bank introduced forms of inequality antithetical to republican ideals.[63] Taylor reminded readers of the maxim, "A democratic republic is endangered by an immense disproportion of wealth," yet here was a system that exacerbated economic inequality by allowing the "rich" to "filch from the poor."[64] In the following decades, claims that the bank distorted the distribution of wealth—and therefore the distribution of power—would be a common refrain in the chorus of complaints against the bank, leading up to Andrew Jackson's veto of the attempt to recharter the bank in 1832.[65]

The Promotion of Manufacturing

The final part of Hamilton's program to create a stronger and more diversified national economy involved government promotion of manufacturing, which was still in an embryonic state. His interest in promoting manufacturing in the United States dated back to his days as a teenager eager to distinguish himself in the colonial struggle against Great Britain.[66] Now he had the opportunity to accelerate the country's industrial development along the path Great Britain had marked out.

To convince Americans of the benefits of manufacturing, he first had to overcome their ideological biases in favor of an agrarian way of life. Many previous attempts to promote manufacturing had failed in part because workers were reluctant to labor under regimented conditions that deprived them of control over the rhythm of work and the flexibility to attend to their domestic responsibilities.[67] Manufacturing also seemed to threaten republican ideals. At this time, Jefferson and perhaps most other Americans believed that a political economy rooted in agriculture was a necessary condition for the preservation and development of republican virtues such as simplicity and frugality. There was also a deep-seated belief that an agrarian way of life was essential to the cultivation of that spirit of independence that made free government itself possible. The top-down structure of industrial manufacturing was associated with a host of vices antithetical to republicanism. Because it was organized around the system of wage labor, the worst effect of manufacturing was its tendency to create and deepen relations of economic dependence that undermined the capacity for self-government.[68]

Hamilton countered these ideas head on by pointing out that the reasons offered in support of a simple agrarian economy were not based on empirical evidence; they were rooted in ideological dogmatism. These outdated theories overstated the economic advantages of an agricultural economy and grossly understated the economic advantages of manufacturing. The evidence of experience demonstrated that manufacturing actually enhances the prosperity and strength of the entire nation. Compared with labor in agriculture, labor in manufacturing is potentially much more productive and efficient thanks to the opportunities for a greater division of labor, it offers more uninterrupted and reliable opportunities for employment because it is not seasonal, it provides employment opportunities for those who might otherwise be excluded from the labor market altogether, it furnishes more opportunities for individuals to develop their diverse "talents and dispositions," it extends the use of machinery, it produces a greater and more steady demand for the produce of agriculture, it encourages immigration from other countries, and it better provides for the national security needs of the nation. Although Hamilton addressed the economic and military advantages of a diversified economy, he never directly addressed the effects an increase of industrial employment and corresponding decrease of agricultural employment would have on the moral or political well-being of the country.

There was simply not enough private capital available to industrialize the country as quickly or as extensively as Hamilton believed would be desirable, so he called on Congress to provide "pecuniary bounties," or subsidies, to promote the development and growth of manufacturing in the United States. The major problem he faced in this instance, as in the battle over the bank, was that the Constitution gave the national government no explicit authority to promote commercial activity, only to regulate it. However, Hamilton believed the government could legitimately take the initiative in directing the economy when other actors could not: "In countries where there is great private wealth much may be effected by the voluntary contributions of patriotic individuals, but in a community situated like that of the United States, the public purse must supply the deficiency of private resource. In what can it be so useful as in prompting and improving the efforts of industry?"[69]

This time, Hamilton's defense of the constitutionality of his proposal relied primarily on the general welfare clause. He acknowledged that the precise status of the general welfare clause is indistinct. It could be understood either as an independent grant of authority or as a qualifying phrase that has the effect of expanding the scope of other powers. Whatever the case, Hamilton was still confident that it allowed the federal government to go beyond those powers expressly enumerated in Article I of the Constitution. "The terms *'general Welfare'* were doubtless intended to signify more than was expressed or imported in those which Preceded; otherwise numerous exigencies incident to the affairs of a Nation would have been left without a provision. The phrase is as comprehensive as any that could have been used; because it was not fit that the constitutional authority of the Union, to appropriate its revenues shou'd have been restricted within narrower limits than the 'General Welfare' and because this necessarily embraces a vast variety of particulars, which are susceptible neither of specification nor of definition."[70] The only inherent limitation the clause imposed on the use of the tax power, according to Hamilton, was a geographical one implied in the idea of "generality" itself. Even this limitation was more of a guideline than a restriction; it simply required that the operation of any money appropriated by Congress extend "in fact, or by possibility, throughout the Union, and not be confined to a particular spot."[71] Likewise, the tax power gives the government the authority to do virtually anything for the general welfare or the common defense as long as it does not violate the three more narrow and expressly stated exceptions that taxes be uniform, that direct taxes be apportioned according to population, and that no taxes be laid on exports from states.

Like the other two major parts of his economic program for the United States, Hamilton's manufacturing plan had the potential to enrich those in the financial and entrepreneurial classes. The possibility that a few private citizens would become (even more) rich as a result of these public policies was widely recognized. Craftsmen in places such as Philadelphia feared that the manufacturing plan was part of a larger Federalist scheme to create new forms of hierarchy.[72] However, unlike his defense of the other two plans, Hamilton's arguments in favor of manufacturing did directly address the potential effects adoption might have on laborers and other members of the so-called lower orders. Speaking from his own experience as a highly talented but disadvantaged young man yearning for opportunities beyond the harsh world of the West Indies, Hamilton suggested that one major advantage of manufacturing is that it offers an escape from the mind-numbing drudgery of agricultural labor by providing opportunities for new and diverse activities that stimulate the mind.[73] He also argued that manufacturing would provide work to "persons who would otherwise be idle (and in many cases a burthen on the community), either from the byass [sic] of temper, habit, infirmity of body, or some other cause, indisposing, or disqualifying them from the toils of the Country." His very next sentence identified "women and Children" as two specific groups who could be "rendered more useful and the latter more early useful by manufacturing establishments, than they would be otherwise."[74] This plan to integrate women and children into the labor force has contributed as much as anything to Hamilton's reputation as a callous capitalist and cold utilitarian, but it should be borne in mind that women and children were already working in large numbers on farms, in shops, at mills, and almost everywhere else there was work to be done—something Hamilton knew very well from his own difficult childhood.[75]

With his report on manufacturing, Hamilton missed an opportunity to discuss the ways in which manufacturing might actually lessen economic inequality. He always returned to the claim that his plan would "increase the real wealth of the community," but he never addressed how this wealth would be distributed within the community.[76] He was preoccupied with the wealth of the nation, but he did not seem particularly concerned about the distribution of that wealth. "It is a truth as important as it is agreeable, and one to which it is not easy to imagine exceptions, that every thing [sic] tending to establish *substantial* and *permanent order*, in the affairs of a Country, to increase the total mass of industry and opulence, is ultimately beneficial to every part of it."[77] Even though he had demanded empirical evidence of the advantages of agriculture from the proponents of agrarianism, he failed to provide any to substantiate his own claim about the wide benefits of manufacturing.

Class and Inequality in Hamilton's Political Thought

Based on the three major reports that constituted the Hamiltonian financial and economic system, it is hard to come away with any conclusion other than that Hamilton's public policies were designed to promote the interests of economic elites. His willingness to use the powers of the national government to advance the interests of the few—even when that required the use of highly controversial principles of interpretation that stretched the meaning of the Constitution—explains why it was so easy for generations of Jeffersonians to portray him as a plutocrat. Any appraisal of Hamilton's views must give great weight to the three famous reports that helped solidify his legacy and, directly or indirectly, steer the direction of the country. However, any account that ends there is incomplete. Although the three reports exemplify Hamilton's constitutional ideals, including his loose constructionist approach, they do not fully capture his views on class and inequality. Other writings and activities from various points of his public career before and after his time as secretary of the treasury reveal a thinker who could be sensitive to the economic hardships of disadvantaged groups and alert to the ways in which government policies can contribute to those hardships.[78] Though he rarely suggested policies aimed at reducing economic inequalities, he often opposed policies that might increase economic inequalities and hardships.

Hamilton's views on economic inequality must be examined in the context of his views on political inequality and the proper role of the people in republican government. Hamilton's reputation for indifference and even hostility to the poor and laboring classes is based in large part on his avowed suspicion of democracy. Even though he was an early and enthusiastic participant in the revolutionary cause, he often complained about how easy it was for popular movements to descend into lawlessness and anarchy. He abhorred the kind of mob action orchestrated by the Sons of Liberty because it fostered disorder.[79] Assaults on Tories left Hamilton with the impression that the "multitude . . . have [sic] not a sufficient stock of reason and knowledge to guide them."[80] Insurgent activity from Shays's Rebellion to the Whiskey Rebellion confirmed his belief that the "multitudes" can easily get carried away when they oppose established policies.[81]

Like many other Federalists, one of his motivations in supporting a new Constitution was to check the "excesses of democracy." The people's susceptibility to manipulation by demagogues was one of the major reasons he favored the indirect system of elections and long terms of office established by the Constitution. In *Federalist* 71 he explained, "The republican principle . . . does not require an unqualified complaisance to every sudden breese [*sic*] of passion, or to every transient impulse which the people may receive from the arts of men, who flatter their prejudices to betray their interests."[82] Hamilton reiterated these ideas at the New York Ratifying Convention, where he noted, "There are certain conjunctures, when it may be necessary and proper to disregard the opinions which the majority of the people have formed."[83] In general, he claimed, experience had proven that the "ancient democracies . . . never possessed one feature of good government."[84] His conception of republicanism emphasized "confidence" in rulers rather than "vigilance" as the chief virtue of the good citizen. According to this ideal, rulers were not directly accountable to the people but to other elites.[85]

Hamilton's occasional remarks on the ignorance and incompetence of the people and on the dangers of democracy leave little doubt that he distrusted the ability of individuals from the lower classes to exercise power responsibly.[86] In casting "Publius" as more fair-minded in his reasoning and more moderate in his rhetoric than the enemies of the Constitution, Hamilton aligned himself with the "wealthy, the well-born, and the great" who had been the objects of popular ire.[87] However, his suspicion of the lower classes did not necessarily translate into confidence in the upper classes. In fact, he was just as apt to question the fitness of the people's representatives, military leaders, and rulers—and often in much harsher terms. He could be particularly scathing toward political elites who failed to live up to his own high standards of integrity and competence.[88] His low opinion of the "masses" reflected his rather low opinion of human nature in general. Even though he cited Shays's Rebellion as an example of the dangers that mobs pose to the foundations of law and order,[89] he acknowledged that the well-heeled often pose the greatest threat to the health of free government. It was just as important for the law to restrain the tyranny of the few as it was to curb the anarchy of the many. As Hamilton described, "An inviolable respect for the Constitution and Laws" was a crucial means of restraining the "rich and powerful" from scheming "against the common liberty."[90] In his view, the danger to free government did not come from one particular class but from class differences in general.

Hamilton's remarks on class during his daylong speech at the Constitutional Convention on June 18 have frequently been cited as evidence of his incurable biases against the lower classes. Critics have pointed to that epic performance as proof he harbored aristocratic (if not monarchical) views and despised popular government. Yates's notes in particular have contributed to the impression that Hamilton trusted the "rich and well-born" with virtually unchecked power. However, the available record indicates that Hamilton doubted the ability of both the many and the few to rise above their own economic interests.[91] In fact, that speech actually indicates the importance of checking all classes, not just the lower ones.

In that June 18 convention speech, Hamilton argued that the tendency of each class to oppress the other makes it imperative to give each the means of defending itself against the other. Hamilton acknowledged that the few "will oppress the many" if they are not checked, but, like other delegates who addressed the conflict between the few and the many, he focused on the dangers posed by the "turbulent and uncontrouling disposition" of the people.[92] He singled out the passage of paper money laws as a prime example of the way in which the many can oppress the few. However, rather than eliminating or reducing popular participation in government, Hamilton suggested that it would be more consistent with republican principles to preserve its role in government but establish a "permanent body [that] can check the imprudence of democracy." Alluding to populist urges that fueled Shays's Rebellion, Hamilton called for the creation of a forceful executive, long terms of office, and other institutional arrangements capable of arresting the "amazing violence & turbulence of the democratic spirit."[93] His most notorious proposals included terms of office during good behavior—essentially for life—for both the executive and an upper house of the legislature. Though these audacious proposals smacked of monarchy, Hamilton insisted both institutions would be consistent with republicanism because their powers would ultimately be derived from the people.[94]

Other remarks he made at the convention reveal that he strongly favored a meaningful, albeit circumscribed, role for the people. He thought it was "essential" for the success of the Constitution that the popular branch of government rest on the broadest possible foundation. According to Madison's notes, Hamilton "expressed himself with great earnestness and anxiety in favor of the motion" by Hugh Williamson of North Carolina to expand the size of the House of Representatives.[95] In addition, Hamilton took a stand against property qualifications. He was the one who proposed to change the basis of representation in the national legislature under the Virginia Plan from "quotas or contribution" or the "number of free inhabitants" to the "number of free inhabitants" alone.[96]

These proposals to expand suffrage for the people were not anomalies. Hamilton's record on measures to protect the voting rights of those with little or no property was far from perfect, but it does belie allegations that he wanted to restrict political power to those with sufficient property.[97] Prior to the Philadelphia Convention, as a member of the New York Assembly, Hamilton spoke out against a provision in an election bill that would have allowed inspectors to question any "unlettered" or "ignorant person" about his ballot as something that "would tend to increase rather than prevent an improper influence."[98] (However, a few days after he made these remarks he raised no objection to the disqualification of "persons absolutely indigent."[99]) Far from seeking to augment the power of the wealthy, Hamilton fought against a proposal that could have allowed them to consolidate their power in the future. He opposed a plan to give the legislature the power to alter the qualifications of either electors or elected on the grounds that such power was subject to abuse by the wealthy: "Commerce it will be admitted leads to an increase of individual property, property begets influence. Though a legislature composed as we are, will always take care of the rights of the middling and lower classes, suppose the majority of the legislature to consist at a future day, of wealthy men, what would hinder them, if the right of innovating on the constitution be admitted, from declaring that no man not worth ten thousand pounds should be eligible to a seat in either house? and [*sic*] would not this introduce a principle of aristocracy fatal to the genius of our present constitution?"[100]

Hamilton never went as far as some of his contemporaries to address the economic preconditions of political participation, but he did occasionally support policies designed to improve the economic condition of those near the bottom of the class structure. He was particularly active in working to increase the pay of those in public service—especially for those in the lower classes. One of his earliest efforts in this regard was a campaign to secure higher pay for soldiers under his command.[101] Just as Hamilton himself had benefited from the meritocratic opportunities the Revolution had made possible, he sought to extend those benefits to others. His support for egalitarian policies extended beyond his (now) well-known proposal to allow blacks to serve in the military in the firm expectation that they would gain their freedom after demonstrating they were just as capable as white soldiers.[102] Hamilton also favored policies that challenged class hierarchies within the military. One biographer explains, "It was Hamilton who broke with the age-old tradition of appointing only gentlemen as officers and never promoting them from the ranks of enlisted men."[103] In addition, he lobbied the Continental Congress to provide disability pensions to "all person[s] disabled in the service of the United States"[104] and worked to get soldiers back pay from a Congress reluctant to make such expenditures.[105]

Hamilton continued to support similar policies following the adoption of the Constitution. In the draft of a speech he wrote for Washington, he urged Congress to offer salaries for public office high enough to attract the most virtuous and capable candidates. He justified this call for higher salaries on the republican principle that offices ought to be open to individuals of all classes, included those who lacked substantial property. Although Jefferson and his allies often proclaimed frugality in government as an indispensable republican value, Hamilton pointed out that penny-pinching in this case would actually undermine republicanism by limiting the opportunities of those who lacked independent means of support.

> If their own private wealth is to supply in the candidates for public office the deficiency of public liberality, then the sphere of those who can be candidates, especially in a country like ours, is much narrowed, and the chance of a choice of able as well as upright men much lessened. Besides that, it would be repugnant to the first principles of our government to exclude men, from the public trusts, because their talents and virtues, however conspicuous, are unaccompanied by wealth. If the rewards of government are too scanty, those who have talents without wealth, and are too virtuous to abuse their stations, cannot accept public offices without a sacrifice of interest.[106]

Some of the policies designed to benefit the poor or working class had little if anything to do with the advancement of republican ideals. Instead, Hamilton justified them in plain humanitarian terms as measures that would ease the burdens faced by specific classes. One example is his proposal in 1792 for the "establishment of one or more marine Hospitals" that would provide medical treatment for sick and disabled seamen. Hamilton stated that the proposal would promote "humanity . . . from its tendency to protect from want and misery, a very useful, and, for the most part, a very needy class of the Community." He added that such a measure would also be advantageous to commerce not only by helping to keep sailors healthy but by attracting them to the profession in the first place. Hamilton proposed that the plan could be funded through a monthly deduction of ten cents from the wages of each seaman. The treasury secretary also recommended that the benefits of the fund "extend, not only to disabled and decrepid [sic] seamen, but to the widows and children of those who may have been killed or drowned, in the course of their service as seamen."[107] As discussed in the next chapter, Congress would eventually act on Hamilton's proposal and establish a system of marine hospitals in major port cities.

Hamilton proposed yet another state-run program to improve the material conditions of the disadvantaged. This time, it concerned assistance for disabled soldiers and their children, a matter he had overseen in 1783 as chairman of a military committee in the Confederation Congress.[108] He recommended the formation of "corps of invalids" as well as an "establishment for the maintenance and education of the children of persons in the army and navy." Corps of invalids, which had been established in France, Great Britain, and in the United States during the Revolutionary War, were units that assigned light duty to disabled soldiers no longer fit for field duty.[109] Sounding much more like Paine than the heartless plutocrat he is often made out to be, Hamilton maintained that "policy, justice, and humanity forbid the abandoning to want and misery men who have spent their best years in the military service of a country, or who, in that service, have contracted infirmities which disqualify them to earn their bread in other modes." Though he insisted that the "corps of invalids" ought to be established by law, he did not think it would be necessary for the public to make any expenditures for "mere maintenance of its members in clothing, lodging, and food" as long as some means of "Employment might be found." Echoing the arguments he had made about the repayment of the national debt being a matter of national honor, Hamilton suggested that the adoption of his proposal was necessary to make the country more re-spectable: "The UStates are [sic] perhaps the only country in which an Institution of this nature is not to be found; a circumstance which if continued will be discreditable. The Establishment as to Children is recommended by similar motives with the additional consider-ation that they may be rendered by it useful members of Society and acquisitions to the army & Navy as Musicians, &c."[110]

At no point did Hamilton bother to offer any justification of these policies on constitutional grounds. He never explained whether the health-care plan for sick seamen or the assistance program for veter-ans with disabilities and their children were authorized by the gen-eral welfare clause, the necessary and proper clause, the commerce clause, or any other provision in the Constitution. It seems it never even crossed his mind that any of these policies would run afoul of the Constitution. After all, he did not even formulate his constitu-tional arguments in favor of the national bank until he was required to do so.

In some instances, Hamilton thought it would be possible to mod-ify relatively uncontroversial policies with no ostensible implica-tions for economic inequality or poverty in ways that would make life easier for the poor. In his *Report on the Establishment of a Mint*, the treasury secretary argued in favor of coining money in smaller denominations so that the poor would be able to purchase smaller quantities of goods (just what they needed at any given time) and escape the inflated prices that tend to result when only large de-nominations are available:

> Pieces of very small value are a great accommodation and the means of a beneficial economy to the Poor; by enabling them to purchase, in small portions, and at a more reasonable rate, the necessaries of which they stand in need. If there are only Cents, the lowest price for any portion of a vendible commodity, how-ever inconsiderable in quantity, will be a Cent; if there are half Cents, it will be a half Cent; and in a great number of cases ex-actly the same things will be sold for a half Cent which if there were none would cost a Cent. But a half Cent is low enough for the *minimum* of price. Excessive minuteness would defeat its object. To enable the poorer classes to procure necessaries cheap [sic] is to enable them with more comfort to themselves to labor for less; the advantages of which need no comment.[111]

A More Progressive Tax System

Hamilton's various statements on taxation throughout his career in public service contain his most sustained engagement with the problems of poverty and inequality. Hardly anyone appreciated the importance of raising as much revenue as possible to fund the national government more than Hamilton did, but he often spoke out in favor of rates and objects of taxation that would minimize the amounts raised from the poor. Although he supported numerous policies designed to benefit members of the upper classes, he also supported policies that would have shifted more of the tax burden onto them.

Hamilton always looked to the experiences of other countries in deciding what would be best for the United States. Sometimes other countries provided positive models he hoped his adopted country would emulate. Sometimes these were negative examples he hoped the United States would avoid. One of the things that bothered him about life in Great Britain and Ireland was that the "common people" there were saddled with onerous taxes on the "necessaries of life."[112] He also found it lamentable that in France taxes fell so hard on certain classes "who are by that means reduced to indigence and misery." There was also much to dislike in the tax policies that existed in different states. Hamilton complained that the need for revenue would force state governments to resort to taxes that "oppress the poor by raising the prices of necessaries."[113] Several years before Shays's Rebellion forced law makers in Massachusetts to confront inequities in the tax system, Hamilton opined that taxes in that state were too high on the lower orders, which led to "real marks of distress among some classes of the people."[114] However, he thought that the more equal distribution of wealth in the United States made it possible to avoid the burdensome levels of taxation that existed in Europe. Thanks to the "much greater equality of fortunes," the tax burden could be distributed more evenly than it was in France, where the "rich have gained so entire an ascendant [*sic*], that there is a constant sacrifice of the ease and happiness of the people to their avarice and luxury: their burthens are in no proportion to those of the middle order, and still less to those of the poor."[115] Even in retirement from public service Hamilton criticized the unfairness of tax policy. In his analysis of the Louisiana Purchase, Hamilton blasted the Jefferson administration for the way it planned to pay for the territory: "*Not by taxing luxury and wealth and whiskey, but by increasing the taxes on the necessaries of life.*"[116]

Hamilton rejected as fanciful the notion that "absolute equality" was attainable, but he did think it was possible to create a tax system that imposed burdens based on the ability to pay rather than demanding an equal quotient from every group.[117] He strongly opposed the use of poll or capitation taxes except in "cases of distressing emergency" for two reasons. One was their susceptibility to abuse by careless or unscrupulous tax collectors. The other was their tendency to hurt the poor. Because a poll tax imposes a "fixed rate" regardless of wealth, it "operates unequally, and injuriously to the industrious poor."[118] An interest in equality was the main reason he supported an impost duty. Under this system, "every class of the community bears its share of the duty in proportion to its consumption; which last is regulated by the compartive [*sic*] wealth of the respective classes in conjunction with their habits of expence or frugality. The rich and luxurious pay in proportion to their riches and luxury, the poor and parsimonious in proportion to their poverty and parsimony." Hamilton went on to explain, "A chief excellence of this mode of revenue is, that it preserves a just measure to the abilities of individuals, promotes frugality and taxes extravagance."[119]

Despite his admonition against the adoption of a poll tax, Hamilton's proposals for new sources of revenue during the Revolutionary War had included a poll tax on all males above the age of fifteen. However, he sought to mitigate the regressive tendencies of this tax by exempting those who performed vital security functions (i.e., "common soldiers" and "common sailors") and those who were too poor to pay (i.e., "day laborers, cottagers, and paupers").[120] The proposed poll tax met with the obvious objection that it would fall equally on rich and poor alike, but Hamilton reminded readers that under his plan the "poor, properly speaking, are not comprehended."[121] He admitted that a poll tax by its nature is not progressive, but he insisted that the legislature could find ways to correct any imbalance. One way to do this would be to institute a luxury tax: "The rich must be made to pay for their luxuries, which is the only proper way of taxing their superior wealth."[122]

Consumption taxes are now widely regarded as being among the most regressive forms of taxation because those closer to the bottom of the economic scale end up paying a far greater percentage of their income in these taxes than do those at the upper end.

When Hamilton served as secretary of the treasury, there was still a widespread assumption that taxes on articles of consumption were fairer than other kinds of taxes because the amount people paid was thought to match their ability to pay: the poor could avoid onerous taxes simply by avoiding those items taxed more heavily. This was the understanding that informed Hamilton's endorsement of consumption taxes in *Federalist* 21, in which he argued that taxes on articles of consumption were least objectionable because the amount individuals paid corresponded to their means, an argument that comported with the prevailing opinion of authorities in political economy from Adam Smith to Malachy Postlethwayt.[123] In addition, consumption taxes were most consistent with the principle of freedom because consumers decided for themselves how much they were willing to pay: "The rich may be extravagant, the poor can be frugal."[124]

The taxes Hamilton proposed as treasury secretary were based on this understanding of the effects of different tax systems. One of the most notorious revenue-raising measures he supported was an excise on certain kinds of spirits, which came to be known as the whiskey tax. In Hamilton's view, a sin tax on alcohol that might discourage consumption of this unwholesome article was a perfectly legitimate exercise of the government's tax power. It was also consistent with fairness in the tax code. He explained,

> Taxes on consumable articles have upon the whole better pretensions to equality than any other. If some of them fall more heavily on particular parts of the community, others of them are chiefly borne by other parts. And the result is an equalization of the burthen as far as it is attainable. Of this class of taxes it is not easy to conceive one which can operate with greater equality than a tax on distilled Spirits. There appears to be no article, as far as the information of the Secretary goes, which is an object of more equal consumption throughout the United States.[125]

Critics complained that excise taxes on alcohol would fall hardest on farmers in the backcountry, but Hamilton adamantly denied any class bias.[126] He remarked snarkily that citizens in the backcountry would pay more in such taxes only if they consumed more alcohol than folks in other parts of the country.[127] Besides, he calculated that the average amount the typical family would pay in a year "would be less than *one dollar and a half*. The citizen who is able to maintain a family and who is the owner or occupier of a farm, cannot feel any inconvenience from so light a contribution, and the industrious poor, whether artisans or laborers are usually allowed spirits or an equivalent in addition to their wages."[128] He dismissed objections about the unfairness of the excise tax on distilled spirits with the observation that this tax operates no more partially than any other.[129] Needless to say, the western Pennsylvania farmers who rose up against the excise taxes during the Whiskey Rebellion vehemently disagreed with Hamilton's assessment. There is no question that the whiskey excise taxed cash-poor grain farmers in frontier communities to benefit the holders of securities concentrated in eastern cities.[130] Even if Hamilton was ultimately wrong about the progressivity of excise taxes, there is no question that he endorsed the principle of progressivity in the tax system.

Many of Hamilton's other tax proposals were indubitably progressive. According to historian Forrest McDonald, Hamilton's position on the proper distribution of taxes reflected the profound influence that French finance minister Jacques Necker exerted on the American statesman's economic ideas. By the time Hamilton became secretary of the treasury, he seems to have internalized Necker's principle that taxes should apply to "objects of luxury and splendor" rather than the necessities of life.[131] Thus, his recommendations to Congress usually imposed higher duties on luxury items than on necessities and other articles heavily consumed by the poor and working classes. For instance, his proposals for additional supplies in 1792 placed higher duties on silk shoes and slippers than on other kinds.[132] He explicitly justified different rates on these and other items as being based on the ability of their most likely consumers to pay. For example, he stated, "Wines generally speaking are the luxury of classes of the community who can afford to pay a considerable [import] duty upon them."[133] The same reasoning applied to other items subject to higher taxes: "With regard to China and Glass there are two weighty reasons for a comparatively high duty upon them. The use of them is very limited except by the wealthier classes. And both their bulk and liability to damage in transportation are great securities against evasions of the Revenue."[134]

Hamilton tended to minimize the additional expenses that protectionist measures would add to the cost of imported goods. He addressed the possibility that these duties would affect different classes differently in the section of his *Report on the Subject of Manufactures* dealing with "printed books." Instead of proposing different rates for different types of books, Hamilton suggested that different consumption patterns would automatically take care of any inequalities. In his estimation, it was unlikely the duties on imported books usually found only in the libraries of wealthy families and professionals would have any effect on their production because these groups could easily afford the added cost. However, when it came to the "books in most general family use," Hamilton expected that the high demand for these texts would stimulate their domestic production so much that those of middling means would, in the long run at least, avoid paying the taxes altogether. In addition, the abundance of printing presses throughout the United States would provide such a steady supply of affordable books that the middling classes could end up paying less for these books than if they imported them without the duty.[135]

The clearest indication of Hamilton's support for progressive taxation appears in two separate proposals to tax dwellings. The first was a plan he submitted to the New York Assembly in January 1787; the other was a plan he proposed in a letter to Oliver Wolcott Jr. of Connecticut, his successor as secretary of the treasury of the United States. Both proposals established graduated tax rates on dwellings and imposed additional taxes on items only the richest citizens were likely to own.

In his draft of "An Act for Raising Yearly Taxes within this State [New York]," Hamilton proposed a variety of direct and indirect taxes that mainly targeted the most affluent citizens of New York. Although he recommended taxes on items such as salt, alcohol, and saddles that were used by rich and poor alike, he also proposed a number of taxes on luxury items that would be borne almost exclusively by the rich: clocks, gold and silver watches, silk and leather shoes, and mahogany furniture. The most progressive feature of the tax applied to homes and furnishings. Assuming that the number of rooms in a dwelling was closely associated with the wealth of its owners or renters, Hamilton recommended different levels of taxation depending on the number of rooms instead of charging a flat rate per room. The more rooms a dwelling had, the higher the tax per room: log houses would be taxed at 2 shillings per apartment, homes with up to three rooms at 3 shillings per apartment, those with four rooms at 4 shillings per apartment, those with five rooms at 6 shillings per apartment, and those with six or more rooms at 8 shillings per apartment. In addition, his proposal imposed additional taxes on the kinds of furnishings only the rich could afford. These included taxes on painted and papered walls; graduated rates on chimneys made of tile (2 shillings), cut stone (10 shillings), and marble (20 shillings); and mahogany staircases. All of these taxes were rather mild in comparison with the taxes that would be levied on pleasure vehicles: two-wheeled carriages would be taxed at 1 pound each; phaetons and other four-wheeled carriages at 3 pounds apiece; chariots at 4 pounds each; and a 5-pound levy would be applied to every coach.[136]

The direct tax proposal Hamilton made to Wolcott in 1797 covered fewer items but was in some respects even more progressive than the one he made to the New York Assembly a decade earlier. He suggested that all log houses be taxed at 20 cents per room but recommended progressively higher rates for other types of homes. Those with two rooms or apartments were to be taxed at 25 cents per room or apartment, those with three were to be taxed at 33.5 cents per room or apartment, those with four were to be taxed at 40 cents per room or apartment, those with five were to be taxed at 60 cents per room or apartment, those with six were to be taxed at 75 cents per room or apartment, and those with seven or more were to be taxed at 100 cents per room or apartment. Hamilton also proposed different tax rates on design elements likely to vary by wealth. Chimneys covered in tile or stone were to be taxed at 50 cents, chimneys faced in expensive marble were to be taxed at 100 cents, and stairs made of cedar or ebony were to be taxed at 50 cents, whereas those constructed with the much more costly mahogany were to be taxed at 100 cents. In addition, Hamilton proposed flat taxes on particular design elements likely to be found only in the most luxurious homes. To top it all off, the proposal called for the outright exemption of "cottages inhabited by paupers" in spite of Hamilton's concern that exempting houses below a certain value from taxation would invite "evasions and partialities" in valuations.[137] As discussed in the next chapter, Congress in 1798 would pass a tax bill structured in much the way Hamilton had proposed. Although many of the details would differ, Congress ended up approving a direct tax on land, dwellings, and slaves that was arguably even more progressive than Hamilton's recommendation.

Conclusion

Hamilton's legacy on the question of economic inequality is decidedly mixed. There is no question that many of his signature programs disproportionately benefited the nation's financial elites and did little directly to advance the interests of the lower classes. However, the three major policy proposals he advanced as secretary of the treasury do not tell the whole story about Hamilton's views on the material conditions of the lower orders. Although this founder was not particularly interested in reducing economic inequalities, he was interested in minimizing the burdens of the disadvantaged. This concern manifested itself both in specific measures targeted toward those in distress and in general tax policies that eased taxes on the poor. Unlike many of his more egalitarian contemporaries, Hamilton's reasons for supporting such measures were not necessarily rooted in republican ideals. Instead, they were grounded in humanitarian concerns for the welfare of particular groups, including soldiers, sick sailors, and people with disabilities.

Hamilton's proposals dominated the domestic agenda of Congress in the years following the ratification of the Constitution. They triggered some of the most important early national debates on the effects of public policy on economic inequality. However, as the next chapter shows, these were hardly the only significant debates that occurred regarding the government's role in the distribution of wealth in the United States.

5

CONSTRUCTING THE CONSTITUTION

How the Early Congresses Understood Their Own
Powers and Tackled Economic Hardship

The financial and economic program laid out in Alexander Hamilton's three major reports set the stage for some of the most significant and heated debates over the impact of public policy on economic inequality during the early years of the Republic. Many of those debates focused on the extent to which Hamilton's program would contribute to existing levels of economic inequality, especially between so-called moneyed men and everyone else. Critics—and even some supporters of Hamilton's plan—worried that policies that disproportionately benefited a few violated core republican principles and ultimately undermined the foundations of popular government. Although proponents of economic equality lost many of their battles to prevent policies they believed would increase the fortunes of the privileged, they won a number of important victories in their efforts to benefit the disadvantaged. Following the lead of state legislators after the Revolution, they often succeeded in structuring the tax system according to the principle that taxes should be allocated on the ability to pay by shifting more of the tax burden onto the wealthy and even exempting those near the bottom.[1] In some instances, they went even further by working for policies designed to improve the material conditions of the disadvantaged. In fact, there were Congress members on both sides of the growing partisan divide between Hamiltonian Federalists and Jeffersonian Republicans who agreed that the government has a legitimate role to play in alleviating the struggles of those near the bottom. However, in determining what the national government ought to do to address the plight of struggling groups, Congress members had to figure out exactly what the Constitution allowed them to do.

It has become customary to look to the courts for definitive answers about the constitutionality of government actions. Despite nearly universal complaints about activist judges, partisan decision making, and overreach by the courts, almost everyone now agrees that the Supreme Court has the final say on the meaning of the Constitution. However, following its ratification by the states, it was Congress that made the first attempts to determine what the Constitution actually permits the federal government to do. From the very beginning, members of Congress had to figure out for themselves the meaning and applicability of vague but significant phrases, including *general welfare, necessary and proper, direct tax, advise and consent,* and a host of others scattered throughout the text. Congress members with drastically different visions for the country and conflicting ideas about the proper role of government made landmark decisions in the six Congresses that met prior to the Jeffersonian revolution of 1800. There was rarely any consensus on the meaning of these or other provisions, let alone the proper interpretive approach to follow, but these early Congresses adopted measures that set important precedents and helped define the meaning of key constitutional clauses. Just as importantly, the first few Congresses established the legitimacy of certain considerations as proper matters of government concern. Even as they worked to restore the public credit of the United States, prepare the nation for armed conflicts, establish a national judiciary, and amend the Constitution itself, members of Congress often took up the cause of economic equality.

Debates in the first six Congresses did not always take place on the plateaus of lofty principle. They frequently descended into the trenches of base interests. Just like legislators today, many of the first members of Congress sought to protect and promote the narrow interests of their own states (or even just segments of their states). However, some debates did prompt members of Congress to expound upon fundamental questions about the proper role of government, the idea of limited government, and the purposes and meaning of the Constitution. One of the principles Congress was forced to confront whenever the issue of taxes came up was the principle of equality. Debates over the most appropriate sources and size of federal revenue implicated other principles as well, but none of the other principles was as central to the republican ideal as equality was. There was widespread if not universal agreement that the United States was an egalitarian country—especially when compared with the highly stratified nations of Europe—and members of Congress generally wanted to keep it that way. For that reason, they were sensitive to the way in which different taxes might affect the distribution of wealth and income in the United States.[2]

Tax policy was not the only subject that prompted discussions of equality and related principles of justice and fairness. Someone would raise questions about the implications of a bill for the "poor" or the "lower classes" almost every time a bill involving spending came up for consideration. Even the decision on where to locate the capital had implications for relations between the classes. James Madison argued that a more central location—that is, one near Virginia's preferred site on the Potomac—would cut down on travel expenses for those without the means to journey to more remote or less accessible locations (September 3, 1789, 1st Cong., 1st sess., 874).[3] Other business led to more protracted debates over economic inequality. Bills dealing with the regulation of the militia, pay and benefits for the military, the sale of lands in the Northwest Territory, the compensation of public officials, and a host of other matters led to lengthy discussions about the financial burdens of the poor, the social distance between the classes, and opportunities to promote economic independence among citizens. Few members of Congress advocated policies designed specifically to promote economic equality, but large numbers did try to formulate policies in ways that would not exacerbate already existing economic inequalities. In the debates over taxes that started with the first session of the First Federal Congress, representatives struggled to develop a system as progressive as possible, consistent with the daunting revenue demands the country faced. Even when they disagreed about which specific policies would best serve the interests of the lower classes, participants on both sides of these debates took it for granted that the promotion of economic equality is a legitimate consideration in public policy making. Even those who opposed policies that might advance economic equality on fiscal or constitutional grounds hardly ever challenged economic equality as a valid consideration or aspiration.

Ever since Charles A. Beard's highly influential and controversial study on the economic origins of the Constitution was written, scholars have devoted enormous attention to the economic theories and interests behind the creation of the Constitution.[4] However, far less attention has been focused on the way the actual implementation of the Constitution affected economic inequality in the years immediately after its ratification. The debate over and impact of

Hamilton's controversial plan to fund the Revolutionary War debt has received the lion's share of attention, but other policies affecting the distribution of wealth and income have received scant attention. Legal scholars have pored over early congressional debates on the meaning of the commerce clause, the necessary and proper clause, the direct tax, and the like—especially those that took place during the First Federal Congress—but seldom with an eye toward understanding how Congress members understood the government's role in dealing with economic inequality or if they thought about it at all.

The aim of this chapter is to fill this rather surprising gap in the scholarly literature on the political thought of the American founding. The debates examined in the following pages reveal that Congress members were acutely sensitive to the ways in which public policy on a range of issues might affect the economic well-being of different groups, especially among the lower classes. Those who sought to ease the burdens faced by distressed groups did not always succeed in getting their colleagues to go along with their ideas, but they did succeed in placing the subject of economic equality on the agenda. If their professions of concern for the poor and other distressed groups are any indication, members of Congress did not fail to act out of a lack of compassion. If they failed, it was mainly because they disagreed about whether the government possessed the financial resources or the constitutional authority to act on behalf of the poor.

Interpreting the Constitution: Deciding on Canons of Construction

Before members of Congress could formulate responses to economic equality or any other perceived problem, they had to figure out exactly what they were authorized to do. Not surprisingly, this was a particularly challenging task for members of the First Federal Congress, which set a precedent with almost every decision it made. Aside from the text of the Constitution itself, they looked for guidance in the history and practices of American and British legislatures, in the writings of luminaries such as William Blackstone and Emmerich de Vattel, in the voluminous commentary produced during the state ratifying debates, and in the first-hand accounts of Madison, Elbridge Gerry, and other framers then serving in Congress. It was not long before they discovered that these sources seldom spoke with a unified voice.

On some matters—at least in the beginning—there was remarkably little dispute over what law makers were constitutionally permitted to do. Questions about the constitutionality of particular measures rarely came up in the earliest discussions concerning the tax and commerce powers of Congress.[5] Both were understood in expansive terms to the extent anyone expressed any thoughts about them at all. No one seemed to doubt that Congress could use those powers to promote good health, protect domestic business interests, stimulate the emergence of new industries, or even encourage republican morals.[6] Those who submitted petitions to Congress to protect certain industries, promote the establishment of others, fund scientific expeditions, provide assistance to widows and orphans, abolish slavery, compensate citizens for property losses, and indemnify heirs against lawsuits certainly believed it had the power to do these things.[7]

It was not long before rifts began to emerge. Anyone hoping to arrive at "a" or "the" original understanding or meaning of the Constitution based on the remarks of those who made the earliest efforts to implement it will be greatly disappointed and overwhelmed by the bewildering diversity of opinions expressed on seemingly basic matters. Not only were there bitter disagreements over what the Constitution permitted, there were also stark differences over the proper mode of interpretation. The various interpretive approaches that divide scholars, judges, and politicians today, from different versions of originalism and textual literalism to structuralism and moral-philosophical approaches, divided members of the first few Congresses as well.[8] There were even disagreements over what actually counts as part of the Constitution. In a debate over possible amendments to the Constitution, representatives including Thomas Tudor Tucker of South Carolina and John Page of Virginia challenged the assumption that the preamble was actually a part of the Constitution (August 14, 1789, 1st Cong., 1st sess., 745, 746). At the start of the second session of the 1st Congress, members of the House of Representatives debated whether they were allowed to pick up where they left off in the previous session or if they had to deal with unfinished business de novo. With changes in membership from one Congress to the next, matters that seemed relatively uncontroversial and well settled in one period sometimes became subjects of heated dispute in another. This was the case with the assumption of state debts, the regulation of the militia, and other measures that struck many small-government advocates as bad policy or even unconstitutional.

Questions about constitutionality usually involved structural questions about the division of power between the legislative and executive branches (e.g., whether Congress could delegate the authority to decide where to build post roads to the president or to the postmaster general), but debates over the more fundamental question of whether the government had the authority to do certain things at all also came up. When questions about the constitutionality of particular measures did emerge, they sometimes involved matters that would not be considered at all controversial today. For instance, Alexander White of Virginia argued that constitutional silence on the compensation of the vice president suggests he was not permitted to receive a salary (July 16, 1789, 1st Cong., 1st sess., 673); William Branch Giles of Virginia contended that the franking privilege is not authorized by the Constitution (December 28, 1791, 2nd Cong., 1st sess., 297); William Findley of Pennsylvania and others suggested that relying on treasury reports was an unconstitutional delegation of legislative authority to the executive branch (March 8, 1792, 2nd Cong., 1st sess.); and Josiah Parker of Virginia argued that it was beyond the legitimate powers of Congress to express gratitude to members of the military for distinguished service (December 4, 1794, 3rd Cong., 2nd sess., 960–961)![9]

Many Congress members openly confessed their utter confusion and uncertainty about the meaning of particular clauses in the Constitution. From the start, a few bold members expressed confidence about the precise meaning of the general welfare clause, the necessary and proper clause, and many other key provisions, but many admitted they simply had no idea what the federal government could and could not do in certain areas. In fact, a good deal of the discussion that took place echoed what "Brutus" and other anti-Federalists had said about the indeterminacy of the Constitution.[10] Some topics presented much more constitutional trouble than others. Many representatives voiced their frustrations over the indeterminacy of the Constitution during a momentous debate over the location of the removal power. Michael Jenifer Stone of Maryland stated he had no idea what something as basic as "executive power" means: "Telling me that this is an executive power, raises no complete idea in my mind" (June 19, 1789, 1st Cong., 1st sess., 589). Other members of Congress expressed consternation that those who actually took part in the Constitutional Convention often proved less than informative about the intent of the framers. In a discussion of the treaty power, Joshua Coit of Connecticut complained that framer Baldwin referred his colleagues to British practices, and Madison, the putative father of the Constitution, could only talk about the difficulties of interpretation (March 22, 1796, 4th Cong., 1st sess., 657–658).[11] Despite the seemingly unambiguous constitutional language placing the treaty power in the hands of the Senate and the president, some members of the House believed the consent of the lower chamber was required (e.g., see debate from August 11, 1789, 1st Cong., 1st sess.). In a particularly contentious debate over support for cod fisheries, Page surmised that some of the textual ambiguity Congress members found so vexing might have been there by design: "Nor will I undertake to deny that it was not the intention of some of the Convention that such ambiguities might be in their Constitution" (February 7, 1792, 2nd Cong., 1st sess., 394).

That lack of clarity and agreement over the meaning of the Constitution led ardent defender of southern interests and states' rights James Jackson to oppose amending the Constitution too quickly.[12] In his view, it was still too early to tell what the new system would be like: "What experience have we had of the good or bad qualities of this constitution? . . . Our constitution, sir, is like a vessel just launched, and lying at the wharf; she is untried, you can hardly discover any one of her properties" (June 8, 1789, 1st Cong., 1st sess., 442).

Whether the Constitution was clear or explicit on a particular point did not necessarily settle matters. At some point, almost every member of Congress resorted to some extraconstitutional principle to persuade colleagues that a particular course of action was justifiable. As David Curie observes, Congress members resorted to just about every tool of construction in use today.[13] Sometimes members tried to argue that their preferred moral, political, or economic principles were supported by the text of the Constitution, if only implicitly. At other times they made no effort whatsoever to locate those principles in the document. Some Congress members simply assumed the Constitution must conform to their own principles.

In the end, members of Congress had to adopt modes of constitutional construction that often had more to do with their political dispositions than with anything that could be found in the text. The methods of "loose constructionism" and "strict constructionism" most closely identified with Hamilton and Thomas Jefferson, respectively, found outspoken, if sometimes inconsistent, adherents in Congress. The two most vocal and capable spokespeople for these competing approaches to constitutional interpretation in the House of Representatives were Massachusetts Federalist Fisher Ames and Madison.

Madison articulated his principles of constitutional construction in major foreign and domestic policy debates involving the national bank, the Jay Treaty, and a host of other subjects. In his efforts to create and ratify a constitution that established a strong and centralized national government, Madison had echoed many of Hamilton's ideas about the need for a government with energetic and expansive powers. However, as partisan divisions began to emerge over the treasury secretary's financial and economic proposals for the country, the Virginia Congressman took the lead in opposing those plans in Congress. Madison articulated his constitutional views most clearly in a debate over cod fisheries that took place during the first session of the 2nd Congress. Responding to those arguing that the power to grant bounties was "implied" by the general welfare clause, the erstwhile Federalist explained that the latitude the doctrine of implied powers would give Congress contradicts the very idea of limited government. Madison stated that he always thought "that this is not an indefinite Government, deriving its powers from the general terms prefixed to the specified powers, but a limited Government, tied down to the specified powers which explain and define the general terms" (February 6, 1792, 2nd Cong., 1st sess., 386). Despite the fact that Madison had made a powerful argument in *Federalist* 37 about the impossibility of precision in matters of politics because of the inherent "obscurity" of language and the objects of study themselves, he became a leading spokesperson for the view that provisions of the Constitution have a definite meaning. Summing up the views of all those who subscribed to the opinion that the only powers possessed by the federal government are those expressly granted to it by the Constitution, Madison argued that the general welfare clause is not an "abstract and indefinite delegation of power extending to all cases whatever" but a "delimitation of specific powers" (February 6, 1792, 2nd Cong., 1st sess., 386). To go beyond the powers specifically enumerated in the Constitution would defeat the very purpose of enumerating those powers in the first place (February 6, 1792, 2nd Cong., 1st sess., 387).

This interpretive doctrine often led Madison and his allies to oppose on constitutional grounds what they otherwise claimed to support on political, economic, or humanitarian grounds. Madison's strict reading of the Constitution even led him to reject means he acknowledged would be conducive to the achievement of legitimate ends if they were not among the specific powers explicitly granted to the national government. For instance, in his critique of the Alien and Sedition Acts, Madison acknowledged, "Provident support for the poor, might be regarded as among the most efficacious" means of preventing insurrections, but he found nothing in the Constitution that allowed Congress to accomplish the specified end of suppressing insurrections in this manner.[14] However, even Madison sometimes had to confess that interpretation of the Constitution was not always so straightforward. In a letter to Samuel Johnston he confided, "The exposition of the Constitution is frequently a copious source, and must continue so until its meaning on all great points shall have been settled by precedents."[15]

The loose constructionists, led by Ames, always found constitutional support for their objectives in a handful of clauses. Confirming the worst suspicions of anti-Federalists such as "Brutus,"[16] Federalist legislators argued that the necessary and proper clause and the general welfare clause did not limit or define the enumerated powers of Congress. Instead, they provided independent grants of general power. Moreover, Federalists believed certain powers were inherent in the very nature of government. Whereas strict constructionists generally confined their arguments to the wording of the Constitution, loose constructionists resorted to a variety of extra-constitutional sources to determine the nature, limits, and location of specific powers. Ames's general approach to the Constitution was to consider the established practices and powers of other legislatures, whether at the state level or in other countries. He did not think the Constitution established a special form of government uniquely limited in its powers but that it empowered the national legislature to do (almost all) the things every other legislature in the world was entitled to do. Ames's rules of interpretation paralleled those Hamilton had outlined near the beginning of his "Opinion on the Constitutionality of a National Bank":

Congress may do what is necessary to the end for which the Constitution was adopted, provided it is not repugnant to the natural rights of man, or to those which they have expressly reserved to themselves, or to the powers which are assigned to the States. This rule of interpretation seems to be a safe, and not a very uncertain one, independently of the Constitution itself. . . . That construction may be maintained to be a safe one which promotes the good of the society, and the ends for which the Government was adopted, without impairing the rights of any man, or the powers of any State. (February 3, 1791, 1st Cong., 3rd sess., 1956)

In contrast with those who believed the greatest danger lies in expansive readings of the governmental powers, Ames argued that narrow readings of those powers could prove just as dangerous. Asking what would happen if the Constitution had omitted any mention of the power to raise armies, Ames declaimed, "Not exercising the powers we have may be as pernicious as usurping those we have not" (February 3, 1791, 1st Cong., 3rd sess., 1955).

Under this theory of interpretation, there was little that Congress or the president could not conceivably do under the right circumstances. The general welfare clause got trotted out so much that after a certain point critics began to treat any reference to it as a tacit admission by its supporters that the measure under consideration was certainly unconstitutional.

In some instances, these competing understandings of the Constitution just became convenient excuses for Congress members to vote the way they wanted to anyway.[17] In other instances, adherents of both approaches genuinely struggled to figure out what they were constitutionally permitted to do. Perhaps the most candid statement on the challenges of interpreting the Constitution came from William Findley. In the protracted and acrimonious debate over the Jay Treaty in the House of Representatives, the western Pennsylvania democrat remarked that the Constitution simply does not provide easy or ready-made answers to many questions because even the most basic terms are subject to widely different interpretations. As he saw it, both sides agree "that the express words of the Constitution will not support either position without a liberty of construction. The difference of opinion is now confined to what construction

is most agreeable to the general principles of the Constitution"
(March 16, 1796, 4th Cong., 1st sess., 588–589).

At some point, almost every member of Congress had to recognize the truth of Findley's observation. That realization was often achieved when representatives tackled issues involving economic inequality. It was always assumed that equality is a republican virtue (e.g., in the May 2, 1794, debate over the excise tax), but that the Constitution provided little guidance on the question of equality. As a consequence, debates over the government's role in dealing with economic inequality often blurred normal party lines. In many instances, Congress members expressed a desire to provide assistance to those in distress that they felt they could not satisfy for constitutional reasons. However, on some occasions, those who ordinarily took a restrictive view of their constitutional authority set aside their misgivings to serve the interests of justice, fairness, compassion, or equality.

Establishing Fairness in the Tax System

After the House of Representatives adopted rules for that chamber, its first order of business was to find ways to raise much-needed revenue. The lack of adequate revenue to repay the Revolutionary War debt and to restore the public credit of the United States was a leading reason for the rejection of the Articles of Confederation and an important impetus behind the adoption of the new Constitution. As Madison explained in a debate on taxing imports, the Constitution was framed specifically to remedy this particular defect under the old system. Just how far Congress could go in exercising its tax power was yet to be determined (May 9, 1789, 1st Cong., 1st sess., 313). Securing enough revenue to finance the debt, provide for national defense, and fund other (still limited) activities of the federal government was the top priority but hardly the only one that mattered to members of Congress and their constituents. Protecting infant industries, encouraging domestic manufacturing, increasing national prosperity, and promoting health and morals were also significant considerations. Yet another consideration factored into congressional debates over the source and size of revenue: equality. As Madison explained early on in these debates, the challenge was to ensure that any tax system the government enacted would be fair: "A national revenue must be obtained; but the system must be such a one, that, while it secures the object of revenue, it shall not be oppressive to our constituents" (April 9, 1789, 1st Cong., 1st sess., 107). Although the other considerations sometimes provoked major philosophical debates over the proper role of government, calls for greater fairness in the tax system seldom generated any controversy—at least in the House. Unlike the other objectives some members hoped to promote through the tax system, no recorded debate over the principle of equality ever took place during the first six Congresses. Nearly every remark made on the subject was on the side of promoting equality.

Taxing Consumption

Congress wasted no time before looking for new sources of revenue. The House of Representatives took up the subject of taxation two days after it achieved a quorum. Within a few months, Congress passed two major revenue bills. One (approved July 20, 1789) was a tonnage bill that required each vessel entering a US port to pay a duty based on its carrying capacity. The other (approved July 4, 1789) was an impost (or tariff) bill that levied specific duties on a list of enumerated goods[18] and imposed a 5 percent duty on all other imported goods.[19] The debate over the impost raised a number of questions. Members had to decide whether the impost should be temporary or permanent, what constituted an appropriate object of taxation, how much revenue could be raised, how high the impost could be before it encouraged evasion through smuggling, and which sections of the country stood to lose and which stood to gain from different arrangements, among others. There was wide agreement that these taxes ought to be laid as "equally" as possible across different segments of the Union. More often than not, the demand for equality in this context referred to equality among the states. Members of Congress in both houses were determined to ensure that their own constituents paid as little as possible—or at least that they paid no more than inhabitants of other states. As a result, representatives from different states frequently argued for and against taxes differently based on the narrow interests of their constituents. One of the most controversial items involved a proposed duty on molasses that provoked a sectional dispute between southerners and New Englanders.

This early debate over the impost is also significant because it prompted members of Congress to consider the impact of different taxes on members of different classes. Only days after the House of Representatives began its official business, its members entered into a discussion on the ways in which the impost would affect the poor. On April 14, representatives from different parts of the country took turns speaking out against proposed taxes on molasses and other goods they believed would either fall disproportionately on the poor or simply add to their burdens. The first to broach the subject was Federalist John Laurance of New York City.[20] In response to Madison's suggestion that the House impose a duty of eight cents per gallon on molasses, Laurance indignantly asked if Congress would "tax articles which are necessaries of life equally as if they were luxuries?" Developing an argument reiterated many times over by various Congress members, Laurance pointed out, "This article [molasses] is used as a necessary among the poorer class of citizens; consequently, if you tax it high, you unequally burthen that part of the community who are least able to bear it" (April 14, 1789, 1st Cong., 1st sess., 134–135).

Much of the debate that ensued focused on the encouragement that duties on imports would give to domestic industry, but it also gave members an opportunity to discuss the economic conditions of different classes and their ability to bear different taxes. Representatives could not always agree on whether certain items were luxuries or necessities (in part because they could not agree on the definitions of these terms), but they did generally support the idea that necessities—along with those goods consumed more heavily by the poor—ought to be taxed more lightly or not at all. Benjamin Goodhue of Salem, Massachusetts, echoed Laurance's point about molasses being a "necessary of life," elaborating that "in the eastern States it entered into the diet of the poorer class of people, who were, from the decay of trade and other adventitious circumstances, totally unable to sustain such a weight as a tax of eight cents would be upon them" (April 14, 1789, 1st Cong., 1st sess., 136–137). George Thatcher, Fisher Ames, and George Partridge, all Federalists, joined Goodhue in expressing concern for the effect of the impost on the poor, but their professions of compassion were probably influenced by the fact that all four hailed from Massachusetts, which would be most adversely affected by the molasses duty (April 14, 1789, 1st Cong., 1st sess., 136–137, 137–138, 142, 144).

Whatever the motives of the Massachusetts delegation, its members' arguments had an effect on the way other members discussed taxes on other goods. If nothing else, they had legitimized the idea that taxes ought to be distributed on the basis of ability to pay. They did not go quite as far as some others would in arguing for a more progressive tax system, but they did establish the principle that regressive taxes ought to be avoided whenever possible. That same day, Philadelphia merchant Thomas Fitzsimons defended a high tax on Madeira wine on the grounds that it was consumed mostly by the well-to-do, who could easily afford the expense (April 14, 1789, 1st Cong., 1st sess., 144–145). Over the next few days, the impact of various duties on the lower classes became a standard debating point for any Congress member who objected to a proposed duty. The validity of the principle became firmly established by the time South Carolina anti-Federalist Tucker proclaimed it was the "duty of the committee to guard against an unequal distribution of the public burthen in every case" (April 15, 1789, 1st Cong., 1st sess., 153). Several weeks later, Tucker restated his opposition to a high duty on molasses as being "oppressive to the poor." He then made perhaps the most progressive statement in the entire debate on the impost when he said, "I do not wish to add to their burthens; on the contrary, *I should be glad to exempt them from taxation altogether, if it was in my power*" (May 8, 1789, 1st Cong., 1st sess., 305; emphasis added).

The idea that the tax system ought to minimize burdens on the poor was the reason perhaps most frequently cited in opposition to a proposed tax on salt. Taxes on salt were extremely common and highly profitable sources of revenue dating back to the ancient world. Because salt is an essential ingredient of economic and biological life used to produce, flavor, and preserve various foods; cure leather; and manufacture different goods, it exemplifies the idea of a necessity.[21] That is exactly what made it such an attractive revenue option for the 1st Congress. It is also what made it such a controversial one. A number of representatives, including anti-Federalists Aedanus Burke of South Carolina and Andrew Moore of Virginia thought it would be "unjust" to tax this necessity (April 16, 1789, 1st Cong., 1st sess., 165, 167). Moore's Federalist colleague in the Virginia delegation, Alexander White, explained that representatives should not pass the tax because their constituents, "particularly the poorer sort of people," expected them to pursue just policies (April 16, 1789,

1st Cong., 1st sess., 171). As others explained, the salt tax would be unjust because the poor would pay a disproportionate share of this tax and they would be entirely unable to avoid it. Tucker strongly objected to the salt tax because it "would bear harder upon the poor than upon the rich." He went on to explain that the "true principle of taxation is, that every man contribute to the public burthens in proportion to the value of his property. But a poor man consumes as much salt as a rich man. In this point of view, it operates as a poll-tax, the most odious of all taxes; it does not operate simply as a poll-tax, but is heavier on the poor than on the rich, because the poor consume greater quantities of salted provision than the rich" (April 16, 1789, 1st Cong., 1st sess., 165–166).

Ames pressed the point again two weeks later. This time he played to national pride in opposing the duties on salt and molasses. He argued that the United States would lose its status as the "best country for the poor to live in" if it resorted to taxes on necessities (April 28, 1789, 1st Cong., 1st sess., 233). He took it for granted that taxes on luxuries should be much higher than taxes on necessities and that the rich should pay more than the "poorest and weakest part of the community" (April 28, 1789, 1st Cong., 1st sess., 234). Later in that same debate Ames launched into a peroration on the struggles of laborers, who often find themselves trapped in poverty. Invoking a nostrum often used in reference to the people of Cape Cod to demonstrate their inability to bear the taxes being contemplated, he noted, "They are too poor to live there, and they are too poor to remove" (April 28, 1789, 1st Cong., 1st sess., 238).

Some of these protestations were probably motivated by little more than regional interests in keeping taxes as low as possible on one's own constituents. However, the persistence of these claims suggests that those making them thought appeals to fairness would be persuasive to members of Congress from other parts of the country. There is evidence that this strategy had some success. Supporters of the salt tax conceded that taxes ought to fall more lightly on the poor, but they defended this tax on the grounds that it was only a small part of a much larger system fairer in its totality. This is the approach Madison took, saying, "I readily agree that, in itself, a tax would be unjust and oppressive that did not fall on the citizens according to their degree of property and ability to pay it." In fact, he perceived the salt tax as a way to "equalize the disproportion [rather] than increase it." However, he supported the salt tax because it would be part of a much broader, and fairer, system of taxation. In making this point, even supporters of the tax acknowledged the validity of taking into account the consequences of policy on the poor (April 17, 1789, 1st Cong., 1st sess., 170).[22] Even when they questioned the sincerity of those whose stated reasons for opposing certain taxes were based on concern for the poor, defenders of these taxes sometimes tried to one-up their opponents. This is essentially what Madison did in responding to Ames's claims that the duties on molasses and salt would further impoverish lower-class New Englanders (April 17, 1789, 1st Cong., 1st sess., 236).

In the end, the House approved duties on salt, molasses, and myriad other items consumed by rich and poor alike. The exigencies of government took priority over relieving the burdens of the poor. Even many of those who feared that the duties would exacerbate the hardships of the poor ended up voting for the Impost Bill because they understood that exempting necessities from taxation altogether would leave the government short of much-needed revenue. However, the "Act for laying a duty on goods, wares, and merchandises, imported into the United States" did achieve a small degree of progressivity by imposing higher duties on items considered high-end luxury items. For instance, shoes and slippers made of silk were taxed three cents more than those made of leather (which few members of the lower classes would have consumed anyway because they generally clothed themselves with homemade or domestically manufactured items).[23] The act also imposed duties on carriages, products made of gold and silver, and other items that tended to be consumed exclusively by the well-to-do.

From what little is known about debates in the Senate, it appears many of the same points were made about the effects of different taxes on the poor. Senators acknowledged the usefulness of the salt tax, but a few raised serious objections to the tax on molasses. The Senate was ready to vote on the molasses tax when Tristram Dalton of Massachusetts called for lowering the duty to three cents. William Samuel Johnson of Connecticut went even further by proposing that molasses be taxed at two cents or not at all because of how heavily it was consumed by the poor.[24] One major difference between debates in the House and the Senate concerned the reaction to proposed duties on luxury items. Although these taxes provoked little controversy in the House, in the Senate Robert Morris demurred over taxes on gold, silver, plated items, and pewter items (but without any explanation or justification).[25]

In spite of repeated entreaties from members of the House, especially those representing the backcountry, Congress maintained the duty on salt and even laid on additional duties throughout the next decade because it was just too good a revenue generator to abolish. The inelastic demand for this good made it an ideal source of revenue, especially as the nation prepared for the possibility of war against Great Britain and then against France. However, the debates that took place over the taxes on salt and molasses established a pattern repeated many times over the next five Congresses. Whenever the subject of revenue came up, some members would propose repealing or lowering taxes on items consumed heavily by the poor. For instance, in a debate on laying an additional duty on salt, Albert Gallatin, Madison's successor as leader of the Jeffersonian party in the House, spoke for many when he railed against the salt tax as "oppressive to certain parts of the Union, and no way affecting others, and therefore wholly unequal, and particularly as it bore heavy on the poorer classes of society" (July 4, 1797, 5th Cong., 1st sess., 442).

Initial failures to scale back regressive taxes on consumption did not discourage members of Congress from seeking other ways to make the tax system more progressive. Proponents of a more progressive tax system often proposed substitutes that would shift more of the tax burden onto wealthy citizens. After the Whiskey Rebellion demonstrated just how fierce popular resistance to regressive excise taxes could be, many Federalists looked to taxes that would fall almost exclusively on the wealthy for new sources of revenue.[26] An important shift in strategy occurred during the first session of the 3rd Congress. George Washington had just been reelected to a second term, but Republicans made substantial gains in the House of Representatives.[27] The election of new members opposed to the Hamiltonian system brought an influx of Congress members who could be expected to be sympathetic to the hardships of small farmers and laborers, especially those in the backcountry. However, it was three-term Federalist Jonathan Dayton of New Jersey who proposed moving away from taxes on common articles consumed heavily by the poor to more creative taxes on items consumed primarily by the rich.

In a debate over a resolution to pay for the costs of a naval armament with an additional duty on imported goods taxed at 7.5 percent, this signer of the US Constitution immediately objected that the existing duty already fell hardest on the poor. He explained that the articles covered "were for the most part purchased and used by the poorer classes of the people, who were less able to bear additional burdens than any other. That indeed very many of those articles, and some of the most important of them were real necessaries, and could not be furnished in this country, but must be brought from abroad, for a long time at least to come; among which he particularly mentioned coarse woolens, &c" (February 21, 1794, 3rd Cong., 1st sess., 459–460). Instead of an additional duty of 1 percent proposed by the select committee that presented the resolution, Dayton suggested laying an additional duty of only .5 percent.

Dayton acknowledged that lowering the duty on articles that affected the poor would result in a revenue shortfall, so he offered a "substitute to remedy that deficiency" (February 21, 1794, 3rd Cong., 1st sess., 460). He listed a large number of articles that could be taxed either because domestic manufacturers could supply them or because they were "luxuries of life, and consequently consumed or used by those who were most able to pay the duties." These included boots, shoes, slippers, artificial flowers and other ornamentation, leather, medicinal drugs, a variety of gold and silver items, diverse spices, cotton goods, and "all marble, slate, and other stone," among other items (February 21, 1794, 3rd Cong., 1st sess., 460–461). After brief debate on exempting some of the items Dayton mentioned, the House adopted his proposal as part of the committee's report (February 21, 1794, 3rd Cong., 1st sess., 461).

After this precedent was established, other members of the House became much more aggressive in pushing for taxes paid primarily by the "propertied classes." A few months after Dayton's proposal, the House took up resolutions to lay taxes on financial transactions. One was a proposal to impose a tax of five cents on the transfer of every $100 of stocks in public funds (i.e., the public debt). The other was to impose a tax of five cents on the transfer of any other bank stock. Supporters quickly pointed out that the sums were relatively small because the volume of transactions was so high (May 1, 1794, 3rd Cong., 1st sess., 617).

The ensuing debate resulted in the first sustained defense of the value and interests of "moneyed men" since the highly contentious debates over Hamilton's financial program. The ordinarily protax

Ames expressed fears that the proposed taxes would make it harder to raise money and would injure public credit. Emphasizing the country's continued dependence on "moneyed men," Ames highlighted the horrors that would surely follow this attempt to raise revenue off this particular breed of the rich: "When we next want to borrow, and shall go to market, the lenders will rise proportionably [sic] in their demands, and refuse a loan on the terms which they before accepted. Hence we shall lose, instead of gaining by it. . . . In the United States, taxation of the Public Funds is nothing more or less than the debtor taxing the creditor; and so questionable an expedient will recoil with tenfold force on the credit of Government itself. The progress of this measure would degrade the Public Debt into a paper rag" (May 1, 1794, 3rd Cong., 1st sess., 617). Ames and others also wondered aloud if a tax on the public debt impaired contracts or violated the government's commitment to creditors.

Federalists were not unified in supporting the interests of the financial class. Ames's fellow Federalist Elias Boudinot responded by pointing to the inherent unfairness of exempting moneyed property, of all things. "He saw no reason why that kind of property should be exempted from the right exercised of taxing other property. So far as the moral principle went, he was satisfied" (May 1, 1794, 3rd Cong., 1st sess., 618). In making his case, Boudinot also defended the congressional taxing power under the Constitution in strong terms. He suggested that the tax power was unqualified, so that Congress would be free to tax public funds just like "any thing [sic] else" (May 1, 1794, 3rd Cong., 1st sess., 619).

Ames conceded, "Property is in general, to be sure, a fair object of taxation," but he argued that this tax would be different. Not only would it be impossible for the government to apply the tax equally because of its inability to monitor every financial transaction, it was also beyond the power of Congress to enact this particular tax (May 1, 1794, 3rd Cong., 1st sess., 620). Ames's attempts to protect the interests of investors were transparent to everyone. South Carolina republican Richard Winn suggested that it was one thing if these creditors were the original holders of the public debt, that is, the "poor soldiers, who gave birth to this country," but it was another entirely if they were speculators. Because creditors mostly constituted the latter, they had no reason to "grumble" (May 1, 1794, 3rd Cong., 1st sess., 620). In the end, fifty-three members voted in favor of the first resolution (to tax the transfer of public funds), and the second one (to tax the transfer of bank stock) passed unanimously (May 1, 1794, 3rd Cong., 1st sess., 620).

Immediately following this debate was another on a resolution to tax snuff and tobacco. Unlike an impost, which could be defended as a protectionist measure that benefited domestic industry, the proposed tax on snuff and tobacco was an "excise" tax, levied on domestically manufactured goods. Like the taxes on financial transactions, this one would fall most heavily on the wealthy.[28] Expressing his support for luxury taxes in general, William Vans Murray of Maryland argued that a tax on these items would be ideal because it would be paid by the rich and because the demand was inelastic: "It is true, that a tax on snuff will not operate upon all men, but those who will be affected by it are well able to bear it. It will be paid by the wealthy, and it will be paid with the less reluctance, because its use is in a habit, which a man does not easily give up" (May 1, 1794, 3rd Cong., 1st sess., 620). In response to the criticism of Nathaniel Macon of North Carolina that this would be the first tax in history "where a raw material was taxed to more than its value," Murray asserted that it would be "easy" for the wealthy to pay (May 1, 1794, 3rd Cong., 1st sess., 621, 622).

Throughout the debates on taxing different articles of consumption up to this point, there was a commonly held assumption that such "indirect" taxes, as they were called, were more desirable than the alternatives. Whatever their political preferences, Congress members understood that what amounted to sales taxes on different items affected different groups in different ways, but they generally considered these taxes fair inasmuch as the consumer ultimately decided whether to pay the tax or not (by deciding whether to purchase the article or not). When the debate on taxing snuff and tobacco resumed the next day, this assumption came under direct attack. For the first time in Congress—but certainly not the last—there was a sustained debate over the relative merits of "indirect" versus "direct" taxes. The alternatives in this case came down to a choice between the tax on snuff and tobacco, on the one hand, and a tax on land, on the other. The tax on snuff and tobacco was approved by a vote of fifty-five to thirty-four (May 2, 1794, 3rd Cong., 1st sess., 631), but the House continued to deliberate on these forms of taxation for the next several days.

The terms of this debate were complicated by sectional disputes over the merits of excise taxes in general and widespread confusion over what actually qualifies as a direct tax (see, e.g., comments made on May 6, 1794, 3rd Cong., 1st sess., 643–644), but at the heart of this debate was a disagreement over which form of taxation was more likely to be regressive. Each side claimed the other favored a policy that would add to the burdens of the poor. Supporters of indirect taxes on snuff argued that a tax on land "is a tax very unequal, and laid on all the necessaries of life, and oppressive to the laborious poor" (Samuel Dexter, May 2, 1794, 3rd Cong., 1st sess., 628), whereas defenders of direct taxes on land retorted that indirect taxes, such as excises, are always unequal. The most eloquent statements for each side were made by Massachusetts Federalist Samuel Dexter and by the leader of the Republicans in the House. After expressing great pride in his home state for the progress it had made in advancing the republican ideal of equality, Madison launched a full frontal assault against taxes that fell disproportionately on the poor:

> It was proper to choose taxes the *least unequal*. Tobacco excise was a burden the *most unequal*. It fell upon the poor, upon sailors, day-laborers, and other people of these classes, while the rich will often escape it. Much had been said about the taxing of luxury. The pleasures of life consisted in a series of innocent gratifications, and he felt no satisfaction in the prospect of their being squeezed. Sumptuary laws had never, he believed, answered any good purpose. (Madison, May 2, 1794, 3rd Cong., 1st sess., 630)

Dexter was just as insistent in arguing that taxes on land were particularly injurious to the poor. He asserted that a "land tax was a tax on the laborious poor. If every acre is to pay the same tax, it must prove very unequal, as poor men generally live on the poorest lands, and must pay oppressive taxes. If the lands are to be valued, the delay and expense must be enormous. Lands increase in value very unequally in different places, and the proportion will be forever altering" (May 6, 1794, 3rd Cong., 1st sess., 646).

The next major tax dispute involved a proposal to tax pleasure carriages. The drawn-out debate on this measure is significant not just because it continued a trend toward taxing luxury items that the wealthy could presumably afford to pay but because it continued the discussion on the constitutional meaning of "direct" tax. The utter state of confusion on this issue was made clear by Murray's confession that the meaning of these terms was totally unclear to him: "The terms in the Constitution, direct and indirect taxes, had never conveyed very distinct or definite ideas to his mind; yet it appeared, as if we were now called on to act under a clear perception of both modes" (May 7, 1794, 3rd Cong., 1st sess., 652). Despite his own uncertainty, Murray was able to explain in the clearest terms exactly what was at stake in defining a tax as a direct tax: if a tax on carriages is a direct tax under the meaning of the Constitution, then it must be apportioned equally among the states. If this was the case, then each state would have to pay an amount based on the size of its population regardless of how many carriages were actually located there. Murray acknowledged that this interpretation of the Constitution would produce "extreme inequality," but he insisted the "Constitution could not be construed to carry such a meaning" in this case. Essentially, he was arguing that the injustice of such an application of the Constitution proved that a tax on carriages could not possibly be a direct tax! Thus, he felt justified in supporting the tax as a revenue measure that would be borne by those who could most afford it: "Coaches and all those splendid vehicles, were evidences of a certain degree of property . . . and, in a moment like this, when we are hunting through all the recesses of revenue which, at any time we had been accustomed to think of, it would be impolitic to tax the humble line of enjoyment and leave the more elevated one free" (May 7, 1794, 3rd Cong., 1st sess., 653). Right before it adjourned for the day, the House voted fifty-four to thirty-four to keep the tax on carriages in the bill (May 7, 1794, 3rd Cong., 1st sess., 656). The debates on the carriage tax that occurred a few weeks later and again in February 1795 focused primarily on the constitutional question, and no one challenged the propriety of a tax that targeted the wealthy. When the bill came up for a final vote, the carriage tax passed by the lopsided vote of forty-nine to twenty-two (May 29, 1794, 3rd Cong., 1st sess., 730). The act that ultimately passed both houses of Congress imposed steep annual taxes ranging from $2 on every "two-wheel, top-carriage" to $8 on every chariot and $10 on every coach.[29]

Proposals to impose or repeal taxes on specific articles of consumption would emerge repeatedly during the next three Congresses. Each time the subject of an impost or excise tax came up, the same arguments were made over and over again. If the tax under consideration would be paid by the poor, someone would make a plea for compassion. If the tax would be paid primarily by the rich, someone would raise constitutional objections. However, in all these debates, participants generally accepted the principle that taxes on the poor should be light or nonexistent.

The only serious challenge to this principle came in a response to one of Findley's numerous attempts to rescue his backcountry constituents in western Pennsylvania from additional taxes (salt, in this instance). It took place during a debate over additional sources of revenue as the country faced the possibility of being drawn into a European war in 1794. Federalist Abraham Clark of New Jersey, ordinarily one of the most reliable champions of economic equality in his generation,[30] launched into a tirade against Findley's implication that the poor should be exempt from taxes altogether. He started by asking Findley exactly what taxes his constituents actually did pay or would be willing to pay. Answering his own question, Clark pointed out that Findley's constituents avoided most taxes because they produced their own goods. Moreover, because they were poor, they did not pay taxes on silk and other luxury items. To top it all off, they objected to every tax measure as being oppressive. Clark concluded by announcing he "was solicitous to learn what taxes the back settlers paid, for, as far as he could understand, they paid none; and their Representative would do well to inform the House on what they were willing to pay a tax. Was Government to be burdened with them, and derive no compensation? Was it a sufficient reason for exempting a district from public burdens to say that the people are poor? Are taxes to be paid exclusively by the rich?" (May 16, 1794, 3rd Cong., 1st sess., 698). Findley replied that his constituents did contribute to the public treasury with the taxes that ladies paid on "silk and other female fineries," so it was unnecessary to burden their poorer neighbors with taxes on necessities. Despite warm expressions of support from several other representatives, Findley's motion to strike out the additional tax on salt failed by a vote of thirty-two to forty-seven (May 16, 1794, 3rd Cong., 1st sess., 698).

A Tax on Bank Notes

Members of the House exhibited willingness to ease the tax burden on the poor up to a point, but many of them were not entirely prepared to shift the tax burden onto the rich. During the first session of the 5th Congress, the House considered a stamp tax to finance military preparations in the event of a war against France. The bill would have laid a tax on various documents, including naturalization certificates, wills, and licenses—but it contained language exempting bank notes. Critics seized on this exemption as an obvious sop to moneyed men. When the bill came up for deliberation on June 27, 1797, Jeffersonian John Nicholas of Virginia moved to strike out the language exempting bank notes because he "could see no reason why notes upon which a profit was made, should be exempted from duty more than others. He trusted all notes would be placed on the same footing" (5th Cong., 1st sess., 393).

Supporters of the provision defended it on a variety of grounds. William L. Smith of South Carolina argued that a duty on bank notes would be unnecessary because banks were taxed in another part of the bill dealing with the transfer of shares, and it would create enormous logistical problems because of the number of additional provisions required to implement such a tax (June 27, 1797, 5th Cong., 1st sess., 394, 397). David Brooks of New York opposed stamping bank notes because it was not done anywhere else in the world. He thought doing so in the United States would be like stamping "dollars or guineas" (June 27, 1797, 5th Cong., 1st sess., 394). Samuel Sitgreaves, a Federalist from Pennsylvania, objected on the grounds that it could discourage their circulation and lower their value (June 27, 1797, 5th Cong., 1st sess., 395).

The response from critics who wanted to tax bank notes just like other documents was furious. Republican Abraham Venable of Virginia observed that the provision grossly violated the ideal of equality because it "was drawn from the doctrine of favoritism—it was meant to favor the moneyed interest, which was already sufficiently encouraged by their [banks'] incorporation" (June 27, 1797, 5th Cong., 1st sess., 394). Gallatin and other Republicans reiterated Venable's remarks on the inherent unfairness and injustice of a measure that exempted the very individuals most capable of contributing to the public revenue. Thomas Claiborne of Virginia explained that the exemption "would be to catch *small fish*, and let the *large ones* pass" (June 27, 1797, 5th Cong., 1st sess., 399). Even South Carolina Federalist John Rutledge joined in the republican critique, saying it would be improper to tax fifty individuals who got together to issue notes, but to exempt a corporation. In his view, stockholders ought to contribute to the government like everyone else (June 27, 1797, 5th Cong., 1st sess., 397).

Despite vehement denials that the exemption was designed to "screen the moneyed interest of this country from paying a tax," Nicholas's motion passed with the support of fifty-five members (Sitgreaves, June 27, 1797, 5th Cong., 1st sess., 399).

The Direct Tax on Land, Houses, and Slaves

The debate over a tax on bank notes was hardly the only one in which members of Congress discussed ways to shift more of the tax burden onto the propertied classes. Near the end of the last session of the 4th Congress, the House considered a direct tax on land, improvements, and slaves. With interruptions to maritime trade expected to increase because of the ongoing conflict in Europe touched off by the French Revolution, many members believed the time had finally come to consider a more predictable—but also more unpopular—source of revenue. As much as they detested it, they felt that the shortfall from taxes on commerce left them no other choice.[31] The main focus of the debate centered on the importance of sufficient revenue to government, but the subject of equality ended up becoming a significant concern as well.

The debate over direct taxes that started in January 1797 and continued into the next Congress made supporters and opponents alike weigh the progressivity of alternative tax systems. The distribution of taxes among the states was an important point of contention, but the effect of different forms of taxation on the poor dominated the debate. All members accepted equality in taxation—across sections and across classes—as an important goal, but they could not agree on which method of taxation was fairest to the poor. Proponents of direct and indirect taxes alike hoped to prevail by convincing their colleagues that their preferred form of taxation best served the interests of the poor. No one challenged the validity of equality as a consideration; instead, the debate revolved around which taxes were most conducive to egalitarian ends.

Opponents of direct taxes immediately attacked them for being "unequal." Not only would they fall unequally on different parts of the country but they would also impose undue burdens on members of the lower class, especially farmers who resided in the interior of the country, where money was scarce. The most impassioned critique of direct taxes was made by the future Speaker of the House from 1807 to 1811, Massachusetts Republican Joseph Bradley Varnum. In a speech that articulated the class divisions at stake in the starkest terms possible, Varnum explained that the direct tax on land proposed by Secretary of the Treasury Oliver Wolcott Jr. would saddle the industrious poor with taxes they could hardly afford to pay and practically exempt wealthy city dwellers who had never once felt the "fatigue of hard labor." It was bad enough that professionals, merchants, and others "living in affluence, [would] be exonerated from any of the burden, except a small pittance for the houses they live in," whereas farmers would have the principal source of their livelihood taxed. What made things even worse was that many of those "swimming in luxury" received their wealth "from the effects of capitals artfully acquired, from the hard earnings of the unwary laborer" (January 16, 1797, 4th Cong., 2nd sess., 1881, 1882). Varnum's speech was exceptional only in the explicitness and vehemence with which he attacked idle capitalists. The underlying assumption that a direct tax would be unfair to the poor was widespread among its opponents.

When outspoken South Carolina Federalist Robert Goodloe Harper and others turned to alternative sources of revenue, they usually singled out objects of taxation more likely to affect the rich than the poor. Though Harper himself did suggest increases to the highly regressive duty on salt, he argued that increased taxes on foreign merchandise would be just because items "in this class were mostly articles of luxury and expense, and consequently fair objects of taxation, since the tax would fall upon the rich consumers" (January 13, 1797, 4th Cong., 2nd sess., 1870). However, there were definite limits to Harper's egalitarianism. He identified a few taxable goods consumed mainly by the rich, but he went on to suggest taxes on stamps and windows (January 13, 1797, 4th Cong., 2nd sess., 1872). New Jersey Federalist Thomas Henderson was much more consistent in proposing indirect taxes that would spare the poor. After expressing his belief that direct taxes would shift the tax burden away from the commercial classes toward the farming classes, Henderson revived the idea of a tax on theatrical exhibitions that he had first introduced on January 10. He urged his colleagues to consider this proposal seriously because it was one of those "articles of convenience or luxury, that are generally used by those who are most able to bear the burdens of Government, and may be used or omitted at

pleasure" (January 16, 1797, 4th Cong., 2nd sess., 1877). He also endorsed a tax on watches and clocks because those items were used
mainly by individuals who could afford to pay extra taxes.

Up to this point in congressional debates, the prevailing assumption was that some indirect taxes were more regressive than others,
not that indirect taxes were inherently regressive. That assumption
finally came under scrutiny after alternatives to the direct tax plan
had been proposed. Republican John Swanwick of Pennsylvania was
the first speaker to make a cogent case that indirect taxes tend by
their nature to be regressive, regardless of the objects being taxed.
As he explained, these taxes tend to heighten inequality because
the poorer a family is, the more of its income it spends. The more
it spends, the more likely it is to spend on items that are taxed:
"All taxes on consumable articles bore very unequally. A large poor
family consumed much more of them than a rich small one" (January 16, 1797, 4th Cong., 2nd sess., 1887). Swanwick singled out the
salt tax as being especially unfair for this reason: "Would not the
poor man be affected in a much greater proportion than the rich?
He certainly would, since some poor families used as much salt as a
rich one." Swanwick suggested that the reason taxes on stamps and
windows were so "hateful" was that the poor already understood
that they paid these taxes disproportionately (January 16, 1797, 4th
Cong., 2nd sess., 1888).[32]

A few days later, Swanwick disputed claims that the poor were
largely exempt from indirect taxes by pointing out that much more
revenue was raised from "articles of general consumption" than
from anything raised "from the luxuries of life" (January 19, 1797,
4th Cong., 2nd sess., 1928). In a subsequent debate over a proposal
to raise revenue by imposing a tax on imported goods including alcohol, footwear, tea, steel, nails, tobacco, snuff, cocoa, chocolate, and
pepper, he reasserted his claim that all taxes on consumption operated unequally: "They fell very unequally upon different classes;
since a poor man, in many instances, paid as much as a rich man;
whereas, it was his opinion, that all taxes should fall upon men according to their ability to pay them—according to their real possessions; but, he said, in this case, a niggardly man pays too little,
and a liberal man too much." Yet another objection to the proposed
additional tax on brown sugar was that it was a necessity widely
used by the poor, so that the "duty would, therefore, fall chiefly
upon a class of the community least able to bear it" (February 16,

1797, 4th Cong., 2nd sess., 2171). This time, Swanwick made the connection between economic equality and republican ideals even more explicit. He noted that the difficulty of procuring fresh milk in the cities meant that the urban poor often relied heavily on tea sweetened with brown sugar for breakfast. "Would it, then, be fair, or consonant with the principles of a Republican Government, he asked, thus to burden the poor of the community? He thought not" (February 16, 1797, 4th Cong., 2nd sess., 2171).[33]

After Swanwick made his initial case, the floodgates opened. When debate resumed on January 18, members took turns observing how regressive a variety of indirect taxes were. Taxes on salt, sugar, tea, licenses, and a host of other items came under assault. Much of the debate shifted to the subject of fairness in the tax system. Federalist representative William Craik of Maryland observed that the current system of taxation was unfair because wealthy, independent farmers could avoid taxes almost entirely by producing their own food, drink, clothing, and other goods (January 18, 1797, 4th Cong., 2nd sess., 1902).

Findley made a key contribution to this discussion when he offered the most powerful egalitarian argument in favor of a direct tax on land. After disposing of the claim that such a tax is impracticable by pointing to experience in his home state of Pennsylvania, Findley argued that a direct tax on land could be highly progressive. The lengthy report on direct taxes by Secretary Wolcott that provided the basis for much of the House deliberation did not specify the exact rates that would be levied, but it did offer levying rates according to different classifications as a possibility—as Hamilton had suggested to him in a 1797 letter.[34] Instead of imposing a uniform tax on all lands and houses regardless of quality or value, this option would impose taxes based on the value of property.[35] Findley seized on this as a way to bring the taxes individuals paid in line with their wealth. He suggested that a direct tax could operate much more equally than an indirect tax because "land would be taxed only in proportion to its value" (January 18, 1797, 4th Cong., 2nd sess., 1908). Another egalitarian advantage of a tax on land is that it would discourage the concentration of land. Citing his home state as an example, Findley observed that the land there tended to be kept in "small tracts" rather than "engrossed" in a few hands (January 18, 1797, 4th Cong., 2nd sess., 1909).

Implicit in much of what Findley said was the belief that property values were a proxy for wealth. As economist Lee Soltow has demonstrated in his detailed analysis of property values in 1798, the available quantitative evidence bears out this belief. The value of a dwelling was very closely correlated with the wealth and income of its owner(s). Because of the expenses associated with furnishing and maintaining a house, the value of a house generally reflected the income a family enjoyed.[36]

It is impossible to know exactly how persuasive the arguments made by Swanwick and Findley were. Whether representatives supported direct taxes because they felt they were the only way to meet the budget shortfall or because they (also) hoped to lessen economic inequality, there was a majority in favor of these taxes each time they came up for a vote on January 20. The Committee of Ways and Means was ordered to prepare a bill in keeping with these votes, but because there were only six weeks left in the session, and so much other pressing business was still to be done, a bill would have to wait until the next Congress.

The House took up the direct tax again after the Committee of Ways and Means reported on May 1, 1798, that it would be "necessary to raise the sum of two millions of dollars by a tax on lands, houses, and slaves, to be apportioned among the several States" (May 1, 1798, 5th Cong., 2nd sess., 1563). The report made it clear that imposts and tonnage duties would not be able to raise the revenue needed because of the "depredations on our commerce" (May 1, 1798, 5th Cong., 2nd sess., 1564). After some debate, the House voted overwhelmingly on May 5 to raise $2 million via a "uniform assessment, on lands, houses, and slaves" (May 5, 1798, 5th Cong., 2nd sess., 1596).

This was hardly the end of the matter. Congress members still had to decide whether a new census was necessary or permitted to apportion the tax among the states, whether the tax should be temporary or permanent, and whether the valuation of houses could be separated from the valuation of lands—not to mention the fact that the occasional member would challenge the necessity of a direct tax at all. One of the most contentious issues to arise while the details of the bill were being worked out concerned the mode of valuation. The thirteenth section of the bill provided for separate valuations of land and houses. Members including Gallatin and Macon contended that it made no sense to do this on practical and normative grounds. Not only would it be difficult to separate the value of a house from the value of the land upon which it sat but also singling out houses from all other improvements on the land would treat owners of homes differently from owners of mills, furnaces, and the like (May 30, 1798, 5th Cong., 2nd sess., 1840).

What makes the debate over this section of the bill relevant to this discussion is that it revolved around the issue of equality. What makes it so interesting is that participants on both sides actually agreed that equality was an important goal. Both proponents and opponents of the section expressed support for the idea that the wealthy should pay a greater share of taxes than the lower classes. In fact, not a single speaker challenged the prevailing idea that the wealthy should pay a greater share of taxes. Many even suggested that the poor should be exempt from these taxes altogether. (Treasury Secretary Wolcott's May 25, 1798, report to the House of Representatives proposed that houses valued under $80 be exempt from the tax; 5th Cong., Appendix, 3595.) The question was, which arrangement, separate or combined valuations, would be most likely to achieve this objective?

Federalist John Williams of New York spoke out in favor of taxing houses separately. He started off by developing a Lockean-cum-Jeffersonian argument that farms are superior to luxurious estates because they make more productive uses of land. Williams was not interested only in promoting industry. He was also interested in promoting a republican ethic of simplicity and modesty: "Perhaps the rage for building elegant houses had gone too far in this country, and, if this tax went to check it, it would not be lamented, as excesses of this kind tend to obstruct agricultural pursuits, which must be considered as the true interest of this country" (May 30, 1798, 5th Cong., 2nd sess., 1840–1841). Williams believed that a direct tax would dampen enthusiasm for extravagant homes and encourage the formation of more farms.

Williams then argued in favor of making taxes as progressive as possible—even if that meant exempting the poor from paying any taxes at all. He declared that it was his wish to "lay taxes upon persons able to pay, and to excuse those who have not money to pay with" (May 30, 1798, 5th Cong., 2nd sess., 1841). In keeping with this principle, he proposed that houses valued at under $80—which constituted roughly 47 percent of all houses in 1798[37]—be exempted from the tax on dwellings. In addition, he suggested that settlers on new lands also be exempt "from public burdens" until they managed to establish themselves in their new places of residence (May 30, 1798, 5th Cong., 2nd sess., 1841). Recognizing that inequality tended to be higher near urban areas (as contemporary research has largely confirmed),[38] Williams said it was important that those concentrations of wealth get taxed (May 30, 1798, 5th Cong., 2nd sess., 1841). He went even further by proposing higher rates of taxation on more luxurious homes, saying "some increase might be made by dividing again some of the higher classes of houses, and adding a higher rate of tax, in proportion to the houses in the higher classes." Though he preferred indirect taxes because the poor could avoid paying them simply by refraining from purchasing the items taxed, he believed that a tax on houses would operate much like an indirect tax in the sense that "every man who built a house would know to what kind of tax it would be subject, and fix his plan accordingly" (May 30, 1798, 5th Cong., 2nd sess., 1841). In case his position was not clear to everyone, Williams concluded by saying that he favored the section of the bill under discussion because it would "relieve the poorer class of our citizens" (May 30, 1798, 5th Cong., 2nd sess., 1842).

Harrison Gray Otis, a Federalist from Massachusetts, was even more explicit than Williams about the progressive objectives of Section 13. Though no tax system could produce perfect equality, he thought this one "would accomplish this purpose in as great a degree as possible" (May 30, 1798, 5th Cong., 2nd sess., 1842). A very important reason for this was that "by the plan proposed, the poorer classes of the community, would be almost wholly exempt from this tax" (May 30, 1798, 5th Cong., 2nd sess., 1843). Another point in its favor was that it would impose higher rates the more expensive a residence was. Otis favored a system of graduated rates even more progressive than what Wolcott had suggested "so that persons possessing these signs of property might be called upon to pay a tax, not merely in an arithmetical proportion to their poorer neighbors, but in a sort of artificial proportion to their poorer neighbors, to be ascertained by experience and observation, which should require from them a larger contribution than their exact proportions, according to the value, splendor, and accommodations of the assumed standard" (May 30, 1798, 5th Cong., 2nd sess., 1842). Critical to Otis's argument was the assumption that the value of a house was a good proxy for wealth: "There would be no better way of levying a tax on all property than by making good houses the standard of opulence.

A good house, though in itself unproductive, is more frequently an indication of the wealth of the occupant, than even a valuable and productive farm" (May 30, 1798, 5th Cong., 2nd sess., 1843). In addition, because this form of property was difficult to conceal, it would help to reduce tax evasion among the wealthy (May 30, 1798, 5th Cong., 2nd sess., 1842). Though a poor man "may live on a farm" in the hopes of eking out an existence, it is hard to believe that a poor man would own a "valuable house. It must add to his difficulties. He ought to sell it and pay his debts, or let it, and save the difference of rent" (May 30, 1798, 5th Cong., 2nd sess., 1843).

The next speaker did not challenge anything Otis had said in principle. Indeed, Varnum of Massachusetts affirmed his belief that taxes should be levied "according to the extent of persons' property" (May 30, 1798, 5th Cong., 2nd sess., 1844). Varnum's only complaint was that *the plan was not progressive enough*. He objected to the possibility that a house valued at $200 would be taxed at the same rate as a house valued at $600, preferring a system that made finer distinctions between different levels of wealth. In addition to recommending a system with more graduated rates, Varnum suggested levying different rates on city dwellers and on those living in the country as being likely to distribute the tax burden "in proportion to their ability to pay" (May 30, 1798, 5th Cong., 2nd sess., 1844). Finally, he proposed taxing other forms of property in addition to houses as the only way to achieve the progressivity sought by supporters. If Congress was not going to tax liquid assets such as "money and moneyed securities," the least it could do was to tax all other real estate (May 30, 1798, 5th Cong., 2nd sess., 1844).

The House members who followed Varnum, including everyone from Federalist Nathaniel Smith of Connecticut to Republican Joseph McDowell of North Carolina, spoke out in support of a more progressive tax system, even if they disagreed with the details of the bill. Sitgreaves of Pennsylvania suggested that one way to make the plan more progressive would be to multiply the classes so that a house valued at $500 would not be taxed at the same rate as one valued at $999. Sitgreaves concluded his remarks by explicating the principle that participants on both sides of the debate seemed to accept: "Upon the principles of justice, it could not be denied that taxes ought not to be collected absolutely equally, but in proportion to persons' wealth; that is to say, a man worth ten thousand dollars a year ought to pay more than ten times the tax that a man pays who is worth only one thousand dollars a year" (May 30, 1798, 5th Cong., 2nd sess., 1847).

The only serious challenge to Section 13 that day came from the leader of the House Democratic-Republican Party. Gallatin raised a number of practical and logistical objections to the bill, but he too expressed strong support for a more egalitarian tax system. After suggesting that those who spoke out in favor of a more progressive tax system were being disingenuous, he pointed out that the rich would not necessarily pay higher rates in all cases (May 30, 1798, 5th Cong., 2nd sess., 1850). Under the current plan, there were situations where those with less wealth would actually end up paying higher rates than those with more. Gallatin found it particularly galling that under this scheme, small farmers, who generally lived on the land they owned, would end up paying more in taxes than wealthy investors who owned large tracts of uncultivated land (May 30, 1798, 5th Cong., 2nd sess., 1852).

Samuel Sewall of Massachusetts immediately accused Gallatin of distorting the facts and arguing in bad faith, suggesting that the Pennsylvanian was only out to derail the bill. In a last-ditch effort to salvage the bill in its present form, Sewall indicated that the figures Gallatin had cited to show that the tax on houses would exacerbate inequality were based on sheer guesswork. Sewall pointed out that the rates for each class were still unknown because the blanks in the bill had yet to be filled (May 30, 1798, 5th Cong., 2nd sess., 1853). In spite of Sewall's attempt to rescue the bill, the House voted forty-five to thirty-nine to strike out Section 13 (May 30, 1798, 5th Cong., 2nd sess., 1854). However, the following day, supporters of the bill won an important victory by getting a postponement after Sewall suggested that the change the House had approved on May 30 altered the entire complexion of the bill.

In the following weeks, the House took up legislation providing for the valuation of houses, land, and slaves. The issue before the House concerned the means of estimating the value of property, but members understood that any valuation that included houses below a certain value could create pressure to tax that property. Various speakers used the opportunity to reiterate their support for a progressive tax system, and a consensus seemed to emerge that houses below a certain value should be excluded from the tax. Gallatin said he favored exempting houses valued below $200 because "they are generally possessed by a description of farmers and laborers, who are not in circumstances to pay such a tax" (June 8, 1798, 5th Cong., 2nd sess., 1894). William Claiborne of Tennessee agreed that "it would be extremely wrong" to tax dwellings valued below $200 because "they are generally the abodes of poverty" (June 8, 1798, 5th Cong., 2nd sess., 1895).[39]

The actual bill to lay and collect direct taxes was taken up on June 26. That bill embodied the progressive principles endorsed in previous discussions and restored the separate valuation on houses struck out of the bill on May 30. It exempted houses below $100 and established a progressive schedule of taxes that laid very steep rates for more expensive houses. For instance, a house valued between $100 and $500 would be taxed up to $1, whereas a house valued between $20,000 and $30,000 would be taxed at $270 (June 26, 1798, 5th Cong., 2nd sess., 2050). Thus, a house valued at $30,000 was worth 60 times more than the most valuable house in the lowest tier, but it would be taxed 270 times more than a house valued at $500.

Although the bill reflected the avowed principles of most members who had spoken on the direct tax question up to this point, it did not sit well with Samuel Smith, a merchant from Baltimore, Maryland. This Democratic-Republican introduced a motion to eliminate the different rates in the hopes of establishing a flat tax on houses. He vehemently objected to the graduated schedule of taxation because he thought the high rates for more expensive homes would discourage construction and mark the end of cities in the United States. He also disputed the assumption that the value of a house was a good indicator of wealth. Although this was generally true in other places, he claimed, it did not hold up in the United States. For example, he claimed, a house valued at $3,000 in the country was often much more splendid than one valued at $10,000 in the city (June 26, 1798, 5th Cong., 2nd sess., 2049). To those who had argued that well-to-do city dwellers should be taxed more, Smith responded that taxes in cities were already high: "As it stood at present, it would fall principally upon the merchants in large cities—a class of men, who, it is well known, always evince a readiness to contribute their full share to the support of Government, and who are now spiritedly advancing their property to build ships for the public service" (June 26, 1798, 5th Cong., 2nd sess., 2051).

After some additional debate in which speakers made final attempts to lower those taxes that would fall hardest on their own constituents (or themselves), as Gallatin suggested they had been doing all along (June 26, 1798, 5th Cong., 2nd sess., 2053), the House voted forty-nine to twenty-eight against Smith's motion to make the tax on houses and land equal (June 26, 1798, 5th Cong., 2nd sess., 2055).[40] A motion by Otis, who had restated his commitment to a progressive tax but proposed that the rates on the most expensive houses be lowered, failed after it received only twenty-three votes (June 26, 1798, 5th Cong., 2nd sess., 2057). The House overwhelmingly approved the direct tax with its steeply progressive tax rates on July 2, 1798, by a vote of sixty-two to eighteen.

The story in the House finally came to a close on July 11. The Senate had voted to approve the direct tax bill but offered several amendments. One of these was an amendment that would have completely eliminated the progressive structure of the house tax. In place of a tax schedule that started at two-tenths of 1 percent and went up to a full 1 percent on the most expensive houses, the Senate proposed a flat rate of four-tenths of 1 percent on all eligible houses. After brief remarks by Gallatin and Samuel Smith, the House voted resoundingly to preserve the progressive structure of the direct tax, with the Senate amendment receiving only seventeen votes (5th Cong., 2nd sess., 2172).

With that, Congress passed the first direct tax in the history of the United States. It also passed a remarkably progressive tax—perhaps even the "world's first effective progressive tax."[41] Although southerners and farmers complained that their wealth was taxed more heavily than the wealth of urban dwellers and merchants under this scheme, the public generally accepted what one scholar of conflict over tax policy in the early Republic has characterized as the law's "radical schedule of progressive duties."[42]

The record of Congress in pursuing a more egalitarian tax system was certainly uneven during the first twelve years of its existence under the Constitution, but it is undeniable that the national legislature struck a blow for equality with the enactment of the direct tax on land, houses, and slaves. The bill John Adams signed into law enshrined the principle that the rate of taxation should be based on the ability to pay. Congress still retained—and in some cases even extended—regressive taxes on consumption, but the records of debates that took place during the first six Congresses reveal that representatives generally strove to promote equality through the tax code.

The Use of Public Expenditures to Ease Private Burdens

Tax policy was one thing. Policy involving spending—public or private—was another. Although Congress managed to enact tax policies conducive to greater economic equality, its record in other areas of public policy was much more mixed. In fact, it failed much more often than it succeeded. However, even when it failed to adopt policies that would have minimized concentrations of wealth or reduced the hardships of the poor, it recognized the legitimacy of those objectives. In fact, the issue of economic equality popped up in some unexpected places and received support from surprising sources.

Regulating and Supplying the Militia

The militia bill that came up for consideration in the third session of the 1st Congress raised a number of political, economic, and constitutional questions. Representatives entered into debates over exemptions for members of Congress, exemptions for conscientious objectors, exemptions from arrest when on active duty, the appropriate age range of militiamen, the proper formation of companies, and the power of the president to call out the militia. One of the lengthiest debates centered on a proposal to supply the poor with weapons at public expense.

The issue of equipping the poor at public expense arose because of a mandate in the militia bill requiring all eligible adult males to supply themselves with the necessary weapons and equipment. At the Virginia Ratifying Convention, outspoken anti-Federalist Patrick Henry had suggested that arming the militia would be the only way to make it useful, but when the House of Representatives took up the matter, it was a fellow anti-Federalist from Virginia who led the effort.[43] Josiah Parker argued the mandate was "impracticable, as it must be well known that there are many persons who are so poor that it is impossible they should comply with the law" (December 16, 1790, 1st Cong., 3rd sess., 1851). He then introduced an amendment "that persons who shall make it appear that they are not able to equip themselves, shall be furnished at the expense of the United States" (December 16, 1790, 1st Cong., 3rd sess., 1852).

The immediate reaction to this proposal was negative. Federalist Jeremiah Wadsworth, a merchant from Connecticut, objected to the amendment on the grounds that the likely expense would be too great, that there were not very many poor people in the United States in any case, and that the measure would be unprecedented. He suggested that it would be better to insert a "clause to excuse them altogether" (December 16, 1790, 1st Cong., 3rd sess., 1853). Parker shot back by pointing out that Wadsworth was mistaken on his last two counts. He noted that there was a law in Virginia "which provides that poor persons, not able to arm themselves, should be equipped at the expense of the State. In every State there are doubtless many such persons, who ought to be provided for by the General Government; and if they are not, the law is rendered impracticable; as you require more than is possible for them to perform." As for excusing the poor from service, Parker reminded his colleague that their contributions might be required in case of emergency (December 16, 1790, 1st Cong., 3rd sess., 1853).

Federalism and other constitutional matters became the focus in the next part of the debate. After Parker modified his amendment so that the individual states rather the federal government would be responsible for subsidizing the purchase of arms, several members raised a variety of constitutional objections. However, the arguments against the revised motion revealed more disagreement than agreement over the meaning of the Constitution. Staunch anti-Federalist Giles argued that the motion constituted an "improper interference with the authority of the State Governments" (December 16, 1790, 1st Cong., 3rd sess., 1854). Roger Sherman, a Federalist from Connecticut who had served as a delegate to the Constitutional Convention, agreed that the amendment was unconstitutional, but for somewhat different reasons. His argument focused on the limits of congressional authority rather than the rights of the states. He pointed out that the Constitution only authorized Congress to *regulate* the militia, not to *supply* it. Sherman also thought the motion was unnecessary because there were so few men incapable of supplying themselves with weapons (December 16, 1790, 1st Cong., 3rd sess., 1854). Tucker of South Carolina agreed with his fellow southerner that Congress could not require the states to make these expenditures, but he disagreed with Sherman about the federal government's authority to make the same expenditures, "for the United States may, without doubt, furnish the arms." Thus, he supported the motion in its original form (December 16, 1790, 1st Cong., 3rd sess., 1855).

The most powerful argument for the constitutionality of the

revised amendment came from John Vining of Delaware, a dependable Hamiltonian Federalist. Vining's argument relied on the same doctrine of implied powers that the leader of his party used to defend his economic and financial program. Vining thought it was absurd to object on the grounds that the motion would be "dictating" to the states. He asked, "What is the whole bill but dictating; a law that affects every individual, touches the whole community?" As for the authority of Congress in this area, he asserted, "With respect to the constitutionality of the measure, there can be no doubt; every grant of power to Congress necessarily implies a conveyance of every incidental power requisite to carry the grant into effect" (December 16, 1790, 1st Cong., 3rd sess., 1855). Despite—or perhaps because of—Vining's argument for a loose construction of congressional powers, the House rejected Parker's amendment (December 16, 1790, 1st Cong., 3rd sess., 1856).

The subject of supplying arms to the poor came up again in the 2nd Congress. On the first of two days of debate on the requirement that all eligible men supply themselves, Murray started things off by drawing attention to the gross inequities of the militia law passed on May 8, 1792. The law provided that every eligible male between the ages of eighteen and forty-five shall "provide himself with a good musket or forelock, sufficient bayonet and belt, two spare flints, and a knapsack, a pouch with a box therein to contain not less than twenty-four cartridges, suited to the bore of his rifle, and a quarter of a pound of powder" (2nd Cong., Appendix, 1392).

Murray railed against this part of the law because it "imposed equal burdens, on shoulders infinitely disproportioned as to their capacity to sustain them; it enjoins duties on the major part of the Militia, of such a nature, as renders the law totally impracticable. A man not worth one farthing, is subjected to the same expense with one who may be worth ten thousand pounds a year; the inequality, evident in the operation of such a requisition, is a glaring instance of injustice, and calls loudly for Legislative interposition and relief" (November 20, 1792, 2nd Cong., 2nd sess., 701–702). Constitutional Convention delegate and anti-Federalist John Francis Mercer agreed with his fellow Marylander concerning the "injustice of the requisition, which enjoins, that a man who is not worth twenty shillings should incur an expense of twenty pounds in equipping himself as a Militia man" (November 20, 1792, 2nd Cong., 2nd sess., 702). Nevertheless, Murray's vaguely worded motion received only fourteen votes in its favor after James Hillhouse of Connecticut, a Federalist, argued that it would be premature to make any alterations to the law as it was just going into effect.

Murray was undeterred. The next day he introduced a new motion to repeal the section of the law requiring militiamen to supply themselves. Once again, his objections rested on egalitarian grounds, not constitutional ones. He invoked a version of the principle that would play a critical role in the debate over direct taxes, namely, "that wherever a tax was levied for the protection of society, its apportionment among individuals should be as exactly as possible correspondent with the property of each individual" (November 21, 1792, 2nd Cong., 2nd sess., 708). According to Murray, the militia law egregiously violated this principle:

> The obligation to arm in a particular manner, as it will produce a uniform expense on men of unequal property, will prove a tax that will act unjustly, because unequally—men will not pay agreeably to their property. . . . By the law, he who has passed his forty-fifth year is exempt from militia duty. It must often happen that men of large fortune will thus contribute nothing towards this species of protection, while the man of very small fortune will be obliged to furnish largely to it, if the father of a family, capable and of age to bear arms. For the sake of harmony and a ready disposition to fall into a patriotic impulse, he much doubted whether his constituents would have murmured much at the violation of the principle; but the impracticability of this clause obliges them to seek relief through their Representatives. . . . The law, in the district he came from, he much feared could not be executed. Each militia-man is to come into the field with a musket or firelock, a bayonet, cartouch-box, and other equipments. These, he verily believed, could not be had. If the citizens—even those who would not think lightly of the burden—could not procure these accoutrements, the law must be violated. Congress, he hoped, would not force his well-inclined fellow-citizens to violate the law; but if the law could not possibly be executed, because impracticable, the Legislature would be answerable for the indignities it brought upon itself, by thus prescribing unnecessary hardships. (November 21, 1792, 2nd Cong., 2nd sess., 709)

Murray observed that there were several different ways to remedy this injustice. One was to furnish arms to all militiamen at public expense. Another was to provide weapons only to those whom officers deemed too poor to provide for themselves. The funds for either option could come from the fines to be levied under the militia law (November 21, 1792, 2nd Cong., 2nd sess., 709).

Murray's motion was very badly defeated by a vote of six to fifty. The critics, which this time including Mercer, complained of the enormous expense that would be incurred, the practical difficulties of implementing the proposal, and the injustice to those capable of furnishing their own arms. Hugh Williamson, a delegate to the Constitutional Convention from North Carolina, asserted that Murray's proposal entailed an unacceptable redistribution of wealth. It would amount to a "most unequal and oppressive species of taxation, especially as it is conceded that more than half of the militia are already armed" (November 21, 1792, 2nd Cong., 2nd sess., 710). However, this time not a single speaker raised any constitutional objections to the proposal to supply the poor with arms.

Various matters relating to the militia would come up again in the next few years, but the subject of providing arms to the militia came up only once more. At the height of tensions with France in June of 1798, the House of Representatives considered a bill to provide arms to the militia throughout the United States. Critics again complained about the expenses and inconveniences involved. As Jonathan Dayton of New Jersey put it, not only would the federal government have to transport these weapons over great distances but also many of them would probably get damaged along the way, rendering them unfit for service (June 14, 1798, 5th Cong., 2nd sess., 1927). Supporters of the bill maintained that its passage was a matter of military necessity. They argued that the federal government had to intervene to supply the southern states, where there was a lack of arms in large part because of the lack of weapons manufacturers in that part of the country. Unless the federal government stepped in, some areas of the United States would be unprepared in the event of emergency. Claiborne of Tennessee, who represented a part of the country that would stand to benefit from passage of the bill, was the only speaker who raised the problem of poverty. Whereas others focused on the unavailability of arms, Claiborne addressed their unaffordability, saying "that those who are not able to pay for them should have them given to them" (June 14, 1798, 5th Cong., 2nd sess., 1931). The next day, without any debate, the House approved the bill providing arms for the militia by a vote of fifty-five to seventeen (June 15, 1798, 5th Cong., 2nd sess., 1938). On July 3, the Senate passed the bill "providing arms for the militia throughout the United States" without amendment (5th Cong., 2nd sess., 597).

Settling Western Lands

Few issues had more far-reaching implications for the distribution of wealth in the United States than the settling of lands west of the Appalachian Mountains. By the time the Constitution went into effect, several important matters had already been settled that provided Congress a general framework for policy making in this area. Under intense pressure from states without any plausible claims to so-called vacant lands (actually inhabited by American Indian nations and small handfuls of white settlers), states that did have claims to trans-Appalachian territory eventually relinquished control over these lands to the government of the United States. This cession resulted in the creation of a "public domain" that came under the jurisdiction of the national government. A series of ordinances adopted by the Confederation Congress established a general framework for the disposition of western lands. The Land Ordinance of 1785 established rules for the surveying and settlement of these lands into square townships divided into thirty-six rectangular sections of 640 acres sold at auction for a minimum price of $1 per acre (with one section reserved for the establishment of a common school). The Northwest Ordinance of 1787 gave the federal government additional powers to decide how to divide and settle the large area north of the Ohio River between the Appalachian Mountains and the Mississippi River. The legislation would have profound consequences for the political structure of the country—particularly its sectional balance of power—because it allowed for the admission of new states on equal terms and outlawed slavery. Settling the lands in the Northwest Territory was a matter of inestimable importance to the future of the country for other reasons as well. How the western lands were distributed would have an enormous impact on the state of the nation's finances. Virtually everyone expected the sale of these lands to play a significant part in repaying the Revolutionary War debt. Just as importantly, how Congress ultimately decided to dispose of these lands would have momentous consequences for the prospects of economic equality and opportunity.[44]

There was broad agreement among political leaders and ordinary citizens that the continued availability of land was the sine qua non of equality in the United States. There was also recognition that the Ordinance of 1785 failed to promote accessibility to these lands because the mechanisms established to sell these lands tended to favor speculators over yeomen, who could not necessarily afford to purchase an entire 640-acre section of land or outbid investors at auctions. In addition, out of desperation for much-needed revenue, the Confederation Congress defied its own law by selling enormous tracts of land to the Ohio Company of Associates, the Scioto Company, and other groups of land speculators for as little as eight cents per acre—far below the legal minimum price of $1 per acre. The urgency of congressional action was compounded by the fact that many who could not afford to purchase land of their own took up residence as squatters. Squatter settlements were so common on the frontiers of states that governments granted the "right of preemption," which conferred legal title on squatters who agreed to purchase their settlements at highly reduced prices.[45] As Thomas Scott of Pennsylvania noted when the House of Representatives took up the matter in May of 1789, if Congress failed to ratify the preemption rights of these settlers either they would move into Spanish-controlled territory and become subjects of a foreign power or they would stay put and compel the government to remove them by force (May 28, 1789, 1st Cong., 1st sess., 412).

Perhaps the most critical question Congress had to settle concerned the size and minimum price of the plots sold to individuals. The government had somewhat conflicting interests in selling off all the land as quickly and as conveniently as possible, on the one hand, and in raising as much revenue as possible, on the other. It could dispose of the lands relatively quickly by establishing very large plot sizes at reduced prices, or it could potentially raise larger sums by selling off the land in smaller but more expensive plots. The first option increased the likelihood that all of the lands would be sold off. Under the second option there was a risk that less desirable land would remain unsold. It was also widely understood that the first option favored wealthy buyers who purchased lands as investments and that the second one favored buyers of middling means who purchased the lands in order to settle them. Many in Congress believed that the future of republicanism was at stake in this choice. The smaller the size of plots for sale, the greater the likelihood that yeomen farmers would be able to settle and achieve a meaningful degree of economic independence. The larger the size of plots, the greater the likelihood speculators would purchase these lands simply to turn a profit.

Despite an earnest attempt to deal with the question of western lands during the 1st Congress and a report by Hamilton laying out a mechanism for the sale of these lands, progress stalled in part because of procedural disputes and disagreements over the proper agency to oversee any program that ultimately got adopted.[46] Meaningful legislative action did not take place until the 4th Congress.[47] On February 15, 1796, the House formed itself into a committee of the whole to consider a bill on establishing a land office that would oversee the sale of lands in the Northwest Territory. From the outset, members expressed worries about putting the land out of the reach of ordinary buyers and enriching speculators in the process. Robert Rutherford of Virginia proclaimed, "There never was a bill of greater importance than that before the House" (February 15, 1796, 4th Cong., 1st sess., 328). If they made the right decisions, they could ensure "that this tract of country should be disposed of to real settlers, industrious, respectable persons, who are ready to pay a reasonable price for it, and not sold to persons who have no other view than engrossing riches" (February 15, 1796, 4th Cong., 1st sess., 329). If they failed to uphold republican principles, they would end up strengthening "that hydra, speculation, which had done the country great harm" (February 15, 1796, 4th Cong., 1st sess., 328–329). Those who spoke after Rutherford that day generally agreed that the best way to ensure the land ended up in the hands of actual settlers would be to break it up into smaller tracts.

Over the next several days and weeks, class became a focal point of debate. Some members believed that they had arrived at a compromise solution that would make the land available for purchase in two different sizes. The motion to sell the land in both small and large plot sizes provided a way to accommodate different classes, but numerous representatives spoke out against this option in the interest of equality. Those who favored selling the land in smaller tracts did so in order to prevent speculators from making windfall profits and to expand economic opportunities for the lower classes. Findley suggested that the tracts should be as small as fifty acres because "it was the interest . . . of every country to encourage freeholders; they are interested in supporting the laws. This, he added, is not only good for Government, but it tends to make the people happy. Land is the most valuable of all property . . . and ought to be brought within the reach of the people" (February 17, 1796, 4th Cong., 1st sess., 339). Others supported Findley's suggestion that Congress had a special obligation to look after the interests of the lower classes. Jeffersonian Jonathan Havens of New York argued that the land should be sold only in "small tracts" because "men who have large capitals will have always an advantage over those who have but little property, though the land be in small tracts. He thought a tract of one mile square large enough" (February 17, 1796, 4th Cong., 1st sess., 339).

Gallatin agreed that the interests of the poor were of special concern, but he argued that their interests might best be served by selling the land in both small and large tracts. Doing so, he indicated, would dispose of the land much more quickly than selling only in small plots. That was something he favored because it would help to pay off the national debt more quickly and help the poor in the process. Gallatin explained that there was "no object of so great importance to the United States as the extinction of the curse of the country, the Public Debt, and no class of citizens would be more benefited by this extinction than the poor" (February 17, 1796, 4th Cong., 1st sess., 340).

What followed over the rest of the day was a largely speculative debate about who was most likely actually to settle, how much it would cost to settle, and which classes would benefit under different arrangements. The members who spoke could not agree on whether the poor, the rich, or the "middling classes" would benefit the most from the mixed-size approach, but they all seemed to agree it was important to accommodate the poor as much as possible, no matter which specific plan they favored. The question was whether the proposals on the table did enough to accommodate wealthy investors. It was feared that much if not most of the land would remain unsold unless it were offered on terms they found attractive.

When the House continued this debate the next day, Williams asserted that it was unnecessary for Congress to go out of its way to protect the interests of investors: "Persons of property, said he, can generally accommodate themselves; we ought to accommodate the lower classes of the people" (February 18, 1796, 4th Cong., 1st sess.,

346). Federalist Jeremiah Crabb of Maryland had grown impatient with the repeated calls for exclusively small tracts. He agreed that "no attention . . . should be paid to moneyed men, [because] they will take care of themselves," but he urged his colleagues not to ignore their interests altogether because the government was still dependent on their support. Crabb explained, "If the Treasury was to be served, it was necessary to accommodate them, as they could not be expected to become purchasers, if obstructions were thrown in their way" (February 18, 1796, 4th Cong., 1st sess., 348).

At the conclusion of the debate, members voted down a proposal to sell the land entirely in small tracts. The proposal to sell the land in a mix of large and small tracts carried (February 18, 1796, 4th Cong., 1st sess., 349), but other questions still remained to be answered. On March 2, 1796, the House voted to have the land sold at auctions, but not before Abraham Baldwin delivered a severe admonition against the glorification of greed.[48] The following day, the House took up a proposal to require at least "one actual settler upon every ____ acres of land" (March 3, 1796, 4th Cong., 1st sess., 408). Gallatin said he favored the amendment as a way to prevent the concentration of land in a few hands by discouraging speculators (March 3, 1796, 4th Cong., 1st sess.). Whereas others suggested that the amendment would actually impede settlement (Nathaniel Smith, March 3, 1796, 4th Cong., 1st sess., 412) or proposed that the same objective could be accomplished by other means (Jonathan Dayton, March 3, 1796, 4th Cong., 1st sess., 409), Gallatin explained that the issue was really about the best way to "promote the general happiness of the whole country." In his view, the happiness of the country up to that point was a result of the fact that the "poor man has been able always to attain his portion of land." If Congress did nothing to discourage speculators from amassing huge concentrations of land, all of that was in jeopardy (March 3, 1796, 4th Cong., 1st sess., 411). Despite Gallatin's entreaties, the motion received only twenty-two affirmative votes (March 3, 1796, 4th Cong., 1st sess., 416).

It appeared that only minor details were left to be worked out when several members made yet another attempt to reduce the size of the plots sold. James Holland, a Democratic-Republican from North Carolina, proposed an amendment to reduce the size of plots from 640 acres to 160 acres "in order to accommodate the poorer class of farmers" (April 4, 1796, 4th Cong., 1st sess., 856–857). The motion was defeated without any debate, but that was still not the end of the matter.

The next day, Crabb introduced a version of Holland's amendment. This one would have sold half the lots rather than all of them in 160-acre tracts. Holland rushed to support what he described as a compromise amendment, saying it would have several beneficial effects. One was that it would "certainly increase competition, and, consequently, the price of the land." Another was that it would "prevent monopoly," well known to be "dangerous to the existence of free Governments." Perhaps the most important "desirable" effect it would have was on economic equality. In describing the way this amendment would promote the interests of the poor, Holland explicated the relation between economic equality and republican freedom in perhaps the clearest terms any member of the first six Congresses had. He explained that selling the plots of land in smaller sizes

> would accommodate, as much as possible, the poorer class of their citizens—a class of men who were the most valuable in a community, because it was upon them they could chiefly rely in cases of emergency, for defence, and, therefore they ought to be accommodated and made happy; to be put into a situation where they might exercise their own will, which they would not be at liberty to do if they were obliged to become tenants to others. To live in that dependent way had a tendency to vitiate and debase their minds, instead of making them free, enlightened, and independent. By this amendment, this class of citizens would be enabled to become possessed of real property—a situation incident to freedom, and desired by all. (April 5, 1796, 4th Cong., 1st sess., 858)

Crabb picked up where Holland left off after two opponents of the amendment challenged the claim that the change in the bill would have its intended effect on the poor. Crabb agreed that increasing opportunities for ownership would promote the republican ideal of independence: "The dividing of the land into small lots would put it into the possession of real proprietors, and have a tendency to make good Republicans instead of servile tenants dependent upon tyrannical landlords" (April 5, 1796, 4th Cong., 1st sess., 860). In response to William Cooper's remark that experience with land sales in New York and Pennsylvania suggested the poor would not purchase land under any of the scenarios under consideration (April 5, 1796, 4th Cong., 1st sess., 859), Crabb theorized that the human instinct for independence would operate as powerful motivation in this case: "The poor and the oppressed had the greatest inducement of all men to emigrate. And the man must know but little of human nature indeed, that did not believe that when a man had been in a state of dependence, and by strenuous exertions of industry, rigid economy, and frugality, had saved a small sum, which would scarcely buy him a garden in the old settled countries where land is so high," he would move (April 5, 1796, 4th Cong., 1st sess., 861).

Most of those who spoke after Crabb supported his amendment for many of the same reasons he and Holland had articulated. Critics such as Democratic-Republican Nicholas and Federalist John E. Van Alen objected to the amendment because of the costs involved (April 5, 1796, 4th Cong., 1st sess., 864), but no one raised any objections to the principles Crabb and Holland had articulated. In fact, Nicholas's main argument against the amendment was that the cost of surveying the land would be so prohibitive for the poor that it would fail to accomplish its aim (April 5, 1796, 4th Cong., 1st sess., 862–863).[49]

The House approved the amendment to sell half the plots in smaller tracts, but it was all for naught (April 5, 1796, 4th Cong., 1st sess., 865). The Senate declined to accept the modification, so the minimum plot size was set at 640 acres. One more attempt was made in the House to restore the smaller 160-acre plot sizes, but that motion failed by the narrow margin of thirty-one to thirty-three with no recorded debate (May 11, 1796, 4th Cong., 1st sess., 1340). The final version of the law, "An Act Providing for the Sale of Lands of the United States in the Territory Northwest of the River Ohio, and above the Mouth of the Kentucky River," provided that the land would be auctioned off in 640-acre sections for no less than $2 per acre (4th Cong., Appendix, 2905–2909). Although these plot sizes greatly exceeded the average farm size at the time, roughly 150 acres, the minimum sale price per acre did somewhat offset any advantages the plot size gave to speculators. At a cost of $2 per acre, the price was several times higher than any previously established or proposed asking price but much closer to the estimated true market value.[50] The effect of pricing land at this level was to discourage some of the speculation feared by many in Congress because any profits gained would be much smaller.[51]

Congress revisited the issue of western lands on several other occasions during the next few decades. Each time it did so, it made changes that would benefit small purchasers, mainly by reducing the minimum size of tracts. This pattern of liberalization began during the 6th Congress. Despite the failure to enshrine the principle of preemption into law, the act passed by Congress in 1800 introduced a number of changes that favored ordinary settlers over speculators. Among other things, Congress reduced the minimum purchase size to 320 acres,[52] liberalized the credit system by allowing purchasers to make payments in installments payable over four years, and established a number of local land offices that would be more accessible to actual settlers. In the coming years, Congress would reduce both the minimum purchase price and the minimum plot size. By 1820, a settler could purchase as few as 80 acres of land for no more than $1.25 per acre.[53]

Providing Relief to Those in Distress

The record of Congress at promoting economic equality between the years 1789 and 1801 was mixed. Although proponents of economically egalitarian policies won important victories in the fight over the direct tax and in a handful of battles over indirect taxes, they enjoyed less success in other areas of public policy. Calls to assist the poor by designing public policies that eased their burdens and expanded their opportunities often relied on appeals to justice and compassion. One of the strategies often used to win support for these policies was to remind members of Congress of the everyday hardships faced by members of the lower classes. Perhaps because the descriptions were not quite vivid enough or because they just did not believe the condition of the poor in the United States was really all that bad, many members were not moved enough to correct these supposed imbalances.

It was an entirely different story when members of Congress were confronted with more discrete groups in need of assistance. They exhibited a much greater willingness to act when presented with moving descriptions of the suffering experienced by narrowly defined

groups than when they were reminded of the everyday hardships
of broadly defined classes of poor farmers and laborers. Congress
did not vote to provide assistance every time it received a petition
for aid, but the more easily identifiable and specific the group, the
more receptive Congress was to pleas for help. In its first few years,
Congress spent an inordinate amount of time dealing with petitions
from individual Revolutionary War veterans, widows, and orphans,
more often than not voting to provide the pensions and other benefits sought.

The three groups that presented the most interesting cases included French refugees from Haiti, victims of a devastating fire in
Savannah, and sick and disabled seamen. Though debates over providing assistance to these groups did not necessarily involve discussions of economic equality, they are relevant to this discussion
because of the way in which constitutional questions were (or were
not) addressed. Debates over whether to provide assistance to these
groups are highly illuminating about the ways in which members
of Congress understood both their powers and their responsibilities
under the Constitution.

The "St. Domingo" Refugees

Members of the 3rd Congress were confronted with a domestic crisis that grew out of foreign events—the slave uprising in the French
West Indian colony of Saint-Domingue. Inspired by the events and
philosophy of the French Revolution,[54] the slave population of
this prosperous colony began an insurrection in August 1791 that
marked the opening stages of what would become the Haitian Revolution. Colonists fleeing violence in the French possession started
to trickle into Norfolk, Charleston, Philadelphia, and other seaports
in the United States shortly after the uprising began. From the first,
the overwhelmingly white refugees relied on various forms of assistance provided by local philanthropic societies and municipal governments. However, what started out as a trickle of exiles in 1791
became a deluge in the summer of 1793 after the fall of Cap Français,
the former capital and an important city located on the northern
coast. Moved by the horrific stories told by these refugees and related in sympathetic newspaper accounts, the citizens of cities that
offered asylum organized relief committees and held fund-raisers
to assist these "unfortunate" exiles. Because many refugees were

aristocrats, they were unable to get any help from French minister Edmond-Charles Genêt, who considered them counterrevolutionaries. With their resources stretched by the overwhelming numbers and no support coming from the French government, cities such as Baltimore, which alone received around 3,000 Saint-Dominguans, looked to the states and the federal government for financial help. The issue came before Congress when it received a petition for federal financial assistance for these displaced French citizens.[55]

The House spent the better part of two days in January debating what to do about the refugees from "St. Domingo" (as they called it). Many of the remarks made on the floor of the House echoed sentiments voiced in local newspapers during the previous two years about the obligations of republican philanthropy and the role of the United States as an asylum.[56] Every single member of the House who spoke out on this matter expressed deep sorrow for the suffering of these refugees. In fact, every single representative supported the idea of providing federal assistance to these French citizens—albeit for different reasons. The familiar cast of loose constructionists found all the justification they needed in the Constitution and in the precedents already established by Congress, whereas the usual proponents of strict constructionism had to resort to a range of extraconstitutional reasons to justify their support for measures they believed would violate the Constitution. A few, such as Clark of New Jersey, simply stated that they had not a "moment's hesitation that relief should be given" (January 10, 1794, 3rd Cong., 1st sess., 170) without offering any constitutional justification whatsoever. Most members of Congress were able to overcome whatever constitutional qualms they had because the plight of the Haitian refugees was framed by an emotionally moving "disaster narrative" that cast them as blameless victims of a sudden and unforeseeable event beyond their control.[57]

Boudinot, a Federalist from New Jersey, saw no difficulty at all. Every consideration of justice, humanity, and friendship supported relief for the distressed Frenchmen:

By the law of Nature, by the law of Nations—in a word, by every moral obligation that could influence mankind, we were bound to relieve the citizens of a Republic who were at present our allies, and who had formerly been our benefactors. . . . When a number of our fellow-creatures had been cast upon our sympathy, in a situation of such unexampled wretchedness, was it possible that gentlemen could make a doubt whether it was our duty to relieve them? (January 10, 1794, 3rd Cong., 1st sess., 172)

Recognizing that moral arguments might not be enough to overcome the constitutional doubts nagging many of his colleagues, Boudinot invoked the general welfare clause and cited a number of precedents to demonstrate that Congress had already taken a relaxed view of the Constitution when it came to providing assistance to the needy. He was convinced that a refusal to provide assistance in this case

would be to act in direct opposition both to the theory and practice of the Constitution. In the first place, as to the practice, it had been said that nothing of this kind had ever occurred before under the Federal Constitution. He was astonished at such an affirmation. Did not the Indians frequently come down to this city, on embassies respecting the regulating of trade, and other business—and did not the Executive, without consulting Congress at all, pay their lodgings for weeks, nay for whole months together? and was not this merely because Indians were unable to pay for themselves? Nobody ever questioned the propriety of that act of charity. Again; when prisoners of war were taken, there was no clause in the Constitution authorizing Congress to provide for their subsistence: yet it was well known that they would not be suffered to starve. Provision was instantly made for them, before we could tell whether the nation to whom they belonged would pay such expenses, or would not pay them. It was very true that an instalment [sic] would soon be due to France, nor did he object to reimbursement in that way, if it could be so obtained. But, in the mean time [sic], relief must be given, for he was convinced that we had still stronger obligations to support the citizens of our allies than either Indians or prisoners of war. In the second place, as to the theory of the Constitution, he referred gentlemen to the first clause of the eighth section of it. By that clause Congress were [sic] warranted to provide for exigencies regarding *the general welfare*, and he was sure this case came under that description. (January 10, 1794, 3rd Cong., 1st sess., 172)

Many of those ordinarily adamant that the Constitution prohibits the government from exercising powers not expressly enumerated in that document admitted they were open to persuasion in this instance. Typical of this position was Nicholas, who initially asserted that an "act of charity, though it would be extremely laudable, was yet beyond their authority," but quickly added that he needed more time to "form a deliberate opinion on the subject" (January 10, 1794, 3rd Cong., 1st sess., 170), practically begging his colleagues to convince him he would not have to violate his own scruples. Later in the debate Nicholas articulated a legislative version of the prerogative power Jefferson would defend in his statements on the duties of the executive in times of emergency. Nicholas said that if he had to vote today, he would vote for the funds, but he would admit that he had "exceeded his powers" and throw himself on the mercy of his constituents (January 10, 1794, 3rd Cong., 1st sess., 172).

Not surprisingly, Madison once again made the strongest case for a narrow reading of the Constitution. Like Jefferson, he doubted the Constitution authorized the federal government to expend money for the relief of exiles. He explained that he

> wished to relieve the sufferers, but was afraid of establishing a dangerous precedent, which might hereafter be perverted to the countenance of purposes very different from those of charity. He acknowledged that he could not undertake to lay his finger on that article in the Federal Constitution which granted a right to Congress of expending, on objects of benevolence, the money of their constituents. And if once they broke down the line laid down before them, for the direction of their conduct, it was impossible to say to what lengths they might go, or to what extremities this practice might be carried. (January 10, 1794, 3rd Cong., 1st sess., 170)

Despite these misgivings, Madison still supported using federal funds to provide charity. He opined that Americans were just as generous as the British, whose Parliament voted to give 100,000 pounds to the victims of the 1755 Lisbon earthquake, but he stated, "This House certainly did not possess an undefined authority correspondent with that of a British Parliament. He wished that some other mode could be devised for assisting the French sufferers than by an act of Congress" (January 10, 1794, 3rd Cong., 1st sess., 171). But rather than stick to his constitutional scruples and vote against federal aid to the French refugees, Madison stated that he needed more time to decide "what line of conduct to pursue" (January 10, 1794, 3rd Cong., 1st sess., 171). Others, including arch-antiadministration critic Giles and staunch Federalist Dexter, agreed that they could use more time to free themselves from their constitutional misgivings (January 10, 1794, 3rd Cong., 1st sess., 173).

When the House resumed the debate on January 28, members were still struggling to come up with some plausible constitutional justification for the assistance they desperately wanted to provide to the refugees. Everyone agreed that considerations of "humanity" or benevolence demanded aid for the refugees, but constitutional doubts continued to agonize a few members. Nicholas reiterated his "compassion for the sufferers" but confessed that he still had not found anything in the Constitution that would allow Congress to provide financial assistance in this case (January 28, 1794, 3rd Cong., 1st sess., 351). He recommended the members of the House give the money requested as an "act of charity," but admit forthrightly that this act would exceed their power (January 28, 1794, 3rd Cong., 1st sess., 351).

Whereas representatives such as Boudinot continued to insist without clarification that the Constitution gave Congress the right to aid the refugees, others offered more specific arguments they hoped would persuade skeptical colleagues. According to one line of reasoning, constitutional limits do not apply in cases of emergency. Clark stated that the extra time helped him come up with a distinction he believed would overcome any constitutional obstacles. Clark suggested matters of life and death supersede ordinary limits on government: "In a case of this kind, we were not to be tied up by the Constitution" (January 28, 1794, 3rd Cong., 1st sess., 350). Another strategy, pursued by Jeffersonian Samuel Smith of Maryland, was to reclassify the assistance as a loan that—it was expected—would be repaid by the French government (January 28, 1794, 3rd Cong., 1st sess., 350). Pennsylvania Federalist Thomas Scott developed a third argument. Instead of considering the requested funds as aid for the distressed refugees, the money could be described as a form of assistance to the residents of Baltimore. If no one would question the federal government's ability to assist a US city from an "army of fighters," reasoned Scott, then no one could challenge its ability to assist such a city from an "army of eaters." Of course, Scott's analogy still begged the question: On what constitutional authority could Congress relieve Americans from economic (as opposed to military) distress? (January 28, 1794, 3rd Cong., 1st sess., 351). The final argument cited recent precedents to justify assistance in this case. Smith reminded his colleagues that Congress repaid both the British consul who had assisted Americans held in captivity in Algiers and a private individual who had aided the crew of an American vessel that ran aground in Portugal (January 28, 1794, 3rd Cong., 1st sess., 351). Smith concluded by suggesting that it would be an embarrassment if Congress were to admit to the "world that we dare not perform an act of benevolence" (January 28, 1794, 3rd Cong., 1st sess., 351), but he cited no specific constitutional authority in support of his position.

At the end of that day's debate the House passed a resolution directing a committee to draw up a bill appropriating funds to assist the exiled Saint-Dominguans. On February 4, 1794, the House passed the bill without debate. It is likely that a solution offered by Madison made it much easier for his allies to endorse the bill without violating their constitutional scruples. He proposed to have any funds used to assist the refugees count as partial payment in fulfillment of the country's outstanding Revolutionary War debt to France.[58] Citing the "humane purposes of this act," the law authorized the president to use up to $15,000 for the relief of persons he thought in need of support, with the money provisionally charged to the government of France (3rd Cong., Appendix, 1417–1418). As it turns out, Congress badly underestimated the extent of the need. The funds were expected to last six months but ran out in just two. For a variety of reasons, including uncertainty surrounding the future of the republican government in France and whether it would actually deduct the amount provided in assistance to refugees as payment toward debt owed to France, Congress did not appropriate any more funds for refugee relief. However, the assistance offered in 1794 would become a precedent cited again and again in future debates over relief to victims of disaster.[59]

The Victims of the Savannah Fire

A similar issue came before the next Congress, but with very different results. On November 26, 1796, a fire in Savannah destroyed well over half the houses in the port city, leaving roughly 400 families homeless. Citing the assistance the 3rd Congress had approved for the relief of the "St. Domingo" refugees less than three years before, South Carolina Federalist William F. Smith introduced a resolution on December 26 to provide assistance to "the sufferers" in Savannah (December 26, 1796, 4th Cong., 2nd sess., 1696).

When the House took up the matter two days later, Smith started off the lengthy discussion by invoking the precedent set by the "St. Domingo" case once again. If the US government could "grant relief to foreigners in distress," he did not see how any "reasonable objection" could be made to helping "our own citizens" (December 28, 1796, 4th Cong., 2nd sess., 1712). In response to concerns that relief in this instance would set an expensive precedent that would put the federal government on the hook every time a disaster struck any part of the country, Smith insisted that this case was entirely different from fires that had destroyed parts of New York and Charleston. In Smith's estimation, this was an "unprecedented calamity" that made the "distress of Savannah . . . more than twenty to one" when compared with other recent disasters (December 28, 1796, 4th Cong., 2nd sess., 1713, 1714). Indeed, Savannah was so badly damaged that any means of relief the city could offer its own residents had been totally destroyed (December 28, 1796, 4th Cong., 2nd sess., 1713).

Those who spoke out in support of Smith's resolution generally echoed his claims about the "unprecedented" nature of this catastrophe. They also extended his claim that the national government has a moral duty to assist those in great distress. They based their claims on a combination of sentiment, justice, and humanity. For instance, fellow Federalist and South Carolinian Robert Goodloe Harper invoked every moral consideration he could think of to make the case for federal assistance: "He believed it a case not merely supported by justice and right, but nearly attached to the finest and most noble feelings of the heart; he believed it would meet the feelings of every man of wisdom to afford relief" (December 28, 1796, 4th Cong., 2nd sess., 1715–1716). Democratic-Republican Rutherford likened the nation to an extended family to support his claim that there is a special obligation to assist any member in great distress (December 28, 1796, 4th Cong., 2nd sess., 1717, 1722). As far as he was concerned, "This idea should be conclusive" (December 28, 1796, 4th Cong., 2nd sess., 1722). Federalist Thomas Hartley of Pennsylvania combined a universalistic appeal to "humanity" with a particularistic appeal to "national honor." If the English government could so generously give 100,000 pounds to the people of Lisbon after the great earthquakes of 1755, there was no good reason for the House to "withhold relief" for the assistance of its own citizens (December 28, 1796, 4th Cong., 2nd sess., 1714).

Sensing that moral considerations might not be enough to convince their colleagues, supporters of assistance also argued that it was in the general interest of the country to aid distressed Savannahans. They did so by pointing out that the city's special status as a "considerable commercial city" affected the general welfare in a unique way (December 28, 1796, 4th Cong., 2nd sess., 1716). Smith and his allies argued that any costs associated with assistance to Savannah's residents would be outweighed by the benefits of restoring the revenue this port city contributed to the national treasury. Refusal to aid Savannah, they argued, would only serve to deprive the nation of much-needed revenue. Besides, the country would get back whatever it spent and more after the city got back to business as usual (December 28, 1796, 4th Cong., 2nd sess., 1718).

Supporters of assistance would have left the Constitution out of the discussion altogether if not forced to address the issue directly. Though a small handful did object to the resolution on policy grounds, alleging that relief in this case would end up making the general government "underwriters to the whole Union," most objections were constitutional in nature (Macon, December 28, 1796, 4th Cong., 2nd sess., 1717). Many participants, including Federalist Aaron Kitchell of New Jersey, Federalist Sitgreaves of Pennsylvania, and Democratic-Republican Claiborne of Virginia (December 28, 1796, 4th Cong., 2nd sess., 1720), seemed genuinely uncertain about what the Constitution actually allowed them to do (December 28, 1796, 4th Cong., 2nd sess., 1714–1715, 1720). A few skeptics were prepared to vote in favor of the resolution based on their perceived moral duty alone, but others asserted that the absence of clear constitutional authorization settled the matter. In characteristically blunt fashion, strict constructionist Giles asserted that they should not consider "what generosity and humanity required, but what the Constitution and their duty required" (December 28, 1796, 4th Cong., 2nd sess., 1724).

The only constitutional language any supporters of the resolution could cite was the general welfare clause. Harper was the only member to advance this argument in a forceful way, but he watered it down by citing precedents that could be defended on other grounds (December 28, 1796, 4th Cong., 2nd sess., 1721).

Georgia representative Baldwin tried a different approach. Instead of pointing to specific language in the Constitution that authorizes Congress to spend money on charity, he discussed the inherent ambiguity and indeterminacy of the text. Adapting claims that had been advanced against ratification of the Constitution, he acknowledged that "it was impossible to obtain absolute directions from it in every case" (December 28, 1796, 4th Cong., 2nd sess., 1721). Although strict constructionists feared that constitutional incompleteness would be subject to abuse, Baldwin (himself a Democratic-Republican) pointed to the many positive—and largely uncontroversial—laws that had already passed without the kind of explicit authorization some were now seeking. He mentioned laws establishing lighthouses, trading houses with Indians, and other acts to "show that though the Constitution was very useful in giving general directions, yet it was not capable of being administered under so rigorous and mechanical a construction as had been sometimes contended for" (December 28, 1796, 4th Cong., 2nd sess., 1722). It was simply unfathomable to Baldwin that the powers of Congress to raise and spend money were limited to the first few purposes listed in Article I, Section 8 but somehow did not include the "general welfare of the United States." He was so sure of this that he turned the tables on his opponents and asked them to explain when they believed the federal government would be justified in providing relief to a distressed part of the country (December 28, 1796, 4th Cong., 2nd sess., 1722).

Nicholas angrily responded that the views of those who, like himself, believed in the "sacredness of the Constitution" had been badly distorted. They had never denied that some degree of latitude in the laws was necessary or claimed "that money should never be expended but for payment of debts or for defence." However, they did insist that the Constitution creates a government of limited and well-defined powers. Nicholas closed his remarks by explaining that the general welfare clause does not permit acts of pure charity. These, he maintained, were reserved to the states. "If the general welfare was to be extended (as it had been insinuated it ought) to objects of charity, it was undefined indeed. Charity was not a proper subject for them to legislate upon; and, if this resolution were to pass, all the power of which they were possessed would not be adequate to raise funds to answer the demands which would be brought against the Treasury" (December 28, 1796, 4th Cong., 2nd sess., 1723).

In the end, the House voted against relief to the refugees by a two-to-one margin. Other than reference to the general welfare clause, no constitutional provision was cited by supporters of the measure. Instead, they cited past precedent (in the case of the Haitian refugees), laudatory foreign examples (England's assistance to the victims of the great Lisbon earthquake), considerations of justice and humanity, and policy benefits (the lost revenue from Savannah's port).

Health Care for Sick and Disabled Seamen

Although victims of disaster during the early years of the Republic could not always count on Congress for aid, the national legislature was often moved to act by the plight of seamen. From the very beginning, the Federal Congress exhibited special concern for the welfare of sailors. Maintaining the well-being of sailors was vital to both the commercial prosperity and national security of a nation that was economically dependent on the transatlantic trade and that relied on ships as the first line of defense in case of war.[60] It should thus come as no surprise that the first labor law ever passed in the United States was designed to improve the working conditions of seamen.[61] Like many other workers on the lowest rungs of the economic ladder, mariners had to contend with the economic hardships brought on by low pay, limited job opportunities, and unsteady seasonal employment. In addition, the nature of their work exposed sailors to a uniquely perilous set of physical dangers and economic insecurities, including the risks of sinking during a storm, attacks from other vessels, exposure to disease in ports and in close quarters on the high seas, and accidents that could result in crippling injury or death. On top of the fact that life expectancy for seamen was much lower than it was for many other laborers, many of them died penniless.[62] Sailors faced such great hardships that Madison made it a topic of discussion in one of the articles he wrote for the Jeffersonian periodical the *National Gazette*:

> The condition, to which the blessings of life are most denied is that of the sailor. His health is continually assailed and his span shortened by the stormy element to which he belongs. . . . In the supply of his wants he often feels a scarcity, seldom more than a bare sustenance. . . . How unfortunate, that in the intercourse, by which nations are enlightened and refined, and their

means of safety extended, the immediate agents should be distinguished by the hardest condition of humanity.[63]

In the first session of the 1st Congress, a committee was appointed to draft a bill "providing for the establishment of hospitals for sick and disabled seamen, and for the regulation of harbors" (July 20, 1789, 1st Cong., 1st sess., 685). There was a British precedent for such an institution in the Greenwich Hospital for disabled seamen established by an act of Parliament in 1696. The US bill was presented to the House in late August and slated for consideration by the committee of the whole on September 15. Unfortunately, the records of the proceedings in the House for that day make no mention of the bill, and no further reference to it appears in the *Annals of Congress* for that term (September 15, 1789, 1st Cong., 1st sess., 927).

On April 17, 1792, near the end of the first session of the 2nd Congress, Hamilton delivered a treasury report that recommended the "establishment of one or more marine Hospitals" on humanitarian and economic grounds. Hamilton stated that the proposal would promote "humanity . . . from its tendency to protect from want and misery, a very useful, and, for the most part, a very needy class of the Community." He added that such a measure would also be advantageous to commerce not only by helping to keep sailors healthy but by attracting them to the profession in the first place. Hamilton proposed that the plan could be funded through a monthly deduction of ten cents from the wages of each seaman. The treasury secretary also recommended that the benefits of the fund "extend, not only to disabled and decrepid [sic] seamen, but to the widows and children of those who may have been killed or drowned, in the course of their service as seamen."[64]

The 2nd Congress took up Hamilton's proposal in its next session. During the debate on a proposal to protect US commerce by increasing the number of American seamen, Williamson recommended that Congress also act to provide medical care to "sick and infirm sailors" (November 19, 1792, 2nd Cong., 2nd sess., 694). Appealing to the "cause of humanity," Williamson proposed that funds left over from tonnage duties could be used to establish public hospitals in two or three major cities to care for these seamen. Citing legislation recently passed in his home state of North Carolina as a potential model, he then proposed a system of wage deductions to help defray expenses: "This fund, however, being contingent, and at most very inadequate to the general use of seamen, it may be necessary to make a small stoppage of their wages as a uniform and certain fund for the support of those very persons when they are sick" (November 19, 1792, 2nd Cong., 2nd sess., 695).

The House appointed a proadministration committee consisting of Williamson, Laurance, Benjamin Goodhue of Massachusetts, Benjamin Bourne of Rhode Island, and Robert Barnwell of South Carolina to draft a bill. According to the *Annals of Congress*, a bill was presented by Williamson's committee and referred to the committee of the whole on January 21, 1793 (2nd Cong., 2nd sess., 830).[65] The House took no further action on the matter until it received a memorial from the merchants and inhabitants of Norfolk and Portsmouth, Virginia, complaining of the "inconvenience under which they labor from the number of sick and disabled seamen that daily frequent that port, and praying that a tax may be imposed upon all vessels or seamen, for the purpose of establishing, in or near the seaport towns of the United States, marine hospitals, for the reception and support of sick and disabled seamen." The memorial was referred to the committee of the whole, which was supposed to take up Williamson's bill (February 8, 1793, 2nd Cong., 2nd sess., 868). Perhaps because the House was so busy with other business, including an appropriations bill, the repayment of loans, and a highly partisan inquiry into Hamilton's official conduct as secretary of the treasury instigated by Giles, it did not return to the subject before the end of the session.[66]

The subject of health care for sick and disabled seamen would come before Congress again (e.g., December 4, 1794, 3rd Cong., 2nd sess., 956), but it was not until the second session of the 5th Congress that meaningful progress was made. On November 29, 1797, the House agreed to a resolution to make deductions from the wages of seamen to establish hospitals and care for their sick and disabled numbers (5th Cong., 2nd sess., 655).

Over the next few months, the House would hear reports from the committee responsible for working out the details, but a full debate did not take place until April 10, 1798. The bill provided that every seaman would pay twenty cents per month out of his wages to provide for the establishment of hospitals and the relief of sick and disabled seamen. Speakers on both sides of the issue expressed deep concern for the well-being of sailors. What seemed to divide them was not any difference of constitutional opinion but a difference of economic interests.

Sewall kicked off the discussion by raising objections to the redistributive effects of the bill. Sewall supported the humanitarian objectives of the bill, but he vigorously disagreed with the methods proposed to achieve those ends. In particular, Sewall objected to the fact that sailors from his home state of Massachusetts would end up paying for a nationwide system of health care that they did not need. He pointed out that some parts of the country, including his own state, already had a system in place to take care of ailing sailors. He suggested that it would be unfair to sailors from any part of the country that had already taken the initiative to address their well-being to have to pay into the one proposed because they would be made to pay twice without any further advantage to themselves (April 10, 1798, 5th Cong., 2nd sess., 1386). Sewall continued along these lines by suggesting that seamen as a class would end up subsidizing the construction of hospitals they would never get to use. Sailors would be the ones supplying all of the funding, but, "in all probability, will receive no advantages from it for fifty years to come, as large and splendid buildings must first be erected, in order to exhibit to the world a specimen of public charity" (April 10, 1798, 5th Cong., 2nd sess., 1386).

Even though Sewall objected to the possibility that sailors from his region of the country would be subject to what he described as a double tax, he perceived no moral or constitutional problems with general public support for sailors. Sewall stated that "he doubted the propriety of taxing seamen only for the support of what ought to be considered a public charity. He thought the laws of reason and charity called upon the public at large in support of unfortunate men of this description, and that the burden ought not to be laid exclusively upon them" (April 10, 1798. 5th Cong., 2nd sess., 1386). Sewall provided no direct constitutional justification for this proposal, but the implication was that the relief of sailors was conducive to the general welfare.

Thomas Pinckney, a Federalist representative from South Carolina, understood Sewall as arguing that the bill would tax a "particular description of men for a general object" (April 10, 1798, 5th Cong., 2nd sess., 1387). If the bill was objectionable because the so-called eastern states already made provisions for sick and disabled seamen, Pinckney suggested that the establishment of a national program would relieve citizens from those states of the burden of supporting the existing systems. Pinckney did not contest Sewall's claim that health care for sailors "would operate [as] a general benefit to the Union," but he did insist that it was "only reasonable and equitable that these persons should pay for the benefit which they were themselves to receive, and that it would be neither just nor fair for other persons to pay it" (April 10, 1798, 5th Cong., 2nd sess., 1387). However, Pinckney did not think sailors would ultimately pay the costs of the program anyway. The costs of the tax, he surmised, would get passed on to consumers in the form of higher prices for merchandise (April 10, 1798, 5th Cong., 2nd sess., 1387).

Democratic-Republican Edward Livingston of New York observed that Pinckney had satisfactorily addressed Sewall's concerns, but he offered additional arguments to justify the program. Livingston maintained that no place that already provided relief to sick and disabled sailors should have any reason to complain because the president would be authorized to reimburse any money spent for that purpose. Livingston also disputed Sewall's suggestion that any sailors would demur at the program. He pointed out that the maritime industry received numerous special benefits from being a part of the Union, including bounties given to fishing vessels (April 10, 1798, 5th Cong., 2nd sess., 1388). However, he then went on to develop perhaps the most paternalistic argument made in the House of Representatives up to that point. It was an argument that relied on a number of stereotypes about the irresponsibility of those who end up in the maritime profession. Because a sailor tends to be a "careless" (carefree) type "concerned only for the present, and is incapable of thinking of, or inattentive to, future welfare; he is, therefore, a proper object for the care of Government, and whilst he can provide an asylum for infirmity or old age, by the sacrifices of a few gills of rum, he will not scruple to do it" (April 10, 1798, 5th Cong., 2nd sess., 1388).

Sewall angrily objected to the paternalistic tone of Livingston's remarks. Sewall asserted that sailors were perfectly capable of taking care of themselves but insisted that he was just looking after their financial interests to make sure they were not paying twice into an otherwise appealing health-care system. Sewall's comments amounted to a balance sheet of costs and benefits involving American seamen. On balance, any benefits American sailors already received or would receive were far outweighed by the benefits they provided to the nation as a whole, so it would be wrong to ask them to contribute any more, even to their own health care. For starters, American seamen were being asked to subsidize hospitals that would also care for foreign sailors (April 10, 1798, 5th Cong., 2nd sess., 1389). In addition, if the fishing industry did receive bounties exceeding what it paid for salt to cure fish, it was still worth the benefits it provided to the nation, especially in times of crisis. Sewall also questioned the claim that New England sailors would benefit from the program by pointing out that they rarely sailed to southern ports. Instead, they exported their catches. Sewall concluded his account with the claim that the tax "would also fall heaviest upon those seamen who have families and are fixed in the country. A foreigner could afford a small deduction from his wages; but a native seaman, with a family, could not afford it" (April 10, 1798, 5th Cong., 2nd sess., 1390).

Parker expressed great disappointment that Sewall took such a parochial view of the subject. He was "sorry" Sewall was looking out only for the financial interests of sailors in his home state but ignoring the needs of sailors in the rest of the country. In Parker's view, the nation had a responsibility to give all of its sailors some sense of security. He recommended that the United States follow the example of Great Britain, which provided its sailors "Greenwich Hospital as an asylum when all his toils are over." "He hoped, therefore, the sailors of this country would not be left to the doubtful benevolence of others; but that, by passing this bill, a permanent relief might be afforded them in case of sickness, disability, or old age" (April 10, 1798, 5th Cong., 2nd sess., 1391).

Sewall's fellow Massachusetts representative, Democratic-Republican Varnum, was the first to raise a constitutional challenge to the bill. Varnum reiterated Sewall's suggestion that the public as a whole ought to pay for the program if sailors were deemed more important than other classes of individuals, but he questioned the government's power to tax one class of individuals even if it was to pay for a program benefiting that group. Varnum also suggested this was a matter best left to the individual states, asking whether "this kind of tax was consistent with federal principles" (April 10, 1798, 5th Cong., 2nd sess., 1391).

Gallatin was the final speaker to weigh in with substantive points. Whereas the representatives from Massachusetts betrayed their narrow sectional interests in opposing the bill, Gallatin raised objections consistent with the principles he had invoked in other debates.

After confessing that the novelty of the measure inclined him to vote against it, Gallatin explained that his general disposition was to vote against any measure when he was unconvinced of the "positive good" likely to arise from it (April 10, 1798, 5th Cong., 2nd sess., 1392). Like Sewall, he also objected to paternalistic assumptions that sailors were more needful of public assistance than other groups. In addition, Gallatin challenged the value of hospitals in general, but said that "supposing the institution to be a good one, he thought it better to leave the business as at present, and suffer this class of people to provide for themselves, or to be provided for in the same way in which other poor and sick or disabled persons are supported" (April 10, 1798, 5th Cong., 2nd sess., 1392). The Democratic-Republican leader then added a constitutional objection. Though "he was inclined to provide relief to sailors," Gallatin argued that the means of raising the funds was impermissible. He said he was opposed to a "tax upon labor, which would, in all cases be a capitation tax" (April 10, 1798, 5th Cong., 2nd sess., 1392).

Gallatin and his allies managed to get a postponement of the bill, but it would be for naught. On April 12, the House approved the bill for the relief of sick sailors with fifty-nine votes in favor (5th Cong., 2nd sess., 1402). "An Act for the Relief of Sick and Disabled Seamen" passed Congress on July 16, 1798 (5th Cong., Appendix, 3787). The marine hospital system that emerged would provide medical treatment to hundreds of thousands of sailors and contribute to the development of general hospitals throughout the country during the nineteenth century.[67]

Conclusion

The temptation to look to the founding for definitive answers to contemporary political questions is very strong. On a few matters, members of the generation that created and implemented the Constitution did speak with a unified voice. However, in most cases they were very much like political actors today: they disagreed vigorously on the political, ideological, economic, moral, and constitutional foundations and implications of the issues they debated. Like disagreements today, disagreements then were grounded in an ever-changing mix of passion, personality, interest, and principle. The meaning and application of the Constitution were hotly contested even by those who participated in its creation.

Nevertheless, the debates that took place over taxes, the militia, commerce, and other contentious issues are still instructive. What these debates show is that members of the first few Congresses agreed on the legitimacy and significance of certain considerations even when they could not agree on the scope of their constitutional authority. Even if they failed to promote economic equality in particular instances, they accepted it as a valid basis for policy making. The United States was far from being the egalitarian country so many Americans imagined, but the relative equality that prevailed among free citizens compared with conditions in the countries of Europe was a mark of distinction members of Congress hoped to preserve. Although they were sometimes unprepared to take affirmative steps to reduce economic inequality, more often than not they sought to avoid policies that would exacerbate existing levels of economic inequality. In that respect, republicanism in this period was defined as much by what law makers sought to avoid as it was by what they sought to achieve.

6

"SILENTLY LESSENING THE INEQUALITY OF PROPERTY"

Thomas Jefferson on the Government's Role in Reducing Economic Inequality

The triumph of Thomas Jefferson and his supporters in the bitterly contested election of 1800 seemed to signify a repudiation of the expansive and potentially expensive role of government envisioned by Alexander Hamilton and his allies in Congress. After all, it was Jefferson who articulated the doctrine of strict constructionism as an alternative to Hamilton's theory of loose construction of the Constitution, spearheaded the fight against the establishment of a national bank, and championed the interests of the states against the encroachments of the federal government. For these reasons, Jefferson is often cited by those who argue that efforts to address economic inequality exceed the constitutional authority of the national government. Although Jefferson is today invoked by political actors from across the ideological spectrum to support an immense variety of causes and positions, perhaps no invocation of this founder is more common in contemporary US politics than a reference to one of his many critical comments on the appropriate size and limits of the federal government. His statements on the excesses of big government have become shibboleths among those who favor a more limited role for government, especially on questions of income and wealth distribution.[1] Critics of the welfare state often quote Jefferson's statements in favor of small, decentralized government and point out that the Declaration of Independence asserts only an unalienable right to "the *pursuit* of Happiness," not a guarantee of any particular outcome in life.[2]

Assertions of Jefferson's supposed hostility to state action to redress economic inequality are not limited to politicians and polemicists. Numerous scholars have also argued that the Virginian would have opposed central pillars of the modern welfare state based on a small government ideology that demands low taxes, frugality in government, and a strict interpretation of constitutional powers.[3] Citing Jefferson's concerns about the dependency engendered by modern market relations, Jean Yarbrough suggests that a "modern-day Jeffersonian" should be troubled by the way "middle-class college students, elderly retirees, the working poor, large-scale corporations, newly arrived immigrants . . . [and] even Jefferson's beloved farmers, all depend on some form of government preferment and/or assistance to insulate them from the risks of daily living."[4] David Mayer contends that the only kinds of economic inequalities that really mattered to Jefferson were "great disparities in wealth" such as those that obtained in Europe.[5] Michael Zuckert argues that even the lofty-sounding pronouncements on human equality contained in the Declaration of Independence merely denied "natural" claims of authority over other persons, so they provide no justification or "mandate for equality of condition." After surveying Jefferson's other writings, Zuckert concludes, "Jefferson's commitment to natural equality and to democratic republicanism does not extend to a commitment to social or economic equality."[6]

Although Jefferson's strict constructionist approach does lend some support to contentions that the US Constitution gives the federal government few if any explicit powers to reduce economic inequality, it would be a mistake to conclude Jefferson was opposed in principle to governmental efforts to minimize economic inequality based on what he had to say about constitutional interpretation. Far from exhibiting hostility to redistributive policies of the kind that generate the most vehement opposition in US politics today, many of Jefferson's writings and signature reforms indicate that minimizing economic inequality was always an important political objective for this founder.

Considerations of charity and benevolence figured into Jefferson's support for measures designed to reduce economic inequality, but his primary reasons were political. Maintaining a degree of economic equality was not an end in itself but a means of preserving political liberty. Jefferson's thinking on the relationship between economic inequality and political freedom reflected and extended both republican and liberal ideas about the preconditions necessary for the effective exercise of individual freedom. In fact, Jefferson believed that strict adherence to a Lockean natural rights philosophy sometimes *requires* affirmative measures to minimize economic inequality. Almost every time he addressed the existence of economic inequality, he described this condition as both a moral and a political problem that calls for state action. Many of the policies he championed—including the establishment of free public education at the local level, a more equal distribution of land to all adult males in his home state of Virginia, and the acquisition of the Louisiana Territory—were designed to create and maintain the conditions for equal opportunity in the United States. Jefferson's preferred means of dealing with the problem of economic inequality was to establish policies that would prevent it from developing in the first place, but he was also willing to adopt measures that would reduce it after the fact.

There were certainly limits to and contradictions in Jefferson's position on equality on questions of race and gender, but when it came to questions of economic inequality among white men, the wealthy Virginia planter was deeply troubled by the implications of inequality for the moral character of individuals and the health of political institutions. In keeping with centuries of republican thought, Jefferson recognized that severe economic inequality is incompatible with free and democratic government because it contributes to "patterns of domination and dependence."[7] Any vertical ordering of society based on artificial distinctions was abhorrent to Jefferson because it threatened the conditions necessary for the maintenance of freedom and independence.[8]

A full examination of Jefferson's views on governmental responses to economic inequality is important not only because his authority is so commonly invoked—and so often distorted—in contemporary debates but also because his reflections show how civic republican and Lockean liberal ideas could be combined to support egalitarian policies ranging from the establishment of a progressive tax system to the redistribution of property. In proposing reforms that would make landed property and education more widely available, for instance, Jefferson developed an analysis of the structural causes of inequality that actually builds on and affirms the very same Lockean rights some contemporary critics of the welfare state claim are threatened by governmental efforts to address economic disparities.[9] Although Jefferson failed to address or even acknowledge certain forms of inequality, many of the reforms he advocated aimed to prevent extremes of economic inequality from developing in the first place.

Poverty and Inequality in Comparative Perspective

As is true of his stance on many issues, Jefferson's record on equality is mixed. Despite his proclamation that "all men are created equal," he harbored racist views toward blacks and did little toward the end of his life to abolish slavery.[10] When asked about the education of women, the southern gentleman confessed that the topic "has never been a subject of systematic contemplation with me."[11] In addition, even though he often professed his admiration for Native Americans as equal to and in some instances even superior to whites, Jefferson tolerated policies that perpetuated their subordination and marginalization.

However, when it came to white men, the patrician planter was an unqualified and consistent proponent of equality. During and after his career in public service Jefferson supported policies that would help make the ideal that "all men are created equal" a reality. That commitment to egalitarianism led to support for institutional reforms that would expand the right to vote and hold office and to economic reforms that would narrow the gap between those at the top and bottom.

As noted in the introduction of this book, it was not unusual for Americans of the founding generation to boast of the liberties and rights they enjoyed compared with their disadvantaged European counterparts. Thomas Paine's proposition in *Common Sense* that America could provide an "asylum" for freedom expressed a sentiment that would come to define the American sense of exceptionalism.[12] However, for Jefferson, the general state of economic equality (at least among white men) was perhaps just as important in defining the United States and setting the country apart from the rest of the world. For him, equality was both the objective political condition of life in the United States and one of its great moral and political objectives.

Never missing an opportunity to demonstrate American superiority to the benighted and corrupt nations of Europe, Jefferson frequently pointed to equality of conditions as a source of pride and mark of distinction. His extensive—and sometimes overblown—claims in this regard show that economic equality ranked very high in his value system because of how much it contributed to the political and social well-being of the country. His appreciation for the contributions economic equality made to American greatness only grew during the time he spent in Europe as a diplomat. Whereas conditions in Europe were so "deplorable" that "every man here must be either the hammer or the anvil," the situation in his native country was so propitious that "happiness . . . is enjoyed in America, by every class of people."[13] While a few in the Old World live in such opulence that it cannot but "dazzle the bulk of spectators," the tranquil blessings of life in the New World are enjoyed by "most of it's [sic] inhabitants."[14] The difference was so great, in fact, that the "poor of Europe" were willing to indenture themselves for up to three years just for the chance to "better their condition."[15]

One of the things that has hampered recognition of Jefferson's egalitarianism when it comes to wealth and income distribution is that he seldom acknowledged the existence of economic inequality in the United States.[16] In fact, he seemed happily oblivious to the existence of significant poverty and inequality in the United States throughout his entire adult life. Typical of this naiveté was his flat assertion to Jean Nicolas Démeunier, "There is no such thing in this country as what would be called wealth in Europe."[17] Much as Alexis de Tocqueville would later insist that there was basic "equality of conditions" in the United States because there was no such thing as a fixed class system established and enforced by laws that protected the rich and suppressed the poor,[18] Jefferson explained approvingly, "The richest are but a little at ease, and obliged to pay the most rigorous attention to their affairs to keep them together."[19] Conveniently ignoring the existence of slavery, he boasted that the only "distinction between man and man [that] had ever been known" in the United States originated solely from the electoral choices of voters. As a result, the "poorest labourer stood on equal ground with the wealthiest Millionary [sic]."[20]

Although Jefferson's description of actual economic conditions in the United States seriously underestimated the extent of inequality and completely overlooked the existence of poverty—especially in urban centers—his idealizations do provide important insights into his views on inequality. Jefferson's unvarying depiction of the distribution of wealth in the United States throughout the decades, regardless of fluctuations in the business cycle and transformations in the economy, suggests that he allowed his political predilections to color his empirical observations. In fact, he presented his ideal distribution of wealth in terms of the conditions that (he believed) prevailed in the United States. In one letter, he proudly described the United States as an overwhelmingly middle-class country where "we have no Paupers" and the "few" who can be called rich possess only "moderate wealth" and "know nothing of what the Europeans call luxury." After concluding that virtually every inhabitant enjoyed a life of modest comfort, Jefferson asked a question that gives the clearest answer to his own views on economic inequality: "Can any condition of society be more desirable than this?"[21] Even though Jefferson's characterizations of the United States as a country with nonexistent or negligible class differences were false, they are indicative of what he believed a healthy political system ought to look like.

Whenever Jefferson did confront the existence of economic inequality, he left no doubt that it spawned a festering sore on the body politic. His anxieties about the negative social and political consequences of economic inequality are expressed most poignantly in those accounts of life in Europe he composed during his diplomatic service abroad. The condition of the lower orders in France was a source of great consternation: "Of twenty millions of people supposed to be in France I am of [the] opinion there are nineteen millions more wretched, more accursed in every circumstance of human existence, than the most conspicuously wretched individual of the whole United states [sic]."[22] Although Jefferson tended to downplay the extent of the violence that convulsed France during its Revolution, he tended to play up the extent of misery and hunger that afflicted its poor.[23] He directed most of his disapproving remarks at France, but no part of Europe was spared from his criticism. The "transition from ease and opulence to extreme poverty . . . between the Dutch and Prussian territories" was "remarkable" enough for Jefferson to record it in his travel journals,[24] but it was only in his epistolary accounts of life in Europe that he seriously considered the causes and consequences of such differences.[25]

Jefferson touched on the deleterious effects of economic inequality in nearly every letter in which the subject came up. Among other things, inequality contributed to and sustained the misery and oppression of the lower orders, stimulated vice and corruption in the upper classes, and undermined the public welfare. However, the worst consequence was the way in which disparities in wealth enabled the rich to "prey" on the poor.[26] In his view, extreme forms of economic inequality sustain and even create the conditions that make domination possible. In these reflections on inequality in

Europe, Jefferson first began to understand how concentrations of wealth often translate into concentrations of power that could be abused to exploit and reinforce the disadvantages of the lower orders. As Hannah Arendt argued, Jefferson doubted that individuals mired in such miserable conditions (as in France) were capable of maintaining a free system of government.[27] Humanitarian concerns for the plight of the poor were always part of Jefferson's critique of inequality, but political concerns for the fate of liberty generally predominated. Even in passing he would note that poverty in Europe was associated with the evils of ignorance, superstition, and "oppression of body and mind in every form."[28] Long after he last laid eyes on Europe the erstwhile traveler continued to draw attention to the fact that the adverse impact of economic inequality on liberty makes it a serious political concern. Comparing conditions in the United States to those in Great Britain while the War of 1812 was still being waged, Jefferson argued that high levels of inequality make it easier for the ruling classes to transform the poor into instruments of their own oppression. Desperate to provide for themselves and left with few other means of support, the poor in Britain often end up seeking employment as soldiers, thereby "furnish[ing] materials" for military aggression abroad as well as social and political oppression at home.[29] Jefferson reiterated these ideas a decade later under very different circumstances. In explaining why people suffered from so many hardships under hereditary and ecclesiastical governments, he noted that "poverty" had been employed as a political tool of subjugation.[30] Moreover, the "inequalities" those hierarchical systems of government produced have "exposed liberty to sufferance."[31]

Though Jefferson was able to give fairly consistent explanations of the negative effects of economic inequality, he did not always provide explanations of its causes. When he did venture possible explanations, the prime suspects were usually specific government policies, not market forces or individual differences. Sometimes he would assign blame to an unfair system of taxation that placed disproportionate burdens on laborers and the poor. For instance, his explanation—and justification—of the "high fermentation" that existed in Paris on the eve of the French Revolution focused on the abuses the people suffered under the "weight of their taxes, and inequality of their distribution."[32] More often than not, though, the biggest culprit was the unequal and unjust distribution of land maintained by a pernicious combination of law and tradition.

Jefferson's most extensive discussion of the evils of economic in-equality appears in a letter he wrote to James Madison while he was serving as ambassador to France. Unlike other letters in which he pondered the oppressive and unequal conditions of life for the lower orders in Europe, this one went much further in diagnosing the causes and effects of "that unequal division of property which occasions the numberless instances of wretchedness which I had ob-served in this country and is to be observed all over Europe."[33] (The letter also inspired its recipient to speculate on the causes of pov-erty and reflect on the negative consequences of economic inequal-ity.[34]) Few of Jefferson's letters have generated as much scholarly disagreement as this one. Whereas some use the letter to support the claim that Jefferson sought a radical democratic alternative to liberal market society,[35] others see no reason it would support "radically egalitarian or redistributionist measures."[36] There is not enough evi-dence in this letter (or any of Jefferson's other writings) to support any claim that he sought a wholesale replacement for liberal market society, but there is ample evidence Jefferson was open to radical redistributive measures in extreme circumstances.

Jefferson informed Madison that his reflections were prompted by a conversation about the "conditions of the laboring poor" he started with a "poor woman" who was traveling in the same direction. He began his account by noting that property in France is "absolutely concentrated in very few hands." He conceded that these concentra-tions of wealth did create various job opportunities in manufactur-ing, commerce, and husbandry, but in drawing attention to the fact that the wealthy "employ the flower of the country as servants" Jefferson seemed to imply that the labor of these servants might have been squandered in such employment. The thought that so many were dependent on a class of idle aristocrats for their liveli-hoods seemed particularly offensive. Indeed, Jefferson's entire public career can be described as a sustained assault on various forms of economic and political dependence because it exposed the depen-dent to material insecurity and made them vulnerable to social and political manipulation. Whether he intended to convey any negative judgments about the way their labor was employed, Jefferson left no doubt that this concentration of wealth deprived the vast majority of economic opportunity. In his estimation, the "most numerous of all classes" was composed of the "poor who cannot find work." He confessed to being puzzled by the fact that "so many should be permitted to beg who are willing to work, in a country where there is a very considerable proportion of uncultivated lands." Then it dawned on him that such concentrations of wealth often lead to unproductive uses of land that reinforce existing class hierarchies. Instead of using the land for cultivation, which would create more food and opportunities for the poor to better their condition, the land is left "undisturbed" so the rich can hunt game and enjoy other forms of unproductive recreation.[37]

At this point Jefferson turned to possible solutions. Though he failed to provide specific details about how any ameliorative measures would actually work, he made it clear "this enormous inequality produc[ed] so much misery to the bulk of mankind" that a governmental response was urgently required. He immediately ruled out an "equal division of property" as "impracticable," but he opened the door to other redistributive measures, including revisions to inheritance laws, the establishment of a progressive tax system, guaranteed employment for the poor, and allotments of land to the unemployed. The condition of the poor in Europe was so desperate that

> legislators cannot invent too many devices for subdividing property, only taking care to let their subdivisions go hand in hand with the natural affections of the human mind. The descent of property of every kind therefore to all the children, or to all the brothers and sisters, or other relations in equal degree is a politic measure, and a practicable one. Another means of silently lessening the inequality of property is to exempt all from taxation below a certain point, and to tax the higher portions of property in geometrical progression as they rise. Whenever there is in any country, uncultivated lands and unemployed poor, it is clear that the laws of property have been so far extended as to violate natural right. The earth is given as a common stock for man to labour and live on. If, for the encouragement of industry we allow it to be appropriated, we must take care that other employment be furnished to those excluded from the appropriation. If we do not, the fundamental right to labour the earth returns to the unemployed. It is too soon yet in our country to say that every man who cannot find employment but who can

find uncultivated land, shall be at liberty to cultivate it, paying a moderate rent. But it is not too soon to provide by every possible means that as few as possible shall be without a little portion of land.[38]

One of most remarkable things about this account is that Jefferson criticized accumulations of property under (feudal) conditions of government in terms very similar to those John Locke had used to defend limits on the accumulation of property in the state of nature. Neither Locke nor Jefferson raised any fundamental objections to the unequal ownership of property—indeed, the very point of Locke's chapter "Of Property" in *The Second Treatise of Government* was to explain and justify "disproportionate and unequal Possession of the Earth"[39]—but both acknowledged that there were limits to how far this inequality could go without violating basic moral principles.

Even though Locke sought to demonstrate that vast accumulations of wealth are morally justifiable on natural law grounds, he pointed to a number of different ways in which those same laws of nature set limits on appropriation.[40] As he put it, "The same Law of Nature, that does by this means give us Property, does also *bound* that *Property*."[41] This is because the right of an individual to appropriate stems from an inherent natural right to the labor of one's own body that is itself subordinate to the fundamental natural law requirement to preserve human life: "Every one [*sic*] as he is *bound to preserve himself*... so by the like reason when his own Preservation comes not in competition, ought he, as much as he can, *to preserve the rest of Mankind*."[42]

This first fundamental law of nature helps explain both the right of appropriation and the limits within which it operates. According to Locke, there are at least three restrictions on the accumulation of property.[43] First is the "spoilage" limitation. Because the earth was given to humans for their enjoyment, any acquisition beyond what an individual can actually use or consume is unjust, for "nothing was made by God for Man to spoil or destroy."[44] Next is the "sufficiency" limitation. This prohibits appropriations that would violate the rights—and duties—of others to self-preservation. Appropriation is permissible only if "there was still enough, and as good left" to others.[45] Finally, there is what Jeremy Waldron labels a "charity" limitation. This permits individuals in desperate circumstances to avail themselves of the property of those who enjoy material comfort: *"Charity* gives every Man a Title to so much out of another's Plenty, as will keep him from extream [*sic*] want, where he has no means to subsist otherwise."[46] In each of these cases, the natural right to life overrides the natural right to otherwise unlimited and unequal accumulations of property.

Like natural law theorists before him, Locke insisted that the laws of nature never change or expire, but the conditions in which they operate vary. In Locke's view, changing circumstances, including technological developments and other innovations, have the potential to render natural law restrictions on human action moot. As Locke went on to argue in his chapter on property, the invention of money enables the propertied to get around the problem of spoilage by allowing them to accumulate wealth in a form that is nonperishable. In addition, because labor accounts for the lion's share of value that exists in the world—perhaps as much as 99 percent, by Locke's generous estimation—it tends to "increase the common stock of mankind" so much that it overcomes the requirement to leave "enough, and as good" as to others.[47] That is to say, the compensation that those without property receive for being deprived of land is the enormous surplus agricultural output that exclusive ownership of property tends to produce.

Although Locke seemed satisfied that these changes are sufficient to overcome most moral constraints on the accumulation of wealth, Jefferson's remarks to Madison suggest that the natural rights of the poor were not adequately protected under existing social and legal arrangements. In making this argument, Jefferson revealed he was much more alert than his philosophical hero to the possibility that violations of natural rights would occur in mature economic systems.

The long quote by Jefferson above contains loud and instantly recognizable echoes of Locke's discussion of property, from the references to "natural right" and the "fundamental right to labour the earth" to the claim that the "earth is given as a common stock for man to labour and live on." Beyond these terminological and rhetorical similarities is a line of reasoning that is also distinctly Lockean. Like Locke, Jefferson acknowledged the legitimacy of unequal possessions. However, the American seemed to imply that property rights are conventional, not natural, by making the appropriation of the earth conditional (*"if* . . . we allow it to be appropriated").[48] The significance of this difference cannot be downplayed, but it does not undermine Jefferson's fundamental agreement with Locke on the moral limitations on economic inequality. Jefferson emphasized the benefits to others (i.e., the unpropertied) when, like Locke, he suggested that the "encouragement of industry" is one of the factors that justifies appropriation and the inevitable inequality that results. Finally, and most importantly, Jefferson also recognized that there are fundamental moral limitations on this very same inequality. Implicit yet unmistakable in Jefferson's remarks is a preoccupation with the sufficiency limitation. Contrary to what Locke had argued (and what might have been predicted), the appropriation of land in France did not improve the welfare of everyone by leading to increases in agricultural output. In fact, it perpetuated the impoverishment of the unpropertied because land was used for the sport of aristocrats rather than the production of food. In Jefferson's view, this clear-cut violation of the natural right of French commoners to have "enough, and as good left" to them justified the redistributive measures he proposed. For when the right to property conflicts with or even threatens the right to life, Jefferson left no doubt which had to yield.[49]

As his list of possible policy responses indicates, Jefferson's preferred approach to dealing with such extremes of inequality was legislative. In most cases of extreme inequality, government intervention would suffice to rectify any resulting injustices. Jefferson gave no indication that the establishment of different tax rates—indeed, the exemption of those below a certain level from taxes altogether—ran afoul of any legal or political principles, such as the rule of law. In fact, he expressed approval of the tax system adopted by Congress shortly after the Constitution went into effect because the duties on imports "fall principally on the rich."[50] As president he reiterated his support for progressive taxation on numerous occasions. For instance, because the government's receipts were exceeding expenses, he proposed in his sixth annual message to Congress that the impost on salt, a "necessary of life," be eliminated but urged the continuance of duties "levied chiefly on luxuries."[51] Despite his preference for low taxes, Jefferson favored higher taxes on the wealthy. As he stated in a letter to Albert Gallatin, he "wish[ed] it were possible to increase the impost on any articles affecting the rich chiefly."[52] In retirement, Jefferson expressed hopes that the elimination of the national debt and the domestic manufacture of salt would result in the elimination of taxes on everything but imported luxuries so that the "farmer will see his government supported, his children educated, & the face of his country made a paradise by the contributions of the rich alone without his being called on to spare a cent from his earnings."[53] Jefferson added that a tax on imports that "falls exclusively on the rich, [combined] with the equal partition of intestate's estates, constitute[s] the best agrarian law."[54]

However, if the government failed to reduce or prevent extreme forms of economic inequality, Jefferson was open to much more direct and radical action by the people themselves: "If we do not [provide adequate means of employment], the fundamental right to labour the earth returns to the unemployed."[55] Jefferson's language is somewhat ambiguous, but it holds out the possibility that those who lack the means to provide for themselves might be entitled to take unused or misused land from unproductive landholders, as the Lockean "charity" principle prescribes. In light of Jefferson's expressions of support for popular uses of violence during Shays's Rebellion, the French Revolution, and the Whiskey Rebellion, it is possible he contemplated the seizure of unproductive land by force. To be sure, his remarks were restricted to the extremes of economic inequality that existed in France on the eve of its Revolution,[56] but they reveal a Jefferson far more willing to accept redistributive measures than his reputation as a champion of property rights would suggest.

Limited Government and Remedies for the Problem of Inequality

Jefferson's reflections on the distribution of property in Europe offer important indications of his views on the legitimacy of economic inequality, but they do not necessarily tell us about the kinds of actions he believed government in the United States could or should take to minimize economic disparities. Jefferson's small-government ideology and narrow reading of the national government's constitutional powers would seem to suggest that his solutions to the problem of economic inequality in the Old World had little if any bearing on American debates.

Many of Jefferson's own words and deeds would suggest that his reflections on European inequality had no applicability in an American context. The notion that the government has either the responsibility or the authority to minimize economic inequality seems to fly in the face of Jefferson's well-known antipathy to what would be called an active or interventionist government. After all, the political party he helped found was formed in direct opposition to the centralizing tendencies of Hamilton's financial system. Jefferson gave powerful expression to his small-government principles in his first Inaugural Address, in which he concluded his catalogue of the ingredients of "good government" with a ringing endorsement of laissez-faire: "A wise and frugal government, which shall restrain men from injuring one another, shall leave them otherwise free to regulate their own pursuits of industry and improvement, and shall not take from the mouth of labor the bread it has earned."[57] In addition, his principles of constitutional construction limit the powers of the federal government to those expressly provided in the text. As he famously argued in his "Opinion on the Constitutionality of a National Bank,"

> The constitution allows only the means which are "necessary" not those which are merely "convenient" for effecting the enumerated powers. If such a latitude of construction be allowed to this phrase as to give any non-enumerated power, it will go to every one [*sic*], for there is no one which ingenuity may not torture into a *convenience, in some way or other*, to *some one* of so long a list of enumerated powers. It would swallow up all the delegated powers, and reduce the whole to one power, as before observed.[58]

Jefferson's opposition to inventive, or "loose," constructions of the Constitution was so severe that he raised questions about the constitutionality of the excise tax,[59] contended that a constitutional amendment would be required to fund internal improvements, and even expressed doubts about the constitutionality of his own Louisiana Purchase.

In addition to his assertions that the powers and functions of the government were narrowly defined, Jefferson sometimes seemed to express reservations about, if not outright antagonism toward, the idea of adopting redistributive policies in the United States. Conservatives often cite a passage in his second Inaugural Address in which the third president affirmed that his administration would maintain "that state of property, equal or unequal, which results to every man from his own industry, or that of his fathers [*sic*]."⁶⁰ Scholars such as Yarbrough can also point to places in which Jefferson denied the idea that an individual could have "too much" property. For instance, in a letter to Joseph Milligan, Jefferson stated, "To take from one, be- cause it is thought that his own industry and that of his fathers [*sic*] has acquired too much, in order to spare to others, who, or whose fathers have not exercised equal industry and skill, is to violate arbi- trarily the first principle of association—the *guarantee* to every one [*sic*] of a free exercise of his industry and the fruits acquired by it."⁶¹ In keeping with these principles, he objected to passing on debts to future generations because he believed it forced later generations to work for earlier ones.⁶²

These remarks offer some powerful evidence that Jefferson op- posed governmental attempts to minimize economic inequality in the United States, regardless of what he had to say about conditions in Europe. However, many of Jefferson's policy proposals—including the ones he considered vital to the long-term welfare of the coun- try—explicitly sought to equalize conditions and/or opportunities in the United States. He never sought perfect equality, but he did believe it was both possible and desirable for the government to pre- vent and minimize those extremes of inequality that threatened the prospects of self-government by the people. Where the health of re- publican government was at stake, Jefferson was willing to set aside his otherwise strict adherence to small-government principles to advance egalitarian policies that contributed to the long-term pres- ervation of freedom.

It is important to contextualize Jefferson's well-known suspicions of centralized and active government to understand his positions on economic policy. Scholars such as Yarbrough might be right in point- ing out that Jefferson's distrust of government exceeded Locke's, but they tend to conflate his insistence on popular vigilance against abuses of government power with unqualified opposition to govern- ment efforts to improve the economic well-being of the people or to preserve their capacity to participate in politics. Much, though by no means all, of his hostility to concentrations of political power, active government, and the like was based on then widely accepted repub- lican assumptions that government tended to represent the inter- ests of the wealthy and powerful at the expense of ordinary citizens. The fact that so much of the support for shifting power away from the states toward the national government in the decades following the Revolution came from urban financiers, merchants, and professionals who, Jefferson believed, stood to gain from these changes reinforced the association between energetic government and the interests of the wealthy. Hamilton's financial plan, from the assumption of state debts to the erection of a national bank, only confirmed Jefferson's worst suspicions. If Jefferson expressed reservations about government intervention in the economy at the national level, it was because he believed that conditions in the United States already allowed even the lowliest laborer or smallest farmer to achieve economic independence, not because he was indifferent to economic inequality.[63]

It is also important to understand that many of the positions Jefferson took on questions of national policy were based on constitutional grounds, not philosophical ones. There is no question that Jefferson's strict constructionism militates against interpretations of constitutional provisions, such as the general welfare clause, that were used to justify internal improvements and many other interventions in the economy. However, just because Jefferson raised constitutional objections to certain federal programs does not necessarily mean he objected to those programs in principle. Indeed, in one of the very same letters in which he condemned such distortions of the Constitution, he indicated his support for the policies those creative interpretations are used to justify by calling for "regular amendment of the constitution."[64] Although he insisted on the strictest adherence to the letter of the Constitution because it stands as the highest expression of the popular will, his belief that "each generation is as independent as the one preceding" led him to endorse the idea of a wholesale revision "every nineteen to twenty years" (roughly the length of a single generation). It is impossible to know definitively what additional powers or responsibilities in government Jefferson himself would have approved under a revised constitution, but there is no doubt he approved of "progressive accommodation to progressive improvement" in human understanding.[65]

An important clue to Jefferson's thinking on the governmental role in addressing economic inequality can be found in his heavy personal investment in a book he translated from French into English, had published in the United States, and promoted heavily. Jefferson frequently recommended works of political philosophy such as Locke's *Treatises* and *The Federalist* to his correspondents and for use in schools, but he endorsed none with as much enthusiasm and energy as Antoine Louis Claude Destutt de Tracy's *A Treatise on Political Economy*. Jefferson admired all of Destutt de Tracy's writings, telling the liberal French author that his commentary on Montesquieu's *Spirit of the Laws* was the "most precious gift the present age has received."[66] The only disagreement Jefferson ever expressed with Destutt de Tracy was over the latter's conception of executive power in that work. However, when it came to *A Treatise on Political Economy*, the Virginian was unreserved in his approval. In a letter to the publisher of the English edition, Jefferson expressed his hope that the book would find its way into the "hands of every reader in [the] country."[67] He addressed the work's numerous merits in a prospectus that lavished praise on its "cogency," rigor, style, and "fearless pursuit of truth, whithersoever it leads."[68]

The appeal of Destutt de Tracy's work for Jefferson is easy to understand. The French liberal invoked an explicitly Lockean conception of individual liberty to develop a social contractarian theory of small, frugal, and limited government that derives its legitimacy from the consent of the governed. Destutt de Tracy's understanding of political economy and the limits of government seems at first to leave little if any room for political intervention in economic matters. Repudiating Physiocratic ideas about the governmental role in managing the economy, he promoted free trade, defended competition, welcomed entrepreneurial risk-taking, opposed government regulation of interest rates, condemned paper money, excoriated public debt, and championed the rights of property. Destutt de Tracy even went as far as to describe economic inequality as an "insuperable" feature of the human condition.[69]

Despite his belief that economic inequality is unavoidable, Destutt de Tracy did favor measures to reduce economic inequality and poverty because they endanger critical political ideals.[70] His support for egalitarian measures was founded on the premise that "all inequality is an evil, because it is a mean of injustice." Combating economic inequality is a matter of justice because inequality in riches "carried to an extreme reproduces that of power," which is "the most grievous" form of inequality.[71] The promotion of economic equality is not a threat to political liberty but a necessary condition of its preservation:

> Since the object of society is to diminish the inequality of power, it ought to aim at its accomplishment, and since its

inconvenience is to favour the inequality of riches, it ought constantly to endeavor to lessen it, always by gentle, and never by violent, means: for it should always be remembered, that the fundamental base of society is a respect for property, and its guarantee against all violence.[72]

Destutt de Tracy's preferred means of tackling inequality was a progressive tax system. Although he favored levels of taxation that were "moderate" overall, he criticized regressive taxes on necessities as being "cruel" to the poor and recommended taxes on luxuries and other items consumed disproportionately by the rich as being full of "advantages without any inconveniences."[73]

It is impossible to know if Jefferson agreed with every part of Destutt de Tracy's discussion of economic inequality, but it is certain that Jefferson did not see any contradiction between the political economist's opposition to interventionist government and his support for measures to minimize economic inequality. If Jefferson had disagreed with Destutt de Tracy's critique of economic inequality or his recommendation to use the tax code to reduce disparities between rich and poor, his express disapproval of Destutt de Tracy's expansive views of executive power suggests he would have voiced his objections. In this instance, Jefferson's silence on the use of public policy to address economic inequality can fairly be construed as tacit approval.

Jefferson's avowed support for policies aimed at reducing economic inequalities and their political effects confirms these impressions. His record in politics—from his time as a member of the Virginia House of Delegates to his two terms as president of the United States—reveals that he took a variety of positive steps to promote economic equality. More often than not, he did so because he believed economic equality is a precondition for liberty. He proposed policies at the local, state, and national levels that would prevent economic inequalities among citizens (white men) from growing so large that they threatened the very existence of republican government. His commitment to equality among citizens was so strong that he promised he would never be diverted from his "intention to fortify the public liberty by every possible means, and to put it out of the power of the few to riot on the labors of the many."[74] The way he endeavored to keep that promise was by making sure government helped secure the conditions that made prosperity—and liberty—possible.

The Establishment of a More Equal Distribution of Land

As a member of the Virginia government following the start of the American Revolution, Jefferson undertook the ambitious project of revising that state's laws to make them more compatible with its "republican form of government."[75] The reforms he endorsed, first as a member of the Virginia House of Delegates and then as governor, included changes to the style of legislative drafting, the liberalization of criminal law, and a plan for the eventual manumission and deportation of slaves, among many others.

Jefferson offered a variety of reasons for supporting each of these reforms, but concern for equality was behind many of them, sometimes in not-so-obvious ways.[76] A case in point is his support for the liberalization of criminal law. Following the ideas of Enlightenment reformers such as Cesare Beccaria, Jefferson proposed changes that would make punishments more proportional to crimes and eliminate some forms of punishment altogether.[77] In explaining why the practice of making a "public spectacle" out of hard labor as a means of rehabilitating criminals was misguided, Jefferson offered a combination of pragmatic and moral arguments. The pragmatic argument relied on experience showing that these practices simply did not work to reduce or deter crime. The moral argument relied on the value of "self-respect." Jefferson explained that the public humiliation of being reduced to such a low state engenders a counterproductive "abandonment of self-respect" that actually has the effect of plunging the punished "into the most desperate & hardened depravity of morals and character."[78] In doing so, these outdated and cruel practices create a second class that lacks the requisite qualities for citizenship in a republic. As Jefferson understood it, that self-respect cannot be sustained unless citizens view themselves as equals.

The notion that a sense of equality is a prerequisite of citizenship informed many of Jefferson's early reform efforts. The kinds of reforms he recommended reflected his recognition that equality is shaped—and potentially undermined—by a variety of social, economic, legal, and political factors. Whereas the changes he proposed to the criminal justice system were aimed at addressing the way in which equality is affected by one's moral status, many of the changes he recommended in other areas were designed to deal with the ways in which equality is affected by one's economic status. Maintaining the economic bases of self-respect was critical to the effective exercise of citizenship.

Of the more than one hundred reforms the Virginia legislature considered after the break with England, Jefferson considered four vital to laying the foundations "for a government truly republican": (1) the abolition of primogeniture, (2) the eradication of entails, (3) a general plan of education, and (4) the establishment of religious freedom.[79] All four were designed to promote equality in some sense, but the first three were designed specifically to undo aristocracy and prevent its further entrenchment.[80] The abolition of entail and primogeniture was a remedial measure that would remove existing legal supports for antiquated forms of economic inequality, and the education bill (discussed below) was a prophylactic measure that would prevent new forms of economic inequality from developing in the first place. As he explained to John Adams decades later, the laws abolishing entail and primogeniture "laid the axe to the root of Pseudo-aristocracy."[81] The discussion with the poor Frenchwoman that prompted Jefferson's reflections on the unequal distribution of land was still a few years away, but he had already come to the conclusion that legal supports for economic inequality are antithetical to the country's political ideals. His attack on these vestiges of feudalism shows that inequality as such—even when it is unconnected to poverty—poses a serious threat to republican government.

The egalitarian motivations behind Jefferson's support for the abolition of entail and primogeniture are spelled out most thoroughly in his *Autobiography*. His principal objection to Virginia's system of entails was that it reinforced and entrenched class hierarchies: "The transmission of this property from generation to generation in the same name raised up a distinct set of families who, being privileged by law in the perpetuation of their wealth were thus formed into a Patrician order."[82] This system of inherited privileges had resulted in an "aristocracy of wealth" antithetical to a "well ordered republic" and inimical to the interests of society.[83] There were additional egalitarian considerations behind Jefferson's opposition to the feudalistic system of primogeniture. In a rare moment of humor, he responded to Edmund Pendleton's proposal to let the eldest son receive a double share of inheritance with the observation "that if the eldest son could eat twice as much, or do double work, it might be a natural evidence of his right to double portion; but being on a par in his powers & wants, with his brothers and sisters, he should be on a par also in the partition of the patrimony."[84] Though he did not impose any requirements on how property should be divided, he did expect each property holder to "divide the property among his children equally, as his affections were divided."[85] Even though there was no guarantee property would, in fact, be passed down equally, the likelihood that this law would promote a rough equality among citizens—that it would place heirs "by natural generation on the level of their fellow citizens"—was the primary political justification in favor of this new arrangement.[86] By removing legal supports for inequality within families, the abolition of entail and primogeniture would lay the groundwork for the diffusion of egalitarian ideals throughout the rest of the social system.

Jefferson's interest in promoting equality in Virginia took even more radical forms. In a provision in his draft constitution for Virginia that was ultimately rejected, Jefferson proposed a plan that would promote the political independence of citizens by guaranteeing each adult white male a minimum share of land. Article IV of his proposed constitution stipulated, "Every person of full age neither owning nor having owned [50] acres of land, shall be entitled to an appropriation of [50] acres or to so much as shall make up what he owns or has owned [50] acres in full and absolute dominion."[87] One of the immediate effects of the plan would have been to enfranchise every white male above the age of twenty-one under the suffrage rules in place in Virginia at that time.[88]

The political consequences of this plan went beyond extending the legal right to vote. It would also have gone a long way toward promoting the material foundations of political independence noted in republican thought from Aristotle to James Harrington.[89] Jefferson could just as easily have accomplished the goal of universal white male suffrage simply by removing existing property qualifications for voting and holding office. However, the proposed system of land distribution would have achieved the additional and ultimately much more critical objective of promoting the economic independence Jefferson believed was vital to free government. Simply opening up the franchise without addressing the underlying foundations of economic independence would not have ensured the free and *independent* exercise of political rights. One of the main reasons Jefferson hoped the United States would remain an agricultural society made up of small freeholders—and why he resisted most forms of manufacturing for so long—was because he believed that widespread ownership of land would help prevent the evils of dependence, which "begets subservience and venality, suffocates the germ of virtue, and prepares fit tools for the designs of ambition."[90]

Jefferson's most significant accomplishment as president was also arguably the one that did the most to foster and extend his egalitarian vision for the United States. The way he saw it, the Louisiana Purchase would make it possible for generations of ordinary Americans to achieve the economic independence necessary for the preservation of political independence. It reflected his long-standing belief that the United States would remain "virtuous" as long as there was enough vacant land to allow independent homesteads.[91] The acquisition of this vast territory would enable Americans to leave the increasingly crowded conditions of life along the eastern seaboard, where limits to affordable land were already exacerbating economic inequality, and settle in sparsely populated areas where the availability of relatively inexpensive land was more conducive to lives of economic independence. The acquisition of the Louisiana Territory was viewed as a way to forestall the Malthusian horrors that awaited Europe and maintain the socioeconomic conditions that made the United States special.[92] It would also help the country avoid the terrible fate that had already befallen the masses in Europe, where aristocratic families who gobbled up this scarce resource for themselves were able to dominate the landless by keeping them in a state of almost perpetual dependence. As Jefferson explained, "The immense extent of uncultivated and fertile lands enables every one [*sic*] who will labor to marry young, and to raise a family of any size."[93] These political economic objectives were so critical to the maintenance of republicanism that they outweighed Jefferson's deep misgivings about the constitutionality of the Louisiana Purchase.[94]

Just how independent these settlers would be in practice is open to question. Even the most ardent supporters of Jeffersonian principles and administration policies—the heads of those "little republics" who worked the land, especially on the frontier—relied on and called upon the national government to achieve the very independence and self-sufficiency they claimed to possess and jealously guarded. Government action—in building roads and canals, delivering the mail, disseminating information about the latest improvements in agriculture, protecting shipping lanes, and securing the frontier from the depredations of foreigners and Native Americans, to name but a few examples—was a necessary precondition for the very possibility of economic self-sufficiency.[95] Nevertheless, it was reasonable for Jefferson to expect these settlers to be free from various forms of economic dependence and domination that ordinary citizens on the eastern seaboard faced as a result of unsteady employment opportunities, competition from other laborers, and the regimentation of working conditions by employers.

Even though Jefferson recognized the economic benefits of internal improvements that would facilitate transportation and communication across the far-flung reaches of the Republic, he opposed many of those measures on both constitutional and political grounds. The lack of clear constitutional authorization for federal construction of roads, canals, and bridges could always be addressed with a constitutional amendment—which Jefferson himself recommended in his sixth annual message to Congress[96]—but the inevitable enrichment of some at taxpayer expense was a political concern much more difficult to address.[97] Jefferson usually numbered anxieties about wasteful government spending and mismanagement in his objections to public projects, but a concern for equality was never far from his mind, either.[98] Indeed, much of his opposition to government expenditures—especially those promoted by Federalists, whom he suspected of nefarious designs to establish aristocratic relations—stemmed from his concern that some government policies would enrich well-connected insiders at the expense of other citizens, thereby exacerbating economic disparities.

Expanding Opportunity through the Ward System

Whenever possible, Jefferson preferred to have local and state governments rather than the national government secure those conditions he thought vital to the maintenance of republicanism. As he indicated in numerous letters to a variety of correspondents over the course of several decades, there was no better way to perpetuate the conditions that make self-government possible than to divide each county into a system of wards. Jefferson described these political subdivisions, modeled after the New England townships in size and function, as the "wisest invention ever devised by the wit of man for the perfect exercise of self-government, and for it's [sic] preservation."[99] Much of Jefferson's enthusiasm for wards can be explained by the democratic opportunities for local control, civic empowerment, and direct participation they opened up to citizens whose political activities would otherwise be limited to periodic voting for representatives. Just as significant to Jefferson was the role they could play in the dissemination of knowledge indispensable to the preservation of a free people. Whatever misgivings he may have had about the possible upward redistributive effects of government expenditures were set aside when considering the benefits of these "little republics."

As noted above, Jefferson's strong interest in public education was an integral part of the legal and political reforms he championed in Virginia. Like Noah Webster and many other advocates of public schooling, Jefferson believed that a proper education is essential to the formation of good republican citizens.[100] The stated aim of his failed "Bill for the More General Diffusion of Knowledge" was to "illuminate, as far as practicable, the minds of the people" so they would be able to keep their republican form of government from being "perverted . . . into tyranny."[101] Like his support for liberalization of the criminal law, Jefferson explained that the bill on education pursued republican aims by elevating the moral status of citizens: it "would have raised the mass of the people to the high ground of moral respectability necessary to their own safety, & to orderly government."[102] Education always had a political aim in Jefferson's thought.[103] The most basic political goal was always to create a more informed citizenry, a goal this devotee of the Enlightenment and champion of republicanism pursued through other means as well, from the establishment of legal protections for a free press to the erection of a public university.[104]

However, like many other republicans of his generation, Jefferson also viewed education as a means of combating the pernicious influence of propertied elites.[105] Education provided a way to loosen the grip of aristocratic privilege in the United States without resorting to more direct redistributionist measures. Like the abolition of entail and primogeniture, his "Bill for the More General Diffusion of Knowledge" was explicitly designed to address the problem of economic inequality. It would have accomplished this most directly by providing a free grammar school education to all indigent children and sending the sons of poor parents who exhibited the "best and most promising genius and disposition" to district-level schools at public expense.[106] The redistributive effects of the proposal were justified by the fact that citizens knowledgeable about their rights would become better guardians of those rights and more "useful instruments for the public." In Jefferson's view, the beneficiaries of a more general diffusion of knowledge were not just the families of children who received a free public education but also the taxpayers and other citizens who valued the preservation of freedom under a republican form of government. The bill failed mainly because of the very conditions it was designed to rectify: the rich in Virginia (as in other states where similar legislation was proposed) resisted the use of their tax dollars to pay for the education of the poor.[107]

Despite the failure of this bill to pass in Virginia, Jefferson never gave up on the idea of free public education as a means of fostering equality. In fact, he continued to promote the establishment of public schools open to children of the rich and poor alike every time he mentioned the ward system. Like wards themselves, the free schools Jefferson hoped to establish were inspired by the example of New England, the only part of the country at the time where provisions for education at public expense were well established. Jefferson's strong insistence on local control was always combined with the requirement that localities fund education for the "few unable to pay."[108] As Jefferson explained to John Adams, this system would establish a "free school for reading, writing and common arithmetic" at the ward level, provide "at the public expense a higher degree of education" for the best students at the district level, and, finally, promote the best of those students to university. In doing so, the ward system would help preserve and extend the kind of upward social mobility that made the United States so different from the rest of the world. As Jefferson went on to explain, "worth and genius would thus have been sought out from every condition of life, and compleatly [sic] prepared by education for defeating the competition of wealth & birth for public trusts."[109] In short, free public education was indispensable to the promotion of a "natural aristocracy" of "virtue & talents" and the prevention of an "artificial aristocracy founded on wealth and birth."[110]

Concern for the public good, not just individual opportunity, motivated Jefferson's support for public schools. In particular, natural talents, which he believed were distributed equally among all classes of men, would be squandered without some support from the state: "We hope to avail the state of those talents which nature has sown as liberally among the poor as the rich, but which perish without use, if not sought for and cultivated."[111] His "Bill for the More General Diffusion of Knowledge" had emphasized the public over the private benefits of free public education. It proclaimed that providing a "liberal education" to indigent children "at the common expense of all" would be "expedient for the publick happiness." The same justifications appeared in Jefferson's "Report of the Commissioners for the University of Virginia." Among the many objectives of a primary education that should be made available to "poor children," Jefferson listed a variety of private and public benefits. This system of education would not only give "every citizen the information he needs for the transaction of his own business," it would also educate citizens in their rights and form the characters of those public officers "on whom public prosperity and individual happiness are so much to depend."[112]

Unfortunately, Jefferson never specified any criteria to determine inability to pay. However, he did indicate that the responsibility to provide public education extends to higher levels of government when lower ones find themselves incapable of meeting their responsibilities. His general preference for local control did not necessarily demand local funding when that proved infeasible. He suggested that the county government could easily shoulder this burden because the expense would not be very great ("it would require too trifling a contribution from the county to be complained of") and would be spread out among a larger population ("the whole county would participate, where necessary").[113]

Despite his general reservations about the role of the central government, Jefferson was also amenable to federal involvement in public education. In his final message to Congress, Jefferson opened up the possibility that the national government could assume some of the responsibility for creating a more informed citizenry. He suggested using the federal surplus to fund various projects including internal improvements, "education, and other great foundations of prosperity and union," even if those measures required the adoption of a constitutional amendment.[114] As he had observed in an earlier message to Congress, even though private enterprise is often superior to government-led efforts, education is one of those concerns a "public institution can alone supply."[115]

However poverty was defined, though, Jefferson made it clear each locality has an obligation to alleviate it. In addition to its responsibilities for public education, the administration of justice, and the maintenance of roads, each ward would also be responsible for the "care of their own poor."[116] Much of what Jefferson had to say on this topic reaffirmed existing practices. In Queries 12 and 14 of his *Notes on the State of Virginia*, he noted that the care of the poor fell to each parish.[117] In a system that obtained throughout the United States, "from Savannah to Portsmouth," localities levied assessments to care for the poor by providing boarding, food, work, and "supplementary aids."[118] He claimed with evident satisfaction that the social safety net in the United States was so strong that he "never yet saw a native American begging in the streets or highways."[119] It was a point of great pride for Jefferson that those stricken by "misfortune" did not have to resort to begging because they could rely on the "comfortable" and "certain" support of their countrymen as administered by local governments.[120]

Yarbrough contends that these passages from the *Notes* do not indicate general support for welfare benefits because the tithe would be limited to communities in which the characters of recipients would be personally known to the "good farmers" tasked with overseeing these programs.[121] According to Yarbrough, Jefferson's reference to the fact that the individuals who administer these programs are "discrete [sic] farmers" indicates he expected them to "make moral distinctions among the poor" in recognition of the fact "that some people are poor because they lack character and will."[122] In Yarbrough's view, Jefferson approved of a system that provided assistance to those with good characters and denied it to those with poor characters.

There is little to no textual support for this reading of Jefferson's *Notes on the State of Virginia*. It would be easy to dismiss his entire discussion of poverty there as irrelevant to understanding his views because he was merely describing existing practices rather than proposing his own ideas, but that would be to ignore his subtle yet undeniable hints of approval—not to mention the fact that he made no distinctions between the deserving and undeserving poor whenever he mentioned this function of his proposed ward system. Indeed, Jefferson's entire discussion of the generous aid provided to the poor has a decidedly self-congratulatory tone about it. It was only when Jefferson's account turned to the subject of "vagabonds" that it might be possible to detect an attempt to distinguish the deserving from the undeserving poor. However, even in this instance, there is no trace of moral condemnation. Although he noted that "vagabonds . . . are placed in workhouses," he also noted that these were places "where they are well cloathed [sic], fed, lodged, and made to labour."[123] Whether or not Jefferson's depiction of life for the poor was accurate, drawing lines of distinction between different types of poor people was never part of his repertoire.

Conclusion

It is fitting that the very last letter Jefferson wrote returned to the problem of inequality. Declining an invitation to attend a celebration in the capital commemorating the fiftieth anniversary of the Declaration of Independence, the elder statesman expounded on the meaning of the document he had drafted. Echoing the final words of the Cromwellian soldier and "leveler" Colonel Richard Rumbold just before he was executed for his part in the failed Rye House Plot to assassinate King Charles II and his brother,[124] Jefferson proclaimed, "The general spread of the light of science has already laid open to every view the palpable truth, that the mass of mankind has not been born with saddles on their backs, nor a favored few booted and spurred, ready to ride them legitimately, by the grace of God."[125] The statement did not directly address the political implications of economic inequality, but it did speak to the dangers inequality can pose to freedom. For the old revolutionary, disparities that become too large threaten the very foundations of republican government because they make it possible for one group to exploit and dominate another.

Many of the reforms Jefferson championed throughout his life can be understood as attempts to minimize artificial distinctions that jeopardize liberty. Even though he accepted and sometimes even condoned certain forms of racial injustice because he ascribed differences between the so-called races to unavoidable "natural" causes, he was far less tolerant of economic inequalities because he generally attributed differences between classes to unacceptable artificial causes. Economic stratification threatened liberty, in his mind, because it was associated with dangerous concentrations of power among the wealthy, on the one hand, and the disempowerment of the lower classes, on the other. In Jefferson's view, minimizing economic inequality did not betray republican principles; it helped fulfill them because it minimized the likelihood of domination, which is destructive of liberty.

Jefferson did not seek to equalize outcomes, but he did attempt to expand and equalize opportunities. Measures to that effect could take either prospective forms aimed at preventing the emergence or increase of economic inequality in the first place or retrospective forms aimed at correcting economic inequalities that already existed. In fact, one of government's primary responsibilities—whether at the local, state, or national levels—was to secure those conditions that would make prosperity and freedom accessible to all. If that required changes in inheritance laws to limit concentrations of wealth, modifications in the tax code to make it more progressive, the establishment of publicly funded schools to educate the children of the poor, and the redistribution of land to ensure economic independence for all, Jefferson gave no indication of any conflict with his political principles.

Scholars are correct in pointing out that Jefferson's most explicit statements in favor of redistributive measures appear in his reflections of the yawning inequalities and appalling misery that existed in prerevolutionary France.[126] However, the question is not (or should not be) what Jefferson wanted for the United States (or France) at that time, but what his principles support. Though conditions in the United States at that time were certainly much more egalitarian than they were in Europe, it is hard to imagine that Jefferson would have exempted his own country from those principles he applied elsewhere. To suggest that Jefferson's policy prescriptions for the United States in the late eighteenth or early nineteenth centuries should not apply in the twenty-first century is to ignore Jefferson's unambiguous and emphatic statements on the need to adjust with the times.[127]

This is not to say that Jefferson's principles are necessarily the right ones, either politically or morally. However, the evidence presented here does suggest that Jefferson cannot be enlisted in the service of causes or policies that would worsen economic inequality without significantly distorting his views. To be sure, the ambiguities and the context within which he developed his views make it difficult to know with certainty exactly what policies he would have supported today. However, if there is a lesson to be taken from Jefferson's reflections on economic inequality, it is that disparities between rich and poor should matter to anyone who professes to share his ideal of freedom.

7

"NOT CHARITY BUT A RIGHT"
Thomas Paine on the Justice of a Welfare State

Among the leading founders, none devoted more attention to the welfare of the working class and the plight of the poor than Thomas Paine. A democratic and egalitarian thinker in both style and substance, Paine eloquently and passionately advocated political reforms aimed at reducing and eliminating the burdens and restrictions aristocratic and monarchical governments had placed on the lower orders, from property qualifications on voting and holding office to various forms of taxation that fell hardest on the poor. However, Paine was also one of the fiercest and most outspoken critics of overactive government. An ardent proponent of limited government in both functions and expenditures, Paine railed against excessive spending, taxation, and debt in government as threats to both liberty and prosperity. The tension between his interest in alleviating the hardships faced by the poor and his interest in limiting the functions and expenses of government has raised questions about just how much Paine was willing to allow the government to do in pursuit of equality. Is it enough for the government to refrain from activities that exacerbate economic inequalities? Or does it have the responsibility to take affirmative steps to reduce economic inequalities?

Commentators have been divided over Paine's stance on the appropriate powers of government. On one side are those who claim Paine was a visionary proponent of welfare-state policies designed to minimize economic inequalities even if that entailed government intrusion into the economy. Generations of radicals championing unionism, abolitionism, women's rights, freethinking, populism, socialism, anarchism, and other progressive causes have found inspiration in Paine.[1] Scholars such as William Christian contend that Paine sought to establish a society in which "all men would enjoy equality of rights and a rough equality of condition."² Biographer John Keane argues, "Paine was no believer in self-regulating 'free markets,' but an advocate of 'nonmarket support mechanisms' inside and outside of government that help nurture the 'civil and political liberties' of citizens."³ Robin West contends that Paine favored an "activist state" that "has an obligation, not just the power, to legislate in a way that guarantees the minimal welfare of all citizens, particularly the poor and the aged."⁴

On the other side stand those who contend that Paine was an antistatist champion of free-market individualism who opposed government involvement in the economy as an encroachment on individual rights and a usurpation of power. Typical of this economic libertarian reading of Paine is Joseph Dorfman, who presents Paine's arguments against the abuses of power by European governments as general repudiations of almost any and all government activity. Dorfman argues that Paine sought the "elimination of all institutions, except those involving property and its security, [that] would permit the expansion of business enterprise."⁵ Eric Foner points to significant ways in which Paine's thought overlapped with Adam Smith's to argue that the former was "extremely receptive to laissez-faire economics."⁶ In a study of theories of economic inequality in the United States, Michael J. Thompson places Paine in a tradition that culminates in the free-market ideology of Milton Friedman.⁷ Modern libertarians such as Murray Rothbard have claimed Paine as one of their own for his adoption of a "sharp quasi-anarchistic distinction between 'society' and 'government.'"⁸

In some instances, the differences between these interpretations are simply unbridgeable. There is just no way to reconcile Dorfman's astounding claim that Paine's "views foreshadow Herbert Spencer's philosophy of a contrast between a system of status and one of free contract"⁹ with Jack Fruchtman Jr.'s contention that Paine adopted the "communitarian, national ideals implicit in the works of Jean-Jacques Rousseau."¹⁰ Although some of these disagreements can be attributed to nakedly partisan efforts to conscript Paine into particular ideological causes, many of the differences among Paine's interpreters depend on the priority given to different texts in his oeuvre. When the emphasis is placed on *Common Sense*, the transplanted revolutionary does strike a decidedly antistatist, almost anarchistic note difficult to harmonize with any positive role for the government. When *Rights of Man* is accented, those same notes sound discordant. Indeed, this is the interpretation offered by Foner, who argues that Paine's views on economic inequality changed significantly between the time he wrote *Common Sense* and "Agrarian Justice," perhaps his most radically egalitarian work.[11]

An important shift certainly did take place during Paine's career as a political pamphleteer, but it had little to do with his stance on economic inequality and poverty. Throughout his career, he opposed policies that tended to reinforce or perpetuate the maldistribution of wealth. Although he consistently opposed price controls, maximum limits on wages, protectionist trade policy, excessive government spending, the use of paper money, and many other forms of government intervention in the economy, he never ruled out the use of political power to correct economic imbalances. What did change was his willingness to accept a more positive role for the government in actually correcting and undoing certain economic inequalities. Indeed, it is precisely because of his egalitarian views that some conservative critics have advised their readers that it is "wise to ignore" Paine as an "English radical who never really understood America"[12] or simply dismiss his status as an American thinker by noting, "He was a recent immigrant."[13]

Paine's arguments in favor of the welfare-state programs he outlined in his later works merit careful consideration today because they suggest that a positive state can still be a limited state. In Paine's view, a good government was not simply one that dutifully observed negative prohibitions but also one that effectively fulfilled a host of positive duties. Even though he employed a wide variety of rhetorical strategies and justifications in defense of these proposals (ranging from humanitarian and sentimental appeals to conscience to consequentialist arguments from interests that even included the threat of violence), his ultimate justification was grounded in a deontological moral argument that appealed to universal rights.

Minimal Government

Paine's reputation as a libertarian antistatist rests largely on the lapidary lines engraved in the opening pages of *Common Sense*: "Society in every state is a blessing, but government, even in its best state, is but a necessary evil; in its worst state an intolerable one" (in vol. 1, 4).[14] Passages such as this one have led one interpreter to remark,

"Paine had nothing positive to say about government" in *Common Sense*.[15] From its ringing tribute to the natural sociability of humans to its stinging rebuke of monarchical government, the rest of the pamphlet seemed to reinforce the message that government functions and powers should be circumscribed as narrowly as possible. The pamphlet was especially critical of the excessive expenditures of governments, which end up leaving future generations saddled with debt (in vol. 1, 21). Indeed, Paine seemed to endorse the idea of the state as a humble night watchman authorized to do little more than maintain basic law and order—and to do it with as little expense as possible: "Wherefore, security being the true design and end of government, it unanswerably follows that whatever form thereof appears most likely to ensure it to us, with the least expence and greatest benefit, is preferable to all others" (in vol. 1, 5).

Paine's remarks undoubtedly expressed a negative attitude toward government, but they did not entirely rule out a more positive role for government. That hostility did not necessarily translate into a detailed specification of the limits of government power. Like social contract theorists before him, Paine investigated the origins of government to ascertain the ends and limits of government. However, his account of the rise of government did not simply reiterate the simple two-stage process (from an authority-free state of nature to a political society with a common authority) delineated by other social contract theorists. Although Paine did employ the state-of-nature concept to explain how individuals join to establish a government, he supplemented his discussion with an evolutionary account of social development. As society grows in size and complexity, the functions of government may have to be adjusted accordingly: "But as the colony increases, the public concerns will increase likewise, and the distance at which the members may be separated, will render it too inconvenient for all of them to meet on every occasion as at first, when their number was small, their habitations near, and the public concerns few and trifling" (in vol. 1, 6). Though Paine explicitly limited the "design and end of government" to the maintenance of "freedom and security," his evolutionary account of social development raised the possibility that the best way for government to accomplish its limited ends might be for it to adapt to changing circumstances rather than to adhere to a fixed set of means.

Paine's views on the nature of limited government in *Common Sense* are not to be found in a detailed enumeration of the proper *functions* of government but in his discussion of the proper *form* of government. Looking to nature for guidance, he argued that the "more simple any thing is, the less liable it is to be disordered, and the easier repaired when disordered" (in vol. 1, 6). Based on this standard of simplicity, Paine recommended a democratic government with a unicameral legislature as the ideal. One of the chief defects of the British Constitution, which deviates sharply from this norm, is that its complexity makes it difficult to hold government officials accountable. The "exceedingly complex" system of checks and balances that divides power between the monarch, the House of Commons, and the House of Lords provides a screen for vice that makes it impossible for the people to "discover in which part the fault lies" (in vol. 1, 7). As these lines suggest, the concept of limited government for Paine was most closely identified with the idea of accountability, not with the idea of enumerated powers.

Much more explicit and emphatic declarations of support for strong government appeared in numerous essays and pamphlets Paine wrote in the decade or so after independence was declared. In 1780 Paine became one of the first Americans to call for an overhaul of the entire political system so that the national government would have enough revenue and powers to fulfill its responsibilities. Throughout that decade Paine called on Congress to adopt a variety of measures that would help ensure the survival of the fledgling Republic. His proposals in this period included a selective tax on those who failed to "render themselves serviceable" to the war effort (*American Crisis 3*, in vol. 1, 98), the redistribution of Loyalist property in Philadelphia to patriots who successfully "repulse the enemy" (*American Crisis 3*, in vol. 1, 100), a plan for increasing the size of the army by lot (*American Crisis 5*, in vol. 1, 128), and the adoption of trade restrictions in retaliation against discriminatory treatment by the British (*A Supernumerary Crisis*, in vol. 1, 239). In addition, by the eve of the Constitutional Convention, Paine was striking a much more positive tone about the role of government in general. In the rules and regulations he drafted for the Philadelphia-based Society for Political Inquiries, he proclaimed, "The moral character and happiness of mankind are so interwoven with the operations of government, and the progress of the arts and sciences is so dependent on the nature of our political institutions that it is essential to the advancement of civilized society to give ample discussion to these topics" (in vol. 2, 41).

Of deepest concern to Paine during this critical period was the inability of Congress to raise sufficient revenue to prosecute the war effort. In *The Crisis Extraordinary*, Paine urged Americans to support a duty on imports as the most convenient means of raising the revenue desperately needed to fund the war effort. One of the chief advantages of a sales tax on imported goods was that it would be easy and relatively inexpensive to administer. However, another consideration important to Paine was its fairness. Though he would later reject taxes on consumption as regressive, in 1780 he, like most Americans, believed that they would be less burdensome to ordinary Americans than the alternatives. Indeed, his views on indirect taxes were virtually indistinguishable from those held by other Americans at the time. He explained that a duty on imports "operates with the greatest ease and equality, because as every one [*sic*] pays in proportion to what he consumes, so people in general consume in proportion to what they can afford; and therefore the tax is regulated by the abilities which every man supposes himself to have, or in other words, every man becomes his own assessor, and pays by a little at a time, when it suits him to buy" (in vol. 1, 183).[16]

One of the most significant things about this essay is the way it highlights Paine's interest in developing public policy with an eye toward protecting and promoting the interests of ordinary citizens— especially of the poor. The merits of a public policy are measured not just by its general effect on the overall population but by its particular effects on specific classes. In subsequent writings, the idea that it is permissible to use government power to pursue egalitarian ends became even more explicit. Whereas Paine had stressed freedom and security as the ends of government in *Common Sense*, he later added equality to the list of objectives a government ought to pursue. In "Dissertation on First Principles of Government," published in July 1795, he explained that government is properly established to do more than just replicate or reinforce the status of individuals in the state of nature. It is also tasked with the responsibility of promoting equality where it does not already exist: "In a state of nature all men are equal in rights, but they are not equal in power; the weak cannot protect themselves against the strong. This being the case, the institution of civil society is for the purpose of making an equalization of powers that shall be parallel to, and a guarantee of, the equality of rights. The laws of a country, when properly constructed, apply to this purpose" (in vol. 2, 583). Paine's principal concern was always the protection of political and legal equality, as evidenced by his support for democratic government and universal male suffrage. However, he came to realize that neither political and legal equality nor political and civil liberty can be guaranteed without some measure of economic equality.

Paine's Critique of Poverty and Inequality

Paine did not set out to eliminate all economic inequality. In fact, he conceded that an unequal division of property was inevitable because differences in individual effort, ability, and disposition will always produce inequalities of wealth. He also acknowledged that "fortunate opportunities, or the opposite," are reasons why "property will ever be unequal" ("Dissertation on First Principles of Government," vol. 2, 580). In spite of this recognition that perfect equality could never be achieved, Paine believed there were moral, economic, and political limits to the levels of inequality acceptable in a decent society.

Paine's interest in minimizing economic inequality is inseparable from his interest in alleviating poverty. Though the two problems are analytically distinct, Paine often discussed them interchangeably when addressing the condition of the lower classes. This may be because he believed that both poverty and inequality threaten important moral, political, and economic values in similar ways. Both poverty and inequality undermine the bases of self-respect, diminish the capacity for autonomy, and lower the material prospects of individuals and society alike.

Paine would eventually become an outspoken deist, but he frequently grounded his calls to aid the poor in claims to a religious duty that reflected his Quaker upbringing.[17] He would often assert that the duties imposed by religion are limited to aiding fellow human beings in this world: "I believe in the equality of man; and I believe that religious duties consist in doing justice, loving mercy, and endeavoring to make our fellow-creatures happy" (*The Age of Reason*, in vol. 1, 464; see also his letter to Samuel Adams, January 1, 1803, in vol. 2, 1438). These religious duties were not rooted in revelation but in conscience: "The Almighty hath implanted in us these unextinguishable [sic] feelings for good and wise purposes. They are the guardians of his image in our hearts. They distinguish us from the herd of common animals" (*Common Sense,* in vol. 1, 30).

Like many other eighteenth-century writers (including Thomas Jefferson), Paine employed the language of moral sentiment to describe the origin and nature of duties toward others. As he indicated in *Common Sense,* reason and feeling are complementary faculties that guide humans in the same direction. Paine's harshest condemnations were always reserved for those he believed were bereft of human feeling and sympathy for the suffering of others, whether that was the coldheartedness of King George toward the entreaties of the American colonists, Edmund Burke's inability to commiserate with the victims of the ancien régime, the callous disregard of priests toward the "many infants [who] are perishing in the hospitals, and aged and infirm poor in the streets, from the want of necessaries" ("Worship and Church Bells," in vol. 2, 758), or even President George Washington's seeming indifference to Paine's unjust imprisonment during the terror in France ("Letter to George Washington," in vol. 2, 698). Feeling enabled Paine to identify the wrongs in capital punishment, the enslavement of blacks, the ravages of war, and above all poverty. In fact, the only time this scourge of the British expressed any sympathy for his native countrymen was when he reflected that the working class in England was being forced to shoulder the burdens of excessive taxation to pay for the war against the Americans (*American Crisis 12,* in vol. 1, 225).

Paine's first serious attempt to alleviate poverty was also his first major foray into politics. He took up the cause of equality in *The Case of the Officers of Excise,* a petition submitted to the English Parliament in 1772. The essay called for improvements in the working conditions and increases in the salaries of these tax collectors. The list of grievances included inadequate pay, the high cost of living where the work was actually carried out, the lack of reimbursement for work-related travel expenses, and the hazards of employment when the officer actually comes upon "contraband goods," among other things (in vol. 2, 4–5). In describing the plight of excise officers, Paine showed signs of those rhetorical talents that would eventually make him one of the most successful authors of the eighteenth century. He painted a pitiful picture of public servants paid so poorly that they often found themselves struggling to make ends meet and unable to set aside any savings during what should be their peak earning years. Because their work required so much traveling they often found themselves unable to start a family and without the aid and comfort of friends and family when they fell on hard times.

Paine also analyzed the unfortunate trade-offs workers were often forced to make. Anticipating the objection that excise officers were not forced to take on this form of employment, Paine argued that the ordinary terms of employment had the tendency to deprive those officials of opportunities to improve their conditions. "The time limited for an admission into an excise employment, is between twenty-one and thirty years of age—the very flower of life. Every other hope and consideration is then given up, and the chance of establishing themselves in any other business becomes in a few years not only lost to them, but they become lost to it" (*Case of the Officers of Excise*, in vol. 2, 7). The general idea was that no one should have been required to work under conditions that deprived them of opportunities to lead a complete and fulfilling life. The inability to start and raise a family was especially grievous to Paine (who himself never had any children).

The material hardships faced by the excise officers dramatized many of the problems associated with poverty. The case of the excise officers also demonstrated some of the problems associated with inequality as such. The absolute condition of these officials was bad enough, but their *relative* standing compounded the difficulties they faced. It was one thing for them to struggle to get by, but it was another for them to lose ground to everyone else. It was outrageous to Paine that national prosperity had increased so much, yet "they are shut out from the general blessing": "To the wealthy and humane it is a matter worthy of concern that their affluence should become the misfortune of others. Were the money in the kingdom to be increased double the salary would in value be reduced one-half. Every step upward is a step downward with them. Not to be partakers of the increase would be a little hard, but to be sufferers by it exceedingly so" (*Case of the Officers of Excise*, in vol. 2, 5). The inability of excise officers to keep up with the rest of the nation was more than just a question of material well-being. It was also a question of self-esteem. A profession that placed them beneath the rest of the population made it an "impossibility" to enjoy "any proper degree of credit and reputation" in society. In terms of contemporary social theory, the problem faced by the excise officers was not only one of inadequate "redistribution" but also of insufficient "recognition."[18] Their pitiful pay deprived them of the material bases of social respect and dignity that every individual deserves and needs to participate fully in the life of the community: "Perhaps an officer will appear more reputable with the same pay than a mechanic or laborer. The difference arises from sentiment, not circumstances. A something like reputable pride makes all the distinction, and the thinking part of mankind well knows that no one suffers so much as they who endeavor to conceal their necessities" (*Case of the Officers of Excise*, in vol. 2, 6).

Some of the arguments Paine developed in *Case of the Officers of Excise* were specific to the condition of these civil servants, but the essay does form the beginnings of a broader critique of poverty and inequality he would develop further in subsequent writings. That critique echoes some of the ideas expressed by Jefferson and others discussed in previous chapters, but Paine developed a more comprehensive argument against inequality than any of his contemporaries. What is most significant about some of these discussions is how much his arguments against economic inequality reiterated the points he made against political inequality. The following sections outline some of those specific and more basic arguments.

Inequality Is Arbitrary

Paine often argued that the level of economic well-being an individual, a family, or even an entire nation enjoys can sometimes be explained by little more than chance. Contrary to the notion sanctified by religion and reinforced by tradition that the status of the poor is a matter of either divine ordination or personal desert, Paine observed that luck all too often plays an outsized role in determining well-being. This sensitivity to rapid and undeserved changes of fortune pervades his writings. For instance, in his critiques of slavery and of British imperialism in India, Paine noted the role of chance in accounting for extreme differences in status: "I see him in the instant when 'To be or not to be,' were equal chances to a human eye. To be a lord or a slave, to return loaded with the spoils, or remain mingled with the dust of India" (in vol. 2, 23). Paine cited the unpredictability in reversals of fortune in arguments against property qualifications for voting and holding office that were directed specifically toward the rich: "Who, fifty or sixty years ago, could have predicted who should be the rich and the poor of the present day; and who, looking forward to the same length of time, can do it now?" ("A Serious Address to the People of Pennsylvania on the Present Situation of Their Affairs," in vol. 2, 289). In "Agrarian Justice," he justified a social security system for the elderly on the grounds that "we often see instances of rich people falling into sudden poverty, even at the age of sixty" (in vol. 1, 616). He noted that even in America, where the distribution of wealth was far more even than it was in Europe, the "varieties of fortune and misfortune are open to all." When the likes of Robert Morris, his business partner John Nicholson, and James Wilson could end up in debtors' prisons, there was no exaggeration in Paine's assertion, "We every day see the rich becoming poor, and those who were poor before, becoming rich" ("Constitutional Reform," in vol. 2, 1001).

Wealth Is Often Acquired Unjustly

The claim that economic status is not entirely deserved took another form as well. Not only is poverty sometimes the result of misfortune but wealth is also sometimes the result of injustice. As Paine explained in his "Dissertation on First Principles of Government," property is often and easily acquired—and lost—through dishonest or coercive means, including theft and fraud. Thus, to make political rights depend on property rights would simply compound the original injustice that produced the unequal division of property. Indeed, the problem of unjustly acquired wealth is so widespread that it was reasonable to conclude, "Wealth is often the presumptive evidence of dishonesty; and poverty the negative evidence of innocence" (in vol. 2, 579).

However, the unjust acquisition of wealth was not just limited to outright theft or dishonesty. Much of the great wealth that has been accumulated by certain individuals, Paine argued, is a result of the exploitation of labor. Like most Americans at the time, Paine subscribed to the idea that workers are entitled to the fruits of their labor.[19] The most egregious violation of this principle is slavery, but any economic relationship in which one individual labors for another is susceptible to abuse. The failure to compensate individuals adequately for their labor is an injustice on par with the theft of their property: "The accumulation of personal property is, in many instances, the effect of paying too little for the labor that produced it; the consequence of which is that the working hand perishes in old age, and the employer abounds in affluence" ("Agrarian Justice," in vol. 1, 620).

Inequality Destroys Solidarity

A recurring theme in Paine's writings is that social distance between individuals tends to weaken their bonds to each other and make it more difficult to experience the sympathy that makes one fully human. The less capable individuals are of being able to identify with each other, the less likely they are to show concern for one another. The most damning version of this argument often appeared in his attacks on monarchy: "You must also see clearly that there must be an entire absence of sympathy between ruler and people. What renders us kind and humane? Is it not sympathy, the power which I have of putting myself in my neighbor's place? How can a monarch have sympathy? He can never put himself in anybody's place, for the simple reason that he can never be in any place but his own" (in vol. 2, 544). One of the implications of this idea is that lack of sympathy makes it much easier to exploit and oppress others. Similar reasoning appears in some of Paine's reflections on economic inequality. In his later writings, he argued that the economic gap between rich and poor—frequently reinforced by patterns of residential segregation—undermined solidarity between these classes. As a result of these attenuated social bonds, it becomes much easier for the rich either to ignore or exploit the poor and much easier for the poor to resent and attack the rich.

Poverty Degrades Character

Paine pointed out that poverty and inequality have a tendency to degrade the character of the downtrodden. One of the most pernicious consequences of this degradation is the corruption of morals. In *The Case of the Officers of Excise*, the former tax collector developed a materialist argument to explain how "downright poverty finishes the character" (in vol. 2, 14). Rejecting essentializing assumptions about the supposedly inherent character flaws of those guilty of corruption or negligence in the performance of their duties, Paine placed the blame for these transgressions squarely on the terrible temptations created by the combination of power and poverty:

Poverty, in defiance of principle, begets a degree of meanness that will stoop to almost anything. A thousand refinements of argument may be brought to prove that the practice of honesty will be still the same, in the most trying and necessitous circumstances. He who never was an hungered [*sic*] may argue finely on the subjection of his appetite; and he who never was distressed, may harangue as beautifully on the power of principle. But poverty, like grief, has an incurable deafness, which never hears; the oration loses all its edge; and *'To be, or not to be'* becomes the only question. (in vol. 2, 11)

Poverty is also a significant factor in the sociology of crime. According to Paine, the adverse effects of poverty are not limited to malfeasance in office but extend to society as a whole. Necessity forces even the "honest man" to violate the law in the struggle for survival.[20]

Poverty and Inequality Undermine National Prosperity

Higher rates of crime were not the only negative side effects of poverty and inequality. Paine also noted that the maldistribution of wealth damages the overall health of the economy. In defending the democratic constitution of Pennsylvania against attacks on its "novelty" (i.e., its lack of property qualifications on voting and officeholding), he contended that states that fail to protect the rights and interests of the poor eventually become impoverished. The main reason for this is that the poor would emigrate, leaving behind a shortage of laborers ("A Serious Address to the People of Pennsylvania on the Present Situation of Their Affairs," in vol. 2, 282–283).

An even more important argument about the connection between equality and prosperity concerns the foundations of economic development. In Paine's view, the economy grows from the bottom up, not the top down. Contrary to those who believed the prosperity of the upper classes was the key to achieving national prosperity, Paine argued that what is good for the poor is also good for the rich. Citing the example of impoverished German aristocrats to illustrate his point, Paine argued that the health of the economy depends first and foremost on laborers, not on the owners of capital ("A Serious Address to the People of Pennsylvania on the Present Situation of Their Affairs," in vol. 2, 282). As discussed below, Paine shared the

Lockean premise that labor is the primary source of value.[21] In a letter to Jefferson dated February 26, 1789, he suggested that the best way to make the French nation more prosperous, and hence increase state revenues, would be to adopt policies that improved the condition of the lower orders:

> To enrich a nation is to enrich the individuals which compose it. To enrich the farmer is to enrich the farm—and consequently the landlord;—for whatever the farmer is the farm will be. The richer the subject, the richer the revenue, because the consumption from which taxes are raised are [sic] in proportion to the abilities of people to consume; therefore the most effectual method to raise both the revenue and the rental of a country is to raise the condition of the people. (in vol. 2, 1282)

Inequality Endangers Republicanism

As important as these moral and economic considerations were in Paine's reflections on poverty and inequality, political considerations go the longest way toward understanding why he believed governmental intervention is legitimate and necessary. In many respects, his political arguments against economic inequality resembled those of his contemporaries. Subscribing to the widely held republican belief that "freedom is destroyed by dependence," Paine suggested that extremes of poverty and inequality often pave the way for despotism.[22] In "A Serious Address to the People of Pennsylvania on the Present Situation of Their Affairs," a wide-ranging diagnosis of the constitutional and political debilities afflicting his adoptive state in 1778, Paine identified economic stratification as a disease that enervates the people. Extreme economic inequality makes the poor more susceptible to despotic government by weakening their defenses against encroachments on their liberty. It does this by infecting them with a growing sense of apathy and disempowerment that could ultimately prove fatal to republicanism.[23] Anyone concerned about keeping the state free ought to support the interests of the poor because they constitute the first line of defense against tyranny (in vol. 2, 284). As Paine went on to explain in "Agrarian Justice," despotism is a disease that feeds off "wretchedness in the mass of the people" (in vol. 1, 621).

Many of Paine's remedies against the ills of poverty and inequality entailed prohibitions against certain types of public policy, including property qualifications for voting and officeholding, tax rates that discriminated against the poor, maximum wage policies, and restrictions on the ownership and alienation of land. However, when he began to understand the problems of poverty and inequality in terms of rights, the emphasis shifted to the affirmative responsibilities of government to alleviate and prevent poverty and inequality. The rights-based arguments he developed in *Rights of Man* and especially in "Agrarian Justice" made it possible for him to justify a more positive role for the state in addressing poverty and economic inequality. This is because proposals to reduce poverty and promote equality could be understood as measures necessary to restore and enforce universal rights.

Realizing the Rights of Man

Paine wrote *Rights of Man* to vindicate the French Revolution against Edmund Burke's excoriating broadside in *Reflections on the Revolution in France*. Paine's work was published in two parts. The first part, which appeared in 1791, was a scathing response to Burke that expanded on many of the arguments in favor of republicanism Paine had first sketched in *Common Sense*. "Part First" presented the French Revolution as an extension of the American Revolution in striving to enact equal human rights, the "natural dignity of man," government by consent, the rule of law, constitutionalism, popular sovereignty, generational independence, and other principles that directly challenge the legitimacy of aristocratic and monarchical rule. This part is filled with declarations of the superiority of American republicanism to the antiquated and unjust systems of hereditary government found in Europe. Paine directed most of his barbs against the British system of government, which he claimed lacked a proper constitution at all—and hence any meaningful protections for the rights of man—because Parliament possesses the unrestricted power to change the laws and form of government at any time.

Rights of Man became an instant best seller in the United States. Whether "Paine wrote both parts of *Rights of Man* with the United States in mind," as one scholar suggests, there is no doubt about the general reception to the book in his adoptive country.[24] It sold more than 100,000 copies in North America and circulated widely among Americans.[25] Republican toasts to Paine and *The Rights of Man* between the years 1791 and 1795 were exceeded only by toasts to President Washington. Even after Paine's reputation in the United States later in the decade suffered as a result of his scathing public attacks on Washington and his blistering critique of Christianity in *The Age of Reason*, Republicans who sought to distance themselves from the controversial writer continued to celebrate the political ideals expressed in his vindication of the French Revolution.[26]

Although most American readers readily embraced the ideas put forth in *Rights of Man*, a few reacted negatively to the democratic tenor of the book. The most sophisticated critique appeared in an eleven-part series penned by John Quincy Adams under the title "Letters of Publicola." The most immediate provocation for this anonymously published attack on *Rights of Man* was the unauthorized appearance of an inflammatory quote by Jefferson in the preface to the first part. In a letter never meant to go public, Jefferson welcomed the work as a timely intervention "against the political heresies which have sprung up among us."[27] The heretical beliefs the secretary of state had in mind were those of Vice President John Adams, whose recently published essays *Discourses on Davila* Jefferson and others deemed unrepublican and even antirepublican for expressing positive sentiments about monarchy, aristocracy, and hereditary succession. The younger Adams mounted an indirect defense of his father's reputation by challenging Paine's ideas as being outside the American mainstream. As John Quincy Adams explained in the final installment of the series, the papers were "simply an examination of certain principles and arguments contained in a late pamphlet of Mr. Paine's, which are supposed to be directly opposite to principles acknowledged by the constitutions of our country."[28]

The younger Adams defended the claim that Paine's ideas were antithetical to American ideals by arguing that an attack on the British Constitution was tantamount to an attack on the US Constitution. This is because key components of American constitutionalism were based on the British constitutional tradition. In particular, the system of checks and balances and other limits on popular sovereignty were essential to both forms of government. Yet Paine rejected this and more. In Adams's interpretation, Paine naively and irresponsibly upheld the untrammeled right of the majority to rule:

"If, therefore, a majority thus constituted are bound by no law human or divine, and have no other rule but their sovereign will and pleasure to direct them, what possible security can any citizen of the nation have for the protection of his unalienable rights? The principles of liberty must still be the sport of arbitrary power, and the hideous form of despotism must lay aside the diadem and the scepter, only to assume the party-colored garments of democracy."[29] Moreover, Paine fell under the spell of Rousseau in suggesting that one legislature has no right to bind a future one.[30]

When the second part of *Rights of Man* was published in 1792, neither Adams bothered to respond. What is striking about this is that the second part actually presents ideas far more radical than anything contained in the first. The second volume laid the foundations for a welfare state that would provide for a progressive income tax, stipends for newly married couples, old-age benefits, free education, and a variety of other reforms aimed at preventing or minimizing economic disparities.

Whereas Paine's criticisms of the British Constitution provoked Adams into mounting a spirited defense of this ancient structure, Paine's novel proposals stirred remarkably little controversy when they were published.[31] The idea that government has a responsibility to mitigate the maldistribution of wealth elicited less controversy among American readers than the ostensibly conventional notion that each generation is entitled to change its government as it sees fit.[32] Even the accessible and democratic style of *Common Sense*, which the elder Adams scorned as a "poor, ignorant, Malicious, short-sighted Crapulous Mass,"[33] drew more criticism from the dour American conservative than the novel policy proposals advocated in "Part Second" of *Rights of Man*. In his previous works, Adams had not hesitated to denounce attempts by the poor to plunder the rich as vicious invasions of their "sacred" property rights (which is why he insisted so strenuously on the importance of an upper legislative house),[34] yet he gave no indication that any specific policy proposed in the last part of *Rights of Man* was either morally or politically objectionable.[35]

In many respects, the reforms proposed in the second part built upon the moral foundations laid in the first. The first volume asserted the natural equality of all individuals in the enjoyment of the same set of natural rights from the very first humans that ever existed to any child born into the world in the present. In Paine's view neither the timing nor the manner of an individual's coming into the world (e.g., "by *creation* instead of *generation*") makes any difference to the rights and obligations owed to that individual (*Rights of Man*, in vol. 1, 274). This theory of equal natural rights helped Paine determine the legitimate ends of government, the proper limits of government, and the ideal form of government. The right of each generation to change the composition and form of government for itself was also based on this conception of natural rights.

However, Paine went further in his discussion of rights by introducing an important distinction that would be used to justify a much more expansive and positive role for the government than he had suggested in his earlier major works. Paine explained that there is an important distinction between natural rights and civil rights: "Natural rights are those which appertain to man in right of his existence. Of this kind are all the intellectual rights, or rights of the mind, and also all those rights of acting as an individual for his own comfort and happiness, which are not injurious to the natural rights of others. Civil rights are those which appertain to man in right of his being a member of society" (*Rights of Man*, in vol. 1, 275–276). Paine continued by pointing out, "Every civil right has for its foundation some natural right pre-existing in the individual," but the difference is that the enjoyment of civil rights ultimately depends on the aid of others (*Rights of Man*, in vol. 1, 276).

This was not an entirely new idea for Paine. In an article that appeared in the June 4, 1777, issue of the *Pennsylvania Journal*, he had argued that whereas natural rights are immutable, civil rights are subject to change, or "improvements," that cannot be anticipated. This distinction between natural and civil rights was grounded in the observation, "*Civil* rights are derived from the assistance or agency of other persons; they form a sort of common stock, which, by the consent of all, may be occasionally used for the benefit of any" ("Candid and Critical Remarks on a Letter Signed Ludlow," in vol. 2, 274). Paine then tried out this idea in a 1789 letter to Jefferson in which he classified the right to property as a civil right, not a natural right, because it depends on the power and protection of others. The distinction is that the full exercise of a natural right falls within the ordinary competence of the individual, whereas the enjoyment of a civil right always depends on the cooperation of others. That is, a civil right obtains only in society. Using the idea of the state of nature to make his point, Paine argued that property rights are not natural rights because, unlike the "rights of thinking, speaking, forming and giving opinions," property rights cannot "be fully exercised by the individual without the aid of exterior assistance" (in vol. 2, 1298). "These I conceive to be civil rights, or rights of compact, and are distinguishable from natural rights because in the one we act wholly in our own person, in the other we agree not to do so, but act under the guarantee of society" (in vol. 2, 1298–1299).

In the first part of *Rights of Man*, Paine used these ideas to compare the British system of government with the new system of government introduced in France. In the second part, this theory of rights helped him lay the foundation for a fourteen-point social reform program outlined in the final chapter.

The first chapter in the second part of *Rights of Man*, "On Society and Civilization," began with Paine's familiar contrast between government and society. He still insisted on the natural sociability of humans and the mutual dependence of individuals in society: "As Nature created him for social life, she fitted him for the station she intended. In all cases she made his natural wants greater than his individual powers. No one man is capable, without the aid of society, of supplying his own wants; and those wants acting upon every individual, impel the whole of them into society, as naturally as gravitation acts to a center" (*Rights of Man*, in vol. 1, 357). Although Paine had emphasized the tensions and even the contradictions between government and society in *Common Sense*, he presented that relationship as much more harmonious this time around. The main reason for the difference seems to be that Paine was engaging in two different types of theorizing in each case. In the first work, his remarks were based on observations about government *as it is*; in the second, his remarks were based on his ideas about government *as it ought to be*. When government is no longer controlled by and operated in the interest of a coterie of aristocrats and oligarchs, Paine did not object in principle to a more active role for government than the mere protection of natural rights. Now the same sociability and mutual dependence that exist in the state of nature helped Paine justify a more expansive vision of governmental responsibilities.

Government was no longer depicted as necessarily being a "necessary evil." In an echo of Rousseau's opening lines from *On the Social Contract*, Paine condemned "such governments as have hitherto existed in the world" as being grounded in "total violation of every principle, sacred and moral," but he pointed to the examples of the

United States and France as providing hope that government *can be* established on proper principles (*Rights of Man*, in vol. 1, 361). The revolutions carried out in these countries demonstrated that it was no longer valid to denigrate government as being fundamentally and hopelessly rooted in injustice. As he explained in his third chapter, "Government on the old system is an assumption of power, for the aggrandizement of itself; on the new, a delegation of power, for the common benefit of society" (*Rights of Man*, in vol. 1, 363). The old system produces countless evils, including unnecessary wars, wasteful spending, burdensome taxes, and a general state of misery among the people. The new system is capable of pursuing more noble and benevolent objectives, including peaceful trade relations among nations, frugal government, manageable taxes, and a general state of knowledge and prosperity throughout the nation.

One of the most objectionable features of the old system is that the people are taxed heavily to support an idle few in hereditary governments. Reiterating a theme he had trumpeted for years, Paine declaimed that there was no greater abuse committed by government "than that of quartering a man and his heirs upon the public, to be maintained at its expense." Though he blasted the idea of supporting a privileged individual at public expense as a mean and ignoble practice, he did not rule out public support for individuals in actual need of assistance. The social position and needs of the individual matter enormously in determining whether public support is permissible or even required. Even as he fulminated against public support for idle and worthless aristocrats and monarchs, he declared, "Humanity dictates a provision for the poor" (*Rights of Man*, in vol. 1, 392–393).

Not until the final chapter did Paine reveal his plan for fulfilling this principle. Contrary to the claim of some interpreters that Paine's welfare plans were limited specifically to "English historical practices"[36] or to "European societies whose governments persist in exploitively taxing the middle class and poor,"[37] Paine commenced his discussion of poverty with the observation that it is a *universal* problem. Although Paine's ruminations were triggered by conditions in England, he insisted that the principles he articulated applied to all countries: "A great portion of mankind in what are called civilized countries, are in a state of poverty and wretchedness, far below the condition of an Indian. *I speak not of one country, but of all.* It is so in England, it is so all over Europe" (*Rights of Man*, in vol. 1, 398; emphasis added).[38]

Before he presented his prescriptions for what government ought
to do, he developed a critique of existing political policies and practices that contributed to poverty and inequality. Drawing his examples primarily from England, he illustrated the numerous ways
in which the existing system of taxation there tended to increase
economic inequality. Even though he had earlier recommended a
tax on articles of consumption as an equitable way to raise revenue,
he came to understand taxes on consumption as inherently regressive taxes that impose unfair burdens on the poor. In particular,
shifting the source of revenue from land to articles of consumption
led to a "constant increase in the number and wretchedness of the
poor, and in the amount of the poor-rates" (*Rights of Man*, in vol. 1,
410–411). He explained that taxes on consumption exacerbate existing inequalities because "men of small or moderate estates . . . consume more of the productive taxable articles, in proportion to their
property, than those of large estates" (*Rights of Man*, in vol. 1, 413).
Then there were taxes on specific items that increased inequality
even more because the wealthy could avoid paying them altogether.
For instance, the tax on beer brewed for sale ended up creating an
exemption for aristocrats, who tended to brew their own beer, and
fell exclusively on those without the means to produce their own
(*Rights of Man*, in vol. 1, 411). As a result, a typical member of the
working class would end up paying such a large share of his income
in taxes that "he is consequently disabled from providing for a family, especially if himself, or any of them, are afflicted with sickness"
(*Rights of Man*, in vol. 1, 424).

Nonmarket forces also contributed to inequalities between rich
and poor. In particular, residential patterns tended to skew the tax
burden even more heavily toward the lower classes. Because aristocrats often lived at a great distance from the poor, usually on large
estates located in the countryside away from urban centers where
concentrations of poverty tend to be greatest, they could avoid the
costs of caring for more needy citizens: "They live apart from distress, and the expense of relieving it. It is in the manufacturing towns
and laboring villages that those burdens press the heaviest; in many
of which it is one class of poor supporting another" (*Rights of Man*,
in vol. 1, 411). Because the poor rates were assessed differently from
one locality to another, members of the lower and middle classes
ended up shouldering a much larger share of the burden for the support of the poor than members of the upper classes (*Rights of Man*,

in vol. 1, 411). To make matters worse, the poor rates did little to assist those in need because so much of the money raised was spent on litigation rather than on direct relief to the distressed (*Rights of Man*, in vol. 1, 423).

Thus, the first step in Paine's plan to provide relief was to "abolish the poor-rates entirely, and, in lieu thereof, to make a remission of taxes to the poor to double the amount of the present poor-rates" (*Rights of Man*, in vol. 1, 424). In fact, four of the fourteen articles that constituted Paine's program dealt with changes in the tax code. Two other articles mandated the abolition of regressive taxes on houses and windows and the abolition of the commutation tax. The fourth point—and the final article in the entire list—involved the establishment of a progressive tax designed to undo the injustices of primogeniture. All of the tax reforms were designed to make the tax system more progressive (*Rights of Man*, in vol. 1, 455).

The eradication of poverty was an important objective of Paine's tax proposals, but the promotion of equality was the primary goal. In Paine's view, simply providing relief to the poor would not do enough to create a more just society. The explicit aim of his system of "progressive taxation" was to lighten the tax burden on the lower and middling classes and to increase it on the upper classes in the interest of fairness: "The object is not so much the produce of the tax [i.e., as a means of raising revenue] as the justice of the measure. The aristocracy has screened itself too much, and *this serves to restore a part of the lost equilibrium*" (*Rights of Man*, in vol. 1, 436; emphasis added). The equalizing effects of the progressive tax would undo some of the unjust gains made by the aristocracy under the existing tax system, which was actually structured to increase rather than narrow the gap between rich and poor. Paine explained, "The chief object of this progressive tax (*besides the justice of rendering taxes more equal than they are*) is, as already stated, to extirpate the overgrown influence arising from the unnatural law of primogeniture, and which is one of the principal sources of corruption at elections" (*Rights of Man*, in vol. 1, 437; emphasis added).

Paine argued that higher taxes on larger estates impose no real hardships because these are not taxes on necessities but on luxuries. Though he admitted the difficulty of determining what is to count as a luxury, noting that the question is answered differently depending on time and place, he suggested that anything above what is required to support a family can be considered a luxury. Indeed, he argued that there is a point at which the accumulation of property is not and cannot possibly be the result merely of "industry," so it is "right" to prohibit the accumulation of property "beyond the probable acquisition to which industry can extend." Indeed, the greater the sum in question, the more justifiable it is to impose higher rates of taxation.

The clearest indication that Paine's ultimate goal was to reduce inequality and not simply to alleviate poverty is that he sought ways to break up concentrations of wealth. One of the ways he aimed to do this was by limiting the ability of families to accumulate fortunes from one generation to the next. Recognizing that the existing class structure becomes more rigid over time, Paine asserted, "There ought to be a limit to property, or the accumulation of it by bequest" (*Rights of Man*, in vol. 1, 437). This final piece of his plan would not have a direct impact on levels of poverty, but it would have a significant and direct impact on the degree of inequality in society. That alone was enough to recommend it.

In order to combat poverty and inequality as effectively as possible, though, it was necessary to develop more targeted programs directed at those who needed the most assistance. In Paine's view, the two groups that constituted the largest number of poor included families with numerous children and individuals too old to work (*Rights of Man*, in vol. 1, 424). Most, but not all, of the remaining ten articles were developed with these two groups in mind.

Paine's plan to assist the elderly set up a system of social insurance that resembled the modern Social Security system both in its justifications and in its operation. He proposed two different levels of support for those who reached a certain age: six pounds per year to those over the age of fifty and ten pounds per year to those over the age of sixty. Considerations of compassion justified both of these articles. Because the physical powers of those who have reached the age of fifty have begun to "decline," they are no longer capable of enduring the exertion and "fatigue" certain kinds of labor require, so they find themselves earning less and feeling "like an old horse, beginning to be turned adrift." Things are even worse for those over the age of sixty, so they should be able to retire altogether without fear of want. "It is painful to see old age working itself to death, in what are called civilized countries, for its daily bread" (*Rights of Man*, in vol. 1, 426).

If Paine's restriction on inherited wealth targeted inequality at the top, his proposals to help ordinary families promoted equality from the bottom up. The plan to assist families consisted of several components. One part of the plan involved annual payments for each child under the age of fourteen as well as free public education for the children of poor families. Two other articles would provide financial assistance to all families, not just those who were already poor. One article recommended a small payment upon the birth of each child, and the other proposed a modest payment to each newly married couple. Like the transfer payments directed to the elderly, these articles were designed to reduce the hardships on families who were already poor. But unlike the two levels of old-age assistance, the assistance offered to families in the form of marriage benefits, child benefits, and free education was also explicitly designed to keep parents and children from falling into poverty in the first place. As Paine explained, "It is certain that if the children are provided for, the parents are relieved of consequence, because it is from the expense of bringing up children that their poverty arises" (*Rights of Man*, in vol. 1, 425).

The family assistance proposals were not just antipoverty measures; they were also proequality measures. By providing families some measure of economic security and opportunity, these proposals would help expand the ranks of the middle class. Each part of his program to aid families was devised to make the class structure less rigid—none more so than providing education to the poor. This part of the plan would allow children to acquire the practical education and skills necessary to escape those cycles of poverty that had perpetuated the class structure in England for centuries. It was not just a remedial program designed to mitigate present levels of poverty but a prophylactic measure designed to prevent poverty from being perpetuated.

> By adopting this method, not only the poverty of the parents will be relieved, but ignorance will be banished from the rising generation, and the number of poor will hereafter become less, because their abilities, by the aid of education, will be greater. Many a youth, with good natural genius, who is apprenticed to a mechanical trade, such as a carpenter, joiner, millwright, blacksmith, etc., is prevented getting forward the whole of his life, from the want of a little common education when a boy. (*Rights of Man*, in vol. 1, 425–426)

Paine went on to argue that the children of the poor would not and should not be the only ones to benefit from this program. He expressed concerns that the children of families in the lower middle class would be excluded from the benefits of education if subsidies were not provided to their families—an oversight that would actually put them "in a worse condition than if their parents were actually poor." In defense of his proposal to expand educational opportunities, Paine suggested two possible justifications with significant political overtones. One of these implied that an education is a right. The assertion that "a nation under a well regulated government should permit none to remain uninstructed" employed the kind of universalistic language Paine ordinarily reserved for discussions of rights. The other implied that education is a prerequisite for republican government. In pointing out that only "monarchical and aristocratic governments . . . require ignorance for their support," he was highlighting the political benefits of education in much the same language Jefferson and other American supporters of public education often used (*Rights of Man*, in vol. 1, 428).

The effects of free education on the economic well-being of the country would not be limited to students and their parents. Making education more widely available could also serve as an indirect jobs program by supporting a "livelihood" for teachers. Paine proposed that the most effective means of educating children and creating job opportunities in local communities would be to make direct transfer payments to parents so that they could pay the salaries of teachers (*Rights of Man*, in vol. 1, 429).

Another major part of Paine's antipoverty program was to provide housing and employment to the unemployed until they got back on their feet (with no restrictions on how often they availed themselves of this opportunity). His proposal was aimed specifically at helping the urban poor, who were much more likely to fall through the cracks than those who resided in the countryside (*Rights of Man*, in vol. 1, 429–430). This part of the plan involved the construction of large facilities that could house and employ "at least six thousand persons" in a wide variety of occupations. In exchange for their labor, these residents would receive "wholesome food, and a warm lodging, at least as good as a barrack." The goal of the plan was not simply to prevent the unemployed from falling further into poverty but to help them become more independent. In addition to free food and lodging, they would receive a lump-sum payment for their work that would enable them to take care of themselves after they left the facility (*Rights of Man*, in vol. 1, 430).

The remaining articles in Paine's plan included subsidies to help cover the "funeral expenses of persons, who, traveling for work, may die at a distance from their friends" (*Rights of Man*, in vol. 1, 429), increases in the salaries of personnel in the army and the navy, and a weekly pension for life to disbanded soldiers and sailors. After concluding his fourteen-point list, Paine added a proposal he first raised in *The Case of the Officers of Excise* by recommending higher salaries for tax officials as something "that justice requires to be made" (*Rights of Man*, in vol. 1, 441).

Paine believed these proposals would be widely acceptable because their benefits would extend throughout society, and he developed a variety of consequentialist arguments to prove the point. One reason was moral-psychological. Assuming moral sentiments operate the same way in nearly all persons, he suggested that relief to the poor would salve the consciences of the nonpoor: "The hearts of the humane will not be shocked by ragged and hungry children, and persons of seventy and eighty years of age begging for bread. The dying poor will not be dragged from place to place to breathe their last, as a reprisal of parish upon parish" (*Rights of Man*, in vol. 1, 431). Another reason was economic. According to Paine's detailed calculations, his plan would be much less expensive than maintaining the existing (failing) system of poor rates. In particular, it would considerably ease the tax burden on the lower and middle classes (*Rights of Man*, in vol. 1, 433). An additional reason was sociological. He predicted that the commission of "petty crimes, the offspring of distress and poverty, will be lessened" when no one is driven to desperation anymore. Additional reasons were political in nature. In particular, Paine suggested that his proposed social policies would contribute to order and stability. Because the poor would begin to feel that the government actually worked for them, they would be more apt to support it. This would be a development advantageous to both the poor and the rich inasmuch as the "cause and apprehension of riots and tumults will cease" (*Rights of Man*, in vol. 1, 431).

Perhaps even more important than these consequentialist considerations was the deontological argument that this support "is not of the nature of charity, but of a right" (*Rights of Man*, in vol. 1, 427). In some instances, Paine resorted to the rather vague insistence that assisting the poor is just the right thing to do. He asked rhetorically if there was anyone who could actually "say, that to provide against the misfortunes to which all human life is subject, by securing six pounds annually for all poor, distressed, and reduced persons of the age of fifty and until sixty, and of ten pounds annually after sixty, is not a *good thing?"* (*Rights of Man,* in vol. 1, 450; emphasis in original). The suggestion that these ambitious proposals were a matter of "rights" belonging to all individuals implied a correlative duty on the part of others. In other words, he understood the various forms of assistance he recommended as "civil rights" that belonged to individuals by virtue of their membership in society. This was a tantalizing idea he would further develop in his next major work on equality.

Compensating for the Loss of a Birthright

The redistributive measures Paine introduced in *Rights of Man* were a prelude to an even more radical idea he would present in "Agrarian Justice." In that essay he made the case that every member of society is entitled to compensation for being deprived of a natural right to common ownership of the earth.

In the English preface to "Agrarian Justice," Paine explained that he was compelled to write the essay in response to the pernicious errors contained in a sermon by the Bishop of Llandaff, "The Wisdom and Goodness of God, in Having Made Both Rich and Poor; with an Appendix, Containing Reflections on the Present State of England and France" (in vol. 1, 609). The specific error that outraged Paine and demanded a refutation was the notion that "God made *rich* and *poor"* (in vol. 1, 609).

Paine began this essay by announcing the universalistic cast of his argument: "The plan contained in this work is not adapted for any particular country alone: the principle on which it is based is general" (in vol. 1, 606). What justified him in making this declaration was his appeal to the state of nature for guidance on the rights of individuals. Like state-of-nature theorists before him, Paine also used this hypothetical device to determine the origins of property and inequality. Though most commentators detect Locke's influence in this discussion,[39] there are even more significant traces of Rousseau.[40] Although all three thinkers agreed that there had been a stage of human development when there was no such thing as private property, they disagreed over the origins of private property and—even more importantly—whether private property is a natural right. Like the Genevan philosopher, cited approvingly in the first part of *Rights of Man* (in vol. 1, 299) and in some of Paine's other writings, Paine argued that property rights are at least partly conventional. This theoretical difference between Paine and Rousseau, on the one hand, and Locke, on the other, had profound implications. For if the right to some kinds of property was not grounded in nature, but in convention, it would be much easier to overcome moral prohibitions against interference with property rights.

Paine's analysis of property rights began with another of his key distinctions. He explained, "There are two kinds of property. Firstly, natural property, or that which comes to us from the Creator of the universe—such as the earth, air, water. Secondly, artificial or acquired property—the invention of men" (in vol. 1, 606). Rejecting the views of more radical contemporaries such as French communist François-Noël "Gracchus" Babeuf, who favored a wholesale redistribution of property, Paine acknowledged that perfect equality of property is impossible because the labor that produces it is never equal. In other words, what he called artificial property could never be equalized.

However, natural property was another matter altogether. With regard to this kind of property, "Every individual in the world is born therein with legitimate claims on a certain kind of property, or its equivalent" (in vol. 1, 606–607). The property to which every individual is entitled is a share of the earth, which is *"the common property of the human race"* (in vol. 1, 613; emphasis in original). The problem, though, is that the natural right of every individual to a share of the earth "or its equivalent" is widely ignored.

To explain how these routine violations came about, Paine followed Rousseau's methodological advice on "tracing things to their origin" (in vol. 1, 612) by examining the condition of individuals in their natural state, before the invention of government. Echoing Rousseau's argument in the *Discourse on Inequality*, Paine maintained that the natural state of man is a state of equality and tranquility. It lacked "those spectacles of human misery which poverty and want present to our eyes in all the towns and streets in Europe" (in vol. 1, 610). The equality that existed in the state of nature was an equality of property that gave every individual an identical share in nature: "It is a position not to be controverted that the earth, in its natural, uncultivated state was, and ever would have continued to be, *the common property of the human race*. In that state every man would have been born to property. He would have been a joint life proprietor with the rest in the property of the soil, and in all its natural productions, vegetable and animal" (in vol. 1, 611; emphasis in original). In explaining the emergence of poverty, Paine agreed with Rousseau's assessment that it is an artificial condition attributable to the rise of civilization. Although this champion of the Enlightenment differed from Rousseau in acknowledging the material and intellectual benefits the rise of the arts and sciences produced, he agreed that the advance of civilization is responsible for producing both dazzling displays of great affluence and shocking "extremes of wretchedness" (in vol. 1, 610).

However, in explaining the precise mechanism by which ownership in land, and therefore inequality in natural property, emerges, Paine avoided the Rousseauvian claim that it was a simple matter of enclosing a plot of land and getting some simpletons to accept this act.[41] Instead, he opted for the Lockean explanation that ownership of land began only with its cultivation (in vol. 1, 611).[42] Paine agreed with Locke's claim that property emerges when individuals mix their labor with a portion of the earth. In other words, an exclusive right developed to what was once common property because of the impossibility of separating the improvements made to land from the land itself (in vol. 1, 611). As a consequence, the individuals who made these improvements gained title to both the value of the improvements and the land itself (in vol. 1, 611–612).

Although Paine agreed with Locke's explanation of how property rights in land emerged, he did not accept Locke's justification of the exclusivity of property rights in land. Although Locke's labor theory of value led him to the conclusion that mixing any portion of one's labor with any part of the unclaimed natural world transforms the whole thing into private property, Paine argued that labor entitles the individual to the "value of the improvement, only, and not the earth itself" (in vol. 1, 611). Thus, the natural right of all others to ownership of land does not disappear entirely with the enclosure or improvement of land, as it does for Locke.

Paine acknowledged that private ownership of land has produced significant social benefits. In fact, he reiterated Locke's estimation that cultivation has increased the value of the earth tenfold (in vol. 1, 612). However, Paine disputed Locke's rosy prediction that this

arrangement ultimately makes everyone better off.[43] He pointed
out that cultivation has also contributed to the concentration of
property, with devastating consequences for the propertyless: "The
landed monopoly that began with it has produced the greatest evil.
It has dispossessed more than half the inhabitants of every nation
of their natural inheritance, without providing for them, as ought
to have been done, an indemnification for that loss, and has thereby
created a species of poverty and wretchedness that did not exist before" (in vol. 1, 612). Although Locke did express concerns about the
dangers of monopolistic ownership when he raised the possibility
that "enough and as good" would not be left to others, he suggested
the increase in value would more than compensate for the loss of the
original common title. However, in Paine's view, no increase in overall prosperity could make up for the fact that the existing "system
of landed property . . . has absorbed the property of all those whom
it dispossessed, without providing, as ought to have been done, an
indemnification for that loss" (in vol. 1, 613). Instead of producing
the prosperity Locke expected to benefit society as a whole, the actual benefits have been concentrated in the hands of a few. Existing
property arrangements have generated so much inequality that the
"great mass of the poor in all countries are become an hereditary
race" (in vol. 1, 619). Justice cries out for a remedy: "The rugged
face of society, checkered with the extremes of affluence and want,
proves that some extraordinary violence has been committed upon
it, and calls on justice for redress" (in vol. 1, 618–619).

Because there was no going back to the state of nature, it would
be necessary to find some way to restore the loss of each individual's
birthright. However, because "it is impossible to separate the improvement made by cultivation from the earth itself, upon which
that improvement is made," Paine argued that each proprietor of
land owes society a fee for the exclusive right to enjoy what is by nature common property. Rather than confiscating and redistributing
land, Paine proposed that anyone who inherits property pay a 10 percent tax on the value of their inheritance into a common fund used
to compensate individuals for the loss of their birthright.[44] Paine described this fee as "ground-rent" every proprietor of cultivated lands
"owes to the community" (in vol. 1, 611). A chief advantage of this
plan over alternatives proposed by the likes of Babeuf is that it could
be implemented in a short period "without diminishing or deranging
the property of any of the present possessors" (in vol. 1, 613). In the

case of a property owner without any heirs, Paine suggested that the entire estate would revert to society because "man is always related to society even if he has no kin" (in vol. 1, 615).[45]

Paine's plan would tax both landed and personal property, but the justification for taxing these two forms of property differed. The tax on land was justifiable because the propertyless deserved to be compensated for the loss of their birthright to an equal share of the earth (in vol. 1, 620). The tax on personal property was justifiable because this form of property would not exist at all without the benefit of society: "Personal property is the *effect of society*; and it is as impossible for an individual to acquire personal property without the aid of society, as it is for him to make land originally" (in vol. 1, 620; emphasis in original). Exploding the atomistic account of the origin of property theorized in works of political philosophy such as Locke's *Second Treatise of Government* and popularized in works of fiction such as *Robinson Crusoe*, Paine explained that certain forms of wealth simply could not exist without the supports society provides. Certainly no one could achieve great wealth without the aid of society:

> Separate an individual from society, and give him an island or a continent to possess, and he cannot acquire personal property. He cannot be rich. So inseparably are the means connected with the end, in all cases, that where the former do not exist the latter cannot be obtained. All accumulation, therefore, of personal property, beyond what a man's own hands produce, is derived to him by living in society; and he owes on every principle of justice, of gratitude, and of civilization, a part of that accumulation back again to society from whence the whole came. (in vol. 1, 620)

Far from exceeding the proper limits on government, Paine insisted that rectifying the inequality established by the introduction of property has become one of the duties of government during the age of revolutions. Now that governments are established to promote the rights of individuals, they can finally begin to enforce a long-neglected right: "In advocating the case of the persons thus dispossessed, *it is a right, and not a charity, that I am pleading for*" (in vol. 1, 612). Paine also argued that these redistributive measures were designed to maintain society itself (in vol. 1, 608). Even though he had spent considerable quantities of ink calling for the contraction of government's involvement in matters of conscience and commerce at earlier points in his career as a writer, here he was calling for an expansion in the government's functions in the interest of equality. Government action in this instance is justified because it involves the enforcement of a natural right, not a constriction of natural rights (as was so often the case under monarchical governments).

This proposed expansion of the government's responsibilities did not necessarily imply a significant expansion in its size or expense, however. Like many of the proposals he advanced in *Rights of Man*, this scheme would involve direct transfer payments without necessarily requiring substantial bureaucratic overhead. In this case, the money paid into the national fund would then be disbursed to two groups—and for two different reasons. The first group would consist of all young adults. Upon reaching the age of twenty-one, individuals would receive a one-time payment "of fifteen pounds sterling, as a compensation in part, for the loss of his or her natural inheritance, by the introduction of the system of landed property." This sum would provide young adults something akin to a small start-up fund to help them achieve a measure of independence. The other group that would benefit was the elderly. Starting at the age of fifty, every individual would receive an annual payment of ten pounds (in vol. 1, 612–613). In the first case, the plan would help individuals get started early in life; in the second, it would help them live out their remaining days in some ease.

In keeping with his claim that this birthright is natural—and therefore universal—Paine proposed that everyone, rich and poor alike, is entitled to these payments. He insisted that the universality of the program was essential to its justice. As he explained, "It is best to make it so, to prevent invidious distinctions. It is also right it should be so, because it is in lieu of the natural inheritance, which, as a right, belongs to every man, over and above the property he may have created, or inherited from those who did" (in vol. 1, 613).

Even though every individual was entitled as a matter of right to receive these payments at the appropriate age, Paine gave individuals the ability to opt out of receiving these benefits—though not the ability to opt out of paying the estate tax that would fund the program (in vol. 1, 613). Paine assumed that a few individuals—perhaps a tenth of the population—would simply decline the portion to which they were entitled because they would not need it (in vol. 1, 616–617). Thus, there would be some money left over that could be put to other uses. Paine proposed that any unclaimed funds could be used to support "blind and lame persons totally incapable of earning a livelihood" no matter what their age (in vol. 1, 617).

Anticipating the skepticism and controversy this plan would generate, Paine reiterated the point (made earlier in the essay and in *Rights of Man*) that justice demands the restoration of equality:

> It is not charity but a right, not bounty but justice, that I am pleading for. The present state of civilization is as odious as it is unjust. It is absolutely the opposite of what it should be, and it is necessary that a revolution should be made in it. The contrast of affluence and wretchedness continually meeting and offending the eye, is like dead and living bodies chained together. Though I care as little about riches as any man, I am a friend to riches because they are capable of good. (in vol. 1, 617)

Paine repeated this point once more only a few paragraphs later. In the preceding passage (and other places) he emphasized the humanitarian considerations that warrant this plan, but in the next one he further developed the claim that such assistance is a matter of universal rights:

> But it is justice, and not charity, that is the principle of the plan. In all great cases it is necessary to have a principle more universally active than charity; and, with respect to justice, it ought not to be left to the choice of detached individuals whether they will do justice or not. Considering, then, the plan on the ground of justice, it ought to be the act of the whole growing spontaneously out of the principles of the revolution, and the reputation of it ought to be national and not individual. (in vol. 1, 618)

In addition to making the case that the problem of the needy should be viewed as a matter of justice, Paine made an argument against understanding the problem or the solution as a matter for charity. He was not opposed to personal acts of charity, but he found them woefully inadequate. The magnitude of the problem is so great that a collective solution is necessary if the "whole weight of misery" is actually going to be removed. Because the problem is systemic, a systemic solution must be found. Charity "may satisfy [the] conscience" of the philanthropist, but it can offer only piecemeal relief and only to a few individuals at a time (in vol. 1, 617–618). Moreover, charity is entirely a matter of individual choice, which leaves the fate of needy people at the mercy of others.

Paine also explained that his plan offered a long-term solution to the problems of inequality by addressing the causes of poverty. Not only would it reduce the poverty that had already reared its ugly head, it would prevent poverty from emerging in the first place because "it will furnish the rising generation with means to prevent their becoming poor; and it will do this without deranging or interfering with any national measures" (in vol. 1, 618). In Paine's view, it would be much more economical in the long run to prevent people from becoming poor in the first place than to offer them assistance later: "It is the practise of what has unjustly obtained the name of civilization (and the practise merits not to be called either charity or policy) to make some provision for persons becoming poor and wretched only at the time they become so. Would it not, even as a matter of economy, be far better to adopt means to prevent their becoming poor?" (in vol. 1, 618). In fact, the plan could contribute significantly to national prosperity by unleashing the productive energies of those who would otherwise be too downtrodden to support themselves. Paine opined that the "consciousness of justice" itself would spur prosperity:

> When a young couple begin the world, the difference is exceedingly great whether they begin with nothing or with fifteen pounds apiece. With this aid they could buy a cow, and implements to cultivate a few acres of land; and instead of becoming burdens upon society, which is always the case where children are produced faster than they can be fed, would be put in the way of becoming useful and profitable citizens. The national domains also would sell the better if pecuniary aids were provided to cultivate them in small lots. (in vol. 1, 618)

That is, society as a whole is better off when everyone—not just the affluent—can prosper and enjoy the blessings of civilization.

Paine outlined several other consequentialist arguments to demonstrate that it would be in society's interest to adopt this plan (in vol. 1, 619). The primary interest that society secures through this plan is stability. Because the exploitative basis of economic inequality cannot be concealed from the masses indefinitely, it is only a matter of time before the rapacious behavior of the propertied classes triggers a violent backlash that would ultimately jeopardize everyone's well-being:

> To remove the danger, it is necessary to remove the antipathies, and this can only be done by making property productive of a national blessing, extending to every individual. When the riches of one man above another shall increase the national fund in the same proportion; when it shall be seen that the prosperity of that fund depends on the prosperity of individuals; when the more riches a man acquires, the better it shall be for the general mass; it is then that antipathies will cease, and property be placed on the permanent basis of national interest and protection. (in vol. 1, 621)

What is most interesting about Paine's argument is the assumption that solidarity among members of different classes would guarantee social stability. By removing the "antipathies" generated by great disparities in wealth, Paine believed his plan could strengthen national unity. If prosperity were no longer viewed as a benefit exclusive to the rich, the poor would begin to feel a stronger sense of common purpose with members of other classes.

A closely related interest promoted by his plan was security. This argument was directed specifically to the propertied classes. Paine raised the specter of violence against the propertied to make the point that greater economic equality actually serves their own material interests. His proposal would serve as an insurance policy against the kinds of confiscatory measures pursued by the Babeuvistes in France. By restoring justice and redressing the grievances of the poor, the program would "form a system that, while it preserves one part of society from wretchedness, shall secure the other from depredation" (in vol. 1, 620). In other words, it is in the interest of the rich as a class to ensure that inequality is kept to a minimum because "it is only in a system of justice that the possessor can contemplate security" (in vol. 1, 621).

The final argument appealed to everyone's interest in a free government. Echoing generations of republican thought, Paine suggested that free government can take root and thrive only if it is planted in the right socioeconomic soil. Where it already exists, free government eventually succumbs to the blight of despotism without the right conditions to sustain it. In his view, poverty paves the way for despotism: "Despotic government supports itself by abject civilization, in which debasement of the human mind, and wretchedness in the mass of the people, are the chief criterions [*sic*]" (in vol. 1, 621). Conversely, free government cannot blossom at all unless every single part of society receives adequate nourishment. For this reason, social and political change must go together. "A revolution in the state of civilization is the necessary companion of revolutions in the system of government" (in vol. 1, 621). Like Marx after him, Paine suggested that a revolution is incomplete if it is political but not social. However, unlike Marx, Paine believed that public policy enacted by republican governments could bring about the social conditions necessary to complete a revolution in politics.

"Prudence and Justice" in the Construction of the Constitution

Paine's vision for a state that would provide economic assistance to its neediest members and guarantee basic social rights undoubtedly challenged prevailing conditions in Europe, but some commentators have wondered whether any of this is relevant to the United States. It is easy to explain away the applicability of Paine's proposals to the United States. Like Jefferson, he was so convinced of the superiority of this country to Europe on so many counts that he sometimes conveyed the impression it was unnecessary to do anything for the lower classes in the young Republic. The very idea that the poor could find greater opportunity anywhere else was unthinkable: "We want not to export our laboring poor, for where can they live better, or where can they be more useful?" (in vol. 2, 204; see also vol. 2, 451). Indeed, like many Americans at the time, he believed his adoptive country was remarkably egalitarian. He remarked that in the United States the "poor are not oppressed, the rich are not privileged. Industry is not mortified by the splendid extravagance of a court rioting at its expense. Their taxes are few, because their government is just; and as there is nothing to render them wretched, there is nothing to engender riots and tumults" (*Rights of Man*, in vol. 1, 360; see also *American Crisis 10*, in vol. 1, 203, and *Rights of Man*, in vol. 1, 375). Paine attributed this state of prosperity to a combination of individual enterprise and prudent public investment, explaining that the money spent on the Revolutionary War was a vital investment in America's economic future.[46]

In spite of these remarks, Paine did recommend egalitarian measures specifically for the United States. In particular, he proposed changes in the tax structure that would make it more progressive. During the war for independence, Paine suggested that the rich should contribute more to the war effort. Part of his reasoning was that those who possess the resources should contribute more, but his primary consideration was humanitarian concern for the lower classes. In a letter written to Blair McClenaghan, he stated, "You are sensible that it is now hard times with many poor people. Several of the back counties are totally disabled to pay taxes; and as it is the rich that will suffer most by the ravages of an Enemy it is not only duty but true policy to do something spirited, and a way may be found to make the backward and the disaffected do their part" (May 1780, in vol. 2, 1185).

Whether Paine recommended egalitarian measures specifically for the United States is ultimately less important than his insistence that the policies proposed in *Rights of Man* and "Agrarian Justice" are universal. He never gave any indication that the United States was exempt from either the principles or the policies he advocated in writings that took up the problem of economic inequality.

However, for those looking to Paine for guidance on the authority of the federal government to adopt and administer egalitarian policies, these statements might seem utterly irrelevant. After all, the US Constitution (in principle) ultimately determines the functions and limits of governmental power in the United States. The fact that Paine played no role in either the creation or the ratification of the Constitution might suggest that he can provide little or no insight into the meaning of that document.

Paine is certainly much less helpful in determining understandings of constitutional functions and limits during the early years of the Republic than, say, Alexander Hamilton, James Madison, or any of the representatives who puzzled over their meanings during the first few Congresses. Unlike these other founders, Paine was not involved in some of those early constitutional controversies over the establishment of a national bank, when the meanings of the commerce clause and the necessary and proper clause were debated.

However, some of the letters he wrote after his return to the United States do offer clues to his possible approach to constitutional interpretation. In particular, his musings on various dimensions of the Louisiana Purchase and its aftermath indicate that he took a rather loose approach to the question of constitutional construction. Perhaps the most noteworthy fact about his numerous letters on this subject is that he never expressed any constitutional misgivings about the Louisiana Purchase. In a comment on the treaty power of the Senate, one of his only remarks on constitutional questions relating to the purchase, he argued that the purchase was not a treaty because it was a one-time act that created no further obligations on the part of the parties to the transaction (Letter to John C. Breckenridge, August 2, 1803, in vol. 2, 1443–1444). Whereas Jefferson was wringing his hands over the constitutionality of the purchase, fearing that the Constitution gave the government no authority to acquire new land, Paine was expressing high hopes for the possibility of expanding the size of the Union without any serious concerns about constitutional authority.

Paine's only other remark on the constitutionality of the Louisiana Purchase acknowledged the indeterminacy of the foundational text in language reminiscent of that used in some early congressional debates over executive power, the direct tax, and other controversial matters. In a letter to Jefferson he stated, "It appears to me to be one of those cases with which the Constitution has nothing to do, and which can be judged only by the circumstances of the times when such a case shall occur" (September 23, 1803, in vol. 2, 1447). The most telling comment of all appeared in another letter to Jefferson, in which Paine wrote that the "cession of Louisiana is a new case not provided for in the Constitution and must be managed by prudence and justice" (January 25, 1805, in vol. 2, 1457). His recommendation to use "prudence and justice" as guides where the Constitution is silent is the closest Paine ever came to offering a principle or standard of constitutional interpretation.

Needless to say, Paine's approach to constitutional construction was considerably more latitudinarian than Jefferson's. Whereas the third president believed the federal government possesses the authority to do only what was explicitly authorized in the Constitution, Paine adopted an approach much closer to Hamilton's in his willingness to look beyond the plain language of the text to ascertain its meaning and purpose. However, in a sense, Paine was being

faithful to his own principles. His comment could be understood as an extension of his thinking about government adaptation to social change. In pointing out that nothing in the Constitution expressly prohibits the acquisition of new territory, Paine suggested that governmental authority extends beyond those powers expressly granted in the Constitution: "The cession makes no alteration in the Constitution; it only extends the principles of it over a larger territory, and this certainly is within the morality of the Constitution, and not contrary to, nor beyond, the expression or intention of any of its articles" (September 23, 1803, in vol. 2, 1447–1448). The reference to the "intentions" of various articles serving as guides to interpretation would place Paine much closer to Hamilton than to his ideological fellow traveler.

One of Paine's greatest concerns relating to Louisiana was populating it with new citizens and laborers. In his letters to Jefferson, he suggested that Congress encourage residents to move to the territory. Though he generally neglected to provide any details about how this ought to be done, he did propose in one instance that Congress should pay for free blacks to move to the territory not only as a means of populating the territory with much-needed laborers but also as a way of improving the condition of free blacks. The plan was not exactly a government-sponsored job-training program, but it did entail the use of subsidies to assist free blacks in getting the knowledge and experience they would need to achieve economic independence. In fact, Paine noted that the inspiration for the idea came from Jefferson himself:

> I recollect when in France that you spoke of a plan of making the Negroes tenants on a plantation, that is, allotting each Negro family a quantity of land for which they were to pay to the owner a certain quantity of produce. I think that numbers of our free Negroes might be provided for in this manner in Louisiana. The best way that occurs to me is for Congress to give them their passage to New Orleans, then for them to hire themselves out to the planters for one or two years; they would by this means learn plantation business, after which to place the men on a tract of land as before mentioned. (January 25, 1805, in vol. 2, 1463–1464)

Paine never identified any specific provision of the Constitution that authorized Congress to do what he was proposing. Where justice was concerned, he appeared to believe the Constitution would impose no barriers.

Conclusion

Of all the founders, Paine provided the most sweeping critique of economic inequality and the most comprehensive plan to reduce it. Much of that critique echoed the points his contemporaries voiced about the damaging consequences of inequality for the dignity and self-respect of those at the bottom, its tendency to weaken the social bonds between classes, and of course its destructive effects on the stability and legitimacy of the political system. To these points he added a deontological argument that framed the pursuit of economic equality as a matter of natural rights. By doing so, Paine was able to make the case that governmental action to promote a more equal distribution of property was not just a way to avoid undesirable outcomes. It was required as a matter of justice. Because the pursuit of justice is a fundamental condition of legitimacy in government, Paine effectively made the pursuit of economic equality a standard of legitimacy. The veteran revolutionary did not have to spell out the consequences for governments that fail the test of legitimacy.

Although there is some truth to one scholar's claim that Paine's welfare "program entails only a marginal expansion of the functions of the minimal state," Paine did not set any limits to the functions or powers of the state in its pursuit of justice.[47] As his numerous social welfare proposals demonstrate, he was willing to expand the role of government when it served the ends of justice. Government did not overreach simply by assuming greater responsibilities; it exceeded its authority when it violated the rights of individuals or worsened their conditions. By demonstrating that individuals possess certain social rights, Paine suggested it was not enough for governments simply to refrain from action to show respect for rights. They would also have to take affirmative action to restore and promote rights.

8

CONCLUSION

When it shall be said in any country in the world, "My poor are happy; neither ignorance nor distress is to be found among them; my jails are empty of prisoners, my streets of beggars; the aged are not in want, the taxes are not oppressive; the rational world is my friend, because I am a friend of its happiness"—when these things can be said, then may that country boast of its constitution and its government.

—Thomas Paine, *Rights of Man*

Americans in the years after the Revolution took enormous pride in the social and political practices that set their young country apart from those in the Old World. The new Republic was still a developing nation without the great fortunes associated with old aristocratic families or the emerging class of industrial and mercantile capitalists, but its vast reserves of unspoiled land promised tremendous economic opportunities, its laws offered almost unparalleled freedom of religion, and the protections guaranteed by its political system provided what Thomas Paine described as an "asylum for mankind."[1] Americans also expressed great pride in the relative economic equality they believed distinguished their country from those in Europe. When they boasted of US economic achievements, they did not mention the impressive estates of men such as Robert Morris, George Washington, or William Bingham. Instead, they boasted that there were no beggars in their streets. When they spoke of the nation's bounty, they envisioned prosperity widely shared across all classes, not spectacular fortunes concentrated in the hands of a select few. The image Americans such as Benjamin Franklin proudly presented to the rest of the world was that of a country where a "general happy Mediocrity . . . prevails."[2] The reality was in many respects very different from America's self-perception and self-presentation.

Americans who claimed that class differences among citizens were negligible were wrong, but their errors reveal a deeper truth about the values that defined the public ethos at the time.

The ideal of economic equality formed the basis of judgments about existing realities and served as a guide for their transformation. Although Americans in the late eighteenth century accepted and enforced forms of inequality generally intolerable today, they were often highly sensitive to the effects of economic inequality on the well-being of individuals, society, the economy, and the political system. In the wake of the American Revolution, Thomas Jefferson, Thomas Paine, Abraham Clark, William Findley, Noah Webster, James Sullivan, and others unleashed a steady volley of criticisms against the ills of economic inequality. As discussed in preceding chapters, arguments against great disparities in wealth focused on both its causes and its effects. Critics argued inequality often arises from unjust forms of acquisition and one's position in the economic system is often the result of morally arbitrary factors such as bad luck or illness, it violates the natural right of individuals to an equal share of the earth's resources, it tends to have corrosive effects on social solidarity, it erodes trust between members of different classes, it undermines the bases of self-respect for those near the bottom, it degrades the character of individuals, it induces the lower classes to seek advancement through unsavory and illegal activities, it impairs economic growth, it reduces opportunities for individuals to achieve economic independence, and most gravely of all, it weakens the foundations of republican government. By the same token, many Americans urged the adoption of policies conducive to greater economic equality because of their belief in its positive effects. Benjamin Rush recommended the emancipation of slaves in the southern colonies because it would "diminish opulence in a few . . . and promote that equal distribution of property, which appears best calculated to promote the welfare of Society."[3]

Republicanism provided an intellectual framework that helped the founders see the political dimensions of economic stratification more clearly than many contemporary perspectives allow. Whereas a major concern today is that public policies designed to reduce poverty and economic inequalities will foster dependence on government, the primary concern around the time of the founding was that poverty and inequality would produce private relations of dependence that would ultimately undermine the capacity of individuals to participate in the political process. Although considerations of fairness, prosperity, and stability figured prominently in disputes over the potential effects of different policies and arrangements on economic inequality, the relation between the distribution of wealth and the distribution of power was of primary concern. No matter which side one took, participants were compelled to address the effects of economic disparities on republican government.

For republican writers such as the anti-Federalist who went by the pen name "Centinel," extreme levels of economic inequality were incompatible with the very idea of free government. "A republic," wrote "Centinel," "can exist only where the body of the people are [*sic*] virtuous, and where property is pretty equally divided."[4] For "Centinel" and his contemporaries, the unequal distribution of wealth was a serious political concern because they understood that inequalities in one sphere tend to spill over into other spheres. Sooner or later, concentrations of economic resources would result in concentrations of political power, and economic vulnerabilities would turn into political vulnerabilities. In other words, economic inequality generates and reinforces corresponding forms of political inequality that enable the haves to dominate the have-nots. Thus, maintaining a rough measure of economic equality was seen as vital to the conditions that make possible the meaningful participation of *all* citizens.

Politics often involves "tragic choices" between values and interests that are not always easy to reconcile. The conventional wisdom nowadays is that equality and freedom are distinct and perhaps even antithetical values. One of the key assumptions underlying much contemporary liberal political thought in particular is that a gain on one dimension often entails a loss on another.[5] In what is arguably the single-most influential US work of political theory published in the last half century, John Rawls's *A Theory of Justice*, equality is treated as a principle separate from—and subordinate to—freedom.[6] However, the political thought of the founders surveyed in this book shows that the two values may actually be mutually dependent. In their view, *a minimum degree of economic equality is a precondition of political liberty.* Relative equality in the social and economic spheres is necessary to enable citizens from all ranks to exercise freedom effectively in the political sphere. Where economic disparities grow too large, the capacity of those near the bottom to share in the collective exercise of popular sovereignty is diminished. By the same token, the freedom to participate in the political process is necessary to preserve and promote social and economic equality. For these reasons, minimizing economic inequality was not simply a moral obligation: it was first and foremost a political imperative.

Almost every major domestic political battle of the postrevolutionary period turned at one point or another to questions about the distribution of wealth. Class politics was an important dimension of disputes over many major issues, including the establishment of state constitutions, qualifications for voting and officeholding, proposals to create public schools, the issuance of paper money and the collection of taxes in the states, the creation of the Constitution for the United States, the repayment of Revolutionary War debt, the erection of a national bank, the disposition of western lands, supplies for the militia, medical care for sick and disabled seamen, and the first federal direct tax. Proponents of greater economic equality did not always prevail in their battles, but they did win the larger rhetorical and ideological war in making the pursuit of economic equality a legitimate and important political consideration. Even though many fought to preserve and extend the privileges and wealth of the upper classes, direct and open challenges to the principle of economic equality were remarkably uncommon.

The most ardent champions of equality were particularly attentive to the ways in which material conditions affect the political engagement of ordinary citizens. They sought to promote that equality mainly by expanding opportunities in education and landownership. Free public education was not simply or even primarily a means of providing students the skills necessary to succeed in the marketplace. For supporters such as William Manning, who argued that "want of knowledge" makes it much easier for the few to dominate the political system, education had a decidedly political purpose connected to the preservation of equality and freedom.[7] From Jefferson's proposal to guarantee every adult citizen of Virginia fifty acres of land and his acquisition of the vast Louisiana Territory to the efforts of numerous Congress members to make western lands as affordable as possible, attempts to maintain easy access to land were often rooted in the belief that economic independence is a precondition for political agency.

The founders scored major victories for equality in the area of taxation. During the transition from dependent colonies to independent states, the idea that taxes should be laid according to the ability to pay gained wide acceptance from citizens and law makers alike. There was a major shift from highly regressive taxes on polls and acreage regardless of value, which worked to the advantage of wealthy landowners who usually owned the most expensive real estate, to more progressive taxes on luxuries and the assessed value of land, which tended to fall more heavily on members of the upper classes. At the national level, egalitarians succeeded in establishing graduated tax rates on a variety of objects and imposing steep levies on items only the wealthy could afford. Among the most significant achievements were the federal taxes on carriages and the graduated rates on land, dwellings, and slaves enacted in 1798. The principle of progressive taxation was still a fairly novel idea at the time, yet it faced no serious opposition.[8] In fact, the principle that taxation should be based on the ability to pay occasionally received support from some of the unlikeliest corners, as the preceding discussions of Robert Morris and Alexander Hamilton have indicated. Even the haughty and aristocratic Gouverneur Morris paid lip service to this idea in his own revenue proposals.

Of all the activities undertaken in the name of economic equality during the founding, perhaps the most significant were those aimed at preventing measures that would contribute to the divide between economic classes. Many of the political leaders discussed in preceding chapters were willing to accept most disparities resulting from the operation of market forces, but they were steadfastly opposed to public policies that would increase existing levels of inequality. Policies that introduced or exacerbated disparities between the classes were widely viewed as illegitimate exercises of government power. To allow government to serve the interests of the wealthy, whether landed aristocrats from the southern states or mercantile elites from the so-called eastern cities, would signify a return to the pernicious practices that flourished during the colonial period and still continued in Europe at the time. Avoiding policies that contributed to economic inequality could be just as important as the pursuit of policies that promoted its opposite. The historical association of active government with the establishment of exclusive privileges and monopolies that benefited the few at the expense of the many helps explain why so many egalitarians at the end of the eighteenth century and throughout much of the nineteenth century favored laissez-faire policies.[9] Sometimes other imperatives—such as the need to raise revenue, restore the credit of the United States, and stabilize the national finances—ultimately took precedence over the pursuit of equality. However, the battles over these policies were particularly fierce because opponents realized that the future of republican institutions was in jeopardy if the government became an instrument of inequality.

For many founders, maintaining the level of economic equality necessary for the preservation of political freedom justified the use of government powers otherwise eyed with suspicion. Many of those who ordinarily wanted to keep the size and scope of government limited were willing to expand its functions to include policies aimed at reducing economic inequalities and providing relief to distressed groups. Writing in support of increases in the money supply and other measures designed to benefit ordinary laborers, Clark reminded legislators, "It is to you that your constituents look for protection and defence—it is your business to help the feeble against the mighty, and deliver the oppressed out of the hands of the oppressor."[10] Paine's famous condemnation of overactive and intrusive government did not extend to the area of social services. Indeed, he outlined an unprecedented plan for a welfare state that would provide assistance to families, the sick, the blind, the poor, the unemployed, and the old. Even some of those, such as Jefferson, who had constitutional reservations about the federal government's authority to intervene in the economy expressed no principled objections to the use of public policy to address inequality and poverty. One of the great ironies of the creation of the Constitution is that the very same national powers that had been augmented to diminish the influence of the lower classes at the state level could later be used to address economic inequality at the national level. The provision of supplies to poor members of the militia and the establishment of hospitals for sick and disabled sailors, who usually populated the very lowest ranks of economic life in urban seaports, reveal that the enhanced powers of the federal government could be used to address the needs of the lower orders as well as the interests of the propertied, in whose interests it was developed.

The Costs of Economic Inequality Today

The belief that economic conditions in the United States were relatively equal, at least compared with those in Europe, helped sustain belief in American exceptionalism during the founding. Although most Americans underestimated the degree of economic inequality—and simply ignored slaves, American Indians, and women in their calculations—they were correct in their claims that social mobility and economic equality for white men were far greater in their own country compared with any in Europe.

What is exceptional about the United States today is how far economic inequality has advanced compared with other advanced industrialized countries. Franklin's boast of a "happy mediocrity of condition" is totally untenable now that the United States leads the advanced industrialized world in disparities between the top and the bottom. In fact, the level of economic inequality in the United States has grown so much that it now rivals that in many parts of the developing world.[11] Since the late 1970s, during a period coming to be known as the Great Divergence, disparities in income and wealth have only accelerated and outpaced those of most other countries on the planet. Although some of this widening inequality is explained by stagnating conditions at the bottom and in the middle, the most significant change by far concerns the spectacular increases in income and wealth at the very top.[12] The 400 wealthiest Americans now control as much wealth as the bottom half of the population combined.[13] Meanwhile, the US middle class—once a sizable and robust majority that used to be the envy of the world in the standard of living it enjoyed—has relinquished its status as the globe's wealthiest middle class to its Canadian counterpart and is quickly losing ground to the middle class in parts of Europe.[14] Even the much-vaunted US reputation as the "land of opportunity" has become something of a myth as economic mobility has stalled. Those born in the lowest economic rungs now have a better chance of ascending the economic ladder in almost every other advanced industrialized country in the world than they do in the United States.[15]

Economic inequality—especially the share of income and wealth going to those at the very top—has often been tolerated and justified on the grounds that economic differences generally reflect differences in natural endowments, individual effort, and acquired skills that ought to be encouraged and rewarded. Economic inequality was the price paid for unrivalled levels of social mobility in the United States. Reducing or eliminating economic inequality, it has been said, would require reducing or eliminating the social mobility that has made it an "exceptional" nation. Many of these long-standing assumptions are now coming into question. Members of the political establishment in both major political parties have begun to acknowledge that growing inequality is starting to undermine upward mobility. In his 2015 State of the Union Address, Democratic president Barack Obama posed the choice facing the country in stark terms: "Will we accept an economy where only a few of us do spectacularly well? Or will we commit ourselves to an economy that generates rising incomes and chances for everyone who makes the effort?"[16] Even on the right some have voiced worries about the political and social effects of economic inequality on social mobility.[17] Prominent Republican members of Congress, including Senator Marco Rubio of Florida and Representative Paul Ryan of Wisconsin, have expressed concerns about diminishing social mobility.[18] During his brief flirtation with a third run at the presidency in early 2015, former Massachusetts governor Mitt Romney declared support for raising the minimum wage as a way to combat growing income inequality.[19]

The idea that unequal outcomes are justified as long as everyone has an equal opportunity to strike it rich is being challenged by growing evidence that the extraordinary levels of economic inequality reached since the start of the Great Divergence are impeding social mobility. Recent studies indicate that parental status is the best predictor of a child's status as an adult. According to some reports, income heritability—the percentage of an individual's earnings that can be explained by their parent's income—has grown from about 20 percent to anywhere between 40 and 60 percent today. The figures are even more skewed at the very top, with children born into the wealthiest families generally maintaining and solidifying their elite status.[20] Spectacular falls like those suffered by James Wilson and Robert Morris have become rare.

Recent scholarship also reveals that economic inequality negatively affects society in many other ways, some of which the founders predicted and others they could not have anticipated. First, there is evidence that heightened levels of economic inequality damage the economy in various ways. Contrary to claims that skewed distributions of income and wealth are a necessary price to pay for expansions in the overall size of the economic pie, there is mounting evidence that higher levels of economic inequality may actually impede economic growth and could even be contributing to economic slowdowns such as the Great Recession of 2008–2009 because the uneven distribution of resources dampens the spending that drives economic activity.[21] In addition, periods with higher levels of inequality tend to experience more financial instability resulting from more risky speculative activities by those seeking to get ahead or merely keep up with the super-rich. Consequently, periods with more economic inequality tend to have higher occurrences of financial bubbles, panics, and crashes.[22] More unequal societies also tend to encourage perverse consumption patterns and unsustainable levels of spending that lead to financial problems for individuals and households. The heightened status consciousness found in less equal societies stimulates the drive to acquire markers of distinction in an escalating arms race of conspicuous consumption that increases levels of anxiety and exacerbates existing levels of inequality.[23] In response to the pressure felt by individuals and families to acquire outward material signs of status, many end up overextending themselves and fall into debt or bankruptcy, which only worsens their condition.[24]

Second, research reveals a strong and consistent negative relationship between economic inequality and various measures of well-being across different countries, states, and cities. Less egalitarian societies exhibit higher infant mortality rates, worse educational attainment among children, lower life expectancy rates, worse status for women, higher levels of mental illness, higher levels of violent crime, higher levels of discrimination, higher levels of teenage pregnancy, higher rates of drug abuse, worse social relations, lower levels of social trust, and less technological innovation.[25] It is not absolute or average levels of income or wealth that explain these results, but how that income is distributed in developed societies. As Richard Wilkinson and Kate Pickett explain, "The problems in rich countries are not caused by the society not being rich enough (or even by being too rich), but by the scale of material differences between people within each society being too big."[26] Although those at the bottom generally have worse outcomes, even those at the top fare more poorly in less equal societies. When it comes to various measures of well-being, relative standing provides a better explanation than absolute levels of income.[27] It is thus no surprise that the United States—the most unequal advanced industrialized country in the world—performs the worst on almost every measure of well-being in comparisons of advanced industrialized countries. Within the United States, those states with the highest levels of economic inequality tend to have the highest rates of teenage pregnancy, the highest levels of obesity, the lowest levels of social trust, the worst educational performance, the highest number of high school drop-outs, the highest levels of imprisonment, and the highest levels of aggression.[28] What is most remarkable about these findings is that outcomes in less equal societies are worse for *everyone, including those at the top.* The negative effects, which very often reflect and reinforce racial disparities, are concentrated at the bottom, but the costs of higher economic inequality across these measures of health and well-being extend across all economic levels.[29]

Third, as many founders suspected, higher levels of economic in-equality tend to undermine social trust and solidarity. There is some dispute among scholars about the direction of causality in the rela-tionship between equality and social capital, but there is no question that the two "move in tandem."[30] The corrosive social effects of eco-nomic inequality are explained in large part by the social and physi-cal distance that emerges between members of different classes. Diminished social contact in the workplace, in places of worship, in voluntary associations, in the marketplace, and at play tends to erode the mutual trust and feelings of fraternity that sustain and invigorate civil life. As income and wealth disparities have grown in the United States, businesses and other institutions have catered their services to the rich in ways that further segregate them from the poor. It has always been possible for the wealthy to minimize their contact with the poor, but now it is possible for the ultra-rich to avoid contact with the lower orders altogether in almost all areas of life. From first-class cabins on airplanes to members-only lounges at airports, from luxury boxes at sporting arenas to exclusive seating areas at concerts, from $100,000-a-plate fund-raisers to ultra-high-end retailers and supermarkets, there are more and more opportuni-ties for the wealthiest Americans to avoid interactions and common experiences with members of other classes. Indeed, the ultra-rich today arguably have much less in common with members of their own countries than they do with the ultra-rich in other countries. As a result, there is now an emerging class of global elites increasingly disconnected from the experiences, concerns, and interests of their fellow citizens.[31] The widening social distance between members of different classes is also transforming the way in which civic or-ganizations (which used to bring people from different backgrounds together) are structured and the way in which they operate. Many associations now focus less on mobilizing their members in local chapters and more on raising money from wealthy supporters nationwide. As a result, civic associations tend to focus less on the issues that matter most to members of the middle and lower classes than they once did.[32]

Fourth, research also confirms the founders' worst suspicions about the effects of economic inequality on the political process. Just as Paine, Jefferson, Clark, William Manning, Findley, Sullivan, and many others feared, concentrations of economic resources are translating into concentrations of political power that enable the wealthy to dominate the political system.

Much as republican thought during the founding predicted, disparities in economic resources are contributing to disparities in rates of political participation between the top and the bottom. The wealthy are more likely than less affluent citizens to engage in every major form of organized political activity, including voting, contacting elected officials, campaigning for candidates, donating money to politicians and causes, and attending political events. They are even more likely to participate in protests and demonstrations, often thought to be "weapons of the weak."[33] Much of the difference can be accounted for by differences in material conditions and working conditions. Aside from the fact that those at or near the top have more money to contribute directly to preferred candidates and causes, they usually have more flexibility to take off time from work, and they can more easily "buy" the time necessary to get involved by hiring others to care for their children and other dependents—a luxury unavailable to most in the lower classes.

Differences in resources are not the only explanation for differences in levels of participation. As a number of founders suggested, economic conditions affect the disposition to get involved in politics too. Whereas those with greater economic clout feel emboldened to assert their interests through their voices and their checkbooks, those closer to the bottom tend to feel more alienated and disempowered. As a result, they become more apathetic and cynical about politics, leading them to withdraw and disengage from politics altogether. The poor—who disproportionately tend to be racial and ethnic minorities—already have to contend with a variety of procedural requirements and electoral rules, such as new voter identification laws and reduced early voting times, that make it harder for them to cast a ballot. However, there is evidence that lower economic status alone tends to discourage political participation.[34]

These different levels of economic clout and political participation have a significant impact on the kinds of policies the government enacts. As economic inequality increases, the treatment of citizens by government also becomes less equal. A major tenet of democracy is that each citizen should have an equal voice, but the effect of economic inequality is to give the wealthy a megaphone that drowns out the speech of the lower classes. Elected officials from both major parties are much more responsive to the interests and preferences of their most affluent constituents than they are to the interests and preferences of their other constituents.[35] Even when controlling for differences in "turnout, knowledge, and contacting," there are still "significant disparities in responsiveness to rich and poor constituents."[36] Political scientists Martin Gilens and Benjamin Page find that "economic elites and organized groups representing business interests have substantial independent impacts on U.S. government policy, while mass-based interest groups and average citizens have little or no independent influence."[37] Larry Bartels's findings are even starker. Based on an examination of the relationship between public opinion and roll-call votes on economic and social issues in the Senate, he concludes, "The views of constituents in the bottom third of the income distribution received no weight at all in the voting decisions of their senators."[38] Thus, even though solid majorities of the US public—including most Republicans—believe the existing distribution of wealth and income is unfair and favor specific policies to reduce economic inequality,[39] little is actually done to address these concerns. Despite consistent—and consistently high—levels of public support for more progressive taxes, hikes in the minimum wage, shoring up the Social Security system, and other policies that would improve the conditions of the middle and lower classes, government often fails to act because these policies tend not to be favored by the highest-income voters.[40] In fact, the government sometimes adopts policies *opposed* by large majorities if they happen to be favored by economic elites. For instance, there has been a trend in the last few decades away from popularly supported progressive taxes on income and property toward regressive consumption taxes that fall more heavily on the poor and middle class.[41]

The dominance of wealth feared by Jefferson, Paine, and many others is not limited to the formation of highly salient public policy. Extreme levels of economic inequality have also contributed to changes in the structure and rules of the political and economic systems. Since the 1970s, both the Democratic and Republican Parties have adopted procedural changes in their nomination systems that have had the effect of overrepresenting the affluent and underrepresenting the poor.[42] Both major parties also reinforce uneven levels of political participation by targeting more and more of their resources and messages to their most affluent supporters and increasingly ignoring less affluent constituents.[43] In addition, the rising cost of political campaigns has elevated the importance of wealthy donors and well-connected bundlers to political parties and individual candidates. The need to cultivate good relationships with campaign contributors has had a profound effect on how and where elected officials spend much of their time. There is evidence that the growing importance of smaller segments of the community may be contributing to the unprecedented rise in political polarization.[44]

When it comes to public policy debates over complex issues that are not especially salient to most citizens, government has adopted rules and regulations with the effect of reinforcing existing inequalities. The deregulation of the financial industry is a case in point. The repeal of the Glass-Steagall Banking Act, the loosening of leverage requirements, the exemption of derivatives and other complex new financial instruments from regulatory oversight, and other recent changes have allowed those in finance to reap huge rewards from taking ever-more-risky ventures with other people's money.[45] Rules affecting corporate governance have also contributed to the spectacular rise in incomes among US CEOs, who, thanks in part to rules regarding stock options, oversight by shareholders, and corporate tax deductions, are far and away the highest paid in the world.[46] Just as significant as policy changes that go largely unnoticed by the majority of the electorate are changes in the agencies charged with enforcing financial and corporate regulations. Thanks to successful lobbying efforts by interested parties, agencies such as the Securities and Exchange Commission (SEC) are often (under)staffed by underqualified or business-friendly regulators, operate with inadequate budgets, and face pressure from many law makers to treat the entities they are supposed to oversee with kid gloves.[47]

Significant rule changes that more directly affect those near the bottom have also reinforced asymmetries in wealth and power. Unions have historically acted as a counterweight to the influence of wealth and business in US politics, but since the 1970s, in response to coordinated lobbying efforts and public relations campaigns by the business community, state and federal governments have generally adopted a hostile attitude toward organized labor. Policies adopted since the 1970s, when the Great Divergence began, have systematically reduced the size and strength of unions by making it harder for workers to organize, slashing the budget of the National Labor Relations Board (NLRB), selectively enforcing labor protection laws, processing unfair labor complaints slowly to create backlogs, and decertifying public unions.[48]

The escalating concentration of wealth has also contributed to changes in the way the so-called fourth branch of government operates. Control of the media by a shrinking number of owners has facilitated many of the shifts in public policy discussed so far. Thanks to the consolidation of the media made possible by growing concentrations of wealth, a small handful of elites is able to exert enormous influence over the dissemination of information and the formation of public opinion.[49] As a result, it is much easier to cast the political alternatives favored by the upper class in a more favorable light and delegitimize or simply ignore the alternatives favored by other classes.

The changes that have occurred in the past few decades point to the development of what Bartels calls a "vicious feedback cycle." Disparities in resources such as power and wealth reinforce each other. Increasing inequality in the economic sphere contributes to increasing inequality in the political sphere, which in turn results in policies that exacerbate inequality in the economic sphere, and so on.[50] As economic inequality has increased, the political power of the wealthy has grown while that of the poor and middle class has diminished. As the political dominance of the super-rich increases, the capacity of those near the bottom to fight back using the standard channels of politics is weakened. As these political losses continue to mount, it would not be surprising if those near the bottom become more disillusioned, disgruntled, and disengaged.

What all of this suggests is that economic inequality jeopardizes the health and stability of democracy. The imbalance of power resulting from huge disparities in wealth is simply incompatible with any normative conception of democracy. One of the central tenets of democracy is that those subject to the laws should have an equal say in the making of those laws: everyone should count the same and no one should count more (or less) than another. However, developments in US politics since the late 1970s demonstrate that expanding economic inequality has made it possible for a few to dominate the political process and exert outsized influence over the formation of laws that affect the well-being of all citizens.

As Paine warned after witnessing the French Revolution, excessive levels of economic inequality and the failure or unwillingness of government to address it ultimately undermine the legitimacy of the political system. The rising levels of distrust and disgust with government lamented by so many today are at least partly attributable to the sense that the political system does not serve all citizens equally. The feeling that money buys access to elected officials and even favored treatment by them only reinforces public cynicism and resentment toward the political system. Americans have been much more tolerant of economic inequality than citizens of other advanced industrialized countries, but it is not clear how long they can sustain their faith in democracy when those disparities result in increasingly unequal political power and ever more unequal treatment at the hands of government.

Looking to the founders for answers to contemporary political problems is always a risky enterprise. After all, no two founders thought exactly alike on any political question, great or small. In addition, their views often changed over time. As a group and as individuals, members of this generation often held complicated and sometimes inconsistent views that could be rethought, revised, and abandoned over time. Moreover, they were often inconsistent and unfaithful representatives of their own ideas. Americans in the late eighteenth century were no different from people in other times and places in living with discrepancies between their ideals and their practices, inconsistencies in their actions and behaviors, and contradictions among their beliefs.

If the political thought at the founding does matter to contemporary debates, it is not because any of the founders provided definitive answers or solutions but because their work can help us better identify and understand certain developments as problems. Because they were undertaking what was still considered an experiment in self-government, they could not afford to take anything for granted. The recognition that this experiment could fail made them highly sensitive to the conditions necessary for its success. As centuries of republican thinkers taught them, the stability and durability of the political order depends on the economic order, and an imbalance in either poses a threat to the other. It is worth heeding these warnings, whether or not we accept the specific solutions they proposed.

As economic inequality receives more attention from scholars, the media, the political establishment, and—most important of all— ordinary citizens, it is well worth considering the emphasis many of the founders placed on the *political* implications of economic inequality. The considerations that tend to receive the most attention in contemporary debates over income and wealth inequality are important in their own right. There is nothing wrong with the current focus on declining standards of living for the poor and middle class, concern about stalled mobility and limited opportunities, worry regarding the mounting debt households accumulate to make ends meet, and press coverage of other economic problems. However, what all too often gets downplayed in contemporary debates is the impact economic inequality has on the political system. That is starting to change, but the implications of economic inequality for political liberty still do not get the attention they deserve. Yet what we are seeing is that excessive levels of economic inequality make it possible for a few to dominate the political system to such an extent that they discourage the participation of others or render that participation moot. What one anonymous New Yorker stated about conditions in 1779 is even truer today: "The security of liberty requires a more equal distribution of property than at present."[51]

To be sure, some would happily welcome further declines in political participation by those in the lower and middle classes. In fact, it is arguable many of the economic changes that have occurred in the last few decades were deliberately undertaken in order to consolidate class power at the top.[52] However, for the vast majority of Americans, participation in the political process is a good they want to encourage. Many of the founders surveyed in this book help us better understand that one of the conditions necessary to promoting meaningful and effective political participation is a more equal distribution of wealth and income. The preservation of democracy in our country may depend on it.

NOTES

Preface and Acknowledgments

1. Emmanuel Saez and Gabriel Zucman, "Wealth Inequality in the United States since 1913: Evidence from Capitalized Income Tax Data," National Bureau of Economic Research Working Paper Series, no. 20625, October 2014, http://www.nber.org/papers/w20625.

2. Tom Kertscher, "Just How Wealthy Is the Wal-Mart Walton Family?" PolitiFact, December 8, 2013, http://www.politifact.com/wisconsin/statements/2013/dec/08/one-wisconsin-now/just-how-wealthy-wal-mart-walton-family/.

3. Anthony B. Atkinson, Thomas Piketty, and Emmanuel Saez, "Top Incomes in the Long Run of History," *Journal of Economic Literature* 49, no. 1 (2011): 7.

4. Emmanuel Saez, "Striking It Richer: The Evolution of Top Incomes in the United States (Updated with 2013 Preliminary Estimates)," January 25, 2015, http://eml.berkeley.edu/~saez/saez-UStopincomes-2013.pdf, 1.

5. Barack Obama, "Remarks by the President on Economic Mobility," December 4, 2013, http://www.whitehouse.gov/the-press-office/2013/12/04/remarks-president-economic-mobility.

6. Jonathan Martin, "On Economy, Jeb Bush Tests Divergent Message," *New York Times*, February 5, 2015, A14.

7. For example, see Thomas Byrne Edsall, *The New Politics of Inequality* (New York: Norton, 1984); Kevin Phillips, *The Politics of Rich and Poor: Wealth and the American Electorate in the Reagan Aftermath* (New York: HarperCollins, 1991); Kevin Phillips, *Wealth and Democracy: A Political History of the American Rich* (New York: Broadway, 2003); Paul Krugman, *The Conscience of a Liberal* (New York: Norton, 2007).

8. For example, see Barry Goldwater, *The Conscience of a Conservative* (New York: Victor, 1960); Milton Friedman, *Capitalism and Freedom* (Chicago: University of Chicago Press, 1969); Robert Nozick, *Anarchy, State, and Utopia* (New York: BasicBooks, 1971); Friedrich A. Hayek, *Law, Legislation, and Liberty*, vol. 2: *The Mirage of Social Justice* (Chicago: University of Chicago Press, 1976).

9. Ronald Reagan, Inaugural Address, January 20, 1981.

10. See David Harvey, *A Brief History of Neoliberalism* (Oxford, UK: Oxford University Press, 2005), 19–31, 42–55.

11. Bill Clinton, "The New Covenant: Responsibility and Rebuilding the American Community," remarks to students at Georgetown University, October 23, 1991.

12. Juana Summers, "Paul Ryan: Stop Dependency Culture," *Politico,* October 24, 2012.

13. Tami Luhby, "Romney: Income Inequality Is Just Envy," CNN Archive, January 12, 2012, http://money.cnn.com/2012/01/12/news/economy/romney_envy/index.htm.

14. This is the central thesis of the best-selling Thomas Piketty, *Capital in the Twenty-First Century*, trans. Arthur Goldhammer (Cambridge, MA: Harvard University Press, 2014).

15. The scholarship on these and other claims is discussed in the conclusion of this volume.

16. Noah Webster, "An Examination into the Leading Principles of the Federal Constitution," in *Friends of the Constitution: Writings of the "Other" Federalists, 1787–1788*, ed. Colleen A. Sheehan and Gary L. McDowell (Indianapolis, IN: Liberty Fund, 1998), 400.

Chapter 1: The American Revolution and the Ideal of Equality

1. Gordon S. Wood, *The Radicalism of the American Revolution* (New York: Vintage, 1991), 24.

2. Seth Rockman, "Class and the History of the Working People in the Early Republic," *Journal of the Early Republic* 25, no. 4 (2005).

3. Class status was not determined according to a single criterion or objective standard (such as a group's relation to the means of production), nor was it always defined with any great precision. Instead, membership in a particular class was determined by a combination of criteria, including literacy and occupation, although the most important criterion by far was wealth. On the indeterminacy of class as a concept in late eighteenth-century America, see Ronald Schultz, "A Class Society? The Nature of Inequality in Early America," in *Inequality in Early America*, ed. Carla Gardina Pestana and Sharon V. Salinger (Hanover, NH: University Press of New England, 1999), 203–221. On the importance of property ownership in determining class, see Jackson Turner Main, *Social Structure of Revolutionary America* (Princeton, NJ: Princeton University Press, 1965), 228–230.

4. Joyce Appleby, *Capitalism and a New Social Order: The Republican Vision of the 1790s* (New York: New York University Press, 1984), 7–8. The stark differences drew disapproving comments from New Englanders such as John Adams: "Gentlemen in other colonies have large plantations of slaves, and the common people among them are very ignorant and very poor. These gentlemen [are more] accustomed, habituated to higher notions

of themselves, and the distinction between them and the common people, than we are." John Adams to Joseph Hawley, letter, November 25, 1775, in *The Works of John Adams, Second President of the United States*, vol. 9 (Boston: Little, Brown, 1865), 367. On other regional differences in attitudes toward equality, see J. R. Pole, *The Pursuit of Equality in American History* (Berkeley: University of California Press, 1978), 30–33.

5. On the different ways in which social rank was enforced, see Wood, *Radicalism of the American Revolution*, 20–21. This is not to say the "lower orders" always adhered to these social norms. Both leaders and visitors in places as different as seventeenth-century New England and late eighteenth-century Philadelphia complained of the insolence of the lower orders. See Thomas N. Ingersoll, "'Riches and Honour Were Rejected by Them as Loathsome Vomit': The Fear of Leveling in New England," in Pestana and Salinger, *Inequality in Early America*, 46–47; Billy G. Smith, *The "Lower Sort": Philadelphia's Laboring People, 1750–1800* (Ithaca, NY: Cornell University Press, 1990), 24. Although such complaints demonstrate that the ideal of deference was not always followed in practice, they do testify to the tenacity of the ideal itself.

6. Main, *Social Structure of Revolutionary America*, 211–213. Economic rewards doled out by the government also flowed to those at the top of various hierarchies. For instance, land grants to veterans of the French and Indian Wars were made according to rank. Wood, *Radicalism of the American Revolution*, 20.

7. Robert A. Becker, *Revolution, Reform, and the Politics of American Taxation, 1763–1783* (Baton Rouge: Louisiana State University Press, 1980).

8. J. G. A. Pocock, "The Classical Theory of Deference," *American Historical Review* 81 (1976). See also John K. Alexander, "Deference in Colonial Pennsylvania and That Man from New Jersey," *Pennsylvania Magazine of History and Biography* 102, no. 4 (1978).

9. "The Preceptor: Vol. 2. Social Duties of the Public Kind," 1772, in *American Political Writings during the Founding Era, 1760–1805*, vol. 1, ed. Charles S. Hyneman and Donald S. Lutz (Indianapolis, IN: Liberty Fund, 1983), 178.

10. Pole, *Pursuit of Equality in American History*, 4.

11. For an overview of these changes in attitude, see Bernard Bailyn, *The Ideological Origins of the American Revolution*, enlarged ed. (Cambridge, MA: Belknap Press of Harvard University Press, 1992), 301–319.

12. For example, *Pennsylvania Evening Post*, April 27, 1776; Democritus, "Loose Thoughts on Government," June 7, 1776, in *The Founders' Constitution*, vol. 1: *Major Themes*, ed. Philip B. Kurland and Ralph Kerner (Indianapolis, IN: Liberty Fund, 1987), 519; "A Watchman," *Pennsylvania Packet*, June 10, 1776, in Kurland and Kerner, *Founders' Constitution*, vol. 1, 520–522; "A Citizen of New Jersey," *Pennsylvania Evening Post*, July 30, 1776, in Kurland and Kerner, *Founders' Constitution*, vol. 1, 524–525.

13. Numerous incidents of direct popular action against economic and political elites in Boston, Philadelphia, and New York City prior to the

Revolution are discussed in Gary B. Nash, *The Urban Crucible: Social Change, Political Consciousness, and the Origins of the American Revolution* (Cambridge, MA: Harvard University Press, 1979), 47–48, 132–133.

14. Wood, *Radicalism of the American Revolution*, 232. See also Main, *Social Structure of Revolutionary America*, 236–239.

15. David McCullough, *1776* (New York: Simon and Schuster, 2005), 31.

16. The author of one article noted that annual elections force the highborn to "come down to our level." *Pennsylvania Evening Post*, April 27, 1776, in Kurland and Kerner, *Founders' Constitution*, vol. 1, 519.

17. Main, *Social Structure of Revolutionary America*, 215–219.

18. Richard B. Morris, "Class Struggle and the American Revolution," *William and Mary Quarterly* 19, no. 1 (1962): 5–7.

19. Samuel Adams to Arthur Lee, letter, April 4, 1774, in *The Writings of Samuel Adams*, vol. 3, ed. Harry Alonzo Cushing (New York: Putnam's Sons, 1906), 102.

20. Terry Bouton, *Taming Democracy: "The People," the Founders, and the Troubled Ending of the American Revolution* (Oxford, UK: Oxford University Press, 2007), 29.

21. Ingersoll, "'Riches and Honour Were Rejected,'" 58–59.

22. As James L. Huston notes, questions about the distribution of wealth did not necessarily "monopolize the concerns of revolutionary leaders" facing the "challenge of building a functioning republican political order [including] the detailing of constitutions, suffrage requirements, legislative powers, executive powers, and the like, not to mention the task of actually winning a war against Europe's most powerful nation," but they did play an "important role in public discourse because the goal of the American revolutionaries was to found a republic that preserved the equality of citizens and individual liberty." Huston, *Securing the Fruits of Labor: The American Concept of Wealth Distribution, 1765–1900* (Baton Rouge: Louisiana State University Press, 1998), 5.

23. Noah Webster, "Miscellaneous Remarks on Divizions of Property, Guvernment, Education, Religion, Agriculture, Slavery, Commerce, Climate, and Diseezes in the United States," in Webster, *A Collection of Essays and Fugitiv* [sic] *Writings: On Moral, Historical, Political, and Literary Subjects* (Boston: I. Thomas and E. T. Andrews, 1790), 327. During the debate over the ratification of the Constitution, Webster reiterated the importance of "equal property" to the preservation of freedom in even stronger language, writing that the rights of the press, to trial by jury, and even of habeas corpus all paled in significance "compared with a general distribution of real property among every class of people." Webster, "An Examination into the Leading Principles of the Federal Constitution," in *Friends of the Constitution: Writings of the "Other" Federalists, 1787–1788*, ed. Colleen A. Sheehan and Gary L. McDowell (Indianapolis, IN: Liberty Fund, 1998), 401.

24. Nash, *Urban Crucible*.

25. See, for example, Maurizio Viroli, *Republicanism* (New York: Hill and Wang, 2002).

26. Samuel Adams to James Warren, letter, February 12, 1779, in Cushing, *Writings of Samuel Adams*, vol. 4, 123.

27. Robert Coram, *Political Inquiries, to Which Is Added a Plan for the Establishment of Schools throughout the United States*, in Hyneman and Lutz, *American Political Writings during the Founding Era*, vol. 2, 809.

28. On the development of republican thought as it was transmitted into the eighteenth-century American context, see Gordon S. Wood, *The Creation of the American Republic, 1776–1787* (Chapel Hill: University of North Carolina Press, 1969); Robert E. Shalhope, "Toward a Republican Synthesis: The Emergence of an Understanding of Republicanism in American Historiography," *William and Mary Quarterly* 29 (1972): 49–80; J. G. A. Pocock, *The Machiavellian Moment: Florentine Political Thought and the Atlantic Republican Tradition* (Princeton, NJ: Princeton University Press, 1975); Lance Banning, *The Jeffersonian Persuasion: Evolution of a Party Ideology* (Ithaca, NY: Cornell University Press, 1978), 25–71; J. G. A. Pocock, *Politics, Language, and Time: Essays on Political Thought and History* (Chicago: University of Chicago Press, 1989), 80–147.

29. Webster, "Miscellaneous Remarks," 331. See also Huston, *Securing the Fruits of Labor*.

30. An important exception is Marcus Tullius Cicero, who represented a more aristocratic strain of republicanism and generally placed much more emphasis on moral and institutional factors than on material ones in his political writings. Indeed, the Roman thinker staunchly defended the importance of maintaining existing distributions of property and gave little thought to their effects on the distribution of power. See Cicero, *On Duties*, ed. M. T. Griffin and E. M. Atkins (Cambridge, UK: Cambridge University Press, 1991), 92–98.

31. James Harrington, *The Commonwealth of Oceania and a System of Politics*, ed. J. G. A. Pocock (Cambridge, UK: Cambridge University Press, 1992), 20.

32. Michael J. Thompson, *The Politics of Inequality: A Political History of Economic Inequality in America* (New York: Columbia University Press, 2007), 4. For a philosophical restatement of republican critiques of domination, see Philip Pettit, *Republicanism: A Theory of Freedom and Government* (Oxford, UK: Oxford University Press, 1997); Philip Pettit, *A Theory of Freedom: From the Psychology to the Politics of Agency* (Oxford, UK: Oxford University Press, 2001).

33. Harrington, *Commonwealth of Oceania*, 57.

34. See, for example, Aristotle, *Politics*, book 5, chap. 3, trans. Ernest Barker, revised trans. R. F. Stalley (Oxford, UK: Oxford University Press, 1995), 183; Aristotle, *Politics*, book 6, chap. 5, 241; Aristotle, *Politics*, book 6, chap. 2, 232; Niccolò Machiavelli, *Discourses on Livy*, trans. Harvey C. Mansfield and Nathan Tarcov (Chicago: University of Chicago Press, 1996), 79, 142, 244, 255; Harrington, *Commonwealth of Oceania*, 33, 99–101; John Trenchard and Thomas Gordon, *Cato's Letters; or, Essays on Liberty, Civil and Religious, and Other Important Subjects*, vol. 1, nos. 3, 35, ed. Ronald

Hamowy (Indianapolis, IN: Liberty Fund, 1995), 44–45, 253–254; Jean-Jacques Rousseau, *Discourse on Political Economy*, in Rousseau, *On the Social Contract with Geneva Manuscript and Political Economy*, trans. Judith R. Masters (New York: St. Martin's, 1978), 221–222, 224, 230–231, 234.

35. Thompson, *Politics of Inequality*, 9, emphasis added.

36. In particular, critics alleged that great disparities in wealth undermine core republican values, including simplicity, modesty, frugality, and virtue.

37. Although many Americans, especially political elites such as Alexander Hamilton, James Madison, John Jay, and Gouverneur Morris, became increasingly skeptical about the ability of ordinary citizens to live up to the demanding ideals of civic virtue, many other republican ideals continued to inform public opinion about political matters because they were compatible with and received support from other intellectual traditions. It appears Americans at the time either did not notice or were untroubled by the theoretical differences scholars have detected between liberalism and republicanism. Indeed, Americans found intellectual support for their conceptions of freedom and self-government in a variety of traditions that shaped American political thought at the time. On the variety of "discourses" that coexisted then, see Isaac Kramnick, "'The Great National Discussion': The Discourse of Politics in 1787," in Kramnick, *Republicanism and Bourgeois Radicalism: Political Ideology in Late Eighteenth-Century England and America* (Ithaca, NY: Cornell University Press, 1990), 260–288.

38. According to Huston, a "consensus" that the survival of a republic depends on a wide, if not exactly equal, distribution of property persisted until the end of the nineteenth century. See Huston, *Securing the Fruits of Labor*.

39. Webster, "Examination into the Leading Principles of the Federal Constitution," 401.

40. Benjamin Trumbull, "Discourse, Delivered at the Anniversary Meeting of the Freemen of the Town of New Haven, April 12, 1773," 30.

41. Ezra Stiles to Thomas Jefferson, letter, September 14, 1786, in *The Papers of Thomas Jefferson*, vol. 10, ed. Julian P. Boyd (Princeton, NJ: Princeton University Press, 1953), 386.

42. "The Remonstrance of the Subscribers, Yeomen, and Citizens of Pennsylvania," quoted in Bouton, *Taming Democracy*, 105.

43. Phillips Payson, "A Sermon," in Hyneman and Lutz, *American Political Writings during the Founding Era*, vol. 1, 526. Payson, a Congregationalist minister from Massachusetts, went even further by discussing how excessive wealth exacerbates the already pernicious effects of vice and corruption on the morals of a community. Ibid., 528.

44. Quoted in Andrew Shankman, *Crucible of American Democracy: The Struggle to Fuse Egalitarianism and Capitalism in Jeffersonian Pennsylvania* (Lawrence: University Press of Kansas, 2004), 5.

45. William Manning, *The Key of Liberty: The Life and Democratic Writings of William Manning, "A Laborer," 1747–1814*, ed. Michael Merrill and Sean Wilentz (Cambridge, MA: Harvard University Press, 1993).

46. Abraham Clark, "The True Policy of New-Jersey, Defined; or, Our Great Strength Led to Exertion, in the Improvement of Agriculture &

Manufactures, by Altering the Mode of Taxation, and by the Emission of Money on Loan, in IX Sections" (Elizabeth-Town, NJ: Shepard Kollock, 1786), 11 (held at Special Collections and University Archives, Rutgers University Library). Ruth Bogin identified Clark as the author of this anonymously published pamphlet in "New Jersey's True Policy: The Radical Republican Vision of Abraham Clark," *William and Mary Quarterly* 35, no. 1 (1978): 100–109. On Clark's political thought and activities, see Bogin, *Abraham Clark and the Quest for Equality in the Revolutionary Era, 1774–1794* (Rutherford, NJ: Farleigh Dickinson University Press, 1982), 34.

47. Clark, "True Policy of New-Jersey," 24.

48. James Sullivan, *The Path to Riches: An Inquiry into the Origins and Use of Money and into the Principles of Stocks and Banks* (Boston: J. Belcher, 1809), 4.

49. Ibid., 45.

50. Gouverneur Morris, "Political Enquiries," in Morris, *To Secure the Blessings of Liberty: Selected Writings of Gouverneur Morris*, ed. J. Jackson Barlow (Indianapolis, IN: Liberty Fund, 2012), 10.

51. John Adams to James Sullivan, letter, May 26, 1776, in Adams, *Works of John Adams*, vol. 9, 376–377. A decade later, Adams reiterated his belief in the connection between economic power and political power, warning, "The rich . . . will destroy *all equality and liberty, with the consent and acclamations of the people themselves*" unless isolated and checked "in a separate assembly." Adams, *A Defence of the Constitutions of Government of the United States of America*, vol. 1 (London: John Stockdale, 1794), 183.

52. Fisher Ames, December 15, 1796: Fourth Congress, 2nd sess., *Annals of Congress* (Washington, DC: Gales and Seaton, 1834), 1642.

53. John Warren, "An Oration, Delivered July 4th, 1783," in *The Rising Glory of America, 1760–1820*, ed. Gordon S. Wood (Boston: Northeastern University Press, 1971), 64.

54. On the background of this controversy and for examples of the reactions it elicited, see the selections in Wood, *Rising Glory of America*, 137–153.

55. Samuel Adams to Samuel P. Savage, letter, July 3, 1778, in *Letters of Delegates to Congress, 1774–1789*, vol. 10, ed. Paul H. Smith (Washington, DC: Library of Congress, 1983), 219.

56. Joseph Lathrop, "The Censor, Number IV," in Hyneman and Lutz, *American Political Writings during the Founding Era*, vol. 1, 663. Lathrop did not, however, believe charity should be provided indiscriminately. Those engaged in charitable activities must distinguish between "those who are really needy" and those who "are spending their time and substance in vain" (674).

57. Sullivan, *Path to Riches*, 24.

58. Manning, *Key of Liberty*, 129.

59. Pole, *Pursuit of Equality in American History*, 28, 35–36.

60. For some southern planters, especially in the highly stratified state of South Carolina, which was dominated by a few wealthy families, the inability of the rich to form a cabal across state lines was enough to qualify

the country as a republic. For instance, Charles Pinckney stated at the Constitutional Convention that there were "not above *100* Men in the United States so rich as to be dangerous" and denied that these great men could "be considered as a distinct Class on a national Scale." John Lansing, "Notes on Debates for June 25, 1787," in *Supplement to Max Farrand's* The Records of the Federal Convention of 1787, ed. James H. Hutson (New Haven, CT: Yale University Press, 1987), 112. James Madison's version of Pinckney's remarks is slightly different, but the substance is the same. See Madison, "Notes for June 25, 1787," in *The Records of the Federal Convention of 1787*, vol. 1, ed. Max Farrand (New Haven, CT: Yale University Press, 1937), 400–401, in which Pinckney favorably contrasts the United States with countries in Europe.

61. Europe provided the context for American thinking on economic equality well into the nineteenth century. See Huston, *Securing the Fruits of Labor*, 184–218.

62. Manning, *Key of Liberty*, 157.

63. Robert Goodloe Harper, March 2, 1798: Fifth Congress, 2nd sess., *Annals of Congress* (Washington, DC: Gales and Seaton, 1834), 1179–1180.

64. Webster, "Miscellaneous Remarks," 327. See also Noah Webster, "Remarks on the Manners, Government, and Debt of the United States," in Webster, *Collection of Essays and Fugitiv* [sic] *Writings*, 88.

65. Benjamin Franklin, "On the Internal State of America," http://franklinpapers.org/franklin/framedVolumes.jsp?vol=43&page=781. The belief that conditions in America were relatively equal was so powerful that it persisted well into the following century. "We have no Paupers," Thomas Jefferson boldly declared in an 1814 letter. "The great mass of our population is of laborers; our rich, who can live without labor, either manual or professional, being few, and of moderate wealth. most [sic] of the laboring class possess property, cultivate their own lands, have families, and from the demand for their labor are enabled to exact from the rich and the competent such prices as enable them to be fed abundantly, clothed above meer [sic] decency, to labor moderately and raise their families." Thomas Jefferson to Thomas Cooper, letter, September 10, 1814, in *The Papers of Thomas Jefferson*, Retirement Series, vol. 7, ed. J. Jefferson Looney (Princeton, NJ: Princeton University Press, 2010), 651.

66. J. Hector St. John de Crèvecœur, *Letters from an American Farmer*, ed. Albert E. Stone (New York: Penguin, 1981), 67.

67. Appleby, *Capitalism and a New Social Order*, 44.

68. David Ramsay, "Oration on the Advantages of American Independence," July 4, 1778, in Robert L. Brunhouse and David Ramsay, "David Ramsay, 1749–1815: Selections from His Writings," *Transactions of the American Philosophical Society*, New Series, vol. 55, no. 4 (1965): 184.

69. Benjamin Franklin, "Appeal for the Hospital," in *Franklin: Writings*, ed. J. A. Leo Lemay (New York: Library of America Press, 1987), 363.

70. Robert Morris to Thomas McKean, letter, August 28, 1781, in *The Papers of Robert Morris, 1781–1784*, vol. 2, ed. E. James Ferguson (Pittsburgh, PA: University of Pittsburgh Press, 1975), 132.

71. On Morris's precipitous fall, see Charles Rappleye, *Robert Morris: Financier of the American Revolution* (New York: Simon and Schuster, 2010), 490–515.

72. Within a generation or two, however, the reality (if not the perception) of class mobility would change dramatically. By the time Alexis de Tocqueville visited the United States, the idea that poverty and wealth were in a constant state of flux had already become a myth—albeit a tenacious one. See Edward Pessen, *Riches, Class, and Power: America before the Civil War* (New Brunswick, NJ: Transaction, 1990).

73. Benjamin Franklin, "Observations Concerning the Increase of Mankind, Peopling of Countries, &c.," in Lemay, *Franklin: Writings*, 368. See also David Ramsay, "Oration on the Advantages of American Independence," July 4, 1778, in Brunhouse and Ramsay, "David Ramsay," 187–188.

74. Noah Webster noted that settlers ventured into the "uncultivated wilderness" to escape the poverty and debt brought on by the growing scarcity of land along the Atlantic Coast. See Webster, "Miscellaneous Remarks," 554.

75. Quoted in Willard Sterne Randall, *Alexander Hamilton: A Life* (New York: Perennial, 2004), 67.

76. Quoted in Henry Adams, *The United States in 1800* (Ithaca, NY: Cornell University Press, 1964), 82.

77. John Adams to Abigail Adams, letter, April 12, 1778, *The Adams Family Correspondence*, vol. 3, ed. L. H. Butterfield (Cambridge, MA: Belknap Press of Harvard University Press, 1973), 10.

78. John Adams, April 6, 1778, diary entry, in Adams, *Works of John Adams*, vol. 3, 121.

79. John Adams, December 30, 1779, diary entry, in Adams, *Works of John Adams*, vol. 3, 244.

80. John Adams to Hendrik Calkoen, letter, October 26, 1780, in Adams, *Works of John Adams*, vol. 7, 305. A few decades later, Adams would revise his claims about the extent of inequality in the United States. See Lee Soltow, *Distribution of Wealth and Income in the United States in 1798* (Pittsburgh, PA: University of Pittsburgh Press, 1989), 18–20.

81. de Crèvecœur, *Letters from an American Farmer*, 240.

82. Franklin contrasted the opulence of the great in Ireland and Scotland with the masses, who were "extreamly [sic] poor, living in the most sordid Wretchedness, in dirty Hovels of Mud and Straw, and cloathed [sic] only in rags." Quoted in Soltow, *Distribution of Wealth and Income*, 10.

83. Melancton Smith, "Speech at the New York State Ratifying Convention, June 21, 1788," in *The Anti-Federalist*, ed. Murray Dry (Chicago: University of Chicago Press, 1981), 340–341.

84. William Manning, "Some Proposals for Making Restitution to the Original Creditors of Government," in Manning, *Key of Liberty*, 112.

85. Manning, *Key of Liberty*, 127, 136.

86. Ibid., 127.

87. Quoted in Alice Hanson Jones, *Wealth of a Nation to Be: The American Colonies on the Eve of the Revolution* (New York: Columbia University Press, 1980), 422–423.

88. Marquis de Chastellux, *Travels in North-America in the Years 1780–1781–1782* (New York: Author, 1828), 291–292.

89. Duc de la Rochefoucault Liancourt, *Travels through the United States of America, and the Country of the Iroquois, and Upper Canada, in the Years 1795, 1796, 1797*, vol. 3 (London: T. Davison, 1799), 484–485.

90. Frontier communities, by definition new or recently settled areas, tended to have far less wealth than older communities, but that wealth also tended to be more equally distributed. According to historian Frederick Jackson Turner, the availability of land on the frontier made it much more conducive to equality than did the more settled parts of the country along the eastern seaboard. Soltow disputes the Turner thesis, arguing that inequality actually increased with distance from the coast. In the easternmost parts of the country, the Gini coefficient was .465, but it increased to .540 at 100 miles away from the coast and grew to .615 at 200 miles away from the Atlantic. Soltow, *Distribution of Wealth and Income*, 79. Based on her sampling of probate records from the year 1774, Jones contends that the level of inequality on the eve of the Revolution was extremely high throughout the colonies: she estimates that the Gini was an astounding .73. However, her findings are in line with that of other scholars who have found that inequality was highest in the South and generally higher in urban areas. Jones, *Wealth of a Nation*, 192, 217.

91. Pessen, *Riches, Class, and Power*, xv.

92. Main, *Social Structure of Revolutionary America*, 36. At the start of the Revolution, 29 percent of Boston residents were too poor to be taxed. Large numbers of the poor often ended up in cities such as Boston because many towns passed laws that prohibited vagrants and others without adequate means of support from remaining within their limits. Pole, *Pursuit of Equality in American History*, 27–28.

93. Sean Wilentz, *Chants Democratic: New York City and the Rise of the American Working Class, 1788–1850* (Oxford, UK: Oxford University Press, 1984), 25–26.

94. John K. Alexander, *Render Them Submissive: Responses to Poverty in Philadelphia, 1760–1800* (Amherst: University of Massachusetts Press, 1980), 12.

95. On the economic structure of the South and the sometimes substantial differences between states, see Main, *Social Structure of Revolutionary America*, 44–67. For the South as a whole, Jones estimates that the top 10 percent owned 69 percent of all physical wealth in the region in 1774. Jones, *Wealth of a Nation*, 258–259.

96. Gloria L. Main, "Inequality in Early America: The Evidence from Probate Records of Massachusetts and Maryland," *Journal of Interdisciplinary History* 7, no. 4 (1977).

97. The confiscation and sale of Loyalist property worth millions of pounds had a major impact on the distribution of wealth in a number of different places. See, for example, Robert S. Lambert, "The Confiscation of Loyalist Property in Georgia, 1782–1786," *William and Mary Quarterly* 20, no. 1 (1963); Richard D. Brown, "The Confiscation and Disposition of

Loyalists' Estates in Suffolk County, Massachusetts," *William and Mary Quarterly* 21, no. 4 (1964).

98. On the nature of these changes and their political impact in Philadelphia, see Shankman, *Crucible of American Democracy*, 160–172.

99. Pessen, *Riches, Class, and Power*, 32.

100. Bouton, *Taming Democracy*, 15.

101. The departure of Loyalists, who made up a significant portion of the wealthiest residents of Philadelphia, helps explain diminished levels of economic inequality in the Quaker City. When they left, their property became "vulnerable to seizure and sale." Smith, *"Lower Sort,"* 87.

102. Bouton, *Taming Democracy*, 101. In his study of social conditions in Philadelphia in the final four decades of the eighteenth century, Alexander finds that inequality in America's leading city was so great that it limited social contact and trust between different economic groups, contributed to class conflict, and hampered upward mobility for the poor. Alexander, *Render Them Submissive.*

103. Soltow calculates that the Gini coefficient for property owners (not including those who had no recorded property) across the country at that time was .588 (compared with .657 on the eve of the Civil War). Soltow finds that there were also significant variations among property owners from one part of the country to another, with the urban South (Gini coefficient of .674) much more unequal than the rural North (Gini coefficient of .503). Perhaps the most surprising finding of all is that a significant percentage of free men owned no real property whatsoever. When free men above the age of twenty-one without property are included in Soltow's analysis, the Gini coefficient for the country as a whole is .797 (compared with .847 in 1860). Soltow, *Distribution of Wealth and Income*, 42–47.

104. Billy G. Smith, ed., *Down and out in Early America* (University Park: Pennsylvania State University Press, 2004).

105. For instance, Philadelphia's poor tended to be concentrated in an area called "Helltown" in the northern part of town along the Delaware River. Smith, *"Lower Sort,"* 21.

106. See, for example, Alexander, *Render Them Submissive*, 48.

107. Smith, *"Lower Sort,"* 124.

108. Based on what is known about consumption patterns in the eighteenth century, standards of living were also generally better for members of the working class in American colonies than they were for their counterparts in England. See Jones, *Wealth of a Nation*, 298, 340–341.

109. Soltow, *Distribution of Wealth and Income*, 126.

110. Main, *Social Structure of Revolutionary America*, 8–11.

111. Dennis P. Ryan, "Landholding, Opportunity, and Mobility in Revolutionary New Jersey," *William and Mary Quarterly* 36, no. 4 (1979).

112. Bouton, *Taming Democracy*, 14.

113. Main, *Social Structure of Revolutionary America*, 184.

114. Even scholars who have documented the extent of poverty in places such as Philadelphia concede that the majority of the poorest residents improved their conditions from one period to the next. Smith, *"Lower Sort,"*

129–134. Because these studies focus on intragenerational mobility (which considers changes in economic conditions over the course of an individual's lifetime) rather than intergenerational mobility (which considers changes from one generation to the next)—the measure favored by scholars of mobility—they may actually understate the degree of upward mobility that existed at the time.

115. Pessen, *Riches, Class, and Power*, 81. Contrary to Alexis de Tocqueville's famous claim that antebellum America was the "era of the common man," the share of wealth possessed by those at the very top continued to grow well into the nineteenth century. In fact, the much-vaunted idea that America was a land of opportunity in the first half of the nineteenth century turns out to be a myth. Relatively few of those born into poverty ever made it into the ranks of the wealthy, and hardly anyone born into great wealth lost it. In fact, catalogues of the richest Americans changed very little from year to year and decade to decade as great fortunes only grew in size. See Pessen, *Riches, Class, and Power*, esp. 84–85.

116. Main, *Social Structure of Revolutionary America*, 194, 271.

117. Nash, *Urban Crucible*, 5, 21–22.

118. To deal with the "lamentable Condition of Widows" left destitute by the death of their husbands, Benjamin Franklin proposed a system of social insurance, the "Intent being to Aid the Poor, not add to the Rich." Franklin, *Silence Dogwood, No. 10*, in Lemay, *Franklin: Writings*, 30.

119. On attitudes toward the poor in Philadelphia, see Alexander, *Render Them Submissive*, 48–60.

120. See Michael B. Katz, *In the Shadow of the Poorhouse: A Social History of Welfare in America*, 10th ed. (New York: BasicBooks, 1996), x.

121. Ibid., 15.

122. Laurel Thatcher Ulrich, "Sheep in the Parlor, Wheels on the Common: Pastoralism and Poverty in Eighteenth-Century Boston," in Pestana and Salinger, *Inequality in Early America*, 182–200.

123. Wilentz, *Chants Democratic*, 38–39.

124. Pessen, *Riches, Class, and Power*, 266–267. Among other things, the dispensary provided free inoculations to thousands of the city's residents. See *An Account of the Philadelphia Dispensary, Instituted for the Medical Relief of the Poor, April 12, 1786* (Philadelphia: Budd and Bartram, 1802). This was a significant establishment because the poor were far more likely to die from disease (and in childbirth) than the rich. Smith, *"Lower Sort,"* 55.

125. Katz, *In the Shadow of the Poorhouse*, xiv–xv.

126. Ibid., xvi.

127. Alexander, *Render Them Submissive*.

128. Benjamin Joseph Klebaner, *Public Poor Relief in America, 1790–1860* (New York: Arno, 1976), 254. Formal institutions dedicated to the relief of the poor were uncommon in the colonial period. See Katz, *In the Shadow of the Poorhouse*, 10.

129. Klebaner, *Public Poor Relief in America*, 360, 351–356.

130. Katz, *In the Shadow of the Poorhouse*, 15, 20.

131. Ibid., 20–21.

132. Klebaner, *Public Poor Relief in America*, 72, 103.

133. Katz, *In the Shadow of the Poorhouse*, 23.

134. Klebaner, *Public Poor Relief in America*, 104.

135. Ibid., 110–111.

136. Ibid., 154–166. On the history of these experiments in Philadelphia between 1760 and 1800, see Alexander, *Render Them Submissive*, 86–121.

137. For a more extensive discussion of Findley's political thought concerning economic inequality and how well it represented the views of other Pennsylvania democrats, see Shankman, *Crucible of American Democracy*, 3–9.

138. Clark, "True Policy of New-Jersey," 32.

139. Sullivan, *Path to Riches*, 4.

140. On republican hostility to laws of entail and primogeniture up to the end of the nineteenth century, see Huston, *Securing the Fruits of Labor*.

141. Thomas Jefferson to James Madison, letter, December 8, 1784, in Boyd, *Papers of Thomas Jefferson*, vol. 7, 557.

142. The best account of this shift away from regressive forms of taxation is Becker, *Revolution, Reform*.

143. Bouton, *Taming Democracy*, 35.

144. Article XIII, A Declaration of Rights, and the Constitution and Form of Government agreed to by the Delegates of Maryland, in Free and Full Convention Assembled, November 11, 1776.

145. Clark, "True Policy of New-Jersey," 10.

146. Gouverneur Morris, "An American: Letters on Public Finance," February 29, 1780, in Barlow, *To Secure the Blessings of Liberty*, 121.

147. Noah Webster, "On the Education of Youth in America," in Webster, *Collection of Essays and Fugitiv* [sic] *Writings*, 24–25.

148. On support for public schooling as a means of promoting republican ideals, see Lorraine Smith Pangle and Thomas L. Pangle, *The Learning of Liberty: The Educational Ideas of the American Founders* (Lawrence: University Press of Kansas, 1993), 91–105, 125–145. In practice, public education was rare outside of New England, but a few places did start to provide educational opportunities for the poor after the Revolution. Reformers in Philadelphia began experimenting with different arrangements in 1785, but from the start there were divisions between those who viewed education as a path to upward mobility and opportunity and those who viewed it as a means of social control. Those in the first group emphasized the importance of education for all classes in fostering equality and promoting republican values. Well-educated citizens, they argued, would be able to think for themselves and resist attempts by the "aristocratic few" to dominate the political process. Those in the latter group had little interest in creating a more egalitarian society. Instead, they supported education for the poor precisely because they believed it would reinforce the existing social order by rooting out vicious behavior, instilling habits of industry, and promoting deference toward social superiors. Alexander, *Render Them Submissive*, 142–159; quote at 153.

149. Quoted in Ira Stoll, *Samuel Adams: A Life* (New York: Free Press, 2008), 227.

150. Benjamin Rush, *A Plan for the Establishment of Public Schools and the Diffusion of Knowledge in Pennsylvania; to Which Are Added, Thoughts upon the Mode of Education, Proper in a Republic,* in Hyneman and Lutz, *American Political Writings during the Founding Era,* vol. 1, 676. On the egalitarian elements of Rush's political philosophy, see Donald J. D'Elia, "Benjamin Rush: Philosopher of the American Revolution," *Transactions of the American Philosophical Society* 64, no. 5 (1974):75, 89, 94, 101–102.

151. Robert Coram, *Political Inquiries, to Which is Added a Plan for the Establishment of Schools throughout the United States,* in Hyneman and Lutz, *American Political Writings during the Founding Era,* vol. 2, 782, 783. Coram also favored a more equal distribution of property, but he did not specify how this would be accomplished beyond a vague recommendation to reform inheritance laws. On the state of inheritance law at the time of the Revolution, which generally followed English practice, and the changes the Revolution prompted, see Stanley N. Katz, "Republicanism and the Law of Inheritance in the American Revolutionary Era," *Michigan Law Review* 76, no. 1 (1977): 1–29.

Chapter 2: Class Conflict and Crisis under the Articles of Confederation

1. Decisions to build public galleries in Boston and Philadelphia were made in 1766 and 1775, respectively. See Gary B. Nash, *The Urban Crucible: Social Change, Political Consciousness, and the Origins of the American Revolution* (Cambridge, MA: Harvard University Press, 1979), 359, 377.

2. On changes in suffrage rules enacted after the start of the Revolution, see Alexander Keyssar, *The Right to Vote: The Contested History of Democracy in the United States* (New York: BasicBooks, 2000), 3–25. Property qualifications varied widely from state to state but were in general low enough to allow a substantial majority of adult white men to vote.

3. Jackson Turner Main, *The Social Structure of Revolutionary America* (Princeton, NJ: Princeton University Press, 1965), 211–213.

4. It should be noted that the interests of debtors and creditors were not necessarily opposed. Economic relations were so complex at the time that the same individual was often simultaneously a creditor and a debtor to different individuals. See Bruce H. Mann, *Republic of Debtors: Bankruptcy in the Age of American Independence* (Cambridge, MA: Harvard University Press, 2002).

5. Many states allowed debtors to repay creditors with goods instead of specie, and some officials even refused to carry out proceedings against debtors. Woody Holton, *Unruly Americans and the Origins of the Constitution* (New York: Hill and Wang, 2007), 7–8. For an overview of the laws that states passed to relieve distressed citizens, see pages 55–64 of Holton's book.

On the shift to more progressive forms of taxation in most states, see Robert E. Becker, *Revolution, Reform, and the Politics of American Taxation, 1763–1783* (Baton Rouge: Louisiana State University Press, 1980). Despite moves toward more progressive forms of taxation, many states continued to rely on regressive poll taxes to raise revenue. On the mix of taxes levied by states during the 1780s, see Roger H. Brown, *Redeeming the Republic: Federalists, Taxation, and the Origins of the Constitution* (Baltimore, MD: Johns Hopkins University Press, 1993), 32–40.

6. On the various forms of resistance employed against unpopular policies and practices during the 1780s, see Terry Bouton, *Taming Democracy: "The People," the Founders, and the Troubled Ending of the American Revolution* (Oxford, UK: Oxford University Press, 2007), 145–167; Holton, *Unruly Americans*, 145–161. On the meaning and uses of crowd action out of doors during this period, see Jason Frank, *Constituent Moments: Enacting the People in Postrevolutionary America* (Durham, NC: Duke University Press, 2010).

7. Neighbors also resisted efforts to raise funds at auctions by honoring "no-bid covenants"—essentially, refusing to bid on items being auctioned. On these and other forms of resistance against efforts to collect delinquent taxes, see Brown, *Redeeming the Republic*, 60–63.

8. Charles Rappleye, *Robert Morris: Financier of the American Revolution* (New York: Simon and Schuster, 2010), 180; John K. Alexander, *Render Them Submissive: Responses to Poverty in Philadelphia, 1760–1800* (Amherst: University of Massachusetts Press, 1980), 34.

9. Holton, *Unruly Americans*, 150–152, 154.

10. Gordon S. Wood, *The Creation of the American Republic, 1776–1787* (Chapel Hill: University of North Carolina Press, 1998), 409–413. My account of the backlash against democracy waged by national elites is heavily indebted to Wood's magisterial study. Other studies that inform my account include Bouton, *Taming Democracy*; Brown, *Redeeming the Republic*; Holton, *Unruly Americans*; and Woody Holton, "Did Democracy Cause the Recession That Led to the Constitution?" *Journal of American History* 92, no. 2 (2005).

11. James Madison, "Vices of the Political System of the United States," in *Madison: Writings*, ed. Jack N. Rakove (Washington, DC: Library of America, 1999), 69–80, quote at 76.

12. For a more detailed examination of Madison's understanding of the tensions between democratic politics and property rights, see Jennifer Nedelsky, *Private Property and the Limits of American Constitutionalism: The Madisonian Framework and Its Legacy* (Chicago: University of Chicago Press, 1990).

13. James Madison to Caleb Wallace, letter, August 23, 1785, in Rakove, *Madison: Writings*, 43.

14. Article IV of the New Jersey Constitution (July 2, 1776) stipulated "that all inhabitants of this Colony, of full age, who are worth fifty pounds proclamation money, clear estate in the same, and have resided within the county in which they claim a vote for twelve months immediately preceding

the election, shall be entitled to vote for Representatives in Council and Assembly; and also for all other public officers, that shall be elected by the people of the county at large." For an overview of the changes introduced by the new state constitutions, see Wood, *Creation of the American Republic,* 127–161.

15. Quoted in Alexander, *Render Them Submissive,* 30.

16. Quoted in Eric Foner, *Tom Paine and Revolutionary America,* updated ed. (Oxford, UK: Oxford University Press, 2005), 130.

17. Quoted in ibid., 133.

18. However, the franchise was still limited to adult men who paid taxes.

19. On these loan offices, see Bouton, *Taming Democracy,* 37–41. Bouton argues that the land bank could be viewed as an "engine of equality" because it capped the size of loans at 100 pounds. Ibid., 40.

20. Jack N. Rakove, *The Beginnings of National Politics: An Interpretive History of the Continental Congress* (Baltimore, MD: Johns Hopkins University Press, 1979), 122.

21. Quoted in Foner, *Tom Paine,* 185.

22. Accusations that Robert Morris had cornered the market on tobacco and other goods and held them from the market until he could sell them at windfall profits dogged him throughout the Revolutionary War. There is evidence that on at least one occasion Morris advised a business partner to keep salt from the market. See Rappleye, *Robert Morris,* 82, 183–184. Critics also charged Morris with profiting from inside information gained from his work on the crucial Secret Committee of Trade in the early part of the Revolution. Rappleye, *Robert Morris,* 45–46.

23. For data on changes in the prices of different food items in Philadelphia during the second half of the century, see Billy G. Smith, *The "Lower Sort": Philadelphia's Laboring People, 1750–1800* (Ithaca, NY: Cornell University Press, 1990), 95–103, 232–237.

24. On the debate that emerged in Philadelphia between advocates of the small producer ethic, on the one hand, and proponents of a laissez-faire philosophy, on the other, see Ronald Schultz, "Small Producer Thought in Early America, Part I: Philadelphia Artisans and Price Control," *Pennsylvania History* 54, no. 2 (1987): 115–147.

25. Quoted in Alexander, *Render Them Submissive,* 34.

26. See John K. Alexander, "The Fort Wilson Incident of 1779: A Case Study of the Revolutionary Crowd," *William and Mary Quarterly* 31, no. 4 (1974); Alexander, *Render Them Submissive,* 34–36; Rappleye, *Robert Morris,* 190–193.

27. Rappleye, *Robert Morris,* 225–236.

28. These and other problems facing the Continental Congress are described in further detail in Rakove, *Beginnings of National Politics,* 275–296.

29. For further details on the rest of Morris's program, see ibid., 298–307.

30. Alexander Hamilton to Robert Morris, letter, April 30, 1781, in *The Papers of Robert Morris, 1781–1784,* vol. 1, ed. E. James Ferguson (Pittsburgh, PA: University of Pittsburgh Press, 1973), 31–60.

31. For reasons like this, historian Terry Bouton describes Robert Morris as a forerunner of trickle-down economics who sought to privatize finance in order to enrich himself and other moneyed men he believed could put wealth to more productive uses than could citizens in the middling and lower ranks. Bouton, *Taming Democracy*, 70–71.

32. On the failed attempt to erect a second bank, see Rappleye, *Robert Morris*, 392–394.

33. Bouton, *Taming Democracy*, 80.

34. Quoted in Rappleye, *Robert Morris*, 394.

35. Quoted in Thomas Paine, "Letters on the Bank," in *The Complete Writings of Thomas Paine*, vol. 2, ed. Philip S. Foner (New York: Citadel Press, 1945), 388.

36. Rappleye, *Robert Morris*, 398.

37. Paine, "Letters on the Bank," 414–439.

38. Quoted in Joseph Blasi, Richard Freeman, and Douglas Kruse, *The Citizen's Share: Putting Ownership Back into Democracy* (New Haven, CT: Yale University Press, 2013), 18.

39. Paine, "Letters on the Bank," 429–430.

40. Quoted in Rappleye, *Robert Morris*, 401.

41. Quoted in ibid., 304.

42. "Remonstrance and Petition to Congress from Blair McClenachan, Charles Petit, John Ewing, and Benjamin Rush," July 8, 1782, in Ferguson, *Papers of Robert Morris*, vol. 6, 695.

43. Ruth Bogin, *Abraham Clark and the Quest for Equality in the Revolutionary Era, 1774–1794* (Rutherford, NJ: Farleigh Dickinson University Press, 1982), 75.

44. For an example of the charge that Robert Morris was an out-of-touch elitist, see the "Lucius" letters, especially the third installment of this five-part series, in Ferguson, *Papers of Robert Morris*, vol. 7, 668. On the background and consequences of these influential essays, see Rappleye, *Robert Morris*, 351–355.

45. Robert Morris to Richard Butler, letter, July 18, 1782, in Ferguson, *Papers of Robert Morris*, vol. 5, 598.

46. Robert Morris to John Hanson, letter, July 29, 1782, in Ferguson, *Papers of Robert Morris*, vol. 6, 67.

47. Robert Morris to the governors of North Carolina, South Carolina, and Georgia, letter, December 19, 1781, in Ferguson, *Papers of Robert Morris*, vol. 3, 414.

48. Morris to Hanson, July 29, 1782, 66.

49. Ibid., 67.

50. Robert Morris to George Washington, letter, September 25, 1782, in Ferguson, *Papers of Robert Morris*, vol. 6, 436.

51. "Such is the Frailty of the human Heart, that very few Men, who have no Property, have any Judgment of their own. They talk and vote as they are directed by Some Man of Property, who has attached their Minds to his Interest." John Adams to James Sullivan, letter, May 26, 1776, in Adams,

The Works of John Adams, Second President of the United States, vol. 9 (Boston: Little, Brown, 1865), 378.

52. Ibid., 378.

53. Wood, *Creation of the American Republic*, 567–592.

54. Ibid., 430–438.

55. John Adams, *The Report of a Constitution, or a Form of Government, for the Commonwealth of Massachusetts*, in *Revolutionary Writings of John Adams*, ed. C. Bradley Thompson (Indianapolis, IN: Liberty Fund, 2000), 305.

56. Ibid., 297–322; Adams, "Thoughts on Government," in Thompson, *Revolutionary Writings of John Adams*, 287–293. Contrary to Joyce Appleby's claim that Adams's expressions of support for balance in his *Defence of the Constitutions of Government of the United States* marked a departure from his earlier thinking on republican government, his draft of the Massachusetts Constitution shows that he had already moved a long way toward the idea that government must give the "few" adequate means of protecting themselves from the depredations of the "many" by the time he drafted the Massachusetts Constitution. Appleby, *Liberalism and Republicanism in the Historical Imagination* (Cambridge, MA: Harvard University Press, 1992), 188–209.

57. See Leonard L. Richards, *Shays's Rebellion: The American Revolution's Final Battle* (Philadelphia: University of Pennsylvania Press, 2003), 71–72.

58. Return of Northampton, Massachusetts, May 22, 1780, in Philip B. Kurland and Ralph Kerner, eds., *The Founders' Constitution*, vol. 1: *Major Themes* (Indianapolis, IN: Liberty Fund, 1987), 528–531.

59. See Richards, *Shays's Rebellion*, 72–74.

60. For instance, sixteen people owned nearly half of the state bonds in Rhode Island in 1786. Holton, *Unruly Americans*, 37.

61. Richards, *Shays's Rebellion*, 75.

62. Ibid., 82–83.

63. Holton, *Unruly Americans*, 29.

64. On the highly regressive distribution of taxes in Massachusetts, see Becker, *Revolution, Reform*, 118–128.

65. The possibility of imprisonment for debt was the norm in every colony and every state until the end of the eighteenth century. See Bruce H. Mann, *Republic of Debtors: Bankruptcy in the Age of American Independence* (Cambridge, MA: Harvard University Press, 2002), 78–108, 180.

66. Richards, *Shays's Rebellion*, 51–52.

67. Wood, *Creation of the American Republic*, 284.

68. Robert E. Moody, "Samuel Ely: Forerunner of Shays," *New England Quarterly* 5, no. 1 (1932).

69. See Brown, *Redeeming the Republic*, 117–120; Richards, *Shays's Rebellion*, 119.

70. Henry Knox, quoted in Richard Beeman, *Plain, Honest Men: The Making of the American Constitution* (New York: Random House, 2009), 17.

71. Henry Lee to George Washington, letter, quoted in Beeman, *Plain, Honest Men*, 17.

72. Elbridge Gerry, in Beeman, *Plain, Honest Men*, 113.

73. Quoted in Richards, *Shays's Rebellion*, 129.

74. See George Washington to James Madison, letter, November 5, 1786, in *George Washington: A Collection*, ed. W. B. Allen (Indianapolis, IN: Liberty Fund, 1988), 339–340.

75. James Madison, quoted in Beeman, *Plain, Honest Men*, 18.

76. The Shays family owned a farm of more than 100 acres, which placed its members in the top 40 percent of landowners in Shutesbury, Massachusetts. See Richards, *Shays's Rebellion*, 6.

77. Ibid., 60.

78. Ibid., 54.

79. Among other things, Rhode Island gave town clerks the discretion to exempt the poor from paying poll taxes, enacted various debtor relief measures, made paper money legal tender for all debts, past and future, and criminalized actions and statements that had the effect of depreciating the value of paper money. See Brown, *Redeeming the Republic*, 86, 90–96.

Chapter 3: The Constitutional Backlash against the "Excesses
of Democracy"

1. Charles A. Beard, *An Economic Interpretation of the Constitution of the United States* (New York: Free Press, 1986), 51.

2. Robert E. Brown, *Charles Beard and the Constitution: A Critical Analysis of* An Economic Interpretation of the Constitution (New York: Norton, 1965); Forrest McDonald, *We the People: The Economic Origins of the Constitution* (New Brunswick, NJ: Transaction, 1991).

3. Robert E. Brown argued that Beard would have been on much more solid ground if he had simply argued that the framers sought protections for property of all kinds instead of focusing on personal property. Brown, *Charles Beard*, 90.

4. Terry Bouton, *Taming Democracy: "The People," the Founders, and the Troubled Ending of the American Revolution* (Oxford, UK: Oxford University Press, 2007), 4, 5. A small sample of other scholars who argue that the Constitution represented a backlash against the popular forms of politics being practiced in the states includes Woody Holton, *Unruly Americans and the Origins of the Constitution* (New York: Hill and Wang, 2007); Jennifer Nedelsky, *Private Property and the Limits of American Constitutionalism: The Madisonian Framework and Its Legacy* (Chicago: University of Chicago Press, 1990); and Sanford Levinson, *Our Undemocratic Constitution: Where the Constitution Goes Wrong (and How We the People Can Correct It)* (Oxford, UK: Oxford University Press, 2006).

5. Morris expressed anxiety as early as April 1774 about the role the laboring classes would play in the political system, when he warned that

the "mob" would eventually turn on the "people of property" if the latter continued to rely on their support in the struggle against Great Britain. Gouverneur Morris to John Penn, letter, May 20, 1774, in *The Founders' Constitution*, vol. 1, ed. Philip B. Kurland and Ralph Kerner (Indianapolis, IN: Liberty Fund, 1987), 343.

6. According to Gordon Wood, for national elites the problem with democracy went beyond its association with class-based politics. Elites objected to the coarse wheeling and dealing of a form of politics grounded in the base pursuit of self-interest rather than a virtuous commitment to the common good. Wood, "Interests and Disinterestedness in the Making of the Constitution," in *Beyond Confederation: Origins of the Constitution and American National Identity*, ed. Richard Beeman, Stephen Botein, and Edward C. Carter (Chapel Hill: University of North Carolina Press, 1987), 69–109.

7. Holton, *Unruly Americans*, 10–12. During the convention itself, protestors in King William and New Kent Counties burned down county buildings that maintained tax records, thereby preventing tax collection. See Roger H. Brown, *Redeeming the Republic: Federalists, Taxation, and the Origins of the Constitution* (Baltimore, MD: Johns Hopkins University Press, 1993), 130.

8. Gouverneur Morris, "Speeches in the Senate on the Repeal of the Judiciary Act of 1801," January 14, 1802, in *To Secure the Blessings of Liberty: Selected Writings of Gouverneur Morris*, ed. J. Jackson Barlow (Indianapolis, IN: Liberty Fund, 2012), 327.

9. Edmund Randolph, May 29, 1787, in *The Records of the Federal Convention of 1787*, vol. 1, ed. Max Farrand (New Haven, CT: Yale University Press, 1937), 27.

10. James Madison, June 6, 1787, in Farrand, *Records of the Federal Convention of 1787*, vol. 1, 134.

11. According to Jennifer Nedelsky, James Wilson made popular sovereignty, not the protection of property rights, "his first and guiding principle." Nedelsky, *Private Property*, 96.

12. Charles Pinckney was able to deny the existence of class conflict only because he subscribed to an exceedingly narrow conception of inequality. He claimed that the United States was the most equal country in the world because it had a dearth of those ultrarich men who dominate politics in Europe. Even though "there are no distinctions of rank, and very few or none of fortune," at least as compared with Europe, there were class differences between professional, commercial, and landed interests. However, Pinckney stressed that there was no conflict between these classes because their interests were actually aligned. Of course, in making the case for social harmony, Pinckney ignored differences and tensions between these interests and economically underprivileged groups made up of artisans, laborers, and small farmers, not to mention slaves, women, and others who lacked property altogether. Pinckney, June 25, 1787, in Farrand, *Records of the Federal Convention of 1787*, vol. 1, 402–403.

13. Elbridge Gerry, May 31, 1787, in Farrand, *Records of the Federal Convention of 1787*, vol. 1, 1, 48.

14. George Mason, May 31, 1787, in Farrand, *Records of the Federal Convention of 1787*, vol. 1, 49.

15. James Madison, June 26, 1787 in Farrand, *Records of the Federal Convention of 1787*, vol. 1, 422.

16. Ibid.

17. Ibid., 421, 423.

18. Robert Yates, "Notes on Debates for June 26, 1787," 431. According to John Lansing's notes, Madison stated, "Distinctions will always exist—that of Debtor and Creditor—Property has made Distinctions in Europe before a Nobility was created—Inequality of Property will produce the same Distinctions here." Lansing, "Notes on Debates, June 26, 1787," in *Supplement to Max Farrand's* The Records of the Federal Convention of 1787, ed. James H. Hutson (New Haven, CT: Yale University Press, 1987), 119.

19. Alexander Hamilton, June 26, 1787, in Farrand, *Records of the Federal Convention of 1787*, vol. 1, 424. See also 432.

20. Gouverneur Morris, July 2, 1787, in Farrand, *Records of the Federal Convention of 1787*, vol. 1, 512. See also Robert Yates, "Notes on Debates, July 2, 1787," 517.

21. Machiavelli, among others, was a strong proponent of this idea. See John P. McCormick, *Machiavellian Democracy* (Cambridge, UK: Cambridge University Press, 2011), 12, 106–107, 180–181.

22. Morris, July 2, 1787, 512–514. According to Yates, Morris also argued that senators should be eligible to hold other offices or else they would undermine the public good: "The wealthy will ever exist; and you can never be safe unless you gratify them as a body, in the pursuit of honor and profit. Prevent them by positive institutions, and they will proceed in some left-handed way." Yates, "Notes on Debates, July 2, 1787," 518.

23. See Jennifer Nedelsky, who argues that Morris's proposals were designed to limit the power of the rich, whom he viewed as the real danger to liberty in a commercial republic. Nedelsky, *Private Property*, 75–90.

24. Gouverneur Morris, July 5, 1787, in Farrand, *Records of the Federal Convention of 1787*, vol. 1, 533.

25. Ibid.

26. John Rutledge, July 5, 1787, in Farrand, *Records of the Federal Convention of 1787*, vol. 1, 534.

27. Elbridge Gerry and Pierce Butler, July 6, 1787, in Farrand, *Records of the Federal Convention of 1787*, vol. 1, 1, 541–542.

28. James Wilson, July 13, 1787, in Farrand, *Records of the Federal Convention of 1787*, vol. 1, 605.

29. July 13, 1787, in Farrand, *Records of the Federal Convention of 1787*, vol. 1, 606.

30. George Mason, July 26, 1787, in Farrand, *Records of the Federal Convention of 1787*, vol. 2, 121.

31. Gouverneur Morris, July 26, 1787, in Farrand, *Records of the Federal Convention of 1787*, vol. 2, 121, 126.

32. Rufus King, July 26, 1787, in Farrand, *Records of the Federal Convention of 1787*, vol. 2, 123. In point of fact, merchants regularly carried

debts on their balance sheets, so even the most prosperous could have found themselves denied the right to vote. See Bruce H. Mann, *Republic of Debtors: Bankruptcy in the Age of American Independence* (Cambridge, MA: Harvard University Press, 2002).

33. John Dickinson, July 26, 1787, in Farrand, *Records of the Federal Convention of 1787*, vol. 2, 123.

34. James Madison, July 26, 1787, in Farrand, *Records of the Federal Convention of 1787*, vol. 2, 124. Emphasis added.

35. July 26, 1787, in Farrand, *Records of the Federal Convention of 1787*, vol. 2, 124–125.

36. Elbridge Gerry, July 26, 1787, in Farrand, *Records of the Federal Convention of 1787*, vol. 2, 125.

37. John Langdon, July 26, 1787, in Farrand, *Records of the Federal Convention of 1787*, vol. 2, 125.

38. King, July 26, 1787, in Farrand, *Records of the Federal Convention of 1787*, vol. 2, 123.

39. Gouverneur Morris, Oliver Ellsworth, and Charles Pinckney, July 26, 1787, in Farrand, *Records of the Federal Convention of 1787*, vol. 2, 126.

40. See Richard K. Matthews, *If Men Were Angels: James Madison and the Heartless Empire of Reason* (Lawrence: University Press of Kansas, 1995); Matthews, "James Madison's Political Theory: Hostage to Democratic Fortune," *Review of Politics* 67, no. 1 (2005): 49–67.

41. Gouverneur Morris, August 7, 1787, in Farrand, *Records of the Federal Convention of 1787*, vol. 2, 203.

42. Ibid., 202.

43. John Dickinson, August 7, 1787, in Farrand, *Records of the Federal Convention of 1787*, vol. 2, 202.

44. James Madison, August 7, 1787, in Farrand, *Records of the Federal Convention of 1787*, vol. 2, 204–205.

45. Oliver Ellsworth, August 7, 1787, in Farrand, *Records of the Federal Convention of 1787*, vol. 2, 202.

46. George Mason, August 7, 1787, in Farrand, *Records of the Federal Convention of 1787*, vol. 2, 203.

47. Benjamin Franklin, August 7, 1787, in Farrand, *Records of the Federal Convention of 1787*, vol. 2, 2, 204–205.

48. John Rutledge, August 7, 1787, in Farrand, *Records of the Federal Convention of 1787*, vol. 2, 205.

49. Benjamin Franklin, August 10, 1787, in Farrand, *Records of the Federal Convention of 1787*, vol. 2, 249.

50. James Madison, June 8, 1787, in Farrand, *Records of the Federal Convention of 1787*, vol. 2, vol. 1, 164.

51. James Madison, Virginia Plan, May 29, 1787, in Farrand, *Records of the Federal Convention of 1787*, vol. 2, 1, 21.

52. James Madison to Thomas Jefferson, letter, March 19, 1787, in *Madison: Writings*, ed. Jack N. Rakove (Washington, DC: Library of America, 1999), 64.

53. Elbridge Gerry, June 8, 1787, in Farrand, *Records of the Federal Convention of 1787*, vol. 1, 165.

54. James Wilson and Roger Sherman, August 28, 1787, in Farrand, *Records of the Federal Convention of 1787*, vol. 2, 439.

55. August 16, 1787, in Farrand, *Records of the Federal Convention of 1787*, vol. 2, 308–310.

56. Pierce Butler, August 23, 1787, in Farrand, *Records of the Federal Convention of 1787*, vol. 2, 392.

57. George Mason, August 25, 1787, in Farrand, *Records of the Federal Convention of 1787*, vol. 2, 413.

58. Gouverneur Morris, August 25, 1787, in Farrand, *Records of the Federal Convention of 1787*, vol. 2, 413.

59. See Isaac Kramnick, *Republicanism and Bourgeois Radicalism: Political Ideology in Late Eighteenth-Century England and America* (Ithaca, NY: Cornell University Press, 1990), 263–265.

60. Patrick Henry, "Speech at the Virginia Ratifying Convention, June 5, 1788," in *The Anti-Federalist*, ed. Murray Dry (Chicago: University of Chicago Press, 1981), 305.

61. On the importance of homogeneity to many anti-Federalists' vision of republicanism, see Herbert Storing, *What the Anti-Federalists Were For* (Chicago: University of Chicago Press, 1981), 19–20.

62. On the reception and populist character of "Centinel," see Saul Cornell, *The Other Founders: Anti-Federalism and the Dissenting Tradition in America, 1788–1828* (Chapel Hill: University of North Carolina Press, 1999), 46–47.

63. "Centinel," Letter 1, in Dry, *Anti-Federalist*, 14.

64. "Centinel," Letter 16, in *Pennsylvania and the Federal Constitution, 1787–1788*, ed. John Bach McMaster and Frederick Stone (Indianapolis, IN: Liberty Fund, 2011), 657, 658–659.

65. The aristocratic bent of the Constitution was a common basis of backcountry grassroots opposition to the Constitution. See Saul Cornell, "Aristocracy Assailed: The Ideology of Backcountry Anti-Federalism," *Journal of American History* 76, no. 4 (1990): 1148–1172.

66. George Mason, "Objections to this Constitution of Government, September 15, 1787," in Farrand, *Records of the Federal Convention of 1787*, vol. 2, 640.

67. "Federal Farmer," Letter 1, in Dry, *Anti-Federalist*, 36.

68. "The Address and Reasons of the Dissent of the Minority of the Convention of Pennsylvania to Their Constituents," in Dry, *Anti-Federalist*, 203.

69. Such complaints were voiced about the Constitution at the Massachusetts Ratifying Convention, which touched off a debate about the connection between property and ability. Pauline Maier, *Ratification: The People Debate the Constitution, 1787–1788* (New York: Simon and Schuster, 2011), 174–175.

70. "Address and Reasons of the Dissent of the Minority," 219.

71. Quoted in Carl J. Richard, "The Classical Roots of the U.S. Congress: Mixed Government Theory," in *Inventing Congress: Origins and Establishment of the First Federal Congress*, ed. Kenneth R. Bowling and Donald R. Kennon (Athens: Ohio University Press, 1999), 25.

72. Melancton Smith, June 21, 1788, in Dry, *Anti-Federalist*, 340.

73. Ibid.

74. Ibid., 341. (Smith reiterated these points in a speech on June 23, 1788.)

75. Ibid., 345, 342.

76. James Madison, *Federalist 10*, in *The Federalist Papers*, ed. Isaac Kramnick (New York: Penguin, 1987), 126.

77. "Brutus" articulated his theory of representation in a number of essays. See essays of "Brutus," in Dry, *Anti-Federalist*, esp. 114–116, 124–132.

78. Despite his claims about the advantages of reputation in this essay, in the next one "Brutus" suggested that the electoral districts would be so large that the people "will have very little acquaintance with those who may be chosen to represent them." "Brutus," Essay 4, in Dry, *Anti-Federalist*, 130.

79. "Brutus," Essay 3, in Dry, *Anti-Federalist*, 125.

80. Ibid., 126.

81. Ibid. "Brutus" also touched on these themes in Essay 4, in Dry, *Anti-Federalist*, 130–131.

82. "Address and Reasons of the Dissent of the Minority," 213.

83. Ibid, 216.

84. Maier, *Ratification*, 287–288.

85. "Brutus," Essay 14, in Dry, *Anti-Federalist*, 179.

86. "Brutus," Essay 6, in Dry, *Anti-Federalist*, 140.

87. "Brutus,' Essay 5, in Dry, *Anti-Federalist*, 138.

88. George Mason, "Speech at the Virginia Ratifying Convention," June 11, 1788, in Kurland and Kerner, *The Founders' Constitution*, 439, 438, 439.

89. "Brutus," Essay 2, in Dry, *Anti-Federalist*, 121.

90. See, for example, "Federal Farmer," Letter 5, in Dry, *Anti-Federalist*, 64.

91. "Federal Farmer," Letter 4, in Dry, *Anti-Federalist*, 60.

92. Henry, "Speech to the Virginia Ratifying Convention," 324.

93. J. R. Pole, *The Pursuit of Equality in American History* (Berkeley: University of California Press, 1978), 112–113.

94. Madison, *Federalist 10*, 127. On the Federalist idea that the purpose of representation was the "filtration of talent," see Wood, *Creation of the American Republic*, 506–518.

95. Alexander Hamilton, "Conjectures about the New Constitution," September 17–30, 1787, in *The Papers of Alexander Hamilton*, vol. 4, ed. Harold C. Syrett (New York: Columbia University Press, 1961), 275–276.

96. "Caesar," Letter 2, in *Friends of the Constitution: Writings of the "Other" Federalists, 1787–1788*, ed. Colleen A. Sheehan and Gary L. McDowell (Indianapolis, IN: Liberty Fund, 1998), 323.

97. "Atticus," Letter 4, in Sheehan and McDowell, *Friends of the Constitution*, 340. In an abbreviated version of the argument Madison made in

Federalist 10, "Atticus" suggested that any attempt to establish equality would be futile because class distinctions were bound to reemerge in any large society: "Were the people actually brought to an equality, you could not keep them so." Ibid., 341.

98. "State Soldier," Essay 4, in Sheehan and McDowell, *Friends of the Constitution*, 367.

99. Noah Webster, "A Citizen of America," in Sheehan and McDowell, *Friends of the Constitution*, 386.

100. Alexander Hamilton, *Federalist* 35, in Kramnick, *Federalist Papers*, 233.

101. Alexander Hamilton, *Federalist* 36, in Kramnick, *Federalist Papers*, 235–236.

102. Alexander Hamilton, "Speech at the New York Ratifying Convention, June 21, 1788," in Syrett, *Papers of Alexander Hamilton*, vol. 5, 43.

103. Nicholas Collin ("A Foreign Spectator"), "An Essay on the Means of Promoting Federal Sentiments in the United States," in Sheehan and McDowell, *Friends of the Constitution*, 422.

104. Benjamin Rush, "Address to the People of the United States," in Sheehan and McDowell, *Friends of the Constitution*, 3. Emphasis in original.

105. James Madison broadened the definition even further to include any "government which derives all its powers *directly* or *indirectly* from the great body of the people." Madison, *Federalist* 39, in Kramnick, *Federalist Papers*, 255. Emphasis added.

106. Madison, *Federalist* 10, 126. According to Richard K. Matthews, Madison's repudiation of democracy stemmed from his "low" regard for the capacity of the people to govern themselves or respect individual rights. Matthews, *If Men Were Angels*.

107. Madison, *Federalist* 10, 128. Madison responded directly to criticisms that the Constitution would result in an aristocracy by reminding readers that offices would be open to all because it established no property qualifications. Madison, *Federalist* 57, in Kramnick, *Federalist Papers*, 343–344. Of course, the states were free to establish their own eligibility rules for voting and officeholding.

108. Madison, *Federalist* 10, 124.

109. Madison, "Vices of the Political System of the United States," in Rackove, *Madison: Writings*, 75.

110. Ibid, 70.

111. Madison, *Federalist* 10, 126. Alexander Hamilton was even more blunt in his defense of a long term of office for the president, writing "that the people commonly *intend* the PUBLIC GOOD," but they sometimes "err." In those instances when the "interests of the people are at variance with their inclinations, it is the duty of the persons whom they have appointed to be the guardians of those interests, to withstand the temporary delusion, in order to give them time and opportunity for more cool and sedate reflection." Hamilton, *Federalist* 71, 410.

112. Madison, *Federalist* 10, 123.

113. Ibid., 124. As Jennifer Nedelsky explains in *Private Property*, this understanding led Madison to subordinate the political right to participation to the civil right to acquire property.

Chapter 4: "Necessary and Proper"

1. Stephen F. Knott, "'Opposed in Death as in Life': Hamilton and Jefferson in American Memory," in *The Many Faces of Alexander Hamilton: The Life and Legacy of America's Most Elusive Founding Father*, ed. Douglas Ambrose and Robert W. T. Martin (New York: New York University Press, 2006), 25–53.

2. Quoted in Stephen F. Knott, *Alexander Hamilton and the Persistence of Myth* (Lawrence: University Press of Kansas, 2002), 24.

3. Michael J. Thompson, *The Politics of Inequality: A Political History of Economic Inequality in America* (New York: Columbia University Press, 2007), 79.

4. Philip S. Foner, "Introduction," *The Complete Writings of Thomas Paine*, vol. 1 (New York: Citadel, 1945), xxv–xxvi.

5. Richard K. Matthews, *The Radical Politics of Thomas Jefferson: A Revisionist View* (Lawrence: University Press of Kansas, 1984), 115.

6. John Patrick Diggins points out that Hamilton disdained those driven by the profit motive alone in "Alexander Hamilton, Abraham Lincoln, and the Spirit of Capitalism," in Ambrose and Martin, *Many Faces of Alexander Hamilton*, 276.

7. Peter McNamara, "Hamilton, Croly, and American Public Philosophy," in Ambrose and Martin, *Many Faces of Alexander Hamilton*, 261.

8. See Terry Bouton, *Taming Democracy: "The People," the Founders, and the Troubled Ending of the American Revolution* (Oxford, UK: Oxford University Press, 2007), 70–87.

9. Alexander Hamilton to James Duane, letter, September 3, 1780, in *The Papers of Alexander Hamilton*, vol. 2, ed. Harold C. Syrett (New York: Columbia University Press, 1961), 401.

10. Alexander Hamilton to James Duane, letter, September 3, 1780, in Syrett, *Papers of Alexander Hamilton*, vol. 2, 407–408.

11. "A Letter from Phocion to the Considerate Citizens of New York on the Politics of the Day," in Syrett, *Papers of Alexander Hamilton*, vol. 3, 490.

12. See McNamara, "Hamilton, Croly, and American Public Philosophy"; Joyce Appleby, *Liberalism and Republicanism in the Historical Imagination* (Cambridge, MA: Harvard University Press, 1992), 185–186.

13. Alexander Hamilton, *Federalist 31*, in *The Federalist Papers*, ed. Isaac Kramnick (New York: Penguin, 1987), 216.

14. Some of these moneyed men had begun lobbying Alexander Hamilton as soon as he became treasury secretary. William Bingham, a Philadelphia merchant and one of the wealthiest men in the country, reminded Hamilton to pay "Great Attention" to public creditors "especially, as they will

constitute an essential part of the monied Interest of the Country to whom Government will often be compelled to have recourse." Bingham to Hamilton, letter, November 25, 1789, in Syrett, *Papers of Alexander Hamilton*, vol. 5, 541.

15. However, some recent scholarship has suggested that, contrary to established opinion, the state of the US economy during the 1790s was rather weak: not only was growth during this period mediocre, the young economy was particularly prone to crises. Carey Roberts calls the period following the adoption of Hamilton's proposals one of "economic malaise" in "Alexander Hamilton and the 1790s Economy: A Reappraisal," in Ambrose and Martin, *Many Faces of Alexander Hamilton*, 212–213.

16. Alexander Hamilton, *Report on Public Credit*, in Syrett, *Papers of Alexander Hamilton*, vol. 6, 68–69.

17. Ibid., 68.

18. Ibid., 74.

19. Ibid., 69.

20. See, for example, Alexander Hamilton to James Duane, letter, September 3, 1780, in Syrett, *Papers of Alexander Hamilton*, vol. 2, 400–418; Hamilton to Robert Morris, letter, April 30, 1781, in Syrett, *Papers of Alexander Hamilton*, vol. 2, 604–635.

21. Alexander Hamilton to George Washington, letter, September 9, 1792, in Syrett, *Papers of Alexander Hamilton*, vol. 12, 349.

22. Alexander Hamilton to George Washington, letter, August 18, 1792, in Syrett, *Papers of Alexander Hamilton*, vol. 12, 247, 248.

23. Ibid., 249.

24. Hamilton, *Report on Public Credit*, vol. 6, 70.

25. Ibid., 88–89.

26. William Manning, "Some Proposals for Making Restitution to the Original Creditors of Government," in *The Key of Liberty: The Life and Democratic Writings of William Manning, "A Laborer," 1747–1814*, ed. Michael Merrill and Sean Wilentz (Cambridge, MA: Harvard University Press, 1993), 99.

27. Ibid., 101.

28. Ibid., 105.

29. All parenthetical notes in the main text refer to the *Annals of Congress* (Washington, DC: Gales and Seaton, 1834), with date, Congress, session, and column number provided.

30. William Maclay, "Notes on Senate Debates for January 14 and 15, 1790," in *The Diary of William Maclay and Other Notes on Senate Debates*, ed. Kenneth R. Bowling and Helen E. Veit (Baltimore, MD: Johns Hopkins University Press, 1988), 183.

31. William Maclay, "Notes on Senate Debates for February 15 and 19, 1790," in Bowling and Veit, *Diary of William Maclay*, 203, 205.

32. William Maclay, untitled essay, *Independent Gazeteer*, February 20, 1790, in Bowling and Veit, *Diary of William Maclay*, 413–414.

33. William Maclay, "Notes on Senate Debates for June 17, 1790," in Bowling and Veit, *Diary of William Maclay*, 296.

34. On the jubilee, see Joseph William Singer, *The Edges of the Field: Lessons on the Obligations of Ownership* (Boston: Beacon, 2000), 50–53.

35. See, for example, William Maclay, "Notes on Senate Debates for July 16, 1790," in Bowling and Veit, *Diary of William Maclay*, 322.

36. See Stanley Elkins and Eric McKitrick, *The Age of Federalism: The Early American Republic, 1788–1800* (Oxford, UK: Oxford University Press, 1993), 89–90, 136–137.

37. For a comprehensive account of the negotiations that took place and the main differences between Hamilton's original plan and the statutes ultimately passed, see Forrest McDonald, *Alexander Hamilton: A Biography* (New York: Norton, 1979), 163–188.

38. Hamilton to Duane, letter, September 3, 1780, 415.

39. Alexander Hamilton, *Report on a National Bank*, in Syrett, *Papers of Alexander Hamilton*, vol. 7, 325.

40. Ibid., 306–310.

41. Ibid., 326.

42. Ibid., 334.

43. For critical assessments of the class politics surrounding the creation of the bank, see Andrew Shankman, *Crucible of American Democracy: The Struggle to Fuse Egalitarianism and Capitalism in Jeffersonian Pennsylvania* (Lawrence: University Press of Kansas, 2004), 27–40.

44. David Cowen, *The Origins and Impact of the First Bank of the United States, 1791–1797* (New York: Routledge, 2000). In his survey of banking institutions in the United States, James Sullivan observed that many of the initial subscribers were unsavory characters who used fraudulent means to acquire more shares than the spirit of the law allowed. Sullivan, *The Path to Riches: An Inquiry into the Origins and Use of Money and into the Principles of Stocks and Banks* (Boston: J. Belcher, 1809), 22–23.

45. Madison then immediately added, "So it has been understood by its friends and its foes, and so it was to be interpreted." Of course, this was plainly false. As Madison well knew from his debates with anti-Federalists during the struggle over ratification, many foes of the Constitution certainly did not understand the Constitution as providing a "grant of particular powers only." In fact, many of them objected to the Constitution precisely because they believed its open-ended and ambiguous language resulted in a general grant of powers that could and would be used in unpredictable and dangerous ways.

46. On the relation of Ames's argument to that of other supporters of the bank, see Benjamin B. Klubes, "The First Federal Congress and the First National Bank: A Case Study in Constitutional Interpretation," *Journal of the Early Republic* 10, no. 1 (1990): 39.

47. Quoted in ibid., 25.

48. William Maclay, "Notes on Senate Debates for December 24, 1790," in Bowling and Veit, *Diary of William Maclay*, 347.

49. William Maclay, "Notes on Senate Debates for January 17, 1791," in Bowling and Veit, *Diary of William Maclay*, 362.

50. Thomas Jefferson, "Opinion on the Constitutionality of the Bill for

Establishing a National Bank," in *The Papers of Thomas Jefferson*, vol. 19, ed. Julian P. Boyd (Princeton: Princeton University Press, 1953), 277.

51. Alexander Hamilton, *Opinion on the Constitutionality of an Act to Establish a National Bank*, in Syrett, *Papers of Alexander Hamilton*, vol. 8, 97.

52. Ibid., 106.

53. Ibid., 103.

54. Ibid.

55. Ibid., 105.

56. In *Federalist* 33, Hamilton had argued that the hysteria aroused by the necessary and proper clause and the supremacy clause was unwarranted because these were simply "declaratory" phrases that did nothing more than explicate truths implicit in the very idea of government. According to Hamilton, "The constitutional operation of the intended government would be precisely the same, if these clauses were entirely obliterated, as if they were repeated in every article." Even though these clauses were constitutionally unnecessary, they were inserted to "guard against all cavilling [sic] refinements in those who might hereafter feel a disposition to curtail and evade the legitimate authorities of the Union." Hamilton, *Federalist* 33, in Kramnick, *Federalist Papers*, 223, 224.

57. Hamilton, *Opinion on the Constitutionality*, 132.

58. Ibid., 100.

59. Ibid.

60. Ibid., 121.

61. Ibid., 129.

62. Ibid., 98. Even when Hamilton argued that the end justifies the means, he noted that certain means were completely off limits: "If the end be clearly comprehended within any of the specified powers, & if the measure have an obvious relation to that end, and is not forbidden by any particular provision of the constitution—it may safely be deemed to come within the compass of the national authority. There is also this further criterion which may materially assist the decision. Does the proposed measure abridge a preexisting right of any State, or of any individual? If it does not, there is a strong presumption in favour of its constitutionality; & slighter relations to any declared object of the constitution may be permitted to turn the scale." Ibid., 107.

63. John Taylor of Caroline, *An Enquiry into the Principles and Tendencies of Certain Public Measures* (Philadelphia: Thomas Dobson, 1794), 48.

64. Ibid., 30, 23. See also Garrett Ward Sheldon, *The Liberal Republicanism of John Taylor of Caroline* (Madison, NJ: Fairleigh Dickinson University Press, 2008), 61–66.

65. See James L. Huston, *Securing the Fruits of Labor: The American Concept of Wealth Distribution, 1765–1900* (Baton Rouge: Louisiana State University Press, 1998), 223–236.

66. Hamilton sang the praises of manufacturing in his very first American publication, "A Full Vindication of the Measures of Congress," in which he predicted that the establishment of manufactures "will pave the way, still

more, to the future grandeur and glory of America." In Syrett, *Papers of Alexander Hamilton*, vol. 1, 56.

67. See Gary B. Nash, *The Urban Crucible: Social Change, Political Consciousness, and the Origins of the American Revolution* (Cambridge, MA: Harvard University Press, 1979), 189–193, 332–337.

68. An excellent account of this agrarian ideology and the ways it informed Jefferson(ians)'s understanding of republicanism can be found in Drew McCoy, *The Elusive Republic: Political Economy in Jeffersonian America* (New York: Norton, 1980).

69. Hamilton, *Report on the Subject of Manufactures*, in Syrett, *Papers of Alexander Hamilton*, vol. 10, 340.

70. Ibid., 303.

71. Ibid.

72. Shankman, *Crucible of American Democracy*, 43.

73. Hamilton, *Report on the Subject of Manufactures*, 254–255.

74. Ibid., 253.

75. After the death of his mother, who had worked as a shopkeeper, Hamilton had to take a job as a clerk at a counting house in St. Croix at the tender age of eleven. On Hamilton's life before emigrating to America, see Ron Chernow, *Alexander Hamilton* (New York: Penguin, 2004), 16–38. The reports of treasury agents who gathered information for Hamilton on the state of manufacturing in the country confirmed the presence of women and children in nascent manufacturing operations. See Nathaniel Gorham to Alexander Hamilton, October 13, 1791, enclosure to letter; "Report of a Committee Appointed to Obtain Information on Manufacturing in Providence," October 10, 1791, in Syrett, *Papers of Alexander Hamilton*, vol. 9, 374, 446.

76. Hamilton, *Report on the Subject of Manufactures*, 282.

77. Ibid., 294.

78. As an attorney in New York, Hamilton occasionally provided pro bono legal representation to the poor in criminal cases. Chernow, *Alexander Hamilton*, 189.

79. Willard Sterne Randall, *Alexander Hamilton: A Life* (New York: Perennial, 2004), 94.

80. Alexander Hamilton to John Jay, letter, November 26, 1775, in Syrett, *Papers of Alexander Hamilton*, vol. 1, 176. For more details on episodes of mob action and Hamilton's reactions, see Chernow, *Alexander Hamilton*, 63–65, 67–70.

81. Chernow argues that the normally loquacious Hamilton "kept silent" about Shays's Rebellion "because he sympathized with the farmers' grievances, however much he despised their methods." Chernow, *Alexander Hamilton*, 225.

82. Hamilton, *Federalist* 71, in Kramnick, *Federalist Papers*, 409–410.

83. Alexander Hamilton, "Speech at the New York Ratifying Convention, June 21, 1788," in Syrett, *Papers of Alexander Hamilton*, vol. 5, 37.

84. Ibid., 39.

85. Robert W. T. Martin, "Reforming Republicanism: Alexander Hamilton's

Theory of Republican Citizenship and Press Liberty," in Ambrose and Martin, *Many Faces of Alexander Hamilton*, 109–133.

86. See, for example, Alexander Hamilton to Gouverneur Morris, letter, May 19, 1777, in Syrett, *Papers of Alexander Hamilton*, vol. 1, 255.

87. Hamilton, *Federalist* 85, in Kramnick, *Federalist Papers*, 483.

88. See, for example, Alexander Hamilton to George Clinton, letter, February 13, 1778, in Syrett, *Papers of Alexander Hamilton*, vol. 1, 425–428; on Lee's incompetence as general, see Hamilton to Elias Boudinot, letter, July 5, 1778, in Syrett, *Papers of Alexander Hamilton*, vol. 1, 510–511. On Hamilton's disappointment with members of the Continental Congress, see McDonald, *Alexander Hamilton*, 17–20.

89. See, for example, *Federalist* 21, in Kramnick, *Federalist Papers*, 173–174.

90. Alexander Hamilton, "Tully," no. 3, in Syrett, *Papers of Alexander Hamilton*, vol. 17, 159.

91. Thomas P. Govan, "The Rich, the Well-born, and Alexander Hamilton," *Mississippi Valley Historical Review* 36, no. 4 (1950): 677–678.

92. Alexander Hamilton, "Speech at the Constitutional Convention, June 18, 1787," in *The Records of the Federal Convention of 1787*, vol. 1, ed. Max Farrand (New Haven, CT: Yale University Press, 1937), 288.

93. Ibid., 289.

94. Ibid., 290.

95. Alexander Hamilton, "Speech at the Constitutional Convention, September 8, 1787," in Farrand, *Records of the Federal Convention of 1787*, vol. 2, 553.

96. Alexander Hamilton, "Speech at the Constitutional Convention, May 30, 1787," in Farrand, *Records of the Federal Convention of 1787*, vol. 1, 36.

97. Hamilton's brief discussion of property qualifications in *The Farmer Refuted* is sometimes cited to show that he wanted to restrict voting to those with property, but it is actually a description rather than an endorsement of policies in England on the eve of the Revolution. Alexander Hamilton, *The Farmer Refuted*, in Syrett, *Papers of Alexander Hamilton*, vol. 1, 105–107.

98. Alexander Hamilton, "New York Assembly. Remarks on an Act for Regulating Elections," January 23, 1787, in Syrett, *Papers of Alexander Hamilton*, vol. 4, 19.

99. Alexander Hamilton, "New York Assembly. Remarks on an Act for Regulating Elections," January 27, 1787, in Syrett, *Papers of Alexander Hamilton*, 26.

100. Ibid., 29.

101. Randall, *Alexander Hamilton*, 101.

102. Alexander Hamilton to John Jay, letter, March 14, 1779, in Syrett, *Papers of Alexander Hamilton*, vol. 2, 17–19.

103. Randall, *Alexander Hamilton*, 103.

104. Ibid., 14.

105. See ibid., 277; Chernow, *Alexander Hamilton*, 73.

106. Alexander Hamilton, "Draft of George Washington's Eighth Annual Address to Congress," November 10, 1796, in Syrett, *Papers of Alexander Hamilton*, vol. 20, 386.

107. Alexander Hamilton, "Report on Marine Hospitals," April 17, 1792, in Syrett, *Papers of Alexander Hamilton*, vol. 11, 295.

108. See Alexander Hamilton, "Continental Congress Report on the Corps of Invalids," May 1, 1783, in Syrett, *Papers of Alexander Hamilton*, vol. 3, 345–346.

109. See Bernard Rostker, *Providing for the Casualties of War: The American Experience through World War II* (Santa Monica, CA: RAND, 2013), 64–65.

110. Alexander Hamilton to James McHenry, letter, September 17, 1799, in Syrett, *Papers of Alexander Hamilton*, vol. 13, 433.

111. Alexander Hamilton, *Report on the Establishment of a Mint*, in Syrett, *Papers of Alexander Hamilton*, vol. 7, 601.

112. Alexander Hamilton, "The Farmer Refuted," in Syrett, *Papers of Alexander Hamilton*, vol. 1, 146–147.

113. Alexander Hamilton, "The Continentalist," no. 6, in Syrett, *Papers of Alexander Hamilton*, vol. 3, 100.

114. Alexander Hamilton to Robert Morris, letter, April 30, 1781, in Syrett, *Papers of Alexander Hamilton*, vol. 2, 612.

115. Ibid., 610.

116. Alexander Hamilton, "Purchase of Louisiana," *New-York Evening Post*, July 5, 1803, in Syrett, *Papers of Alexander Hamilton*, vol. 26, 135. Emphasis in original.

117. Alexander Hamilton, "Continental Congress Report on a Letter from the Speaker of the Rhode Island Assembly," December 16, 1782, in Syrett, *Papers of Alexander Hamilton*, vol. 3, 215.

118. Hamilton, *Report on the Subject of Manufactures*, 312.

119. Hamilton, "Continental Congress Report," 214.

120. Alexander Hamilton, "The Continentalist," no. 4, in Syrett, *Papers of Alexander Hamilton*, vol. 2, 670.

121. Hamilton, "The Continentalist," no. 6, 103.

122. Ibid., 104.

123. William D. Barber, "'Among the Most *Techy Articles of Civil Police*': Federal Taxation and the Adoption of the Whiskey Excise," *William and Mary Quarterly* 25, no. 1 (1968): 59.

124. Hamilton, *Federalist* 21, 175–176.

125. Alexander Hamilton, "Report on the Difficulties in the Execution of the Act Laying Duties on Distilled Spirits," March 5, 1792, in Syrett, *Papers of Alexander Hamilton*, vol. 11, 96–97.

126. For example, a petition to Congress from residents of western Pennsylvania contended that the excise on "spirituous liquors" would be "unequal in its operation, as a duty laid on the common drink of a nation, instead of taxing the citizens in proportion to their property, falls as heavy on the poorest class as on the rich." Albert Gallatin, "Petition against Excise," in

The Writings of Albert Gallatin, vol. 1, ed. Henry Adams (Philadelphia: Lippincott, 1879), 3.

127. Hamilton, "Report on the Difficulties," 97.

128. Ibid., 99.

129. Hamilton to Washington, letter, August 18, 1792, 234–235.

130. On the political and economic effects of the whiskey tax, see Dall W. Forsythe, *Taxation and Political Change in the Young Nation, 1781–1833* (New York: Columbia University Press, 1977), 39–51.

131. Quoted in McDonald, *Alexander Hamilton,* 136. On Necker's general influence on Hamilton, see ibid., 84–85, 135–136.

132. Alexander Hamilton, "Report Relative to the Additional Supplies for the Ensuing Year," in Syrett, *Papers of Alexander Hamilton,* vol. 11, 144.

133. Ibid., 146.

134. Ibid., 148.

135. Hamilton, *Report on the Subject of Manufactures,* 335.

136. Alexander Hamilton, "An Act for Raising Yearly Taxes within This State," in Syrett, *Papers of Alexander Hamilton,* vol. 4, 40–50.

137. Alexander Hamilton to Theodore Sedgwick, enclosure to letter, in Syrett, *Papers of Alexander Hamilton,* vol. 20, 502–504. On Hamilton's objections to exemptions, see ibid., 501.

Chapter 5: Constructing the Constitution

1. On reforms at the state level that structured taxes according to ability to pay, see Robert A. Becker, *Revolution, Reform, and the Politics of American Taxation, 1763–1783* (Baton Rouge: Louisiana State University Press, 1980).

2. Whether every member who expressed concern for economic equality was being sincere is unknowable—and also beside the point. These expressions of concern for the condition of the poor are indicative of the weight the speakers assumed this point had with their audience inside and outside of Congress.

3. All parenthetical notes in the main text refer to the *Annals of Congress* (Washington, DC: Gales and Seaton, 1834), with date, Congress, session, and column number provided.

4. In addition to Charles Beard's *An Economic Interpretation of the Constitution of the United States* (New York: Free Press, 1986), see for example, Forrest McDonald, *We the People: The Economic Origins of the Constitution* (New Brunswick, NJ: Transaction, 1991); McDonald, *E Pluribus Unum: The Formation of the American Republic, 1776–1790* (Indianapolis, IN: Liberty Fund, 1979); Jack N. Rakove, *The Beginnings of National Politics: An Interpretive History of the Continental Congress* (Baltimore, MD: Johns Hopkins University Press, 1979), 275–329; Robert A. Goldwin and William A. Schambra, eds., *How Capitalistic Is the Constitution?* (Washington, DC: American Enterprise Institute, 1982); Jennifer Nedelsky, *Private Property*

and the Limits of American Constitutionalism: The Madisonian Framework and Its Legacy (Chicago: University of Chicago Press, 1990); Carl J. Richard, "The Classical Roots of the U.S. Congress: Mixed Government Theory," in *Inventing Congress: Origins and Establishment of the First Federal Congress*, ed. Kenneth R. Bowling and Donald R. Kennon (Athens: Ohio University Press, 1999); and Sotirios A. Barber, *Welfare and the Constitution* (Princeton, NJ: Princeton University Press, 2003).

5. For an overview of the constitutional debates that did take place on the scope of the commerce power, see David P. Currie, *The Constitution in Congress: The Federalist Period, 1789–1801* (Chicago: University of Chicago Press, 1997), 55–67.

6. On the promotion of morality in the 1st Congress, see William C. diGiacomantonio, "To Form the Character of the American People: Public Support for the Arts, Sciences, and Morality in the First Federal Congress," in Bowling and Kennon, *Inventing Congress*.

7. According to Charlene Bangs Bickford and Kenneth R. Bowling, of the more than 600 petitions received by the 1st Congress alone, "the vast majority sought resolution of private claims." Bickford and Bowling, *Birth of the Nation: The First Federal Congress, 1789–1791* (Madison, WI: Madison House, 1989), 6. See also ibid., 31.

8. For an overview of different approaches to constitutional interpretation, see Sotirios A. Barber and James E. Fleming, *Constitutional Interpretation: The Basic Questions* (Oxford, UK: Oxford University Press, 2007).

9. Even James Madison admitted it was hard to distinguish between deliberative and ministerial functions, but he did insist such a line actually exists (November 19, 1792, 2nd Cong., 2nd sess., 700).

10. See, for example, "Brutus," Essay 5 and Essay 11, in *The Anti-Federalist*, ed. Murray Dry (Chicago: University of Chicago Press, 1981), 134 and 165–166, respectively.

11. The exact same complaint was made by Thomas Henderson of New Jersey (April, 22, 1796, 4th Cong., 1st sess., 1165).

12. On James Jackson's political thought and leanings, see Marie Sauer Lambremont, "Rep. James Jackson of Georgia and the Establishment of the Southern States' Rights Tradition in Congress," in Bowling and Kennon, *Inventing Congress*, 191–207.

13. Currie, *Constitution in Congress*, 117.

14. James Madison, *Report on the Alien and Sedition Acts*, in *Madison: Writings*, ed. Jack N. Rakove (Washington, DC: Library of America, 1999), 627–628.

15. James Madison to Samuel Johnston, letter, June 21, 1789, in Rakove, *Madison: Writings*. This echoed Madison's claim in *Federalist* 37, "All new laws [including the Constitution], though penned with the greatest technical skill, and passed on the fullest and most mature deliberation, are considered as more or less obscure and equivocal, until their meaning be liquidated and ascertained by a series of particular discussions and adjudications." Madison, *Federalist* 37, in *The Federalist Papers*, ed. Isaac Kramnick (New York: Penguin, 1987).

16. See "Brutus," Essay 6, in Dry, *Anti-Federalist*, 139.

17. David Currie has concluded that members were increasingly "tailoring their arguments to their conclusions" after the 1st Congress. Currie, *Constitution in Congress*, 171.

18. Duties were laid on dozens of goods, including distilled spirits, molasses, brown sugar, candles, boots, silk and leather shoes, nails and spikes, snuff, and various teas. "An Act for Laying a Duty on Goods, Wares, and Merchandises, Imported into the United States," *Annals of Congress*, 1st Cong., 2183–2186.

19. See Stanley Elkins and Eric McKitrick, *The Age of Federalism: The Early American Republic, 1788–1800* (Oxford, UK: Oxford University Press, 1993), 65–74.

20. In the *Annals of Congress*, his last name is incorrectly given as "Lawrence."

21. Mark Kurlansky, *Salt: A World History* (New York: Penguin, 2003).

22. John Laurance was one of the only members to dispute the claim that the salt tax would fall more heavily on the poor. He suggested that the rich actually end up paying much more because they have to provide for so many servants and dependents who consume salt (April 17, 1789, 1st Cong., 1st sess., 168). However, he also defended the salt tax on the basis of its universality. In principle, he argued, everyone should pay some tax, and the salt tax was the best way to ensure that no one would be completely exempt from any taxes at all (April 17, 1789, 1st Cong., 1st sess., 169).

23. On the consumption habits of ordinary citizens and the republican ideology that supported it, see Drew R. McCoy, *The Elusive Republic: Political Economy in Jeffersonian America* (New York: Norton, 1980).

24. William Maclay, "Notes on Senate Debates for June 4, 1789," in *The Diary of William Maclay and Other Notes on Senate Debates*, ed. Kenneth R. Bowling and Helen E. Veit (Baltimore, MD: Johns Hopkins University Press, 1988), 66.

25. Maclay, "Notes on Senate Debates for June 2, 1789," in Bowling and Veit, *Diary of William Maclay*, 64.

26. W. Elliot Brownlee, *Federal Taxation in America: A Short History*, new ed. (Cambridge, UK: Cambridge University Press, 2004), 24.

27. On the election of 1792 and its aftermath, see Elkins and McKitrick, *Age of Federalism*, 288.

28. However, domestic manufacturers of the items subject to excise taxes, usually small production, independent craftsmen, complained that these taxes hurt them most of all. See Andrew Shankman, *Crucible of American Democracy: The Struggle to Fuse Egalitarianism and Capitalism in Jeffersonian Pennsylvania* (Lawrence: University Press of Kansas, 2004), 47–48.

29. "An Act Laying Duties upon Carriages for the Conveyance of Persons," June 5, 1794, 3rd Cong., 1st sess., 1452. A motion by William Branch Giles of Virginia in the next session of Congress to have the carriage tax repealed lost by a vote of twenty-nine to fifty-five. February 6, 1795, 3rd Cong., 2nd sess., 1204. In the first case reviewing the constitutionality of

an act of Congress, the US Supreme Court ruled in *Hylton v. United States* (1796) that the carriage tax was not a direct tax but an excise tax.

30. Ruth Bogin, *Abraham Clark and the Quest for Equality in the Revolutionary Era, 1774–1794* (Rutherford, NJ: Farleigh Dickinson University Press, 1982).

31. Proponents of the direct tax hoped to overcome resistance by emphasizing the "urgency" and "necessity" of the situation the country faced as it prepared for a naval war that could prove devastating to trans-Atlantic trade.

32. Samuel Smith contradicted the idea that consumers are aware of just how regressive and "oppressive" indirect taxes are, but he insisted, "Those who do know it ought to endeavor to relieve them from it" (May 5, 1798, 5th Cong., 2nd sess., 1604).

33. Swanwick also made positive, if sometimes idiosyncratic, arguments in favor of direct taxes. Perhaps his most original was the argument that a direct tax would produce a positive civic effect by stimulating greater interest in the operations and expenses of government. In contrast to many indirect taxes, which can operate imperceptibly, a direct tax "would awaken the attention of the farmer to its operations, to inquire of the why and the wherefore" (January 16, 1797, 4th Cong., 2nd sess., 1888–1889).

34. For details of Alexander Hamilton's proposal, see the discussion at the end of chapter 4.

35. Oliver Wolcott's Report on Direct Taxes can be found in *Annals of Congress*, 4th Cong., Appendix, 2635.

36. Lee Soltow, *Distribution of Wealth and Income in the United States in 1798* (Pittsburgh, PA: University of Pittsburgh Press, 1989).

37. This percentage is derived from a table, "Distribution of Housing Values in the United States, 1798" in ibid., 51.

38. See ibid., 41.

39. In his May 25, 1798, report to the House of Representatives, Oliver Wolcott cited new settlements as evidence in support of his claim that "dwelling-houses of small value ought not to be considered as indications of poverty" (5th Cong., Appendix, 3595).

40. The House also rejected a second attempt by Samuel Smith to equalize the tax on houses and land by a vote of forty-six to thirty-two (June 29, 1798, 5th Cong., 2nd sess., 2059).

41. Soltow, *Distribution of Wealth and Income,* 109.

42. Dall W. Forsythe, *Taxation and Political Change in the Young Nation, 1781–1833* (New York: Columbia University Press, 1977), 122.

43. Patrick Henry, "Speech at the Virginia Ratifying Convention, June 5, 1788," in Dry, *Anti-Federalist,* 304.

44. On land policy during the 1780s, see Roy M. Robbins, *Our Landed Heritage: The Public Domain, 1776–1936* (Lincoln: University of Nebraska Press, 1962), 1–11.

45. Ibid., 9–11.

46. Alexander Hamilton, "Report on Vacant Lands," July 20, 1790, in *The Papers of Alexander Hamilton,* Vol. 6, ed. Harold C. Syrett (New York: Columbia University Press, 1962), 502–506.

47. On early legislative action concerning the Northwest Territory, see Benjamin Horace Hibbard, *A History of the Public Land Policies* (New York: Macmillan, 1924), 56–81.

48. Abraham Baldwin lamented that philosophers used to appeal to virtue, honor, patriotism, and public interest, but "have of late made their most importunate and successful addresses to other passions, and have excited the insatiable sordid passion of avarice to an unusual degree. Speculation and making money are rarely found in a more raging extreme, and persons whom we have supposed worthy of our confidence and esteem, publicly practising the meanest and most disgraceful tricks of swindling; and instead of being exhibited to public infamy in the pillory, they sow an unblushing front in a very different situation. When such men, said he, are publicly patronized and treated with respect, it is necessary to take care how we suffer the execution of our land law to depend on the disinterestedness of an individual" (March 2, 1796, 4th Cong., 1st sess., 402–403).

49. The relatively large size of plots did offset somewhat the surveying cost borne by purchasers. See Farley Grubb, "U.S. Land Policy: Founding Choices and Outcomes, 1781–1802," in *Founding Choices: American Economic Policy in the 1790s*, ed. Douglas Irwin and Richard Sylla (Chicago: University of Chicago Press, 2011), 260.

50. Ibid., 266–268, 284–285.

51. Hibbard, *History of the Public Land Policies*, 64. As it turns out, the price did discourage speculation, with the result that land sales flagged far below expectations. Ibid., 68–69.

52. An attempt during the 6th Congress by Albert Gallatin and his allies to subdivide the land into 320- and 160-acre sections failed (March 31–April 1, 1800, 6th Cong., 1st sess., 651–652).

53. On changes in land policy between 1800 and 1820, see Robbins, *Our Landed Heritage*, 18–34.

54. For details on the general background and development of these events, see C. L. R. James, *The Black Jacobins: Toussaint L'Ouverture and the San Domingo Revolution*, 2nd ed., rev. (New York: Vintage, 1989).

55. On the reception, treatment, and activities of refugees in the United States, see Ashli White, *Encountering Revolution: Haiti and the Making of the Early Republic* (Baltimore, MD: Johns Hopkins University Press, 2012).

56. On the sometimes self-congratulatory tone of these claims, see ibid., 53–61.

57. On the use and development of "disaster narratives" to justify federal assistance to those who could be portrayed as blameless victims, see Michele Landis Dauber, *The Sympathetic State: Disaster Relief and the Origins of the American Welfare State* (Chicago: University of Chicago Press, 2013).

58. See Currie, *Constitution in Congress*, 189.

59. On the immediate aftermath of the relief bill, see White, *Encountering Revolution*, 73–78.

60. On the importance of sailors to both the economic and naval strength of the country, see Alexander Hamilton, *Federalist* 11, in Kramnick, *Federalist Papers*, 131–132.

61. The law, "An Act for the Government and Regulation of Seamen in the Merchant Service," passed on July 20, 1790, specified the rights, benefits, and remedies to which sailors would be entitled (1st Cong., 2nd sess., Appendix, 2294–2299). See also Currie, *Constitution in Congress*, 65.

62. On the economic insecurity of seamen, see Billy G. Smith, *The "Lower Sort": Philadelphia's Laboring People, 1750–1800* (Ithaca, NY: Cornell University Press, 1990), 112–115.

63. James Madison, "Republican Distribution of Citizens," *National Gazette*, March 5, 1792, in Rackove, *Madison: Writings*, 512.

64. Alexander Hamilton, "Report on Marine Hospitals," April 17, 1792, in Syrett, *Papers of Alexander Hamilton*, vol. 11, 295.

65. Unfortunately, the *Annals of Congress* for the 2nd Congress are very sketchy, so there is no record of any further debates.

66. For details on Giles's resolutions against Hamilton and his exoneration, see Elkins and McKitrick, *Age of Federalism*, 295–302.

67. See John Odin Jensen, *Bulwarks against a Human Tide: Government, Mariners, and the Rise of General Hospitals in the Midwest Frontier, 1800–1900*, PhD diss., Carnegie Mellon University, 2000; Gautham Rao, "Sailors' Health and National Wealth: Marine Hospitals in the Early Republic," *Common-Place* 9, no. 1 (October 2008).

Chapter 6: "Silently Lessening the Inequality of Property"

1. Conservative books, magazines, websites, and speeches are chock-full of quotations from Jefferson purporting to show that the founder steadfastly opposed any and all governmental attempts to minimize economic inequality on both constitutional and ideological grounds. A few examples are given in the section titled "Limited Government and Remedies for the Problem of Inequality."

2. For instance, while arguing on the floor of the House of Representatives that the general welfare clause of the US Constitution refers to the "general welfare of the nation, not welfare of individuals," Republican representative R. Paul Broun of Georgia stood next to an easel that quoted Jefferson as saying "Congress has not unlimited powers to provide for the general welfare, but only those specifically enumerated." Speech delivered on April 12, 2011.

3. On Jefferson's small-government ideology, see, for example, John Lauritz Larson, "Jefferson's Union and the Problem of Internal Improvements," in *Jeffersonian Legacies*, ed. Peter S. Onuf (Charlottesville: University of Virginia Press, 1993), 340–369.

4. Jean M. Yarbrough, *American Virtues: Thomas Jefferson on the Character of a Free People* (Lawrence: University Press of Kansas, 1998), 86.

5. David N. Mayer, *The Constitutional Thought of Thomas Jefferson* (Charlottesville: University of Virginia Press, 1994), 82.

6. Michael P. Zuckert, *The Natural Rights Republic: Studies in the Foundation of the American Political Tradition* (Notre Dame, IN: University of Notre Dame Press, 1996), 21, 225. Zuckert now takes a more nuanced

position but still maintains that the problem of economic inequality did not "impinge" on Jefferson's thinking in the same way it did for someone such as Paine because of the confidence the Virginian placed in the ability of available land in the United States to forestall the kinds of social and political ills that afflicted France. See Zuckert, "Two Paths from Revolution: Jefferson, Paine, and the Radicalization of Enlightenment Thought," in *Paine and Jefferson in the Age of Revolutions*, ed. Simon P. Newman and Peter S. Onuf (Charlottesville: University of Virginia Press, 2013), 267.

7. Michael J. Thompson, *The Politics of Inequality: A Political History of Economic Inequality in America* (New York: Columbia University Press, 2007), 186.

8. Perhaps the reason Jefferson could live with existing racial and gender relations, including the subordination of blacks, was because he believed those relations were grounded in "natural" and not just conventional distinctions between the races. See, for example, Jefferson, *Notes on the State of Virginia*, Query 14, in *Jefferson: Writings*, ed. Merrill D. Peterson (New York: Library of America, 1984), 264–270.

9. See, for example, Robert Nozick, *Anarchy, State, and Utopia* (New York: BasicBooks, 1971).

10. On Jefferson's inconsistencies on questions of slavery and race, see Paul Finkelman, "Jefferson and Slavery: 'Treason against the Hopes of the World,'" in Onuf, *Jeffersonian Legacies*, 181–221.

11. See, for example, Thomas Jefferson to Nathaniel Burwell, letter, March 14, 1818, in Peterson, *Jefferson: Writings*, 1411–1413.

12. Thomas Paine, *Common Sense*, in *The Complete Writings of Thomas Paine*, vol. 1, ed. Philip S. Foner (New York: Citadel, 1945), 31.

13. Thomas Jefferson to Charles Bellini, letter, September 30, 1785, in *The Papers of Thomas Jefferson*, vol. 8, ed. Julian P. Boyd (Princeton, NJ: Princeton University Press, 1953), 568.

14. Ibid., 568, 569.

15. Thomas Jefferson, "Observations on Démeunier's Manuscript," in Boyd, *Papers of Thomas Jefferson*, vol. 10, 31.

16. Even when Thomas Jefferson did acknowledge the existence of different classes in the United States, he still maintained that there was a "lovely equality which the poor enjoy with the rich." Jefferson to John Bannister Jr., letter, October 15, 1785, in Boyd, *Papers of Thomas Jefferson*, vol. 8, 636.

17. Thomas Jefferson to Jean Nicolas Démeunier, letter, April 29, 1795, in Boyd, *Papers of Thomas Jefferson*, vol. 28, 341.

18. Alexis de Tocqueville, *Democracy in America*, trans. and ed. Harvey C. Mansfield and Delba Winthrop (Chicago: University of Chicago Press, 2000), 3–15, 45–53.

19. Jefferson to Démeunier, April 29, 1795, 341.

20. Jefferson, "Observations on Démeunier's Manuscript," 52.

21. Thomas Jefferson to Thomas Cooper, letter, September 10, 1814, in *The Papers of Thomas Jefferson*, Retirement Series, vol. 7, ed. J. Jefferson Looney (Princeton, NJ: Princeton University Press, 2010), 651.

22. Thomas Jefferson to Eliza House Trist, August 18, 1785, letter, in Boyd, *Papers of Thomas Jefferson*, vol. 8, 404.

23. Thomas Jefferson, *Autobiography*, in Peterson, *Jefferson: Writings*, 81.

24. Thomas Jefferson, "Notes of a Tour through Holland and the Rhine Valley," in Boyd, *Papers of Thomas Jefferson*, vol. 13, 13.

25. For example, Thomas Jefferson to John Page, letter, May 4, 1786, in Boyd, *Papers of Thomas Jefferson*, vol. 9, 444–446.

26. Thomas Jefferson to Edward Carrington, letter, January 16, 1787, in Boyd, *Papers of Thomas Jefferson*, vol. 11, 49.

27. Hannah Arendt, *On Revolution* (New York: Penguin, 1965), 67.

28. Thomas Jefferson to George Wythe, letter, August 13, 1786, in Boyd, *Papers of Thomas Jefferson*, vol. 10, 244.

29. Jefferson to Cooper, September 10, 1814, 650.

30. Thomas Jefferson to William Johnson, letter, June 12, 1823, in Peterson, *Jefferson: Writings*, 1470.

31. Ibid., 1471.

32. Jefferson, *Autobiography*, 78. In fact, he explicitly approved of the "objects" pursued by the "mobs" of Paris. See Jefferson to Diodati, August 3, 1789, letter, in Boyd, *Papers of Thomas Jefferson*, vol. 15, 325.

33. Thomas Jefferson to James Madison, October 28, 1785, letter, in Boyd, *Papers of Thomas Jefferson*, vol. 8, 681.

34. In addition to an unequal division of land, James Madison identified overpopulation as a major cause of the "misery" that afflicts the masses. Madison to Thomas Jefferson, letter, June 19, 1786, in Boyd, *Papers of Thomas Jefferson*, vol. 9, 659–665.

35. Richard K. Matthews, *The Radical Politics of Thomas Jefferson: A Revisionist View* (Lawrence: University Press of Kansas, 1984).

36. Yarbrough, *American Virtues*, 95.

37. Jefferson to Madison, October 28, 1785, 681–682.

38. Ibid., 682.

39. John Locke, *Two Treatises of Government*, ed. Peter Laslett (Cambridge, UK: Cambridge University Press, 1988), 302. The classic case for Locke as an apologist for unlimited and unequal acquisition is C. B. Macpherson, *The Political Theory of Possessive Individualism: Hobbes to Locke* (Oxford, UK: Oxford University Press, 1962), 194–262.

40. See Macpherson, who claims that Locke actually "remove[s] all the natural law limits from the property right." Macpherson, *Political Theory of Possessive Individualism*, 199.

41. Locke, *Two Treatises of Government*, 290.

42. Ibid., 271.

43. The following discussion is indebted to the insightful analysis in Jeremy Waldron, *God, Locke, and Equality: Christian Foundations in Locke's Political Thought* (Cambridge, UK: Cambridge University Press, 2002), 151–187.

44. Locke, *Two Treatises of Government*, 290.

45. Ibid., 291.

46. Ibid., 170.

47. Ibid., 294.

48. Emphasis added. This is a point of great controversy among scholars.

David Mayer contends that Thomas Jefferson viewed property acquired by one's own labor as a natural right (*Constitutional Thought of Thomas Jefferson*, 79–80), whereas Richard Matthews argues that Jefferson viewed property rights as originating in positive law rather than natural right (*Radical Politics of Thomas Jefferson*, 20, 26, 50).

49. As Michael Zuckert explains with reference to another letter by Thomas Jefferson, the right to property is derived from and in the service of the right to life. See Zuckert, *Natural Rights Republic*, 79–81.

50. Thomas Jefferson to Comte de Moustier, letter, December 3, 1790, in Boyd, *Papers of Thomas Jefferson*, vol. 18, 119.

51. Thomas Jefferson went on to argue that the surplus gained from the continuation of imposts, most of which is applied to "foreign luxuries, purchased by those only who are rich enough to afford themselves the use of them" could be used to fund the "great purposes of the [*sic*] public education, roads, rivers, canals, and such other objects of public improvement as it may be thought proper to add to the constitutional enumeration of federal powers." Jefferson, sixth annual message, in Peterson, *Jefferson: Writings*, 529. Jefferson opined, "Those who can afford to add foreign luxuries to domestic comforts" would "cheerfully" pay taxes on these items. Jefferson, second Inaugural Address, in ibid., 518–519.

52. Thomas Jefferson to Albert Gallatin, letter, September 13, 1802, in Boyd, *Papers of Thomas Jefferson*, vol. 38, 390.

53. Thomas Jefferson to Monsieur Dupont de Nemours, letter, April 15, 1811, in Looney, *Papers of Thomas Jefferson*, Retirement Series, vol. 3, 560. Jefferson repeated these sentiments almost word for word a few days later. See Jefferson to Thaddeus Kosciusko, letter, April 16, 1811, in Boyd, *Papers of Thomas Jefferson*, 566.

54. Jefferson to Dupont de Nemours, letter, April 15, 1811, 560. As debates over taxes on imports during the first six Congresses suggest, exactly what constitutes a luxury and what is considered a necessity is in the eye of the beholder (or palate of the consumer). Jefferson, a free-spending oenophile, rejected the idea that duties on wine were "merely a tax on the rich" and looked forward to their reduction in hopes (he claimed) of making this beverage a more affordable alternative to the "bane of whiskey." Jefferson to Jean Guillaume Hyde de Neuville, letter, December 13, 1818, in *The Writings of Thomas Jefferson*, vol. 3, ed. Albert Ellery Bergh (Washington, DC: Thomas Jefferson Memorial Association, 1907), 177.

55. In Richard Matthews's view, this passage reveals Thomas Jefferson's willingness to go even further than Thomas Paine in "Agrarian Justice" and "redistribute property with every generation." Matthews, *Radical Politics of Thomas Jefferson*, 33.

56. Yarbrough vehemently disputes readings of Jefferson as a radical or redistributionist even in this letter to James Madison because, she argues, Jefferson did not object to "inequality per se but the inequality of aristocratic property laws that result in 'so much misery to the bulk of mankind.'" Though Yarbrough is correct in claiming that Jefferson never called for a totally "egalitarian redistribution of wealth," her claim rests on a false choice

between perfect equality, on the one hand, and acquiescence to all degrees of inequality, on the other. Yarbrough, *American Virtues*, 96. She ignores the possibility that Jefferson was unwilling to accept inequality that exceeded a particular threshold. Though he never specified with mathematical exactitude where that threshold might be, his refusal to accept inequality beyond a particular (if unspecified) point does buttress his egalitarian bona fides.

57. Thomas Jefferson, first Inaugural Address, in Boyd, *Papers of Thomas Jefferson*, vol. 33, 150.

58. Thomas Jefferson, "Opinion on the Constitutionality of the Bill for Establishing a National Bank," in Boyd, *Papers of Thomas Jefferson*, vol. 19, 278. Emphasis in original.

59. Thomas Jefferson to James Madison, letter, December 28, 1794, in Boyd, *Papers of Thomas Jefferson*, vol. 28, 229.

60. Jefferson, second Inaugural Address, 522.

61. Quoted in Yarbrough, *American Virtues*, 97.

62. See Herbert Sloan, "'The Earth Belongs in Usufruct to the Living,'" in Onuf, *Jeffersonian Legacies*, 283.

63. Michael J. Thompson, *The Politics of Inequality: A Political History of Economic Inequality in America* (New York: Columbia University Press, 2007), 76–77.

64. See, for example, Thomas Jefferson to William Branch Giles, December 26, 1825, in Peterson, *Jefferson: Writings*, 1510–1511.

65. Thomas Jefferson to Samuel Kercheval, July 12, 1816, in Looney, *Papers of Thomas Jefferson*, Retirement Series, vol. 10, 227. See also Jefferson to James Madison, September 6, 1789, in Boyd, *Papers of Thomas Jefferson*, vol. 15, 392–398. On Jefferson's understanding that the "earth belongs to the living," see Matthews, *Radical Politics of Thomas Jefferson*, 19–29.

66. Quoted in Antoine Louis Claude Destutt de Tracy, *A Treatise on Political Economy*, trans. Thomas Jefferson, ed. Jeremy Jennings (Indianapolis, IN: Liberty Fund, 2011), xv.

67. Thomas Jefferson to Joseph Milligan, October 25, 1818, in Jefferson and Jennings, *Treatise on Political Economy*, 3.

68. Thomas Jefferson to Antoine Louis Claude Destutt de Tracy, prospectus, in Jefferson and Jennings, *Treatise on Political Economy*, 6.

69. Destutt de Tracy, *Treatise on Political Economy*, 24.

70. Destutt de Tracy argued that special solicitude should be shown toward the poor: "Humanity, justice, and policy, equally require that of all interests, those of the poor should always be the most consulted, and the most constantly respected." Ibid., 179.

71. Ibid., 26.

72. Ibid., 192.

73. Ibid., 241, 234, 240.

74. Thomas Jefferson to John Tyler, letter, June 28, 1804, in Peterson, *Jefferson: Writings*, 1147.

75. Jefferson, *Autobiography*, 37.

76. Ralph Lerner argues that the legal reforms undertaken by Jefferson provide an important glimpse into his thinking on the "character of an

emerging republican society as it was and as it might be." Despite the republican aspirations of the legal revisal, though, Lerner contends that many of the changes "preserve[d] and confirm[ed]" many "long-standing inequalities" between the races, sexes, and classes. Lerner, *The Thinking Revolutionary: Principle and Practice in the New Republic* (Ithaca, NY: Cornell University Press, 1987), 63. However, as Lerner himself observes, the legislature did take up measures to address relations between the classes by making public assistance available to the poor and disabled, providing arms at public expense to militiamen who could not afford to supply themselves, and guaranteeing ownership of fifty acres of land to adult males. Ibid., 65–66.

77. See, for example, Cesare Beccaria, *On Crimes and Punishments*, trans. David Young (Indianapolis, IN: Hackett, 1986), 14–16.

78. Jefferson, *Autobiography*, 41.

79. Ibid., 44.

80. Looking back on these attempts decades later, Thomas Jefferson pointed out that there was a class dimension to the controversy over his bill to establish religious freedom: "The establishment was truly the religion of the rich, the dissenting sects being entirely composed of the less wealthy people." Jefferson, *Autobiography*, 44.

81. Thomas Jefferson to John Adams, October 28, 1813, in Looney, *Papers of Thomas Jefferson*, Retirement Series, vol. 6, 565.

82. Jefferson, *Autobiography*, 32.

83. Ibid.

84. Ibid., 39.

85. Ibid., 32–33.

86. Ibid., 33.

87. Thomas Jefferson, third draft of the Constitution for Virginia, June 1776, in Boyd, *Papers of Thomas Jefferson*, vol. 1, 362.

88. Matthews, *Radical Politics of Thomas Jefferson*, 80.

89. Harrington's influence on Jefferson's thinking in this respect is discussed in Lance Banning, *The Jeffersonian Persuasion: Evolution of a Party Ideology* (Ithaca, NY: Cornell University Press, 1978), 25–41.

90. Jefferson, *Notes on the State of Virginia*, Query 19, in Peterson, *Jefferson: Writings*, 290–291.

91. Thomas Jefferson to James Madison, December 20, 1787, in Boyd, *Papers of Thomas Jefferson*, vol. 12, 442.

92. Drew R. McCoy, *The Elusive Republic: Political Economy in Jeffersonian America* (New York: Norton, 1980), 195.

93. Thomas Jefferson to Jean Baptiste Say, letter, February 1, 1804, in Peterson, *Jefferson: Writings*, 1144.

94. See, for example, Mayer, *Constitutional Thought of Thomas Jefferson*, 244–251; Joseph J. Ellis, *American Sphinx: The Character of Thomas Jefferson* (New York: Vintage, 1996), 242–253; Jeremy D. Bailey, *Thomas Jefferson and Executive Power* (Cambridge, UK: Cambridge University Press, 2007), 171–194.

95. Peter S. Onuf and Leonard J. Sadosky, *Jeffersonian America* (Oxford, UK: Blackwell, 2002), 6–7.

96. Jefferson, sixth annual message, 530.

97. See Larson, "Jefferson's Union and the Problem of Internal Improvements," 360–361.

98. See, for example, Thomas Jefferson to George Washington, letter, March 15, 1784, in Boyd, *Papers of Thomas Jefferson*, vol. 7, 27.

99. Jefferson to Kercheval, July 12, 1816, 225.

100. Noah Webster argued, "Education in a great measure, forms the moral characters of men, and morals are the basis of government." See Webster, *The Rising Glory of America, 1760–1820*, rev. ed., ed. Gordon S. Wood (Boston: Northeastern University Press, 1990), 162.

101. Thomas Jefferson, "A Bill for the More General Diffusion of Knowledge," in Peterson, *Jefferson: Writings*, 365.

102. Jefferson to Adams, October 28, 1813, 565.

103. See, for example, Lorraine Smith Pangle and Thomas L. Pangle, *The Learning of Liberty: The Educational Ideas of the American Founders* (Lawrence: University Press of Kansas, 1993), 106–124; Richard D. Brown, *The Strength of a People: The Idea of an Informed Citizenry in America, 1650–1870* (Chapel Hill: University of North Carolina Press, 1996), 75–77; and Yarbrough, *American Virtues*, 125.

104. On Jefferson's efforts to produce a more informed citizenry, see Brown, *Strength of a People*, 75–77.

105. Onuf and Sadosky, *Jeffersonian America*, 81.

106. Jefferson, "Bill for the More General Diffusion of Knowledge," 365, 372.

107. Brown, *Strength of a People*, 98–99. In some other states, similar proposals to provide public funding for education actually went down to defeat because of a belief that the sons of rich men would benefit disproportionately. See Jackson Turner Main, *The Social Structure of Revolutionary America* (Princeton, NJ: Princeton University Press, 1965), 248–249.

108. Thomas Jefferson to Joseph C. Cabell, letter, February 2, 1816, in Looney, *Papers of Thomas Jefferson*, Retirement Series, vol. 9, 436.

109. Jefferson to Adams, October 28, 1813, 565.

110. Ibid., 563. Notwithstanding their well-known differences, these proposals would have been congenial to John Adams, who had himself promoted the notion that the rich should pay for the education of the poor as far back as 1765 in his "Dissertation on the Canon and Feudal Law." Responding to those "high churchmen and high statesmen" who criticized New England's tradition of supporting public education "as a needless expense, and an imposition upon the rich in favor of the poor," Adams intoned that "liberty must at all hazards be supported." Adams, "A Dissertation on the Canon and Feudal Law," in *The Revolutionary Writings of John Adams*, ed. C. Bradley Thompson (Indianapolis, IN: Liberty Fund, 2000), 28. On Adams's commitment to public education, see Brown, *Strength of a People*, 54–58, 77–82.

111. Jefferson, *Notes on the State of Virginia*, Query 14, in Peterson, *Jefferson: Writings*, 274.

112. Thomas Jefferson, "Report of the Commissioners for the University of Virginia," in Peterson, *Jefferson: Writings*, 459.

113. Jefferson to Cabell, February 2, 1816, 436.

114. Thomas Jefferson, eighth annual message, in Peterson, *Jefferson: Writings*, 549.

115. Jefferson, sixth annual message, 529–530.

116. Jefferson to Kercheval, July 12, 1816, 225. Jefferson listed the same responsibilities every time he brought up the subject of wards. See also Jefferson to John Tyler, letter, May 26, 1810, in Looney, *Papers of Thomas Jefferson*, Retirement Series, vol. 2, 420–421; Jefferson to Major John Cartwright, letter, June 5, 1824, in Peterson, *Jefferson: Writings*, 1492.

117. Jefferson, *Notes on the State of Virginia*, 233, 259.

118. Ibid., 259.

119. Ibid., 259.

120. Ibid., 259.

121. Yarbrough, *American Virtues*, 68.

122. Ibid. Jefferson's actual spelling in the quotation Yarbrough uses from *Notes on the State of Virginia* is "discreet" not "discrete."

123. Jefferson, *Notes on the State of Virginia*, 259.

124. See Douglass Adair, "Rumbold's Dying Speech, 1685, and Jefferson's Last Words on Democracy, 1826," in Adair, *Fame and the Founding Fathers*, ed. Trevor Colbourn (Indianapolis, IN: Liberty Fund, 1998).

125. Thomas Jefferson to Roger C. Weightman, June 24, 1826, in Peterson, *Jefferson: Writings*, 1517.

126. Yarbrough, *American Virtues*, 96.

127. See, for example, Jefferson to Kercheval, July 12, 1816, 226–227.

Chapter 7: "Not Charity but a Right"

1. For a survey of Thomas Paine's influence on radical movements in the United States and elsewhere, see Harvey J. Kaye, *Thomas Paine and the Promise of America* (New York: Hill and Wang, 2005). E. P. Thompson notes that Paine's *Rights of Man* became a "foundation-text of the English working-class movement." See Thompson, *The Making of the English Working Class* (New York: Vintage, 1966), 90.

2. William Christian, "The Moral Economics of Tom Paine," *Journal of the History of Ideas* 34, no. 3 (1973): 378.

3. John Keane, *Tom Paine: A Political Life* (New York: Grove, 1995), 190–191.

4. Robin West, "Tom Paine's Constitution," *Virginia Law Review* 89, no. 6 (2003): 1457.

5. Joseph Dorfman, "The Economic Philosophy of Thomas Paine," *Political Science Quarterly* 53 (September 1938): 386.

6. See Eric Foner, *Tom Paine and Revolutionary America*, updated ed. (Oxford, UK: Oxford University Press, 2005), 153–158, quote at 93.

7. Michael J. Thompson, *The Politics of Inequality: A Political History of the Idea of Economic Inequality in America* (New York: Columbia University Press, 2007), 159–160.

8. Murray N. Rothbard, "The Sudden Emergence of Tom Paine," in Rothbard, *Conceived in Liberty* (Auburn, AL: Ludwig von Mises Institute, 2011), 1251.

9. Dorfman, "Economic Philosophy of Thomas Paine," 386.

10. Jack Fruchtman Jr., *Thomas Paine: Apostle of Freedom* (New York: Four Walls Eight Windows, 1994), 253.

11. Foner, *Tom Paine and Revolutionary America*, 94.

12. Irving Kristol, "The American Revolution as a Successful Revolution," *Reflections of a Neo-Conservative: Looking Back, Looking Ahead* (New York: BasicBooks, 1983), 87.

13. Larry Schweikart, *What Would the Founders Say? A Patriot's Answers to America's Most Pressing Problems* (New York: Sentinel, 2011).

14. All references to Thomas Paine's works are from *The Complete Writings of Thomas Paine*, ed. Philip S. Foner (New York: Citadel, 1945) by volume and page number.

15. Fruchtman, *Thomas Paine*, 66.

16. In one of his letters on the infamous Silas Deane affair, Thomas Paine suggested that it was not taxes in themselves that are objectionable, but the manner in which they are distributed: "Let expenses be ever so great, only let them be fair and necessary, and no good citizen will grumble." Paine, "To the Public on Mr. Deane's Affair," in Foner, *Complete Writings of Thomas Paine*, vol. 2, 125.

17. Thomas Paine believed that the Quakers' solicitude for the poor was a significant mark in their favor compared with other religions. Paine, "Worship and Church Bells," in Foner, *Complete Writings of Thomas Paine*, vol. 2, 759.

18. For an overview of debates over these terms, see Nancy Fraser and Axel Honneth, *Redistribution or Recognition? A Political-Philosophical Exchange* (New York: Verso, 2003).

19. James L. Huston, *Securing the Fruits of Labor: The American Concept of Wealth Distribution, 1765–1900* (Baton Rouge: Louisiana State University Press, 1998), 33, 61–62.

20. Noah Webster drew similar conclusions about the relation between inequality and crime, suggesting that the great disparities that existed in England and Ireland caused some members of the lower classes to "become desperate, and turn highwaymen." Webster, "On the Education of Youth in America," *A Collection of Essays and Fugitiv* [sic] *Writings: On Moral, Historical, Political, and Literary Subjects* (Boston: I. Thomas and E. T. Andrews, 1790), 26.

21. In John T. Meng's view, Thomas Paine's intervention in the debate over the Pennsylvania Constitution presents some of Paine's strongest statements on the importance of laws favorable to the poor. Meng, "The Constitutional Theories of Thomas Paine," *Review of Politics* 8, no. 3 (1946): 287.

22. Foner, *Tom Paine and Revolutionary America*, 98.

23. See Craig Nelson, *Thomas Paine: Enlightenment, Revolution, and the Birth of Modern Nations* (New York: Penguin, 2006), 141–142.

24. Kaye, *Thomas Paine and the Promise of America*, 98.

25. Nelson, *Thomas Paine*, 207–208, 220.

26. On toasts to Paine and *Rights of Man* during the 1790s, see Simon P. Newman, "Paine, Jefferson, and Revolutionary Radicalism in Early National America," in *Paine and Jefferson in the Age of Revolutions*, ed. Simon P. Newman and Peter S. Onuf (Charlottesville: University of Virginia Press, 2013), 73–83.

27. Thomas Jefferson to George Washington, letter, May 8, 1791, in *The Papers of Thomas Jefferson*, vol. 20, ed. Julian P. Boyd (Princeton, NJ: Princeton University Press, 1953), 291.

28. John Quincy Adams, "Letters of Publicola XI," in *Writings of John Quincy Adams*, vol. 1, ed. Worthington Chauncey Ford (New York: Macmillan, 1913), 107–108.

29. Ibid., 71.

30. Ibid., 76.

31. Eric Foner suggests that the "social chapter" did not provoke a greater response in America because "it was not relevant to the New World." Foner, *Tom Paine and Revolutionary America*, 233. Although Thomas Paine himself observed that levels of inequality were far lower in America than they were in Europe, his assertions about the universality of his ideas indicates that the remedies he prescribed for this social ill would be just as applicable in America as anywhere else if conditions changed.

32. The attacks that did appear on the book's supposed "leveling system" focused as much on the implications for "subordination in government" as they did on threats to property. For examples of these attacks, see Newman, "Paine, Jefferson, and Revolutionary Radicalism," 79–80.

33. John Adams to Thomas Jefferson, letter, June 22, 1819, *The Adams-Jefferson Letters*, ed. Lester J. Cappon (Chapel Hill: University of North Carolina Press, 1959), 542.

34. John Adams, *The Works of John Adams*, vol. 6, ed. Charles Francis Adams (Boston: Little, Brown, 1851), 65–66.

35. Conservative attacks on the egalitarian ideas in *Rights of Man* intensified at the height of tensions between the United States and France later in the 1790s. Though he never mentioned Thomas Paine by name, Baptist preacher and college president Jonathan Maxcy condemned the "rights of man" and other slogans promoted by "modern levelers" for instigating class warfare. See Maxcy, "An Oration," in *American Political Writings during the Founding Era, 1760–1805*, vol. 2, ed. Charles S. Hyneman and Donald S. Lutz (Indianapolis, IN: Liberty Fund, 1983).

36. Michael Zuckert, "Two Paths from Revolution: Jefferson, Paine, and the Radicalization of Enlightenment Thought," in Newman and Onuf, *Paine and Jefferson in the Age of Revolutions*, 256.

37. John W. Seaman, "Thomas Paine: Ransom, Civil Peace, and the Natural Right to Welfare," *Political Theory* 16, no. 1 (February 1988): 128.

38. The universalistic cast of Thomas Paine's political ideas arguably goes

back to *Common Sense,* which called for global changes that could be inspired by events in America. See Jack Fruchtman Jr., "Thomas Paine's Early Radicalism, 1768–1783," in Newman and Onuf, *Paine and Jefferson in the Age of Revolutions,* 49, 57–60. Although Paine's reflections were always written in response to the conditions specific to particular places, the normative foundations and practical applications of his political thought were universal in character, just as the principles in *Common Sense* also applied to Europe and the principles in *Rights of Man* applied to the United States.

39. Michael Zuckert makes a strong argument that Thomas Paine's defense of welfare rights in "Agrarian Justice" ultimately rests on a Lockean natural rights foundation—albeit with a significant difference over the possibility of converting the earth into private property. See Zuckert, "Two Paths from Revolution," 254–266.

40. Fruchtman, *Thomas Paine,* 8.

41. Jean-Jacques Rousseau, *Discourse on the Origin and Foundations of Inequality,* in Rousseau, *The First and Second Discourses,* trans. Roger D. and Judith R. Masters (New York: St. Martin's, 1964), 141.

42. The Lockean turn in Thomas Paine's thinking was well recognized when the pamphlet first appeared. Radical English egalitarian Thomas Spence credited Paine for finally accepting the "indisputable" truth articulated by Locke that *"God hath given the earth to the children of men, given it to mankind in common,"* but chastised him for having "erected an execrable fabric of compromissory expediency" that does not go far enough to restore the universal rights of humankind. Spence, "The Rights of Infants: Or, the Imprescriptable [*sic*] Right of Mothers to Such a Share of the Elements as Is Sufficient to Enable Them to Suckle and Bring Up Their Young" (London: Author, March 19, 1797), preface. Spence went on to make the point that the right of a human mother to provide for her young from the bounty of nature is at least as great as the right any animal has to provide for itself.

43. See Zuckert, "Two Paths from Revolution," 263–264.

44. Thomas Paine rejected some of the more radical redistributionist plans championed in his time because they would involve indiscriminate violations of the natural rights of proprietors who actually earned their property: "While, therefore, I advocate the right, and interest myself in the hard case of all those who have been thrown out of their natural inheritance by the introduction of the system of landed property, I equally defend the right of the possessor to the part which is his." In Foner, *Complete Writings of Thomas Paine,* vol. 1, 612.

45. Newspaper editor Robert Coram had developed a similar explanation for the rise of inequality in a 1791 pamphlet, but he proposed a general tax to fund a system of free public education as the best way to promote the personal independence that economic inequality tends to undermine. See Coram, *Political Inquiries, to Which Is Added a Plan for the Establishment of Schools throughout the United States,* in *American Political Writings during the Founding Era, 1760–1805,* vol. 2, ed. Charles S. Hyneman and Donald S. Lutz (Indianapolis, IN: Liberty Fund, 1983), 756–811.

46. "Yet, notwithstanding those advantages on the part of America, true it is, that *had it not been for the operation of taxes for our necessary defence, we had sunk into a state of sloth and poverty.*" Paine, *American Crisis 10,* in Foner, *Complete Writings of Thomas Paine,* vol. 1, 203. Emphasis added.

47. Seaman, "Thomas Paine," 133.

Chapter 8: Conclusion

1. Thomas Paine, *Common Sense,* in *The Complete Writings of Thomas Paine,* vol. 1, ed. Philip S. Foner (New York: Citadel, 1945), 31.

2. Benjamin Franklin, "Information to Those Who Would Remove to America," in *Franklin: Writings,* ed. J. A. Leo Lemay (New York: Library of America, 1987), 975.

3. Benjamin Rush, "An Address to the Inhabitants of the British Settlements in America, upon Slave-Keeping," in *American Political Writings during the Founding Era, 1760–1805,* vol. 1, ed. Charles S. Hyneman and Donald S. Lutz (Indianapolis, IN: Liberty Fund, 1983), 220.

4. "Centinel," Letter 1, in *The Anti-Federalist,* ed. Murray Dry (Chicago: University of Chicago Press, 1981), 16.

5. The classic statement of this idea appears in Isaiah Berlin, "Two Concepts of Liberty," in Berlin, *Four Essays on Liberty* (Oxford, UK: Oxford University Press, 1969).

6. John Rawls, *A Theory of Justice,* rev. ed. (Cambridge, MA: Belknap Press of Harvard University Press, 1999).

7. William Manning, *The Key of Liberty: The Life and Democratic Writings of William Manning, "A Laborer," 1747–1814,* ed. Michael Merrill and Sean Wilentz (Cambridge, MA: Harvard University Press, 1993), 154.

8. Edward R. A. Seligman, "Progressive Taxation in Theory and Practice," *Publications of the American Economic Association* 9, nos. 1–2 (1894).

9. See James L. Huston, *Securing the Fruits of Labor: The American Concept of Wealth Distribution, 1765–1900* (Baton Rouge: Louisiana State University Press, 1998), 69–80.

10. Abraham Clark, "The True Policy of New-Jersey, Defined; or, Our Great Strength Led to Exertion, in the Improvement of Agriculture & Manufactures, by Altering the Mode of Taxation, and by the Emission of Money on Loan, in IX Sections" (Elizabeth-Town, NJ: Shepard Kollock, 1786), 11 (held at "Special Collections and University Archives, Rutgers University Libraries), 33–34.

11. See, for example, Branko Milanovic, *The Haves and the Have-Nots: A Brief and Idiosyncratic History of Global Inequality* (New York: BasicBooks, 2011), 176–181; Central Intelligence Agency, *The World Factbook: Country Comparison: Distribution of Family Income—Gini Coefficient,* https://www .cia.gov/library/publications/the-world-factbook/rankorder/2172rank .html.

12. Timothy Noah, *The Great Divergence: America's Growing Inequality Crisis and What We Can Do about It* (New York: Bloomsbury, 2103);

Emmanuel Saez, "Striking It Richer: The Evolution of Top Incomes in the United States (Updated with 2012 Preliminary Estimates)," September 3, 2013, http://eml.berkeley.edu/~saez/saez-UStopincomes-2012.pdf; Heather Boushey and Christian E. Weller, "What the Numbers Tell Us," in *Inequality Matters: The Growing Economic Divide in America and Its Poisonous Consequences*, ed. James Lardner and David A. Smith (New York: New Press, 2005), 27–40; Joseph E. Stiglitz, *The Price of Inequality: How Today's Divided Society Endangers Our Future* (New York: Norton, 2013), 1–34.

13. PolitiFact, "Michael Moore Says 400 Americans Have More Wealth Than Half of All Americans Combined," http://www.politifact .com/wisconsin/statements/2011/mar/10/michael-moore/michael -moore-says-400-americans-have-more-wealth-/.

14. David Leonhardt and Kevin Quealy, "The American Middle Class Is No Longer the World's Richest," *New York Times*, April 22, 2014.

15. Milanovic, *Haves and the Have-Nots*, 120–123; Stiglitz, *Price of Inequality*, 35–64.

16. Barack Obama, State of the Union Address, January 20, 2015, http:// www.whitehouse.gov/the-press-office/2015/01/20/remarks-president -state-union-address-january-20-2015.

17. As Republican strategist and former US representative Vin Weber explained, "Mobility ought to be a big Republican concern, because that has always been the argument that we had against the inequality argument: 'Yeah, we have a lot of inequality, we have maldistribution of income. But the good news is, we're a very mobile society. People can move up.' That's not the case anymore." Quoted in Jackie Calmesjan, "Address May Hint at Compromise on Ways to Fight Inequality," *New York Times*, January 23, 2014.

18. Sean McElwee, "Republicans Suddenly Can't Stop Talking about 'Mobility,'" *New Republic*, February 19, 2014, http://www.newrepublic.com /article/116670/republicans-focus-mobility-over-inequality-has-major-flaw.

19. Jonathan Weisman and Ashley Parker, "Talk of Wealth Gap Prods the G.O.P. to Refocus," *New York Times*, January 22, 2015, A1.

20. Noah, *Great Divergence*, 28–43; John E. Roemer, *Equality of Opportunity* (Cambridge, MA: Harvard University Press, 1998).

21. Stiglitz, *Price of Inequality*; Barry Z. Cynamon and Steven M. Fazzari, "Inequality, the Great Recession, and Slow Recovery," January 23, 2014, http://ssrn.com/abstract=2205524 or http://dx.doi.org/10.2139/ssrn .2205524.

22. Charles P. Kindleberger, *Manias, Panics, and Crashes: A History of Financial Crises*, 6th ed. (New York: Palgrave Macmillan, 2011).

23. Pierre Bourdieu, *Distinction: A Social Critique of the Judgment of Taste*, trans. Richard Nice (Cambridge, MA: Harvard University Press, 1984).

24. Richard Wilkinson, *The Impact of Inequality: How to Make Sick Societies Healthier* (New York: New Press, 2005), 171–177. See also Robert H. Frank, *Falling Behind: How Rising Inequality Harms the Middle Class* (Berkeley: University of California Press, 2007); Robert H. Frank, *Luxury Fever: Weighing the Cost of Excess* (Princeton, NJ: Princeton University

Press, 2010); Juliet B. Schor, *The Overspent American: Why We Want What We Don't Need* (New York HarperPerennial, 1999).

25. Results from studies on the relationship between economic inequality and various measures of well-being are summarized in Richard Wilkinson, *Impact of Inequality*, and Richard Wilkinson and Kate Pickett, *The Spirit Level: Why Greater Equality Makes Societies Stronger* (New York: Bloomsbury, 2009). According to Wilkinson, the psychosocial effects of greater inequality help explain these outcomes. One of the major factors that accounts for the inferior health outcomes of unequal societies across all economic levels is the higher levels of stress everyone experiences from the acute status consciousness and competitiveness promoted in stratified societies. Among other things, the conflictual nature of social relations contributes to increases in the production of cortisol, an endocrine hormone that increases blood sugar levels and suppresses the immune system, and fibrinogen, a blood-clotting factor associated with cardiovascular disease. Wilkinson, *Impact of Inequality*, 162–164, 275–277.

26. Wilkinson and Pickett, *Spirit Level*, 25.

27. Wilkinson, *Impact of Inequality*, 69.

28. Robert D. Putnam finds that places with lower levels of social capital—which also happen to be the places with the highest levels of inequality—tend to be more belligerent and violent. Putnam, *Bowling Alone: The Collapse and Revival of American Community* (New York: Simon and Schuster, 2000), 308–313.

29. Wilkinson, *Impact of Inequality*, 105, 228–231.

30. Putnam, *Bowling Alone*, 358–360.

31. See Chrystia Freeland, *Plutocrats: The Rise of the New Global Super-Rich and the Fall of Everyone Else* (New York: Penguin, 2012).

32. Theda Skocpol, "Voice and Inequality: The Transformation of American Civic Democracy," *Perspectives on Politics* 2, no. 1 (2004): 3–20.

33. Task Force on Inequality and American Democracy, "American Democracy in an Age of Rising Inequality," American Political Science Association (2004), https://www.apsanet.org/imgtest/taskforcereport.pdf..

34. Ibid., 5.

35. See Martin Gilens, *Affluence and Influence: Economic Inequality and Political Power*, rep. ed. (Princeton, NJ: Princeton University Press, 2014); Pablo Beramendi and Christopher Anderson, "Income Inequality and Democratic Representation," in Beramendi and Anderson, *Democracy, Inequality, and Representation* (New York: Russell Sage Foundation, 2008).

36. Larry M. Bartels, *Unequal Democracy: The Political Economy of the New Gilded Age* (Princeton, NJ: Princeton University Press, 2010), 277.

37. Martin Gilens and Benjamin Page, "Testing Theories of American Politics: Elites, Interest Groups, and Average Citizens," *Perspectives on Politics* 12, no. 3 (2014), 565.

38. Bartels, *Unequal Democracy*, 254.

39. Benjamin I. Page and Lawrence R. Jacobs, *Class War? What Americans Really Think about Economic Inequality* (Chicago: University of Chicago Press, 2009), 40–48. In a poll conducted by the Pew Research Center between

January 15 and January 19, 2014, 69 percent of Americans responded that the government should do either "a lot" or "some" to "reduce the gap" between the rich and everyone else. There was a significant partisan difference in the survey. Democratic respondents expressed support for government action by 90 percent, whereas only 45 percent of self-described Republicans indicated support. Pew Research Center for the People and the Press, "Most See Inequality Growing, but Partisans Differ over Solutions," January 23, 2014, http://www.people-press.org/2014/01/23/most-see-inequality-growing-but-partisans-differ-over-solutions/.

40. Bartels, *Unequal Democracy*, 223–282; Page and Jacobs, *Class War?*

41. Katherine S. Newman, *Taxing the Poor: Doing Damage to the Truly Disadvantaged* (Berkeley: University of California Press, 2011).

42. Thomas Byrne Edsall, *The New Politics of Inequality* (New York: Norton, 1984).

43. Task Force on Inequality and American Democracy, "American Democracy in an Age of Rising Inequality," 10.

44. Nolan McCarty, Keith T. Poole, and Howard Rosenthal, *Polarized America: The Dance of Ideology and Unequal Riches* (Cambridge: Massachusetts Institute of Technology Press, 2006).

45. For an overview of these changes, see Jacob S. Hacker and Paul S. Pierson, *Winner-Take-All Politics: How Washington Made the Rich Richer—and Turned Its Back on the Middle Class* (New York: Simon and Schuster, 2010), 66–72.

46. Ibid., 61–66. Preliminary reports suggest that reforms empowering shareholders to rein in chief executive officer (CEO) pay have fallen short of expectations. Compensation for CEOs at major corporations has continued to increase in spite of changes introduced by the Dodd-Frank Wall Street Reform and Consumer Protection Act of 2010. David Gelles, "For the Highest-Paid C.E.O.s, the Party Goes On," *New York Times*, May 17, 2015, BU1.

47. Lawrence Jacobs and Desmond King, "America's Political Crisis: The Unsustainable State in a Time of Unraveling," *PS: Political Science and Politics* 42, no. 2 (2009): 277–285.

48. Edsall, *New Politics of Inequality*, 141–178; Noah, *Great Divergence*, 138–143; Hacker and Pierson, *Winner-Take-All Politics*, 56–61, 127–132, 139–143.

49. C. Edwin Baker, *Media Concentration and Democracy: Why Ownership Matters* (Cambridge, UK: Cambridge University Press, 2006).

50. Bartels, *Unequal Democracy*, 286.

51. Quoted in Robert A. Becker, *Revolution, Reform, and the Politics of American Taxation, 1763–1783* (Baton Rouge: Louisiana State University Press, 1980), 161.

52. See, for example, David Harvey, *A Brief History of Neoliberalism* (Oxford, UK: Oxford University Press, 2005), 16, 19, 31–36.

INDEX

and *Rights of Man*, 222, 235–247,
    252, 253, 257, 323n35
on state of nature, 224, 226, 238–239,
    247–250
on taxes, 225, 226, 228, 234, 240–
    243, 246, 250–252, 257, 322n16
universalism of, 223, 240, 245, 247–
    257, 323n31, 323–324n38
on wealthy, 229, 230–232, 241,
    256, 257
welfare state, 33, 221–222, 235, 237,
    243–247, 252–254, 260, 266
Parker, Josiah
    on constitutional interpretation, 131
    on marine hospitals, 188
    on militia, 161–162
Partridge, George, 138
Pendleton, Edmund, 210
Pennsylvania
    class politics in, 39–45, 122
    Constitution of, 40–41
    Constitutional Party in, 41, 44
    democratic reforms in, 39–40
    influence of, in national politics, 38
    representation in, 73
    Republican Party in, 41, 45
    taxes in, 31, 308n126
Philadelphia
    economic troubles in, 41–42
    inequality in, 21, 22, 287nn101–102
    mobility in, 24
    national significance of, 38
    poverty in, 26–27
Pinckney, Charles
    on America compared to Europe,
        296n12
    on economic inequality, 61, 284n60
    on suffrage, 65, 67, 68
Pinckney, Thomas, 186–187
poor, 118
    attitudes toward, 4, 25–26, 56, 60–63,
        74, 79, 283n56, 309n2
    beliefs about existence of, 19–20
    Hamilton on, 87, 113–114, 116–118,
        119, 120, 125
    Jefferson on, 195–200, 202, 214–219,
        284n65, 315n16
    and militia bill, 161–166
    numbers of, 23, 286n92
    Paine on, 226–230, 232–234, 240–
        242, 243–246, 256
    political participation of, 2–3, 9, 52,
        75–76, 271–273
    and public debt, 93–94, 99
    relief for, 25–28, 32, 289n148,
        295n79
    Robert Morris on, 47–49

and taxes, 31, 36, 47–49, 77, 119–122,
    138–144, 146, 147–148, 150–153,
    155–157, 308n126, 311n22
and western land, 168–172
See also class; economic inequality
Postlethwayt, Malachy, 121
poverty
    actual levels of, 21, 23
    beliefs about, 13, 15, 17–20
    policies regarding, 25–28, 32
property rights, 32
    in Constitutional Convention, 57–
        58, 62–64, 66–69
    defended, 6, 12, 37–38, 49–50, 54–55,
        56, 60, 63–64, 66–68, 79, 82–83,
        92, 94, 98, 237, 302n113
    limits on, 40, 96, 199–203, 238–239,
        242–243, 247–251
protest, popular, 36–37, 53–54, 59–60,
    296n7

Ramsay, David, 16
Randolph, Edmund, 60, 105
Rawls, John, 263
representation
    anti-Federalists on, 57, 70–71, 73–76
    and Constitutional Convention,
        debates in, 60–68
    Federalists on, 78–83, 115
    in states, 4, 35–36, 37–38
republicanism, 8–10, 109, 282n37
    and equality, 7, 8–9, 12, 108, 136,
        153, 168, 171, 255–256, 262–
        263, 266
    meaning of, 7
    and philanthropy, 175
    power and property, relation
        between, 9–10, 11–12, 66, 108
    and simplicity, 13, 108, 155, 282n36
    and virtue, 8, 14, 75–76
Romney, Mitt, 268
Rousseau, Jean-Jacques, 8, 81, 237, 239,
    247–249
Rubio, Marco, 268
Rush, Benjamin, 26, 32, 80–81, 262
Rutherford, Robert, 168, 180
Rutledge, John, 64, 67, 149
Ryan, Paul, 268

sailors. *See* seamen
Savannah fire, 179–183
Scott, Thomas, 95, 167, 178
seamen, 33, 37, 117–118, 146, 174, 183–
    189. *See also* marine hospitals
Sedgwick, Theodore, 95, 99, 102
Sewall, Samuel, 158, 186–189
Shays, Daniel, 55, 295n76